THE THEFT ACTS 1968 AND 1978

AUSTRALIA
The Law Book Company Ltd.
Sydney : Melbourne : Brisbane

CANADA AND U.S.A.
The Carswell Company Ltd.
Agincourt, Ontario

INDIA
N. M. Tripathi Private Ltd.
Bombay
and
Eastern Law House Private Ltd.
Calcutta *and* Delhi
M.P.P. House
Bangalore

ISRAEL
Steimatzky's Agency Ltd.
Jerusalem : Tel Aviv : Haifa

MALAYSIA : SINGAPORE : BRUNEI
Malayan Law Journal (Pte.) Ltd.
Singapore

NEW ZEALAND
Sweet & Maxwell (N.Z.) Ltd.
Auckland

PAKISTAN
Pakistan Law House
Karachi

THE THEFT ACTS
1968 AND 1978

By

EDWARD GRIEW, M.A., LL.B.

of Gray's Inn, Barrister
Professor of Law at the
University of Leicester

FOURTH EDITION

LONDON

SWEET & MAXWELL

1982

First Edition	1968
Second Edition	1974
Second Impression	1975
Third Edition	1978
Fourth Edition	1982

Published by
Sweet & Maxwell Limited of
11 New Fetter Lane, London
and printed in Scotland.

British Library Cataloguing in Publication Data
Griew, Edward
The Theft Acts 1968 and 1978.—4th ed.
1. Great Britain. Theft Act 1968
2. Great Britain. Theft Act 1978
3. Larceny—England
I. Title   II. Great Britain. Theft Act 1968
III. Great Britain. Theft Act 1978
344.205'262   KD 7992
ISBN 0-421-28640-7
ISBN 0-421-28650-4 Pbk

PREFACE TO THE FOURTH EDITION

Many decisions have been reported since the last edition of this book went to press, and the body of learned commentary on the Theft Acts and on the rather unhappy case law on the 1968 Act has continued to grow. This edition has been thought necessary to take account of these routine developments; the previous edition had come to have a decidedly out of date appearance.

I have taken the opportunity to refer, at many points, to Professor Glanville Williams' remarkable treatment of the subject in his *Textbook of Criminal Law*, which appeared shortly after the previous edition went to press; and I have occasionally ventured to respond to his arguments. The offences under the Theft Act 1978, formerly relegated to a stop-press type of Appendix, are now, of course, raised to the body of the text. A good many passages of the book are substantially rewritten; some are entirely new; and there has been a good deal of reorganisation. It would be tedious to try to itemise the changes. I mention only the fact that I have been able to take account of the Court of Appeal's decision in *McIvor* (on the issue of dishonesty), which was reported just after work on the proofs was, as I thought, completed. In consequence I can express the hope that the book will be found to be up to date to November 18, 1981.

Looking back at earlier Prefaces, I see that I have omitted to thank the publishers for relieving me (as they have consistently done) of the task of preparing the index and tables. The truth is that they do so out of self-interest; there are departments in which they are confident of their authors' incompetence. It is a nice question in ethics whether gratitude can be earned by a self-interested act. Happily it is a question that I need not resolve. I have had much else in recent years for which to be grateful to my friends at Sweet and Maxwell Ltd. This I record here with pleasure and without qualification.

I wish also to thank my secretary, Barbara Harris, for all her cheerful help in the preparation of this edition.

E.J.G.
November 1981

CONTENTS

Preface		*page* v
Table of Cases		xi
Table of Statutes		XXV

		PARA.
1.	PRELIMINARY AND MISCELLANEOUS	
	1. Abbreviations	1–01
	2. The Background to the Acts	1–04
	3. The Contents of This Book	1–06
	4. Mode of Trial. Verdicts	1–07
	5. Interpretation	1–12
2.	THEFT	
	1. Introduction	2–01
	2. Basic Definition of Theft	2–02
	3. "Property"	2–03
	4. "Belonging to Another"	2–18
	5. "Appropriates"	2–37
	6. "With the Intention of Permanently Depriving the Other of it"	2–71
	7. "Dishonestly"	2–79
	8. Informations and Indictments	2–92
	9. Abstracting of Electricity; Dishonest Use of Public Telephone or Telex System	2–98
3.	ROBBERY	
	1. Definition	3–01
	2. The Details of the Offence	3–02
4.	BURGLARY AND AGGRAVATED BURGLARY	
	1. Introduction	4–01
	2. Burglary	4–02
	3. Aggravated Burglary	4–28
5.	OFFENCES OF TAKING NOT AMOUNTING TO THEFT	5–01
	1. Removal of an Article from a Place Open to the Public	5–02
	2. Taking a Conveyance without Authority	5–11
6.	OBTAINING PROPERTY BY DECEPTION	
	1. Introduction to the Fraud Offences	6–01
	2. The Offence of Obtaining Property by Deception	6–08
	3. "Obtains Property Belonging to Another"	6–09
	4. Deception	6–12

		PARA.
5.	Relation Between the False Representation and the Obtaining	6–30
6.	The Mental Element	6–41
7.	Jurisdiction	6–49
8.	Liability of Company Officers, etc.	6–53

7. OBTAINING SERVICES BY DECEPTION

1.	The Offence	7–01
2.	"By Any Deception Dishonestly Obtains"	7–03
3.	"Obtains Services from Another"	7–05

8. EVASION OF LIABILITY BY DECEPTION

1.	The Offence	8–01
2.	"By any Deception Dishonestly Secures/Induces/ Obtains"	8–04
3.	"Liability to Make a Payment"	8–06
4.	Securing Remission of Existing Liability	8–11
5.	Inducing Creditor to Wait for or Forgo Payment	8–13
6.	Obtaining Exemption from or Abatement of Liability	8–17

9. OBTAINING A PECUNIARY ADVANTAGE BY DECEPTION

1.	The Offence	9–01
2.	"By any Deception Dishonestly Obtains for Himself or Another"	9–04
3.	Overdrafts, Insurance Policies and Annuity Contracts	9–06
4.	Opportunity to Earn Remuneration or to win Money by Betting	9–09

10. OTHER FRAUD OFFENCES

1.	False Accounting	10–01
2.	False Statements by Company Directors, etc.	10–08
3.	Suppression of Documents. Procuring Execution of Valuable Securities	10–09

11. MAKING OFF WITHOUT PAYMENT

1.	The Offence. Power of Arrest	11–01
2.	The Details of the Offence	11–05

12. BLACKMAIL

1.	Introduction	12–01
2.	Definition of Blackmail. General Observations	12–04
3.	The Making of a Demand with Menaces	12–08
4.	The Demand with Menaces must be "Unwarranted"	12–20
5.	A View to Gain or an Intent to Cause Loss	12–32

13. HANDLING

1.	Definition	13–01
2.	Stolen Goods	13–02

CONTENTS

			PARA.
	3.	What Conduct Amounts to Handling	13–12
	4.	The Mental Element	13–18
	5.	The Relationship between Handling and Theft	13–27
	6.	Informations and Indictments	13–32
	7.	Advertising Rewards for Return of Goods Stolen or Lost	13–35
14.	GOING EQUIPPED		
	1.	Definition. Power of Arrest	14–01
	2.	The Details of the Offence	14–02
15.	HUSBAND AND WIFE		
	1.	The Spouse as Offender	15–01
	2.	The Spouse as Prosecutor. The Prosecution of Spouses	15–02
	3.	The Spouse as Witness	15–04
16.	RESTITUTION AND COMPENSATION		
	1.	Title to Property	16–01
	2.	Restitution and Compensation	16–02
APPENDICES			
	1.	The Theft Act 1968	17–01
	2.	The Theft Act 1978	18–01
Index			*page* 235

TABLE OF CASES

Abbott (1847) 1 Den. 273; 2 Car. & Kir. 630; 2 Cox C.C. 430 6–37
Agbim [1979] Crim.L.R. 171, C.A. 6–28
Airlie [1973] Crim.L.R. 310 13–25
Allsop (1976) 64 Cr.App.R. 29 6–48
Alt (1972) 136 J.P. 751; (1972) 56 Cr.App.R. 457; [1972] Crim.L.R. 552 .... 13–22, 13–32
Ambler [1979] R.T.R. 217, C.A. 5–21
Amos [1971] Crim.L.R. 352 13–32
Anderson [1978] Crim.L.R. 223 13–25
Anderton v. Wish (1980) 72 Cr.App.R. 23; [1980] Crim.L.R. 319, D.C. 2–37, 2–50, 2–58
Andrews and Craig [1962] 1 W.L.R. 1474; [1962] 3 All E.R. 961; 127 J.P. 64; 106 S.J.
   1013; 47 Cr.App.R. 32 13–31
Andrews and Hedges [1981] Crim.L.R. 106 8–15
Ardley (1871) L.R.I.C.C.R. 301; 40 L.J.M.C. 85; 24 L.T. 193; 19 W.R. 478; 35 J.P.
   550 6–16
Ashmore, Benson, Pease & Co. Ltd. v. A. V. Dawson Ltd. [1973] 1 W.L.R. 828; 117
   S.J. 203; [1973] 2 All E.R. 856; [1973] 2 Lloyd's Rep. 21; [1973] R.T.R. 473,
   C.A. 11–08
Aspinall (1876) 2 Q.B.D. 48 6–31
Attorney-General's Reference (No. 1 of 1974) [1974] Q.B. 744; 1974 2 W.L.R. 891;
   118 S.J. 345; [1974] 2 All E.R. 899; 59 Cr.App.R. 203; [1974] Crim.L.R. 427 ... 13–10
Attorney-General's References (Nos. 1 and 2 of 1979) [1980] Q.B. 180; [1979] 3
   W.L.R. 577; (1979) 123 S.J. 472; [1979] 3 All E.R. 143; (1979) 69 Cr.App.R.
   266; [1979] Crim.L.R. 585, C.A. 4–25
Attorney-General's Reference (No. 4 of 1979) (1980) 71 Cr.App.R. 341; [1981]
   Crim.L.R. 51, C.A... 13–06, 13–07
Attorney-General's Reference (No. 1 of 1980) [1981] 1 All E.R. 366 (1980) 124 S.J.
   881; The Times, October 30, 1980, C.A. 10–02
Atwal v. Massey (1971) 56 Cr.App.R. 6; [1971] 3 All E.R. 881...................... 13–18, 13–21

B. and S. v. Leathley [1979] Crim.L.R. 314 4–17
Balls (1871) L.R. 1 C.C.R. 328; 40 L.J.M.C. 148; 24 L.T. 760; 35 J.P. 820; 12 Cox
   96 2–95
Ballysingh (1953) 37 Cr.App.R. 28 .... 2–93, 2–96
Banaster (1978) 68 Cr.App.R. 272; [1979] R.T.R. 113, C.A. 6–17
Barnard (1837) 7 C. & P. 784 6–19
Barnard (1979) 70 Cr.App.R. 28; (1979) 123 S.J. 803; [1980] Crim.L.R. 235, C.A. 1–09
Barr [1978] Crim.L.R. 244 .... 5–05, 5–08
Bates v. Bulman [1979] 1 W.L.R. 1190; (1978) 123 S.J. 688; [1979] 3 All E.R. 170;
   (1978) 68 Cr.App.R. 21; [1979] Crim.L.R. 531, D.C. 4–34
Bayley and Easterbrook [1980] Crim.L.R. 503, C.A. 2–78
Baxter [1972] 1 Q.B. 1; [1971] 2 W.L.R. 1138; 115 S.J. 246; [1971] 2 All E.R. 359;
   [1971] Crim.L.R. 281; 55 Cr.App.R. 214 .... 1–12, 6–52, 12–14
Bellenie [1980] Crim.L.R. 437, C.A. 13–18, 13–21
Bernhard [1938] 2 K.B. 264; 107 L.J.K.B. 449; 159 L.T. 22; 54 T.L.R. 137; 102 J.P.
   282; 82 S.J. 257; [1938] 2 All E.R. 140; 36 Cr.App.R. 137; 36 L.G.R. 333; 31
   Cox 61... 2–82, 12–24, 12–29
Bhachu (1976) 65 Cr.App.R. 261, C.A. 2–55
Billing v. Pill [1954] 1 Q.B. 70; [1953] 3 W.L.R. 788; 117 J.P. 569; 97 S.J. 764; [1953] 2
   All E.R. 1061; 37 Cr.App.R. 174 2–04
Birshirgian (1936) 25 Cr.App.R. 176 10–06
Blackpool J.J., ex p. Charlson and Gregory [1972] 1 W.L.R. 1456; 116 S.J. 729; [1972]
   3 All E.R. 854; 56 Cr.App.R. 823 16–02
Blades v. Higgs (1865) 11 H.L.C. 621 2–08

Blayney v. Knight (1975) 60 Cr.App.R. 269; [1975] R.T.R. 279; [1975] Crim.L.R. 237......5–14, 5–19

Bleasdale (1848) 2 Car. & K. 765 2–94

Bloxham (1943) 29 Cr.App.R. 37......2–56, 2–76

Bloxham [1981] 1 W.L.R. 659; [1981] 2 All E.R. 647......13–15, 13–16, 13–22

Bogacki [1973] Q.B. 832; [1973] 2 W.L.R. 937; 117 S.J. 355; [1973] 2 All E.R. 864; [1973] R.T.R. 384; [1973] Crim.L.R. 385 5–14

Boggeln v. Williams [1978] 1 W.L.R. 873; (1978) 122 S.J. 94; [1978] 2 All E.R. 1061; (1978) 67 Cr.App.R. 50; [1978] Crim.L.R. 242, D.C. 2–88, 2–98

Bone [1968] 1 W.L.R. 983; 132 J.P. 420; 112 S.J. 480; [1968] 2 All E.R. 644; 52 Cr.App.R. 546 12–21

Bonner [1970] 1 W.L.R. 838; 114 S.J. 188; [1970] 2 All E.R. 97n; sub nom. R. v. Bonner (George Andrew); R. v. Town (Anthony Stuart); R. v. Anderson (William); R. v. Town (Michael Barry) 54 Cr.App.R. 257 ......1–12, 2–21, 2–37, 2–40, 2–42

Bott [1968] 1 All E.R. 1119; 132 J.P. 199 13–25

Bow [1977] R.T.R. 6; (1976) 64 Cr.App.R. 54; [1977] Crim.L.R. 176, C.A. 5–17

Bozickovic [1978] Crim.L.R. 686 4–25

Boyle and Merchant [1914] 2 K.B. 339; 83 L.J.K.B. 1801; 111 L.T. 638; 30 T.L.R. 521; 78 J.P. 390; 58 S.J. 673; 10 Cr.App.R. 180; 24 Cox 406 12–16

Bradburn (1973) 57 Cr.App.R. 948; [1973] Crim.L.R. 705 16–16

Bradley (1979) 70 Cr.App.R. 200; [1980] Crim.L.R. 173, C.A. 13–24

Brangwynne v. Evans [1962] 1 W.L.R. 267; [1962] 1 All E.R. 446 2–92

Bratty v. Att.-Gen. for Northern Ireland [1963] A.C. 386; [1961] 3 W.L.R. 965; 105 S.J. 865; [1961] 3 All E.R. 523; 46 Cr.App.R. 1 12–21

Brewster (1979) 69 Cr.App.R. 375; [1979] Crim.L.R. 798, C.A. 2–27

Bridges v. Hawkesworth (1852) 21 L.J.Q.B. 75; 18 L.T.(o.s.) 154 2–19

British Airways Board v. Taylor [1976] 1 W.L.R. 13; [1976] 1 All E.R. 65; (1975) 120 S.J. 7; [1976] 1 Lloyd's Rep. 167; (1975) 62 Cr.App.R. 174; 18 Man.Law 146 6–13

Brown [1965] Crim.L.R. 108......13–16, 13–31

Brutus v. Cozens [1973] A.C. 854; [1972] 3 W.L.R. 521; [1972] 2 All E.R. 1297; 56 Cr.App.R. 799; [1973] Crim.L.R. 56; sub nom. Cozens v. Brutus, 116 S.J. 647; reversing Cozens v. Brutus [1972] 1 W.L.R. 484; 116 S.J. 217; [1972] 2 All E.R. 1 2–87

Bryan (1857) Dears & B. 265; 26 L.J.M.C. 34; 5 W.R. 598; 21 J.P. 372; 3 Jur.(N.S.) 620; 7 Cox C.C. 312 6–16

Bryce (1955) 40 Cr.App.R. 62 2–28

Byrne v. Kinematograph Renters Society Ltd. [1958] 1 W.L.R. 762; 102 S.J. 509; [1958] 2 All E.R. 579 4–07

Bullock v. Dunlap (1876) 2 Ex.D. 43; 36 L.T. 194; 25 W.R. 293; 13 Cox 581 16–03

Bunce (1977) 66 Cr.App.R. 109; [1978] Crim.L.R. 236, C.A. 16–16

Bundy [1977] 1 W.L.R. 914; [1977] 2 All E.R. 382 14–03

Button [1900] 2 Q.B. 597; 69 L.J.Q.B. 901; 83 L.T. 288; 16 T.L.R. 525; 64 J.P. 600; 48 W.R. 703; 44 S.J. 659; 19 Cox C.C. 568......6–39, 9–11

C. (A Minor) v. Hume [1979] Crim.L.R. 328; sub nom. A.C. (A Minor) v. Hume [1979] R.T.R. 424, D.C. 5–18

Cadamarteris [1977] Crim.L.R. 236, C.A. 16–16

Caise v. Wright [1981] R.T.R. 49 5–19

Caldwell [1981] 2 W.L.R. 509; [1981] 1 All E.R. 961; (1981) 73 Cr.App.R. 13; [1981] Crim.L.R. 392, H.L.; affirming (1980) 71 Cr.App.R. 237; [1980] Crim.L.R. 572, C.A. 4–12, 6–43

Carpenter (1911) 76 J.P. 158; (1911) 22 Cox 618 6–48

Carter Patersons and Pickfords Carriers Ltd. v. Wessel [1947] K.B. 849; 177 L.T. 448; 91 S.J. 446; sub nom. Wessel v. Carter Paterson and Pickfords Carriers Ltd. [1947] L.J.R. 1370; 63 T.L.R. 517; 111 J.P. 474; [1947] 2 All E.R. 280 13–29

Chan Wan Lam v. The Queen [1981] Crim.L.R. 497 6–46

Chapman [1974] Crim.L.R. 488 2–67

Charles [1977] A.C. 177; (1976) 68 Cr.App.R. 334, *sub nom.* Metropolitan Police
    Commissioner *v.* Charles [1977] Crim.L.R. 615, H.L......6–21, 6–22, 6–32, 6–40, 9–07
Chatwood [1980] 1 W.L.R. 874; (1979) 124 S.J. 396; [1980] 1 All E.R. 467; [1980]
    Crim.L.R. 46; *sub nom.* R. *v.* Chatwood; R. *v.* Egan; R. *v.* Flaherty; R. *v.*
    Proctor; R. *v.* Walker (1979) 70 Cr.App.R. 39, C.A. 13–07
Christou [1971] Crim.L.R. 653; (1971) 115 S.J. 687 6–21
Church (1970) 55 Cr.App.R. 65 ....16–04, 16–09, 16–10
Clear [1968] 1 Q.B. 670; [1968] 2 W.L.R. 122; 112 S.J. 67; [1968] 1 All E.R.
    74 ....12–16, 12–18
Clegg [1977] C.L.Y. 619 6–40
Close [1977] Crim.L.R. 107, C.A. 13–08
Clotworthy [1981] Crim.L.R. 501 5–23
Clucas [1949] 2 K.B. 226; [1949] L.J.R. 1571; 65 T.L.R. 346; 113 J.P. 355; 93 S.J. 407;
    [1949] 2 All E.R. 40; 33 Cr.App.R. 136; 47 L.R.G. 563 .... 6–38, 6–39, 9–09
Cockburn [1968] 1 W.L.R. 281; [1968] 1 All E.R. 466; 132 J.P. 166; 112 S.J. 91; 52
    Cr.App.R. 134 2–86
Cocks (1976) 63 Cr.App.R. 79 2–73
Cohen (1907) 71 J.P. 1901 16–04
Collings (*Re*) [1933] Ch. 920 2–09
Collins [1973] Q.B. 100; [1972] 3 W.L.R. 243; 116 S.J. 432; [1972] 2 All E.R. 1105; 56
    Cr.App.R. 554 .... 4–06, 4–08, 4–12, 4–13, 4–14, 4–27
Collins (Christopher) [1976] Crim.L.R. 249 4–27
Collis-Smith [1971] Crim.L.R. 716 6–30
Collister and Warhurst (1955) 39 Cr.App.R. 100 12–08
Colonial Bank *v.* Whinney (1885) 30 Ch.D. 261 2–10
Copley (1979) 1 Cr.App.R.(S.) 55 16–16
Corbyn *v.* Saunders [1978] 1 W.L.R. 400; (1977) S.J. 15; [1978] 2 All E.R. 697; (1977)
    67 Cr.App.R. 7; [1978] Crim.L.R. 169 D.C. 11–14
Corcoran *v.* Whent [1977] Crim.L.R. 52 2–35
Corcoran *v.* Anderton (1980) 71 Cr.App.R. 104; [1980] Crim.L.R. 385, D.C.......2–49, 3–03
Cornwell (1979) 1 Cr.App.R.(S.) 19; [1979] Crim.L.R. 399, C.A. 16–16
Cottee *v.* Douglas Seaton (Used Cars) Ltd. [1972] 1 W.L.R. 1408; 116 S.J. 821; [1972]
    3 All E.R. 750; [1972] R.T.R. 509; [1972] Crim.L.R. 590 6–23
Cugullère [1961] 1 W.L.R. 858; [1961] 2 All E.R. 343; 125 J.P. 414; 105 S.J. 386; 45
    Cr.App.R. 108 4–35
Cullum (1873) L.R. 2 C.C.R. 28; 42 L.J.M.C. 64; 28 L.T. 571; 37 J.P. 442; 21 W.R.
    687; 12 Cox 469 2–29
Cunningham [1957] 2 Q.B. 396; [1957] 3 W.L.R. 76; 121 J.P. 451; 101 S.J. 503; [1957]
    2 All E.R. 412; 41 Cr.App.R. 155 4–26

Dabek [1973] Crim.L.R. 527 13–03
Daly [1974] 1 W.L.R. 133; 118 S.J. 66; [1974] 1 All E.R. 290; *sub nom.* R. *v.* Daly
    (James Joseph) (1973) 58 Cr.App.R. 333; [1974] Crim.L.R. 263 16–16
Davenport [1954] 1 W.L.R. 569; 118 J.P. 241; 98 S.J. 217; [1954] 1 All E.R. 602; 38
    Cr.App.R. 37 2–28
Davies (1823) R. & R. 499 4–14
Davies, *The Times*, November 7, 1981 2–63
Davies *v.* Alexander (1970) 54 Cr.App.R. 398 4–32
Davies *v.* Flackett (1972) 116 S.J. 526; [1973] R.T.R. 8; [1972] Crim.L.R. 708 6–12
Davies *v.* Leighton (1978) 68 Cr.App.R. 4; (1978) 122 S.J. 641; [1978] Crim.L.R. 575,
    D.C. 2–35
Davis [1972] Crim.L.R. 431 13–24
Davison, *Ex p.* (1896) 60 J.P. 808; 13 T.L.R. 93 16–14
Dawson (1976) 64 Cr.App.R. 170; (1976) R.T.R. 533; [1976] Crim.L.R. 692.......3–01, 3–04
Deakin [1972] 1 W.L.R. 1618; [1972] 3 All E.R. 803 ....13–14, 13–16, 13–32, 13–33
Deller (1952) 36 Cr.App.R. 184 6–27
Derry *v.* Peek (1889) 14 App.Cas. 337; 58 L.J.Ch. 864; 61 L.T. 265; 5 T.L.R. 625; 58
    W.R. 33; 54 J.P. 148; 1 Meg. 292; reversing *sub nom.* Peek *v.* Derry (1887) 37
    Ch.D. 541 6–43

Diggin (1980) 72 Cr.App.R. 204; [1980] Crim.L.R. 656, C.A. 5–20
D.P.P. v. Anderson [1978] A.C. 964; (1978) 122 S.J. 400; [1978] 2 All E.R. 512; (1978)
    67 Cr.App.R. 185; [1978] Crim.L.R. 568; H.L.; *sub nom.* R. v. Anderson
    (Keith) [1978] 2 W.L.R. 798; (1977) 121 S.J. 848; [1978] 2 All E.R. 8; (1978) 66
    Cr.App.R. 134, C.A. 16–02, 16–15
D.P.P. v. Humphrys [1977] A.C. 1; [1976] 2 W.L.R. 857; 120 S.J. 420; [1976] 2 All
    E.R. 497; [1976] R.T.R. 339; 63 Cr.App.R. 95; [1977] Crim.L.R. 421, H.L.;
    reversing *sub nom.* R. v. Humphrys [1976] Q.B. 191 4–27
D.P.P. v. Majewski [1977] A.C. 443; [1976] 2 W.L.R. 623; 120 S.J. 299; [1976] 2 All
    E.R. 142; (1976) 62 Cr.App.R. 262; [1976] Crim.L.R. 374, H.L.; affirming *sub*
    nom. R. v. Majewski [1975] 3 W.L.R. 401 5–23
D.P.P. v. Merriman [1973] A.C. 584; [1972] 3 W.L.R. 545; 116 S.J. 745; [1972] 3 All
    E.R. 42; 56 Cr.App.R. 766; [1972] Crim.L.R. 784, H.L.; reversing *sub nom.* R.
    v. Merriman [1971] 2 Q.B. 310 2–93
D.P.P. v. Morgan [1976] A.C. 182; [1975] 2 W.L.R. 913; 119 S.J. 319; 61 Cr.App.R.
    136; *sub nom.* D.P.P. v. Morgan [1975] 2 All E.R. 347; [1975] Crim.L.R. 717,
    H.L.; affirming *sub nom.* R. v. Morgan [1975] 1 All E.R. 8, C.A. 4–12
D.P.P. v. Nieser [1959] 1 Q.B. 254; [1958] 3 W.L.R. 757; 123 J.P. 105; 102 S.J. 955;
    [1958] 3 All E.R. 662; 43 Cr.App.R. 35 13–23
D.P.P. v. Nock [1978] A.C. 979; [1978] 3 W.L.R. 57; (1978) 122 S.J. 417; [1978] 2 All
    E.R. 654; (1978) 67 Cr.App.R. 116; [1978] Crim.L.R. 483, H.L.; reversing
    (1978) 122 S.J. 128 4–25
D.P.P. v. Ray [1974] A.C. 370; [1973] 3 W.L.R. 359; 117 S.J. 663; [1973] 3 All E.R.
    131; 58 Cr.App.R. 130 *sub nom.* Ray v. Sempers [1974] Crim.L.R. 181, H.L.;
    reversing *sub nom.* Ray v. Sempers [1973] 1 W.L.R. 317; [1973] 1 All E.R. 860;
    (1972) 57 Cr.App.R. 324; [1973] Crim.L.R. 182 .... 6–20, 6–25, 6–26,
                                            6–31, 6–36, 8–02, 11–03
D.P.P. v. Schildkamp [1971] A.C. 1; [1970] 2 W.L.R. 279; 114 S.J. 54; [1969] 3 All
    E.R. 1640; 54 Cr.App.R. 90; H.L. affirming [1969] 1 W.L.R. 818; 113 S.J. 486;
    [1969] 2 All E.R. 835n. 14–04
D.P.P. v. Stonehouse [1978] A.C. 55; [1977] 3 W.L.R. 143; (1977) 121 S.J. 491; [1977]
    2 All E.R. 909; (1977) 65 Cr.App.R. 192; [1977] Crim.L.R. 544, H.L. 6–49, 6–52
D.P.P. v. Turner [1974] A.C. 357; [1973] 3 W.L.R. 352; 117 S.J. 664; [1973] 3 All E.R.
    124; 57 Cr.App.R. 932; [1974] Crim.L.R. 186; H.L. reversing *sub nom.* R. v.
    Turner [1973] 1 W.L.R. 653; 117 S.J. 303; [1973] 2 All E.R. 826; [1973]
    Crim.L.R. 370; *sub nom.* R. v. Turner (John Eric) 57 Cr.App.R. 650,
    C.A. 1–14, 6–21, 8–02, 8–15
Dolan (1975) 62 Cr.App.R. 36; [1976] Crim.L.R. 145, C.A. 13–29
Donaghy and Marshall [1981] Crim.L.R. 644 3–10
Doodeward v. Spence (1908) 6 C.L.R. 406 2–16
Doukas [1978] 1 W.L.R. 372; (1978) 122 S.J. 30; [1978] 1 All E.R. 1061; (1977) 66
    Cr.App.R. 228; [1978] Crim.L.R. 177, C.A. 6–32, 14–07
Durkin [1973] Q.B. 786; [1973] 2 W.L.R. 741; 117 S.J. 355; [1973] 2 All E.R. 782 5–09
Durn [1974] 1 W.L.R. 2; [1973] 3 All E.R. 715 .... 2–14, 2–74, 6–11, 6–44, 6–45
Dymond [1920] 2 K.B. 260; 89 L.J.K.B. 876; 123 L.T. 336; 36 T.L.R. 421; 84 J.P. 103;
    64 S.J. 571; 26 Cox C.C. 621; 15 Cr.App.R. 1 12–29

Eagling v. Wheatley [1977] Crim.L.R. 165, D.C. 2–82
Easom [1971] 2 Q.B. 315; [1971] 3 W.L.R. 82; 115 S.J. 485; [1971] 2 All E.R. 445; 55
    Cr.App.R. 410 .... 2–76, 2–78
Eddy v. Niman [1981] Crim.L.R. 502 .... 2–50, 2–58
Eden (1971) 55 Cr.App.R. 193, C.A. 10–01, 10–03
Edgington v. Fitzmaurice (1885) 29 Ch.D. 459; 65 L.J.Ch. 650; 53 L.T. 369; 1 T.L.R.
    326; 33 W.R. 911; 50 J.P. 52 6–13
Edmonds [1963] 2 Q.B. 143; [1963] 2 W.L.R. 715; 127 J.P. 283; 107 S.J. 196; [1963] 1
    All E.R. 828; 47 Cr.App.R. 114 4–33
Edwards [1978] Crim.L.R. 49, C.A 6–19, 6–34

Edwards v. Clinch [1981] 3 W.L.R. 707; (1980) 124 S.J. 397; [1980] 3 All E.R. 278;
    [1980] S.T.C. 438, C.A.; reversing [1979] 1 W.L.R. 338; (1978) 122 S.J. 863;
    [1979] 1 All E.R. 648; [1979] S.T.C. 148; [1978] T.R. 417 9–10
Edwards v. Ddin [1976] 1 W.L.R. 942; 120 S.J. 587; [1976] 3 All E.R. 705; (1976) 63
    Cr.App.R. 218; [1976] R.T.R. 508; [1976] Crim.L.R. 580......................2–18, 2–36
Ellames [1974] 1 W.L.R. 1391; 118 S.J. 578; [1974] 3 All E.R. 130; [1974] Crim.L.R.
    554; sub nom R. v. Ellames (Charles John); (1974) 60 Cr.App.R. 7, C.A. 14–05
Elliot [1908] 2 K.B. 452 16–12
Ellis [1899] 1 Q.B. 230 6–49
Etim v. Hatfield [1975] Crim.L.R. 234..6–10, 6–36

Falconer-Atlee (1973) 58 Cr.App.R. 348, C.A. 2–80
Farrell [1975] 2 N.Z.L.R. 753 13–08
Feely [1973] 1 Q.B. 530; [1973] 2 W.L.R. 201; 117 S.J. 54; [1973] 1 All E.R. 341;
    [1973] Crim.L.R. 193; sub nom. R. v. Feely (David) (1972) 57 Cr.App.R. 312,
    C.A. 2–86, 2–87, 2–88, 2–88a, 2–89, 2–90, 2–91, 2–98, 6–47, 6–48, 11–16, 13–26
Ferguson [1970] 1 W.L.R. 1246; 114 S.J. 472; [1970] 2 All E.R. 820; 54 Cr.App.R.
    410..16–04, 16–07, 16–09
Ferris [1973] Crim.L.R. 642, C.A. 14–06
Figures [1976] Crim.L.R. 744 .... 2–45, 13–16
Firth (1869) L.R.I.C.C.R. 173; 38 L.J.M.C. 54; 19 L.T. 746; 33 J.P. 212; 17 W.R. 327;
    11 Cox 234 2–94
Flower Freight Co. Ltd. v. Hammond [1963] 1 Q.B. 275; [1962] 3 W.L.R. 1371; 127
    J.P. 42; 106 S.J. 919; [1962] 3 All E.R. 950; 61 L.G.R. 67 ....4–32, 5–13
Floyd v. Bush [1953] 1 W.L.R. 242; 117 J.P. 88; 97 S.J. 80; [1953] 1 All E.R. 265; 51
    L.G.R. 162; [1953] 1 Lloyd's Rep. 64...5–19, 5–24
Foley v. Hill (1848) 2 H.L.C. 28 2–09
French [1973] Crim.L.R. 632 13–34
French v. Champkin [1920] 1 K.B. 76; 89 L.J.K.B. 131; 122 L.T. 95; 36 T.L.R. 14; 83
    J.P. 258; 17 L.G.R. 761 5–13
Frost and Hale (1964) 108 S.J. 321; (1964) 48 Cr.App.R. 284 13–13
Fuschillo [1940] 2 All E.R. 489; 27 Cr.App.R. 193 13–07

Gale (1876) 2 Q.B.D. 141; 46 L.J.M.C. 134; 35 L.T. 526; 41 J.P. 119; 13 Cox 340 2–28
George (1901) 65 J.P. 729 16–04
Gibbons [1971] V.R. 79 13–07
Gilks [1972] 1 W.L.R. 1341; 116 S.J. 632; [1972] 3 All E.R. 280; 56 Cr.App.R.
    734..2–26, 2–31, 2–42, 2–88, 2–97
Governor of Pentonville Prison, ex p. Khubchandani (1980) 124 S.J. 275; (1980) 71
    Cr.App.R. 241; [1980] Crim.L.R. 436, C.A. 6–49
Grainge [1974] 1 W.L.R. 619; 118 S.J. 116; [1974] 1 All E.R. 928; sub nom. R. v.
    Grainge (Albert Robert) (1973) 59 Cr.App.R. 3; [1974] Crim.L.R. 180,
    C.A. 13–21, 13–22
Graham (1913) 8 Cr.App.R. 149 10–11
Grail (1944) 30 Cr.App.R. 81 6–31
Greater London Metropolitan Police Commissioner v. Streeter (1980) 71 Cr.App.R.
    113, D.C. 2–59, 13–09
Greenberg [1972] Crim.L.R. 331 2–36
Greenhoff [1979] Crim.L.R. 108 4–25
Greenstein; R. v. Green [1975] 1 W.L.R. 1353; [1976] 119 S.J. 742; [1976] 1 All E.R.
    1; sub nom. R. v. Greenstein (Allan); R. v. Green (Monty) (1975) 61
    Cr.App.R. 296; [1975] Crim.L.R. 714, C.A..............................2–88, 6–47, 6–48
Gregory [1972] 1 W.L.R. 991; 116 S.J. 506; [1972] 2 All E.R. 861; [1972] Crim.L.R.
    509; (1972) 56 Cr.App.R. 441, C.A. 13–33
Griffiths (1974) 60 Cr.App.R. 14, C.A. 13–21, 13–23
Griffiths v. Freeman; Same v. Same; Same v. Jones [1970] 1 W.L.R. 659; sub nom.
    Griffiths v. Freeman, 114 S.J. 263; sub nom. Griffiths v. Freeman; Jones v.
    Freeman [1970] 1 All E.R. 1117, D.C.....................................13–01, 13–32
Grundy (Teddington) Ltd. v. Fulton, The Times, July 2, 1981 2–58

Grundy and Moorhouse [1974] 1 W.L.R. 139; 118 S.J. 34; [1974] 1 All E.R. 292; [1974]
  Crim.L.R. 128, C.A. 16–16

Hack [1978] Crim.L.R. 359 13–07
Hale (1978) 68 Cr.App.R. 415; [1979] Crim.L.R. 596, C.A..................... 2–45, 2–49, 3–08,
                                                                                                3–09, 3–10, 13–28
Hall [1973] 1 Q.B. 126; [1972] 3 W.L.R. 381; 116 S.J. 598; [1972] 2 All E.R. 1009;
  [1972] Crim.L.R. 453; sub nom. R. v. Hall (Geoffrey) 56 Cr.App.R. 547,
  C.A. 2–25, 2–26
Halstead v. Patel [1972] 1 W.L.R. 661; 116 S.J. 218; [1972] 2 All E.R. 147; 56
  Cr.App.R. 334; [1972] Crim.L.R. 255 .... 2–73, 2–86, 2–89, 6–44, 6–47, 6–48
Hammer [1923] 2 K.B. 786 13–03
Hannah v. Peel [1945] K.B. 509; 114 L.J.K.B. 533; 61 T.L.R. 502; 89 S.J. 307; [1945] 2
  All E.R. 288 2–19
Harden [1963] 1 Q.B. 8; [1962] 2 W.L.R. 553; 126 J.P. 130; 106 S.J. 264; [1962] 1 All
  E.R. 286; 46 Cr.App.R. 90, C.C.A. 6–49
Harris [1961] Crim.L.R. 256; 111 S.J. 224 14–04
Harris [1966] 1 Q.B. 184; [1965] 3 W.L.R. 1040; 129 J.P. 542; 109 S.J 572; [1965] 3 All
  E.R. 206n; 49 Cr.App.R. 330, C.C.A. 10–06
Harrison [1970] Crim.L.R. 415, C.A. 14–10
Harry [1974] Crim.L.R. 32 12–17
Harvey (1980) 72 Cr.App.R. 139...12–22, 12–27, 12–28
Haughton v. Smith [1975] A.C. 476; [1974] 3 W.L.R. 1; [1973] 3 All E.R. 1109; (1973)
  58 Cr.App.R. 198; sub nom. R. v. Smith (Roger) (1973) 118 S.J. 7; [1974]
  Crim.L.R. 305, H.L.; affirming sub nom. R. v. Smith (Roger) (1973) 2 W.L.R.
  942; sub nom. R. v. Smith (R.D.) 117 S.J. 429; sub nom. R. v. Smith (Roger
  Daniel) [1973] 2 All E.R. 896; 57 Cr.App.R. 666; [1973] Crim.L.R. 508,
  C.A. 1–09, 2–26, 2–27, 2–78, 6–27, 13–02
Hayes (1977) 64 Cr.App.R. 82, [1977] Crim.L.R. 691, C.A. 2–80
Hazelton (1874) L.R. 2 C.C.R. 134; 44 L.J.M.C. 11; 31 L.T. 451; 39 J.P. 37; 23 W.R.
  139; 13 Cox, C.C. 1, C.C.R. 6–21
Hensler (1870) 22 L.T. 691; 34 J.P. 533; 19 W.R. 108; 11 Cox C.C. 570, C.C.R. 6–34
Henwood (1870) 22 L.J. 486; 34 J.P. 580; 11 Cox 526 2–94
Herron [1967] 1 Q.B. 107; [1966] 3 W.L.R. 374; 130 J.P. 266; 110 S.J. 544; [1966] 2 All
  E.R. 26; 50 Cr.App.R. 132, C.C.A. 13–25
Hibbert v. McKiernan [1948] 2 K.B. 142; [1948] L.J.R. 1521; 64 T.L.R. 256; 112 J.P.
  287; 92 S.J. 259; [1948] 1 All E.R. 860; 40 L.G.R. 238 2–19
Hillen and Pettigrew v. I.C.I. (Alkali) Ltd. [1936] A.C. 65 4–07
Hircock (1978) 67 Cr.App.R. 278; [1978] Crim.L.R. 184, C.A. 2–61, 2–62, 2–65, 2–66
Hobson v. Impett (1957) 41 Cr.App.R. 138, D.C. 13–13
Hogdon [1962] Crim.L.R. 563, C.C.A. 5–22
Holland v. Hodgson (1872) L.R. 7 C.P. 328; 41 L.J.C.P. 146; 26 L.T. 709; 20 W.R.
  990 2–04
Hollis [1971] Crim.L.R. 525, C.A.. 4–23, 4–35, 4–36
Holt and Lee [1981] 1 W.L.R. 1000; [1982] 2 All E.R. 854...........................8–02, 8–15
Hoskyn v. Metropolitan Police Commissioner [1979] A.C. 474; [1978] 2 W.L.R. 695;
  [1978] 2 All E.R. 136; (1978) 67 Cr.App.R. 88; [1978] Crim.L.R. 429, H.L.;
  reversing [1978] Crim.L.R. 225 15–04
Howell (A) (1978) 66 Cr.App.R. 179; [1978] Crim.L.R. 567, C.A. 16–16
Howlett; R. v. Howlett (1968) 112 S.J. 150; sub nom. R. v. Howlett and Howlett
  [1968] Crim.L.R. 222, C.A. 2–07
Hubbard v. Messenger [1938] 1 K.B. 300 ....4–32, 5–13
Hughes [1956] Crim.L.R. 835, C.A. 2–28
Hulbert (1979) 69 Cr.App.R. 243, C.A. 13–07
Humphreys [1977] Crim.L.R. 225, C.A. 4–34
Husseyn (1977) 67 Cr.App.R. 131; sub nom. R. v. Hussein [1978] Crim.L.R. 219,
  C.A. 4–25

Ikpong [1972] Crim.L.R. 432, C.A. 13–32
Ingram [1975] Crim.L.R. 457, C.A. 2–43

Inwood (1974) 60 Cr.App.R. 70, C.A. 16–16
Ironfield (1971) 55 Cr.App.R. 91, C.A. 16–16
Ismail [1977] Crim.L.R. 557, C.A. 13–21

Jackson (Peter) Pty. Ltd. v. Consolidated Insurance of Australia Ltd. [1975] V.R.
    781 2–61
Jaggard v. Dickinson [1981] 2 W.L.R. 118; (1980) 124 S.J. 847; [1980] 3 All E.R. 716;
    [1980] Crim.L.R. 717, D.C. 2–81, 5–23
Jemmison v. Priddle [1972] 1 Q.B. 489; [1972] 2 W.L.R. 293; (1971) 116 S.J. 99; [1972]
    1 All E.R. 539; (1971) 56 Cr.App.R. 229; [1972] Crim.L.R. 182, D.C. 2–93
Jones (1884) 50 L.T. 726; 48 J.P. 616; 15 Cox C.C. 475, C.C.R. 6–31
Jones (1948) 33 Cr.App.R. 11 2–28
Jones (John); R. v. Tomlinson; R. v. Warren; R. v. O'Shea; R. v. Carpenter; R. v.
    Llywarch [1974] I.C.R. 310; 118 S.J. 277; (1974) 59 Cr.App.R. 120; [1974]
    I.R.L.R. 117; [1974] Crim.L.R. 663, C.A. 2–93
Jones [1979] C.L.Y. 411 .... 4–35, 14–04
Jones and Smith [1976] 1 W.L.R. 672; [1976] 3 All E.R. 54.................. 4–07, 4–08, 4–13

Kaur v. Chief Constable for Hampshire [1981] 1 W.L.R. 578; [1981] 2 All E.R.
    430... 2–33, 2–35, 2–65
Keatley [1980] Crim.L.R. 505... 2–29, 10–02
Kelt [1977] 1 W.L.R. 1365; (1977) 121 S.J. 423; [1977] 3 All E.R. 1099; (1977) 65
    Cr.App.R. 74; [1977] Crim.L.R. 556, C.A. 4–35, 14–04
King [1979] Crim.L.R. 122 6–17
King [1938] 2 All E.R. 662 13–10
Kirby (1972) 56 Cr.App.R. 758, C.A. 13–32
Kneeshaw [1975] Q.B. 57; [1974] 2 W.L.R. 432; 118 S.J. 218; [1974] 1 All E.R. 896;
    sub nom. R. v. Kneeshaw (Michael Brian) 58 Cr.App.R. 439; [1974] Crim.L.R.
    263, C.A. 16–16
Knott [1973] Crim.L.R. 36, C.A. 13–25
Kohn (1979) 69 Cr.App.R. 395; [1979] Crim.L.R. 675, C.A.................. 2–13, 2–14, 2–74
Kovacs [1974] 1 W.L.R. 370; 118 S.J. 116; [1974] 1 All E.R. 1236; sub nom. R. v.
    Kovacs (Stephanie Javika) (1973) 58 Cr.App.R. 412; [1974] Crim.L.R. 183,
    C.A. 6–40, 9–07
Kylsant [1932] 1 K.B. 442 .... 6–17, 10–06

Lambert [1972] Crim.L.R. 422 12–28
Lambie [1981] 3 W.L.R. 88; [1981] 2 All E.R. 776 .... 6–22, 6–31, 6–32, 6–36, 14–07
Landy [1981] 1 W.L.R. 355; [1981] 1 All E.R. 1172.............. 2–88, 2–88a, 2–98, 6–48, 11–16
Lapworth [1931] 1 K.B. 117 15–04
Laverty [1970] 3 All E.R. 432; 54 Cr.App.R. 495; [1971] R.T.R. 124, C.A. 6–36
Lawrence v. Howlett [1952] W.N. 308; [1952] 1 T.L.R. 1476; 116 J.P. 391; 96 S.J. 397;
    [1952] 2 All E.R. 74; 50 L.G.R. 531; [1952] 1 Lloyd's Rep. 483, D.C. 5–24
Lawrence v. Metropolitan Police Commissioner [1972] A.C. 626; [1971] 3 W.L.R. 225;
    115 S.J. 565; 55 Cr.App.R. 471; sub nom. Lawrence v. Commissioner of Police
    for the Metropolis [1971] 2 All E.R. 1253; affirming sub nom. R. v. Lawrence
    (Alan) [1971] 1 Q.B. 373; [1970] 3 W.L.R. 1103; sub nom. R. v. Lawrence, 114
    S.J. 864; [1970] 3 All E.R. 933; 55 Cr.App.R. 73.................. 2–31, 2–57, 2–60, 2–61,
                       2–62, 2–63, 2–64, 2–65, 2–66, 2–67, 2–76, 2–79, 2–83, 6–43
Lawrence and Pomroy (1971) 57 Cr.App.R. 64; [1971] Crim.L.R. 645 ...12–17, 12–22, 12–34
Lawson [1952] 1 T.L.R. 889; 116 J.P. 195; [1952] 1 All E.R. 804; 36 Cr.App.R. 30 2–95
Leach v. R. [1912] A.C. 305; sub nom. Leach v. D.P.P. 81 L.J.K.B. 616; 106 L.T. 281;
    28 T.L.R. 289; 76 J.P. 203; 56 S.J. 342; 7 Cr.App.R. 157; 22 Cox 721 ....15–04, 15–05
Lester and Byast (1955) 39 Cr.App.R. 157 14–04
Levene v. Pearcey [1976] Crim.L.R. 63, D.C................................... 2–97, 6–09
Lewis (1922), unreported.. 6–39, 9–09
Lewis (1975) 62 Cr.App.R. 206; [1976] Crim.L.R. 383, C.A. 2–89, 6–47, 16–06

Lillis [1972] 2 Q.B. 236; [1972] 2 W.L.R. 1409; 16 S.J. 432; [1972] 2 All E.R. 1209; [1972] Crim.L.R. 458; *sub nom.* R. *v.* Lillis (Michael Joseph Patrick) 56 Cr.App.R. 573, C.A. 1–08, 1–09
Lince (1873) 28 L.T. 570; 37 J.P. 710; 12 Cox 451, C.C.R. 6–34
List [1966] 1 W.L.R. 9; [1965] 3 All E.R. 710; 12 Cox, C.C. 451, C.C.R. 13–25
Lobell [1957] 1 Q.B. 547; [1957] 2 W.L.R. 524; 121 J.P. 282; 101 S.J. 268; [1957] 1 All E.R. 734; 41 Cr.App.R. 100 12–21
Locker [1971] 2 Q.B. 321; [1971] 2 W.L.R. 1302; 115 S.J. 346; [1971] 2 All E.R. 875; *sub nom.* R. *v.* Locker (John Victor Daniel) 55 Cr.App.R. 378, C.A. 8–05
London County JJ., *ex p.* Dettmer & Co. (1908) 72 J.P. 513 16–12
London and Globe Finance Corporation, *Re* [1903] 1 Ch. 728 6–31
Lovett (1870) 23 L.T. 95; (1870) 11 Cox 602 16–16
Low *v.* Blease (1975) 119 S.J. 695; [1975] Crim.L.R. 513........................ 2–15, 2–98, 4–28
Lyons (Raymond) & Co. Ltd. *v.* Metropolitan Police Commissioner [1975] Q.B. 321; [1975] 2 W.L.R. 197; 119 S.J. 82; [1975] 1 All E.R. 335; [1975] Crim.L.R. 92 D.C. 16–14
Lyttle [1969] Crim.L.R. 213, C.A. 1–09

McCall (1970) 55 Cr.App.R. 175, C.A. 6–48
McCullum (1973) 57 Cr.App.R. 708, C.A. 13–18
MacDonagh [1974] Q.B. 448; [1974] 2 W.L.R. 529; 118 S.J. 222; [1974] 2 All E.R. 257; [1974] R.T.R. 372; *sub nom.* R. *v.* MacDonagh (Brian) 59 Crim.App.R. 55; [1974] Crim.L.R. 317, C.A. 5–19
McDonald (1980) 70 Cr.App.R. 288; [1980] Crim.L.R. 242, C.A. 13–07
McDonough (1962) 106 S.J. 961; (1962) 47 Cr.App.R. 37, C.C.A. 13–05
McGill *v.* Shepherd (1976) Victoria, unreported. 2–05
McHugh [1977] R.T.R.1; [1977] Crim.L.R. 174 1–11
McIvor, *The Times,* November 18, 1981; C.A. No. 3488/A/80 ....2–88, 2–88a, 6–48
McKnight *v.* Davies [1974] R.T.R. 4; 117 S.J. 940; [1974] Crim.L.R. 62, D.C.......5–15, 5–16
McPherson [1973] Crim.L.R. 191; 117 S.J. 13 ....2–50, 2–58
MacPherson [1973] R.T.R. 157; [1973] Crim.L.R. 457, C.A. 5–23
McQuaid *v.* Anderton [1981] 1 W.L.R. 154; [1980] 3 All E.R. 540 5–19
Machent *v.* Quinn [1970] 2 All E.R. 255 2–97
Macklin (1850) 5 Cox 216 16–09
Mallett [1978] 1 W.L.R. 820; (1978) 122 S.J. 295; [1978] 3 All E.R. 10; (1978) 67 Cr.App.R. 239, C.A. 10–06
Malone *v.* Metropolitan Police Commissioner [1980] Q.B. 49; [1978] 3 W.L.R. 936; (1978) 122 S.J. 433; (1978) Cr.App.R. 4; *sub nom.* Malone *v.* Commissioner of Police of the Metropolis [1979] 1 All E.R. 256; *sub nom.* Malone *v.* Commissioner of Metropolitan Police [1978] Crim.L.R. 555, C.A. 16–07
Mandry and Wooster [1973] 1 W.L.R. 1232; 117 S.J. 760; [1973] 3 All E.R. 996; [1974] Crim.L.R. 49; *sub nom.* R. *v.* Mandry (Michael John); R. *v.* Wooster (Roger John) 58 Cr.App.R. 27, C.A. 6–29
Manning *v.* Purcell (1855) 7 DeG.M. & G. 55 2–09
Mansfield [1975] Crim.L.R. 101, C.A. 14–07
Marshall (1971) 56 Cr.App.R. 263 13–32
Marshall [1977] Crim.L.R. 106 13–07
Martin (1867) L.R. 1 C.C.R. 56; 36 L.J.M.C. 20; 15 L.T. 541; 31 J.P. 164; 15 W.R. 358; 10 Cox C.C. 383, C.C.R..6–37, 6–38
Martin [1911] 2 K.B. 90 4–15
Mason [1980] 3 W.L.R. 617; [1980] 3 All E.R. 777; (1980) 71 Cr.App.R. 157, C.A. 13–23
Meech; R. *v.* Parslow; R. *v.* Jolliffe [1974] Q.B. 549; [1973] 3 W.L.R. 507; 117 S.J. *sub nom.* R. *v.* Meech (Arthur James); R. *v.* Parslow (Jonathan Joseph); R. *v.* Jolliffe (Peter William), 58 Cr.App.R. 74, C.A. 2–27, 2–58
Meredith [1973] Crim.L.R. 253 2–42
Metharam (1961) 45 Cr.App. 304; 125 J.P. 518; 105 S.J. 632; [1961] 3 All E.R. 200, C.A. 4–25
Metropolitan Police Commissioner *v.* Charles. *See* R. *v.* Charles.

Middleton (1873) L.R. 2 C.C.R. 38; 42 L.J.M.C. 73; 28 L.T. 777; 37 J.P. 629; 12 Cox
    417 2–31
Miller [1976] Crim.L.R. 147, C.A. 5–20
Miller (1976) 68 Cr.App.R. 56n, C.A. 16–16
Monaghan [1979] Crim.L.R. 673, C.A. 2–50
Moran (1952) 116 J.P. 216; [1952] 1 All E.R. 803n.; (1952) 36 Cr.App.R. 10; 15
    M.L.R. 345, C.A. 12–15
Morgan v. Ashcroft [1938] 1 K.B. 49 2–31
Morgan v. Russell & Sons [1909] 1 K.B. 357; 78 L.J.K.B. 187; 100 L.T. 118; 25 T.L.R.
    120; 53 S.J. 136 2–04
Moss v. Hancock [1899] 2 Q.B. 11 16–04
Mowatt [1968] 1 Q.B. 421; [1967] 3 W.L.R. 1192; 131 J.P. 463; 111 S.J. 716; [1967] 3
    All E.R. 47; 51 Cr.App.R. 402 4–26
Mowe v. Perraton (1952) 116 J.P. 139; 96 S.J. 182; [1952] 1 All E.R. 423; 35
    Cr.App.R. 194, D.C. 5–16
Moynes v. Coopper [1956] 1 Q.B. 439; [1956] 2 W.L.R. 562; 120 J.P. 147; 100 S.J. 171;
    [1956] 1 All E.R. 450; 40 Cr.App.R. 20 2–30

Naguib [1917] 1 K.B. 359; 86 L.J.K.B. 709; 116 L.T. 640; 81 J.P. 116; 25 Cox C.C. 712;
    12 Cr.App.R. 187; C.C.A. 13–03
Naylor (1865) L.R. 1 C.C.R. 41; 35 L.J.M.C. 61; 13 L.T. 381; 30 J.P. 6; 1 Jur.N.S.
    910; 14 W.R. 58; 10 Cox, C.C. 149, C.C.R. 6–48
Neal v. Gribble (1978) 68 Cr.App.R. 9; [1978] R.T.R. 409; [1978] Crim.L.R. 500,
    D.C. 5–13
Nicklin [1977] 1 W.L.R. 403; 121 S.J. 286; [1977] 2 All E.R. 444; (1977) 64 Cr.App.R.
    205; [1977] Crim.L.R. 221, C.A. 13–32
Noble [1974] 1 W.L.R. 894; 118 S.J. 442; [1974] 2 All E.R. 811; [1974] Crim.L.R. 545;
    sub nom. R. v. Noble (Irene), 59 Cr.App.R. 209, C.A.; affirming [1974]
    Crim.L.R. 42 15–04
Nordeng [1976] Crim.L.R. 194; sub nom. R. v. Nordeng (Jarl) (1975) 62 Cr.App.R.
    123, C.A. 6–25
Norreys v. Zeffert (1939) 83 S.J. 456; [1939] 2 All E.R. 187 12–16

Oddy [1974] 1 W.L.R. 1212; 118 S.J. 239; [1974] 2 All E.R. 666; sub nom. R. v. Oddy
    (Julian Farrar), 59 Cr.App.R. 66; [1974] Crim.L.R. 435, C.A. 16–16
O'Donaghue (1974) 66 Cr.App.R. 116n 16–16
Ohlson v. Hylton [1975] 1 W.L.R. 724; 119 S.J. 255; [1975] 2 All E.R. 490; [1975]
    Crim.L.R. 292, D.C. 4–34
Overington [1978] Crim.L.R. 692, C.A. 13–07
Oxford v. Moss (1978) 68 Cr.App.R. 183; [1979] Crim.L.R. 119, D.C. 2–17
Oxford v. Peers (1980) 42 Cr.App.R. 19 2–50

Page [1971] 2 Q.B. 330; [1971] 2 W.L.R. 1308; 115 S.J. 385; [1971] 2 All E.R. 870; sub
    nom. R. v. Page (Gregory Arthur), 55 Cr.App.R. 184, C.A. 6–21
Page [1971] Crim.L.R. 713, C.A. 1–08
Parker [1970] 1 W.L.R. 1003; [1970] 2 All E.R. 458; sub nom. R. v. Parker (Harry)
    (1970) 54 Cr.App.R. 339, C.A. 16–06, 16–12
Parkes [1973] Crim.L.R. 358 12–34
Partington v. Williams (1975) 120 S.J. 80; (1975) 62 Cr.App.R. 220 2–78
Paterson [1976] 2 N.Z.L.R. 394 4–15
Pearce [1973] Crim.L.R. 321, C.A. 5–17
Pearlman v. Harrow School (Keepers and Governors of) [1979] Q.B. 56; [1978] 3
    W.L.R. 736; [1979] 1 All E.R. 365; (1978) 38 P. & C.R. 136; (1978) 247 E.G.
    1173; [1978] J.P.L. 829, C.A. 1–14
Peart [1970] 2 Q.B. 672; [1970] 3 W.L.R. 63; 114 S.J. 418; [1970] 2 All E.R. 823; sub
    nom. R. v. Peart (Frank) (1970) 54 Cr.App.R. 374, C.A. 5–16, 5–22
Perry (Howard E.) Ltd. v. British Railways Board [1980] I.C.R. 743; [1980] 1 W.L.R.
    1375; [1980] 2 All E.R. 579; (1980) 124 S.J. 591; [1980] 2 All E.R. 579 2–50
Pethick [1980] Crim.L.R. 242, C.A. 13–21

Petrie [1961] 1 W.L.R. 358; 125 J.P. 198; 105 S.J. 131; [1961] 1 All E.R. 466; 45
    Cr.App.R. 72..4–31, 4–32, 4–33
Phipps and McGill (1970) 54 Cr.App.R. 301; *sub nom.* R. *v.* Phipps; R. *v.* McGill
    [1970] R.T.R. 209; *sub nom.* R. *v.* McGill [1970] Crim.L.R. 290, C.A. 5–16, 5–22
Pilgram *v.* Rice-Smith [1977] 1 W.L.R. 671; [1977] 2 All E.R. 658; (1977) 65
    Cr.App.R. 142; [1977] Crim.L.R. 371, D.C...2–50, 2–97
Pitchley (1972) 57 Cr.App.R. 30; 1972 Crim.L.R. 705, C.A. 2–09, 13–16, 13–22, 13–32
Pitham and Hehl (1976) 65 Cr.App.R. 45; [1977] Crim.L.R. 285, C.A. 2–37, 2–50, 2–56
Porter [1976] Crim.L.R. 58 13–07
Potger (1970) 55 Cr.App.R. 42; 114 S.J. 906..................................... 2–86, 6–47, 6–48
Powell *v.* McRae [1977] Crim.L.R. 571, D.C. 2–29
Pratt (1855) 4 E. & B. 860 4–15
Price (1884) 12 Q.B.D. 247 2–16

Quigley *v.* Stokes [1977] 1 W.L.R. 434; 121 S.J. 224; (1976) 64 Cr.App.R. 198; [1977]
    2 All E.R. 317; [1977] R.T.R. 333; [1977] Crim.L.R. 282, D.C. 16–15

Rank Film Distributors Ltd. *v.* Video Information Centre [1981] 2 W.L.R. 668; [1981]
    2 All E.R. 76 2–10
Rao [1972] Crim.L.R. 451 2–86
Rapier (1979) 70 Cr.App.R. 17; [1980] Crim.L.R. 48, C.A.............................4–32, 4–33
Rashid [1977] 1 W.L.R. 298; [1977] 2 All E.R. 237; (1976) 64 Cr.App.R. 201; [1977]
    Crim.L.R. 237, C.A. 14–07, 14–09
Reader (1977) 66 Cr.App.R. 33, C.A. 13–21
Reeves (1978) 68 Cr.App.R. 331; [1979] Crim.L.R. 459, C.A. 13–21
Rice *v.* Connolly [1966] 2 Q.B. 414; [1966] 3 W.L.R. 17; 130 J.P. 322; 110 S.J. 371;
    [1966] 2 All E.R. 649, D.C. 13–16
Roberts (No. 2) [1965] 1 Q.B. 85; [1964] 3 W.L.R. 180; 128 J.P. 395; [1964] 2 All E.R.
    541; 48 Cr.App.R. 296; 235 L.T. 385, C.C.A. 5–19
Robertson, Stanley [1977] Crim.L.R. 629 2–28
Robinson (1796) 2 Leach 749; 2 East P.C. 1110 12–08
Robinson [1977] Crim.L.R. 173, C.A..2–82, 3–02
Rogers *v.* Arnott [1960] 2 Q.B. 244; [1960] 2 W.L.R. 73; 124 J.P. 349; 104 S.J. 508;
    [1960] 2 All E.R. 417; 44 Cr.App.R. 195, D.C. 2–40, 2–50
Roper *v.* Taylor's Central Garage (Exeter) [1951] 2 T.L.R. 284, D.C. 13–20
Rothery [1976] R.T.R. 550; [1976] Crim.L.R. 691, *sub nom.* R. *v.* Rothery (Henry
    Michael) (1976) 63 Cr.App.R. 231, C.A. 2–16
Royle [1971] 1 W.L.R. 1764; 115 S.J. 910; [1971] 3 All E.R. 1359; 56 Cr.App.R. 131,
    C.A. 6–04, 6–43, 8–05

Sainthouse [1980] Crim.L.R. 506, C.A. 2–52, 2–70, 13–27, 13–30
St. John Shipping Corporation *v.* Joseph Rank Ltd. [1957] 1 Q.B. 267; [1956] 3
    W.L.R. 870; 100 S.J. 841; [1956] 3 All E.R. 683; [1956] 2 Lloyd's Rep. 413 11–08
Salvo [1980] V.R. 401 ....2–87, 6–47
Sanders [1919] 1 K.B. 550 6–37
Saycell *v.* Bool [1948] W.N. 232; 63 T.L.R. 421; 112 J.P. 341; 92 S.J. 311; [1948] 2 All
    E.R. 83; 46 L.G.R. 447, D.C. 5–19
Sbarra (1918) 13 Cr.App.R. 118 13–07
Scattergood *v.* Sylvester (1850) 15 Q.B. 506 16–14
Schama and Abramovitch (1914) 112 L.T. 480; (1914) 11 Cr.App.R. 45 13–23
Schmidt (1866) L.R. 1 C.C.R. 15; 35 L.J.M.C. 94; 13 L.T. 679; 30 J.P. 100; 12 Jur.
    (N.S.) 149; 14 W.R. 786; 10 Cox 172 13–09
Schofield [1978] 1 W.L.R. 979; (1978) 122 S.J. 128; [1978] 2 All E.R. 705; (1978) 67
    Cr.App.R. 282, C.A. 16–16
Scudder *v.* Barrett; Miles *v.* Clovis [1980] Q.B. 195n; [1979] 3 W.L.R. 591; (1979) 69
    Cr.App.R. 277, D.C. 2–78
Seagrave (1910) 4 Cr.App.R. 156 6–31
Seamark *v.* Prouse [1980] 1 W.L.R. 698; (1980) 124 S.J. 167; [1980] 3 All E.R. 26;
    (1980) 70 Cr.App.R. 236; [1980] Crim.L.R. 240, D.C. 4–29

Sergeant (1826) Ry. & M. 352 15–04
Seymour [1954] 1 W.L.R. 678; 118 J.P. 311; 98 S.J. 288; [1954] 1 All E.R. 1006; 38
    Cr.App.R. 68; 118 J.P.J. 635, C.C.A. 13–23
Sharkey [1976] Crim.L.R. 388; 120 S.J. 95 16–16
Sharpe (1857) Dears & Bell 160 2–16
Shendley, 113 S.J. 834; [1970] Crim.L.R. 49, C.A. 3–10
Shepherd (1868) L.R. 1 C.C.R. 118; 37 L.J.M.C. 45; 17 L.T. 482; 32 J.P. 116; 16 W.R.
    373; 11 Cox 119 2–94
Shenton (1979) 1 Cr.App.R. (S.) 81 16–16
Skipp [1975] Crim.L.R. 114, C.A. 2–61, 2–62, 2–66, 2–93
Skivington [1968] 1 Q.B. 166; [1967] 2 W.L.R. 665; 131 J.P. 265; 111 S.J. 72; [1967] 1
    All E.R. 483; 51 Cr.App.R. 167...2–82, 3–02
Skujins [1956] Crim.L.R. 266 2–04
Sloggett [1972] 1 Q.B. 430; [1971] 3 W.L.R. 628; 115 S.J. 655; [1971] 3 All E.R. 264;
    sub nom. R. v. Sloggett (Sydney Ernest), 55 Cr.App.R. 532, C.A........13–15, 13–23,
                                                                                13–32
Smith (1850) 1 Den. 510; T. & M. 214; 2 Car. & Kir. 882; 19 L.J.M.C. 80; 14 J.P. 69;
    14 Jur. 92; 4 Cox C.C. 42 12–19
Smith (1915) 11 Cr.App.R. 81 6–31
Smith [1924] 2 K.B. 194; 93 L.J.K.B. 1006; 131 L.T. 28; 88 J.P. 108; 69 S.J. 37; 18
    Cr.App.R. 76; 27 Cox 618 2–24
Smith (Albert) (1976) 64 Cr.App.R. 217, C.A. 13–21
Smith v. Komourou [1979] R.T.R. 355; [1979] Crim.L.R. 116, D.C. 6–40
Smith v. Land and House Property Corporation (1884) 28 Ch.D. 7 6–18
Smythe (1981) 72 Cr.App.R. 8................... 13–01, 13–13, 13–22, 13–32, 13–33
Solomons [1909] 2 K.B. 980 10–02
Southwark London Borough Council v. Williams, Southwark London Borough
    Council v. Anderson [1971] Ch. 734; [1971] 2 W.L.R. 467; [1971] 2 All E.R.
    175; 69 L.G.R. 145, C.A. 2–91
Springfield (1969) 53 Cr.App.R. 608; 113 S.J. 670; [1969] Crim.L.R. 557, C.A. ... 1–08, 1–09
Stagg [1978] Crim.L.R. 227, C.A. 13–18
Staines (1974) 60 Cr.App.R. 160; [1975] Crim.L.R. 651, C.A. 6–43
Stamp v. United Dominions Trust (Commercial) Ltd. [1967] 1 Q.B. 418; [1967] 2
    W.L.R. 541; 131 J.P. 177; 110 S.J. 904; [1967] 1 All E.R. 251; [1966] C.L.Y.
    7650, D.C...16–04, 16–12
Stapylton v. O'Callaghan [1973] 2 All E.R. 782; [1974] Crim.L.R. 63, D.C. 2–37, 2–52,
                                                                                2–70, 13–23, 13–30
Stapleton and Lawrie [1977] Crim.L.R. 366, C.A. 16–16
Stevens v. Gourley (1859) 7 C.B. (N.S.) 99 4–17
Studer (1915) 11 Cr.App.R. 307; 85 L.J.K.B. 1017; 114 L.T. 424; 25 Cox C.C.
    312...12–08, 12–19
Sullivan (1945) 30 Cr.App.R. 132...6–31, 6–36
Sunair Holidays Ltd. [1973] 1 W.L.R. 1105; 117 S.J. 429; [1973] 2 All E.R. 1233; 57
    Cr.App.R. 782; [1973] Crim.L.R. 587, C.A. 6–13
Swift (1980) unreported 1–14

Tamm [1973] Crim. L.R. 115 13–16
Tarling v. Government of the Republic of Singapore (1979) 70 Cr.App.R. 77; [1978]
    Crim.L.R. 490, H.L.; reversing The Times, April 26 & 27, July 30, 1977,
    D.C. 2–22, 2–29
Taylor [1979] Crim.L.R. 649; C.A. 4–23
Taylor v. Mead [1961] 1 W.L.R. 435; 125 J.P. 286; 105 S.J. 159; [1961] 1 All E.R. 626;
    59 L.G.R. 202; 25 J.P.J. 201, D.C. 5–13
Tennant [1976] Crim.L.R. 133 1–09
Thompson (1869) 21 L.T. 397; 33 J.P. 791; 11 Cox C.C. 362, C.C.R...................... 14–04
Thompson [1914] 2 K.B. 99 2–96
Thorne v. Motor Trade Association [1937] A.C. 797 ....12–16, 12–25
Thornton [1964] 2 Q.B. 176; [1963] 3 W.L.R. 444; 127 J.P. 113; [1963] 1 All E.R. 170;
    47 Cr.App.R. 1, C.C.A. 10–12

Tideswell [1905] 2 K.B. 273 2–97
Tirado (1974) 59 Cr.App.R. 80, C.A. 6–36, 6–49
Tolhurst and Woodhouse; R. *v.* Woodhouse, (1961) 106 S.J. 16; *sub nom.* R. *v.*
    Tolhurst and Woodhouse [1962] Crim.L.R. 489, C.C.A. 5–21
Tolley *v.* Giddings [1964] 2 Q.B. 354; [1964] 2 W.L.R. 471; 128 J.P. 182; 108 S.J. 36;
    [1964] 1 All E.R. 201; 48 Cr.App.R. 105; 62 L.G.R. 158, D.C. 5–20
Tomlin [1954] 2 Q.B. 274; [1954] 2 W.L.R. 1140; 118 J.P. 354; 98 S.J. 374; [1954] 2 All
    E.R. 272; 38 Cr.App.R. 82 2–95
Torkington *v.* Magee [1902] 2 K.B. 427 2–10
Treacy *v.* D.P.P [1971] A.C. 537; [1971] 2 W.L.R. 112; (1970) 115 S.J. 12; [1971] 1 All
    E.R. 110; (1970) 55 Cr.App.R. 113; 115 S.J. 239, H.L.; affirming *sub nom.* R.
    v. Treacy [1970] 3 W.L.R. 592 .... 1–14, 6–49, 12–12, 12–13, 12–14, 12–15
Turner (No. 2) [1971] 1 W.L.R. 901; [1971] 2 All E.R. 441; [1971] R.T.R. 396; *sub
    nom.* R. *v.* Turner, 115 S.J. 405; *sub nom.* R. *v.* Turner (Frank Richard) 55
    Cr.App.R. 336 .... 2–31, 2–42, 2–79

Villensky [1892] 2 Q.B. 597 13–09
Vivian [1979] 1 W.L.R. 291; (1978) 122 S.J. 680; [1979] 1 All E.R. 48; [1979] R.T.R.
    106; (1978) 68 Cr.App.R. 53, C.A. 16–16

Walkington [1979] 1 W.L.R. 1169; (1979) 123 S.J. 704; [1979] 2 All E.R. 716; (1979) 68
    Cr.App.R. 427; [1979] Crim.L.R. 526, C.A. 4–20, 4–25
Walters *v.* Lunt [1951] W.N. 472; 115 J.P. 512; 95 S.J. 625; [1951] 2 All E.R. 645; 35
    Cr.App.R. 94; 49 L.G.R. 809, D.C. 13–08
Wakeman (1912) 8 Cr.App.R. 18 2–55
Wakeman *v.* Farrar [1974] Crim.L.R. 136, D.C. 2–28
Warner (1970) 55 Cr.App.R. 93, C.A. 2–73
Warner *v.* Metropolitan Police Commissioner [1969] A.C. 256; [1968] 2 W.L.R. 1303;
    (1968) 132 J.P. 378; 112 S.J. 378; [1968] 2 All E.R. 356; 52 Cr.App.R. 373,
    H.L. 4–35
Waterfall [1970] 1 Q.B. 148; [1969] 3 W.L.R. 947; 113 S.J. 872; [1969] 3 All E.R. 1048;
    53 Cr.App.R. 596, C.A. 2–89, 6–43, 6–47, 8–05
Watkins [1976] 1 All E.R. 578 .... 9–06, 9–07
Webb (1979) 1 Cr.App.R.(S.) 16; [1979] Crim.L.R. 466, C.A. 16–16
Webley *v.* Buxton [1977] Q.B. 481; [1977] 2 W.L.R. 766; 121 S.J. 153; [1977] 2 All
    E.R. 895; [1977] R.T.R. 193; (1977) 65 Cr.App.R. 136; [1977] Crim.L.R. 160,
    D.C. 1–10
Webley *v.* Webley [1967] Crim.L.R. 300; 111 S.J. 111 .... 4–35, 14–04
Welham *v.* D.P.P. [1961] A.C. 103; [1960] 2 W.L.R. 669; 124 J.P. 280; 104 S.J. 308;
    [1960] 1 All E.R. 805; 44 Cr.App.R. 124, H.L.; affirming *sub norm.* R. *v.*
    Welham [1960] 2 Q.B. 445; [1960] 2 W.L.R. 333; 124 J.P. 156; 104 S.J. 108;
    [1960] 1 All E.R. 260; 44 Cr.App.R. 79, C.C.A. 10–05
Welsh [1974] R.T.R. 479 2–16
Whenman [1977] Crim.L.R. 450, C.A. 16–16
Wibberley [1966] 2 Q.B. 214; [1966] 2 W.L.R. 1; 130 J.P. 58; 109 S.J. 877; [1965] 3 All
    E.R. 718; 50 Cr.App.R. 51, C.C.A. 5–15, 5–16
Wilkins [1975] 2 All E.R. 734; [1975] Crim.L.R. 343; *sub nom.* R. *v.* Wilkins (Betty
    Margaret) 60 Cr.App.R. 300, C.A. 13–25
Wilkinson (1979) 1 Cr.App.R.(S.) 69 16–16
Williams (1836) 7 C. & P. 354 6–47
Williams [1953] 1 Q.B. 660; [1953] 2 W.L.R. 937; 117 J.P. 251; 97 S.J. 318; [1953] 1 All
    E.R. 1068; 37 Cr.App.R. 71 2–86
Williams [1962] Crim.L.R. 111 2–81
Williams [1980] Crim.L.R. 589, C.A. 2–33, 2–63
Williams *v.* Williams (1882) 20 Ch.D. 659 2–16
Williamson (1977) 67 Cr.App.R. 35; (1977) 121 S.J. 812; [1978] Crim.L.R. 228,
    C.A. 4–31
Willis and Syme [1972] 1 W.L.R. 1605; 116 S.J. 944; [1972] 3 All E.R. 797; 57
    Cr.App.R. 1, C.A. 13–32

Wilson v. Read; Blyth v. Read [1956] Crim.L.R. 418, D.C. 2–95
Wines [1954] 1 W.L.R. 64; 118 J.P. 49; [1953] 2 All E.R. 1497; 37 Cr.App.R. 197,
    C.C.A. 10–04, 12–34
Winter v. Bancks (1901) 84 L.T. 504; 17 T.L.R. 446; 65 J.P. 468; 49 W.R. 574; 19 Cox
    687 16–03
Withers [1975] Crim.L.R. 647 15–02
Wollez (1860) 8 Cox 337 16–13
Woodley v. Woodley [1978] Crim.L.R. 629; (1978) 8 Fam. Law 207, D.C. 15–03
Woodman [1974] Q.B. 745; [1974] 2 W.L.R. 821; 118 S.J. 346; [1974] 2 All E.R. 955;
    [1974] Crim.L.R. 441; sub nom. R. v. Woodman (George Eli) (1974) 59
    Cr.App.R. 105, C.C.A. 2–19
Woods [1969] 1 Q.B. 447; [1968] 3 W.L.R. 1192; 112 S.J. 839; 133 J.P. 51; [1968] 3 All
    E.R. 709; sub nom. R. v. Woods (Patrick Thomas) 53 Cr.App.R. 30, C.A. 1–09
Woolmington v. D.P.P. [1935] A.C. 462 12–21
Workman (1979) 1 Cr.App.R.(S.) 335; [1980] Crim.L.R. 189, C.A. 16–16
Wylie [1975] R.T.R. 94; [1974] Crim.L.R. 608, C.A. 16–16

Young v. Spiers (1952) 36 Cr.App.R. 200 13–07

TABLE OF STATUTES

1831 Game Act (1 & 2 Will. 4,
   c. 32)
   s. 30 4–15
1832 Anatomy Act (2 & 3 Will. 4,
   c. 75)
   s. 7 2–16
   s. 10 2–16
1861 Larceny Act (24 & 25 Vict.
   c. 96)........... 2–08, 10–09, 17–32
   s. 84...................... 6–17, 10–08
   Offences against the Person
   Act (24 & 25 Vict. c. 100)
   s. 18 4–03
   s. 20......................4–03, 4–26
1869 Debtors Act (32 & 33 Vict.
   c. 62)
   s. 13 6–02
1870 Extradition Act (33 & 34 Vict.,
   c. 52) Sched. 1 17–33
1873 Extradition Act (36 & 37 Vict.
   c. 60)................... 17–33, 18–05
1874 Infants Relief Act (37 & 38
   Vict. c. 62) 8–07
1875 Falsification of Accounts Act
   (38 & 39 Vict. c. 24) 10–02,
           10–04
   s. 2 6–03
1890 Partnership Act (53 & 54 Vict.
   c. 39)
   s. 20(1) 2–42
1893 Sale of Goods Act (56 & 57
   Vict. c. 71)
   s. 24(1) 16–01
1897 Police (Property) Act (60 & 61
   Vict. c. 30) 16–03, 16–14
   s. 1(1) 16–14
   (2) 16–14
   s. 2(1) 16–14
1898 Criminal Evidence Act (61 &
   62 Vict. c. 36)
   s. 4(1) 15–04
1913 Forgery Act (3 & 4 Geo. 5,
   c. 27)................... 10–05, 15–04
   s. 6 10–06
   (2) 10–06
1915 Indictments Act (c. 90) 2–94,
           13–33
1916 Larceny Act (6 & 7 Geo. 5,
   c. 50)....................1–04, 2–31,
      2–86, 2–95, 3–01, 6–13,
          10–09, 12–02
   s. 1(1)......................2–39, 2–57
   (3)(b) 2–07

1916 Larceny Act—cont.
   s. 20(1)(i) 2–39
   s. 21 2–39
   s. 23(1)(b) 3–08
   ss. 24–27 4–01
   s. 28 4–01
   (2) 14–04, 14–06
   s. 29(1)(i)............... 12–03, 12–12,
         12–16, 12–25
   ss. 29–31 12–01
   s. 30...................... 12–03, 12–16,
         12–18, 12–24
   s. 32................. 6–02, 6–08, 6–49
   (1) 6–12
   s. 33 13–01
   s. 44(3) 2–66
   (4) 2–66
   s. 45...................... 16–01, 16–04
1920 Administration of Justice Act
   (10 & 11 Geo. 5, c. 81)
   s. 15 13–03
1925 Criminal Justice Act (15 & 16
   Geo. 5, c. 86)
   s. 47 15–01
1952 Magistrates' Courts Act (15 &
   16 Geo. 6 & 1 Eliz. 2,
   c. 10)
   s. 33 16–04
1952 Visiting Forces Act (15 & 16
   Geo. 6 & 1 Eliz. 2, c. 67)   18–05
1953 Prevention of Crime Act (1 &
   2 Eliz. 2, c. 14) 4–30,
         4–31, 4–34
   s. 1(1)...................... 4–30, 4–35
   (4) 4–30
   Post Office Act (1 & 2 Eliz. 2,
   c. 36) 17–33
   Sched. 2, Part I, para. 8 2–98
1956 Sexual Offences Act (4 & 5
   Eliz. 2, c. 69)
   s. 1 4–03
   Copyright Act (4 & 5 Eliz. 2,
   c. 74)
   s. 1(1) 2–69
   s. 2(5) 2–69
1958 Prevention of Fraud (Investments) Act (6 & 7 Eliz. 2,
   c. 45)
   s. 13 6–03
1960 Road Traffic Act (8 & 9 Eliz.
   2, c. 16)
   s. 191(1) 5–13
   s. 217(1) 5–15

1960	Charities Act (8 & 9 Eliz. 2, c. 58)	
	s. 28	2–23
	(1)	2–23
	(2)	2–23
1961	Mock Auctions Act (9 & 10 Eliz. 2, c. 46)	11–07
	Human Tissue Act (9 & 10 Eliz. 2, c. 54)	
	s. 1	2–16
1962	Vehicles (Excise) Act (10 & 11 Eliz. 2, c. 13)	
	Sched. 4, Pt. I, para. 7	5–13
1967	Criminal Law Act (c. 58)	4–01
	s. 2	5–12, 14–01
	(1)	11–04
	(3)	11–04
	(4)	11–04
	s. 4(1)	13–31, 16–02
	(7)	13–01
	s. 6	1–08
	(3)	1–08, 1–09, 4–23, 5–12
	(4)	1–08, 1–09, 1–10
	Fugitive Offenders Act (c. 68)	
	Sched. 1	18–05
	Road Traffic Regulation Act (c. 76)	
	s. 20	5–21
	Sched. 5, para. 2	5–13
	Criminal Justice Act (c. 80)	
	s. 8	4–33, 10–05
	s. 56(5)	16–02
1968	Criminal Appeal Act (c. 19)	
	s. 2(1)	2–96
	s. 9	16–12
	s. 30	16–11, 17–28
	(1)	16–11
	(2)	16–12
	(4)	16–12
	s. 42	17–28
	(1)	16–11
	(2)(a)	16–12
	s. 50(1)	16–12
	Firearms Act (c. 27)	4–29, 14–04
	s. 18(1)	4–35
	s. 57(1)	4–29
	Trade Descriptions Act (c. 29)	6–13, 6–23
	Theft Act (c. 60)	1–01, **1–04**, 1–06, 1–11, 2–89, 2–91, **6–02**, 6–03, 6–04
	s. 1	2–02, 2–64, 2–66, 2–89, 4–23, 6–07, 13–03, **17–01**
	(1)	2–02, 2–22, 2–27, 2–44, 2–65, 13–09
	(2)	2–05, 2–91, 13–30
	(3)	2–98, 6–46

1968	Theft Act—cont.	
	s. 2	2–86, 2–98, 6–47, **17–02**
	(1)	2–45, 2–80, 2–86, 2–87, 2–89, 6–48
	(a)	2–81, 2–82, 2–98, 3–02, 5–10, 5–23, 6–47, 12–24
	(b)	2–83, 2–91, 2–98, 5–10, 5–23
	(c)	2–46, 2–52, 2–53, 2–84
	(2)	2–40, 2–85
	ss. 2–6	2–02
	s. 3	2–80, 17–03
	(1)	2–12, 2–37, 2–38, 2–41, 2–45, 2–48, 2–53, 2–54, 2–55, 2–61, 2–72, 2–74
	(2)	2–54
	(19)	2–48
	s. 4	2–03, **17–04**
	(1)	2–03, 2–17, 2–69, 6–09
	(2)	2–04, 2–05, 6–46
	(a)	2–05
	(b)	2–05, 2–51
	(c)	2–05
	(3)	2–05
	(4)	2–03, 2–07, 2–08
	s. 5	2–18, 2–35, 2–81, 13–09, **17–05**
	(1)	2–05, 2–09, 2–18, 2–19, 2–24, 2–25, 2–27, 2–28, 2–32, 2–72, 2–82, 6–01, 13–09, 15–02
	(2)	2–05, 2–23, 2–24, 2–25, 4–29
	(3)	2–09, 2–24, 2–25, 2–27, 2–28, 2–29
	(4)	2–26, 2–30, 2–31, 2–32, 2–33, 2–81, 11–02
	(5)	2–34
	s. 6	2–71, **2–73**, 6–45, 6–46, **17–06**
	(1)	2–73, **2–74**, 2–76, 2–77, 5–02, 6–45, 6–46
	(2)	2–73, 2–77, 6–45
	s. 7	2–02, **17–07**
	s. 8	3–02, 3–04, 3–07, **17–08**
	(1)	2–40, 3–01
	(2)	1–10, 3–01
	s. 9	4–02, 4–08, 4–14, **17–09**
	(1)	4–10, 4–15
	(a)	4–02, 4–08, 4–23, 4–25
	(b)	4–02, 4–23, 4–24, 4–26, 4–36
	(2)	4–02, 4–23, 4–24
	(3)	4–02
	(4)	4–02

1968   Theft Act—*cont.*
 s. 10.............. 4–36, 14–09, **17–10**
  (1)..................... 4–28, 4–35
   (*b*) 14–09
  (2)..................... 4–02, 4–28
 s. 11......... 5–01, 5–02, **5–03, 17–11**
  (1) 5–09
  (2) 2–40, 5–04, 5–09
  (3) 5–10
  (4) 5–03
 s. 12................ 5–01, 5–11, 5–12,
   5–15, 5–17, 5–24, 16–15,
   17–12
  (1) 5–01, 5–12, 5–13,
   5–19, 14–01, 14–06
  (2) 5–12
  (3) 5–12
  (4) 1–11
  (5) 5–13, 5–24
  (6) 5–10, 5–21, 5–23, 5–24
  (7)(*a*) 5–13, 5–19
   (*b*) 5–21
 s. 13.................2–15, 2–98, **17–13**
 s. 14...................... 1–06, **17–14**
  (1) 1–06
  (2) 1–06
 s. 15................ 2–14, 2–36, 2–62,
   2–63, 2–65, 2–66, 2–74,
   2–89, 6–05, 6–07, 6–09,
   6–10, 6–14, 6–22, 6–23,
   6–25, 6–27, 6–34, 6–40,
   6–41, 6–43, 6–44, 6–45,
   6–46, 6–48, 6–53, 7–02,
   7–03, 7–04, 7–07, 8–03,
   8–04, 8–05, 9–04, 9–05,
   9–06, 9–11, 11–02, 13–03,
   14–01, 14–07, **17–15**,
   18–05
  (1) 2–29, 2–60,
   2–65, 6–08, 13–09
  (2) 6–08, 6–10,
   6–11, 6–46, 6–52
  (3) 6–45
  (4) 6–08, 6–12, 6–26,
   6–42, 7–03, 8–04, 9–04,
   14–07
 s. 16................. 6–02, 6–04, 6–07,
   6–39, 6–40, 8–05, 8–11,
   9–03, 9–05, 9–11, 11–03,
   16–16, **17–16**
  (1) 6–40, 9–01
  (2) 9–01, 9–02, 9–09
   (*a*) 1–05, 6–05, 6–22,
   6–25, 8–01, 8–02, 8–15,
   9–01, 9–02, 18–05
   (*b*) 6–22, 6–40, 9–01,
   9–04, **9–06**, 9–07
   (*c*) 9–01, 9–04,
   9–09, 9–11

1968   Theft Act—*cont.*
  (3) 9–04
 s. 17................2–47, 6–03, 10–01,
   10–07, 12–32, **17–17**
  (1)(*a*) 10–01, 10–02,
   10–03, 10–06, 10–10,
   10–11
   (*b*) 10–01, 10–03,
   10–06
  (2) 10–02, 10–03
 s. 18................ 6–53, 7–02, 8–03,
   10–07, **17–18**, 18–05
  (1) 6–53
  (2) 6–53
 s. 19.............. 6–03, 10–08, **17–19**
 s. 20...................... 6–03, **17–20**
  (1) 10–10
  (2) 6–28, 10–11, 10–12
  (3) 10–11
 s. 21................3–02, 3–06, 12–02,
   12–04, 12–05, 12–11, 12–14,
   12–16, 12–18, 12–22,
   12–25, 12–32, 13–03,
   17–21
  (1) 12–04, 12–20,
   12–21, 12–22
  (2) 12–04, 12–10,
   12–19, 12–34
  (3) 12–04
 s. 22.................2–52, 2–70, 13–19,
   13–20, 13–24, **17–22**
  (1) 2–45, 2–70, 11–04,
   13–01, 13–26, 13–27,
   13–29, 13–32
  (2) 13–01
 s. 23......................13–35, **17–23**
 s. 24 .... **17–24**
  (1) 13–03
  (2) 13–04, 13–16
   (*a*) 13–05, 13–06
   (*b*) 13–05, 13–16
  (3) 13–06, 13–09
  (4) 13–03
 s. 25......................14–01, 14–04,
   14–06, **17–25**
  (1) 14–01
  (2) 14–01
  (3) 14–08, 14–09, 14–10
  (4) 14–01
  (5) 14–01, 14–06
 s. 26.................. 1–06, **17–26**
 s. 27......................13–34, 17–27
  (1) 13–34
   (*a*) 13–24
  (2) 13–34
  (3) 13–24, 13–25
  (4) 13–07
  (5) 13–24

1968 Theft Act—*cont.*
      s. 28......................16–02, 16–04,
                        16–09, 16–10, 16–11,
                        16–12, **16–13**, 16–14,
                                      17–28
        (1)....................16–02, 16–10
          (*a*)..............16–03, 16–05,
                        16–08, 16–09, 16–11
          (*b*)......16–04, 16–05, 16–11
          (*c*)..............16–05, 16–06,
                              16–07, 16–08
        (2).........................16–05
        (3).........................16–08
        (4).........................16–10
        (5)..................16–11, 16–12
        (6).........................16–02
      s. 29 ....**17–29**
        (1)(i).......................12–12
        (2).........................4–03
      s. 30 ....**17–30**
        (1)....................15–01, 18–05
        (2)....................15–02, 15–05
        (3)....................15–04, 15–05
        (4)....................15–02, 15–03
        (5).........................14–03
      s. 31 ....**17–31**
        (1)....................1–06, 18–05
        (2)....................16–01, 16–04
      s. 32 ....**17–32**
      s. 33 ....**17–33**
      s. 34......................**17–34**, 18–05
        (1)....................6–08, 6–09,
                              6–10, 15–02
        (2)(*a*)..............10–04, 12–03,
                              12–07, 12–33
          (i) 12–33
          (ii) 10–05
          (*b*)..............11–05, 13–04,
                        13–06, 16–02, 16–04
      s. 35 ....**17–35**
      s. 36 ....**17–36**
      Sched. 1 ....**17–37**
      Sched. 1 2–08
1970 Income and Corporation Taxes
      Act (c. 10)
      s. 181(1) 9–10
1971 Vehicles (Excise) Act (c. 10)
      Sched. 4, Pt. I, para. 9 5–13
      Courts Act (c. 23)
      s. 56 17–29
      Sched. 11 17–29
      Criminal Damage Act (c. 48)
                              2–43, 5–23
        s. 1 4–27
        s. 5 4–27
          (2).....................2–81, 5–23
1972 Road Traffic Act (c. 20)
        s. 2 6–43
        s. 93 5–12

1972 Road Traffic Act—*cont.*
        s. 196(1) 5–13
        Sched. 2, para. 2 5–13
        Sched. 4, Pt. III 5–12
                para. 3 14–01
      Criminal Justice Act (c. 71)
        s. 6 16–02
          (3) 16–08
          (4)(*a*) 16–12
            (*b*) 16–12
          (5) 16–11
        s. 36 13–10
        s. 64(1) 17–28
        Sched. 5...................16–02, 17–28
1973 Northern Ireland Constitution
      Act (c. 36)
        s. 41(1) 17–36
        Sched. 6 17–36
      Powers of Criminal Courts Act
        (c. 62)
        s. 34 16–16
        s. 35 16–15
          (1).....................16–15, 16–16
          (2) 16–15
          (4) 16–16
          (5) 16–15
        s. 39 16–02
        s. 43 14–01
1974 Juries Act (c. 23)
        s. 17 6–28
      Northern Ireland Act (c. 28)
        Sched. 1, para. 1(1)(*b*) 18–06
                (4) 18–06
                (5) 18–06
1974 Consumer Credit Act (c. 39)
        s. 40(1) 8–07
1975 Conservation   of   Wild
        Creatures and Wild Plants
        Act (c. 48)
        s. 4 2–05
        s. 5 2–05
        Sched. 2 2–05
      Criminal   Jurisdiction   Act
        (c. 59)
        s. 14(4)...................15–03, 17–30
          (5) 17–30
        Sched. 5 15–03
        Sched. 6 17–30
1976 Sexual Offences (Amendment)
        Act (c. 82)
        s. 1(1) 4–27
1977 Torts   (Interference   with
        Goods) Act (c. 32)
        s. 6(1) 16–04
        s. 10(1) 2–40
          (*a*) 2–40
          (*b*).................2–40, 2–42
      Patents Act (c. 37)
        s. 30(1) 2–10

1977 Criminal Law Act (c. 45)
s. 2(2)(a) 15–01
s. 5(2) 6–20
s. 60 16–15
s. 65 16–02
(4) 17–28
(5) 17–29
Sched. 12 .... 16–02, 17–28
Sched. 13 17–29
1978 Refuse Disposal (Amenity)
Act (c. 3)
s. 3 5–21
Theft Act (c. 31)............ **1–05, 6–04,**
8–01, 9–01
s. 1 .... 1–05, 6–05,
6–06, 6–12, 7–03, 7–08,
7–09, 8–01, 8–07, 9–08,
11–02, 11–04, **18–01**
(1) 7–01
(2).............. 7–05, 7–06, 7–08,
7–09, 7–11, 7–13, 8–18
s. 2 .... 6–06, 6–12, 8–01,
8–02, 8–05, 8–07, 9–05,
11–04, **18–02**
(1)..................... 8–06, 8–10,
8–11, 8–13, 8–17
(a)........... 8–05, **8–11**, 8–12
(b)....8–02, 8–05, 8–10, 8–11,
8–13, 9–07, 11–10, 11–13,
11–14
(c) 8–05, 8–06,
8–07, 8–12, **8–17**
(2) 8–07
(3)........... 8–15, 11–10, 11–13
(4) 8–17
s. 3 .... 6–12, 6–25, 8–02,
11–02, 11–05, 11–08,
11–10, 11–12, 11–13,
11–14, **18–03**
(1)........... 11–01, **11–10**, 11–13
(2) 11–11
(3) 11–07
(4) 11–04
s. 4 .... **18–04**
(2).................... 8–01, 11–01
(3)..............7–01, 8–01, 11–01
s. 5 18–05
(1)..................... 7–02, 8–03
(2)....... 1–06, 7–03, 8–04, 11–05
s. 6 .... **18–06**

1978 Theft Act—cont.
s. 7 .... **18–07**
1979 Prosecution of Offences Act
(c. 31)
s. 6 17–30
(2)(a) 15–03
s. 11(1) 15–03, 17–30
Sched. 1................... 15–03, 17–30
Estate Agents Act (c. 38)
s. 13(1) 2–27
Sale of Goods Act (c. 54)
s. 17 2–35
s. 18.........................2–67, 6–10
(1) 2–36
s. 23........................ 6–10, 16–04
1980 Magistrates' Court Act (c. 43)
s. 32 18–04
s. 63(3) 16–13
s. 75 16–16
s. 108(1) 16–12
(3) 16–12
s. 111 16–12
s. 154(1) 18–04
Sched. 1, para. 28 1–05,
13–01
(a) 3–01,
4–27, 12–04
(b) 4–03
(c) 4–03
Sched. 7 18–04
Deer Act (c. 49)
s. 1 .... 2–08, 17–37
s. 9(2) 17–37
Limitation Act (c. 58)
s. 2 13–11
s. 3(2) 13–11
s. 4 13–11
1981 Forgery and Counterfeiting
Act (c. 45)............. 6–03, 10–01
s. 3 10–06
Criminal Attempts Act (c. 47)
s. 1 ....6–34, 6–43
(1).........2–48, 2–59, 4–03, 6–51
(2)....................2–78, 6–27
(3)....................2–59, 6–27
(4) 6–51
s. 4(2) 2–92
Wildlife and Countryside Act
(c. 69)
s. 13 2–05

CHAPTER 1

PRELIMINARY AND MISCELLANEOUS

1. ABBREVIATIONS

THROUGHOUT this book the following abbreviations will be used: **1–01**
"The Act," unless the context otherwise requires, means the Theft Act
1968. References to sections and Schedules, except in §§ 6–05 to 6–07 and
in Chapters 7, 8 and 11 and unless otherwise indicated, are references to
sections of and Schedules to that Act.

"The Bill," except in § 6–05, means the Theft Bill introduced in the
House of Lords in December 1967. This Bill became the Theft Act 1968.

"The Committee" means the Criminal Law Revision Committee.

"The draft Bill," except in § 6–05, means the Draft Theft Bill annexed to
the Committee's *Eighth Report*.

"The *Eighth Report*" means the Committee's *Eighth Report: Theft and
Related Offences* (Cmnd. 2977).

"The *Thirteenth Report*" means the Committee's *Thirteenth Report:
Section 16 of the Theft Act 1968* (Cmnd. 6733).

Two invaluable works will be referred to in abbreviated form: **1–02**

"Smith, *Theft*" means J.C. Smith, *The Law of Theft* (4th ed. 1979).

"Williams, *Textbook*" means Glanville Williams, *Textbook of Criminal Law* (1978 and Supplement 1979).

Parties will be found referred to much of the time in the conventional   **1–03**
modern manner: "D" is the person whose possible criminal liability is
under discussion; "P" is the victim of D's conduct.

2. THE BACKGROUND TO THE ACTS

The Theft Act 1968

Before the passing of the Act, the law of theft and related offences was   **1–04**
largely contained in the Larceny Act 1916. That statute enshrined most of
the indictable offences of dishonesty. It stated, but did not reform, the
complex law of larceny and other common law offences; and it consolidated, but did not rationalise, numerous accretions to the statute book in
the form of special offences of larceny and other crimes.

In March 1959 Mr. R.A. Butler, the Home Secretary, asked the newly
created Criminal Law Revision Committee

"to consider, with a view to providing a simpler and more effective
system of law, what alterations in the criminal law are desirable with
reference to larceny and kindred offences and to such other acts
involving fraud or dishonesty as, in the opinion of the committee,

1

could conveniently be dealt with in legislation giving effect to the committee's recommendations on the law of larceny."

There was then no talk of a general codification of a revised criminal law. But this reference of "larceny and kindred offences" to the Committee was well justified; the law in this area was generally acknowledged to be in an unsatisfactory state. It is not necessary now to conduct a post-mortem on the old law, but an indication of some of its outstanding deficiencies will be given as necessary in the introductory passages to later chapters of this book.

The subject occupied the Committee for seven years. Their *Eighth Report: Theft and Related Offences* was presented to Parliament in May 1966. The draft Bill annexed to this Report, slightly amended, was the basis of the Theft Bill introduced in the House of Lords in December 1967. After further amendments during its passage, that Bill received the Royal Assent in July 1968. The Act came into force on January 1, 1969.

The Theft Act 1978

1–05   It was, before long, a matter of general agreement that section 16(2)(*a*) of the Act required replacing. The highly unsatisfactory nature of that provision justified special amending legislation in advance of a general review of fraud offences promised by the Law Commission.[1] Proposals for such legislation were made by the Committee on a reference from the Home Secretary. The outcome was the Theft Act 1978, which came into force on 20 October 1978.[2]

3.   THE CONTENTS OF THIS BOOK

1–06   The texts of the Acts are printed in the Appendices. Most of their provisions are examined in detail in the ensuing chapters. But some provisions of the 1968 Act are not dealt with elsewhere in this chapter or in those that follow. In particular:

(a) Section 14. This is a jurisdictional provision concerned with offences of theft or robbery committed outside England and Wales in relation to mail bags or postal packets in the course of transmission between different jurisdictions in the British postal area (as defined in section 14(2)). Section 14(1) renders the offender amenable to justice in England and Wales.

(b) Section 26. This section confers powers on justices to issue warrants, and on senior police officers to give written authorities to constables, for the purpose of searching for and seizing goods believed to be stolen. Although these powers are important and replace powers existing under legislation repealed by the Act, discussion of them is not felt to be appropriate to this book and they are not mentioned hereafter.

(c) Section 31(1). This mainly concerns the liability of a person to answer

[1] See Law Com. No. 76, *Report on Conspiracy and Criminal Law Reform* (1976), para. 1.15; *Thirteenth Report*, para. 3.
[2] The background to the 1978 Act is more fully treated below, at §§ 6–04 to 6–07 and §§ 11–02, 11–03.

incriminating questions in certain non-criminal proceedings and the effect of such answers in the event of the prosecution of that person or of his or her spouse for an offence under the Act (or under the 1978 Act: see s. 5(2) thereof).

4. MODE OF TRIAL. VERDICTS

Mode of trial

Most indictable offences under the Act are triable either way.[3] The exceptions are referred to in the relevant chapters.

1–07

Verdicts on trial on indictment

The Criminal Law Act 1967, s. 6, contains provisions of general application which it is preferable to mention here rather than repeatedly throughout the book. These provisions apply only on trial on indictment.

1–08

Section 6(3) of the Criminal Law Act 1967 confers important powers on a jury who find an accused not guilty of an offence with which he is specifically charged. If "the allegations in the indictment amount to or include (expressly or by implication) an allegation of another offence" within the trial court's jurisdiction, the jury can find him guilty of that other offence; or they can find him guilty of an offence of which he could be found guilty if he were specifically indicted for that other offence. For the purposes of section 6(3) an allegation of an offence always includes an allegation of an attempt to commit it (s. 6(4)).

In order to tell whether an allegation of an offence (the "lesser offence") is included *by implication* in an indictment charging another offence (the "major offence"), the test to be applied is

> "to see whether it is a necessary step towards establishing the major offence to prove the commission of the lesser offence: in other words is the lesser offence an essential ingredient of the major offence?"[4]

A lesser offence may be found to be *expressly* included in an indictment by applying "the red pencil test"—that is, by "striking out all the averments which have not been proved"[5] and seeing whether what is left amounts to the allegation of a lesser offence.

Here follow some applications of these principles, the heading in each case indicating the offence charged in the indictment.

1–09

Theft

An allegation of theft does not by implication include an allegation of handling by receiving[6] or by any other means.

---

[3] Magistrates' Courts Act 1980, Sched. 1, para. 28.
[4] *Springfield* (1969) 53 Cr.App.R. 608 at p. 611; *Lillis* [1972] 2 Q.B. 236 at p. 241. For an illustration, see *Page* [1971] Crim.L.R. 713.
[5] *Lillis*, above, at pp. 241–242.
[6] *Woods* [1969] 1 Q.B. 447.

Robbery; *assault with intent to rob*

Robbery, as we shall see, involves theft as an essential ingredient. On a charge of robbery, therefore, the jury may find the accused not guilty of robbery but guilty of theft.[7] The other ingredient of robbery is the use of force or the putting or seeking to put any person in fear of being then and there subjected to force. But an assault is not an essential ingredient of robbery, if only because one who seeks to put another in fear of being subjected to force may fail to put the other in fear and if so will not commit an assault. There cannot, therefore, on a charge of robbery, be a conviction of common assault[8] or of assault with intent to rob.

Burglary and aggravated burglary

A person charged with aggravated burglary may be convicted of burglary as described in the indictment or of any offence of which he could be found guilty on an indictment charging burglary so described.

Burglary may be committed by entering a building as a trespasser with intent to commit one of a number of offences. On an indictment charging burglary of this kind, it is not possible to convict of an attempt to commit the specified intended offence; entry with intent to rape, for instance, does not necessarily imply conduct that has got so far as an attempt to rape.[9]

Another mode of committing burglary[10] is to enter a building as a trespasser and to steal or attempt to steal therein or to inflict or attempt to inflict on any person therein any grievous bodily harm. An allegation of entering a building as a trespasser and stealing therein includes an allegation of theft. If the trespass is not proved, the allegation of it may be struck out, as may the word "therein" and even the date alleged, to reveal an express allegation of theft committed wheresoever and whensoever.[11]

Handling

Many (maybe most) persons guilty of handling stolen goods are also guilty of theft. But a handling charge does not imply an allegation that the accused intended to deprive the victim permanently of the goods, which is essential for theft, and this alone suffices to make a verdict of theft impossible on a handling indictment.[12]

1–10   Section 6(4) of the Criminal Law Act 1967 goes on to provide for the situation in which an indictment charges a mere attempt or an assault or

---

[7] Similarly, a conviction of conspiracy to steal should be available on a charge of conspiracy to rob (where all that is not proved is the agreement to use force); but see to the contrary, unconvincingly, *Barnard* (1979) 70 Cr.App.R. 28 at p. 33.

[8] So ruled on this ground in *Tennant* [1976] Crim.L.R. 133. Moreover, P may be put in fear by words alone, which possibly will not constitute an assault: see *Springfield*, above, at p. 612.

[9] *Cf. Lyttle* [1969] Crim.L.R. 213.

[10] For the position where the wrong mode is charged, see below, § 4–23, at n. 45.

[11] *Lillis*, above; criticised by J.C. Smith at [1972] Crim.L.R. 459. The Court of Appeal indicated in *Lillis* that the application of s.6(3) of the 1967 Act is discretionary. Oddly enough this is not expressly stated by the subsection; contrast s.6(4).

[12] *Cf. Haughton* v. *Smith* [1975] A.C. 476, *per* Lord Hailsham of St. Marylebone L.C. at pp. 489–490, as to a verdict of theft or attempted theft on a charge of attempted handling.

other act preliminary to an offence, but in which it is proved that the accused was in fact guilty of the completed offence. In such a case the accused can be convicted of the attempt[13] or other preliminary offence charged, or the court can discharge the jury so that an indictment for the completed offence can be preferred. An example under the present Act might arise from a charge of assault with intent to rob under section 8(2) where the jury find that the accused in fact committed the full offence of robbery.

Only in one case does the Theft Act 1968 itself provide for conviction of   **1–11** one offence on an indictment charging another: a person charged with theft may be found guilty of taking a conveyance.[14] Further provision of this kind might perhaps have been included with advantage and without risk of injustice—for instance, to permit a verdict of guilty of assault with intent to rob on an indictment for robbery. The Act nowhere provides for conviction of the offence charged where some other offence, but not the offence charged, is found to have been committed. Yet the Court of Appeal has on one occasion allowed a conviction of theft to stand on the ground that, if that offence was not committed, the appellant was guilty of obtaining a pecuniary advantage by deception, so that (as the court asserted) no miscarriage of justice had occurred.[15] To convict a person of an offence not proved to have been committed because he has committed an offence with which he has not been charged surely requires statutory warrant. The decision should be regarded as an aberration.

5. INTERPRETATION[16]

The Theft Act, as has been judicially observed in several cases, "is an Act   **1–12** designed to simplify the law."[17] There is no controversy about this. The Act greatly reduces the number of offences employed to cover the range of conduct penalised; it employs, on the whole, simpler, more modern and less technical language than was formerly used; and it removes a good many "technicalities and subtleties"[18] that had marred the old law.

Two further points ought to be beyond controversy. First, the Act's aim of simplifying the law should not be frustrated by gratuitous subtlety in its interpretation. The courts for their part may be expected to reject a subtle reading in favour of a simple reading where both are truly available, and they will be right to do so. Still, it is a practitioner's proper function to take a subtle point on behalf of his client when the need arises; and a commentator will occasionally feel bound to suggest an analysis of the Act that appears to be available, even if he regards it as unattractive on the ground of undue subtlety or otherwise.

---

[13] Similarly on summary trial, for the attempt does not merge in the completed offence: *Webley* v. *Buxton* [1977] Q.B. 481.
[14] s.12(4).
[15] *McHugh* [1977] R.T.R. 1; [1977] Crim.L.R. 174.
[16] Brazier, "The Theft Act: Three Principles of Interpretation" [1974] Crim.L.R. 701.
[17] *Baxter* [1972] 1 Q.B. 1 at p. 13, *per* Sachs L.J.
[18] *Bonner* [1970] 1 W.L.R. 838 at p. 843; [1970] 2 All E.R. 97n. at p. 99, *per* Edmund-Davies L.J.

Secondly, judicial exegesis should be clear and consistent. If a series of decisions is unrelated and incoherent, the result will be uncertainty and obscurity rather than simplicity. This, unhappily, has been the tendency of some of the case law on the Act. It is especially true of important appellate decisions on the vital phrase "appropriates property belonging to another" in the definition of theft, which have suffered from serious defects. In particular, previous relevant authority has been consistently ignored, so that the case law has become more and more confused; and judgments have been casually and obscurely phrased, and decisions therefore hard to interpret.[19] If the Act is to be kept simple, decisions upon it require internal clarity and collective consistency.

1-13   Closely associated with the view of the Act as one designed to simplify the law is the proposition (which does not follow from it) that it ought to be capable of being understood by the layman. From this proposition proceeds the notion (which also does not follow) that the Act should receive a plain man's interpretation; and the feeling seems to be that, the plain man being no lawyer, there is something disreputable about construing it in a lawyerly way. This, it is thought, contributes to the defects in the case law mentioned above. It also leads, it is submitted, to an insupportable doctrine concerning the relation between the criminal law in this Act and other principles of law. In the case of *Baxter*,[20] Sachs L.J. elaborated the statement that the Act is one "designed to simplify the law" by saying that

> "it uses words in their natural meaning and is to be construed thus to produce sensible results; when [the] Act is under examination this court deprecates attempts to bring into too close consideration the finer distinctions in civil law as to the precise moment when contractual communications take effect or when property passes."

The major difficulty with this benignly-intentioned approach is that the Act inevitably defines offences against property in terms of the categories of the civil law (see, for instance, ss. 4, 5, 9 and 15). Words by means of which reference to those categories is made (such as "things in action," "ownership," "possession," "proprietary right or interest," "trespasser") do not have "natural" meanings but technical ones. This is helpful, not harmful; it makes for certainty in the criminal law. The Act should of course be read sensibly; but that does not mean that there is a painless plain man's route to its meaning. There are bound, in particular, to be cases in which the practitioner cannot do his full duty without an adequate grasp of relevant principles of the civil law. And the courts should be prepared to make careful application of those principles, for two reasons: as an indispensable means of fixing the boundaries of criminal liability with

---

[19] See, *e.g.*, §§ 2–20, 2–31, 2–57 *et seq.*
[20] See n. 17, above; *cf Nordeng* (1975) 62 Cr.App.R. 123 at p. 128 (and commentary by J. C. Smith [1976] Crim.L.R. at p. 195).

adequate certainty; and to avoid incongruous and even unjust conflict between the respective demands on citizens of the civil and criminal law.[21]

There has, in fact, been a judicial tendency to leave the interpretation of **1–14** particular statutory words to the lay tribunal. The relevant doctrine is that an "ordinary word" does not need judicial explanation; its "natural" or "ordinary" meaning is known to the jury. This view has been pervasive, though it is not always given effect.[22] Its application is sometimes very puzzling, as when the identification of an "obligation" is said to be a matter for the jury although the word means "legal obligation."[23] And generally—and especially in relation to the central word "dishonestly"[24]—the doctrine has proved controversial.[25] It will be contended, on the one hand, that there is much to be said for the criminal law's being able to reflect community values, as represented by justices and juries, and to respond to changes in those values; and that there is a real difficulty about tying down the meaning of words by judicial pronouncement. On the other hand, it may be argued that a person's liability to conviction should not depend upon the accidental composition of the bench or jury that tries him when it might depend upon a proposition of law[26]; that the prevailing view makes unjustified assumptions about the existence of clear community norms in a morally and socially plural society, and also about the existence of generally apprehended "natural meanings" of words[27]; and that it is the business of the judiciary, gradually by a course of decisions, to help the lay tribunal to as consistent an application of the criminal law as can reasonably be achieved. The present book will be found to reflect a rather strong inclination to the latter view—though the matter is a difficult one upon which a dogmatic position would be unjustified.

---

[21] See J. C. Smith, "Civil Law Concepts in the Criminal Law" [1972 B] C.L.J. 197, *passim* and especially at pp. 197–198; Williams, "Theft, Consent and Illegality" [1977] Crim.L.R. 127 at pp. 128 *et seq*; Williams, *Textbook*, Chap. 34.

[22] See as to the impact of the doctrine in Theft Act cases, D. W. Elliott, "Law and Fact in Theft Act Cases" [1976] Crim.L.R. 707.

[23] For "legal obligation," see below, §§ 2–27, 2–31, and for the suggested jury function, see § 2–26.

[24] See below, §§ 2–86 *et seq*.

[25] See Williams, "Law and Fact" [1976] Crim.L.R. 472 and 532; and, as to the issue of dishonesty, see the references in § 2–87, n. 57.

[26] *Cf.*, in other contexts, Criminal Law Revision Committee, *Fourteenth Report: Offences against the Person* (1980: Cmnd. 7844), para. 7; *Pearlman* v. *Harrow School* [1979] Q.B. 56 at pp. 66–67, *per* Lord Denning M.R.

[27] For there are several references in Theft Act cases to the "natural meaning" of words (*e.g.* *Baxter*, n. 17, above; *Treacy* [1971] A.C. 537 at p. 543, *per* John Stephenson J.; *D.P.P.* v. *Turner* [1974] A.C. 357 at p. 364, *per* Lord Reid). Nevertheless, it is thought that scepticism about this notion is permissible. In one case the jury asked for and were granted the use of a dictionary, probably to look up the word "dishonestly." The conviction was quashed; the jury should have been told to apply the "ordinary meaning" of the word, which was said to be "quite clear": *Swift* (1980: Court of Appeal No. 1396/B/79), unreported.

1. INTRODUCTION

2–01 THE offences replaced by the present offence of theft are now a matter of history. There is no need to recall them in detail here, although it will be necessary to refer to some aspects of them in the ensuing pages. The following brief account of some of the leading principles should suffice by way of general explanation.

Historically, *larceny* was an offence against another man's possession of goods. It involved a violation of that possession by "taking and carrying away" his goods without his consent, with the intention of permanently depriving him of them. Such a "taking" could not occur where there was a consensual delivery; nor could it occur where the offender was himself already in possession, for instance as a bailee. But one who induced a delivery by fraud was regarded as "taking" without consent because the fraud was treated as negativing the victim's apparent consent; and a bailee became capable of larceny (by conversion of the goods bailed) by a statutory extension of the offence. The element of "carrying away" (or "asportation") required some physical removal of the goods, however slight. Another important limitation on the scope of larceny was the requirement that the intention to deprive the victim permanently should exist at the moment of the taking, though this rule was somewhat mitigated by intellectual ingenuity on the part of the judges.

Embezzlement was an offence of statutory origin designed to deal with the dishonest misappropriation by a servant of any chattel, money or valuable security delivered to the servant on account of his employer; for such misappropriation could not be larceny if it occurred before the property was reduced into the employer's possession.

Fraudulent conversion was another statutory creation. Its main *raison d'être* was the fact that, whereas a bailee could by statute be guilty of larceny by misappropriating the property bailed, one who had ownership of property could not, even though he had been entrusted with it otherwise than for his own beneficial enjoyment. The offence covered absconding trustees, club treasurers and the like. Unlike larceny and embezzlement it extended to any kind of property.

In the notion of a fraudulent conversion of any property (now thinly disguised in the language of dishonest appropriation) the model was found for a single new offence of theft to replace the three crimes mentioned above. Or rather to replace a great many crimes, for under the old law there was a large number of different forms of larceny with different maximum penalties. There is now one offence of theft—though robbery, which is no mere aggravated theft but rather theft-plus-force, is preserved as a distinct crime and is entitled to its own chapter.

2.   BASIC DEFINITION OF THEFT

Section 1(1) provides that a person   **2–02**

> "is guilty of theft if he dishonestly appropriates property belonging to another with the intention of permanently depriving the other of it";

and section 7 provides a maximum penalty of 10 years' imprisonment on conviction on indictment of this offence.

The various constituent phrases in the basic definition of theft in section 1 are defined or partially defined in sections 2 to 6. Detailed consideration of the scope of theft can therefore be undertaken largely by way of a treatment of those sections. It will be convenient to consider first the subject-matter of theft ("property belonging to another"). Having established that there is something that can be stolen, we can then examine the kinds of conduct which, assuming the necessary state of mind in the actor, may amount to theft ("appropriates"). The third general question will be: Given an appropriation of property belonging to another, under what mental conditions is that appropriation a theft ("dishonestly . . . with the intention of permanently depriving the other of it")?

3.   "PROPERTY"

" 'Property' includes money and all other property, real or personal,   **2–03** including things in action and other intangible property" (s. 4(1)); and wild creatures, tamed or untamed, are to be regarded as property (s. 4(4)). Section 4 provides specially for land and wild creatures by limiting the circumstances in which they can be stolen. These special cases will be dealt with below. Subject to them, anything falling within the very wide definition in section 4(1) can, in theory at least, be stolen.

Land; and things growing wild thereon

Land can be stolen, but only by certain persons in certain particular   **2–04** ways. A person who appropriates "land, or things forming part of land and severed from it by him or by his directions," is not guilty of theft unless he falls within one of the exceptional cases mentioned below, or unless what he appropriates is an incorporeal hereditament (s. 4(2)).[1]

Land is not defined in the Act. Any difficulty that exists concerns the meaning of the phrase "things forming part of land." Problems can arise in connection with (i) things annexed to the land and (ii) materials deposited on the land.

(i)   As to *things annexed to the land*, "the general maxim of the law is, that what is annexed to the land becomes part of the land; but it is very

---

[1] The most important incorporeal hereditaments are easements, *profits à prendre* and rent charges. See Megarry and Wade, *The Law of Real Property* (4th ed.), Chap. 13.

difficult, if not impossible, to say with precision what constitutes an annexation sufficient for this purpose."[2] There is no difficulty with houses and similar permanent structures or with things that are clearly integral parts of such structures.[3] In the case of anything resting on or attached to land or to a building thereon, the tests to be applied are those applied in the law relating to fixtures: whether such a thing forms part of the land depends in part upon the degree of annexation and in part upon the object of annexation.[4] In *Billing* v. *Pill*[5] the floor of an army hut built in seven sections was secured to concrete foundations by bolts let into the concrete. It was held that although the foundations formed part of the realty, the hut, in the light of the evidence as to the temporary object of its attachment to the land, did not. On the other hand "blocks of stone placed one on top of another without any mortar or cement for the purpose of forming a dry stone wall would become part of the land,"[6] at least if the wall was not purely temporary.

(ii) *Materials deposited on land*, such as sand and cinders, will not form part of the land if they lie in heaps on the ground; but if they are spread on the land they are likely to be found to have become part of the soil.[7]

Nice questions can clearly arise, then, as to whether something on or attached to land forms part of that land.

2–05   Section 4(2) provides that land can exceptionally be stolen in the following situations.

(a) A trustee or personal representative or one authorised[8] to sell or dispose of land belonging to another[9] can steal the land or anything forming part of it by dealing with it in breach of the confidence[10] reposed in him (s. 4(2) (*a*)).

(b) A person not in possession[11] of land can in general steal something forming part of the land: he can appropriate it by severing it or causing it to be severed, or after it has been severed[12] (s. 4(2)(*b*)). To come onto a man's property and take the tiles from his roof (severing) is obviously as

---

[2] *Holland* v. *Hodgson* (1872) L.R. 7 C.P. 328 at p. 334, *per* Blackburn J.
[3] See *per* Lord Goddard C.J. in *Billing* v. *Pill* [1954] 1 Q.B. 70 at p. 75.
[4] See, as to the meaning of fixtures, Megarry and Wade, *op. cit.*, pp. 711–715; Halsbury, *Laws of England* (3rd ed.), Vol. 23, p. 490 (quoted with approval in *Billing* v. *Pill* [1954] 1 Q.B. 70 at p. 75).
[5] [1954] 1 Q.B. 70.
[6] *Holland* v. *Hodgson* (1872) L.R. 7 C.P. 328 at p. 335, *per* Blackburn J. Compare *Skujins* [1956] Crim. L.R. 266 (a decision of quarter sessions): farm gate held to form part of the realty.
[7] As in *Morgan* v. *Russell & Sons* [1909] 1 K.B. 357.
[8] "by power of attorney, or as liquidator of a company, or otherwise . . . ."
[9] See s. 5(1)(2). Land held on trust, for instance, will belong to the beneficiaries.
[10] The word "confidence" is purposely used in preference to "trust," which might have been understood in a technical sense. It would seem that an agent authorised to sell land will commit theft if, for instance, he sells to his own nominee at an undervalue for the purpose of making a profit by then selling to a sub-purchaser on his own account.
[11] The phrase "not in possession" no doubt includes a member of the household of one in possession.
[12] After it has been severed it will surely not form part of the land.

much theft as to take the books from his shelves; and one may steal another's pasture by grazing cattle on his land[13] (causing to be severed).

The general rule that a person not in possession of land can steal by severance is subject to a large exception, provided by section 4(3), in relation to things growing wild. Save in one class of case, no one steals if he picks mushrooms[14] growing wild or if he picks flowers, fruit or foliage from a plant[15] growing wild. The excepted case is that in which the picking is done "for reward or for sale or other commercial purpose."

This piling of exception upon exception is very confusing. We may approach these provisions in another way by observing that the Act makes a series of distinctions:

(i)   One who is in possession of land and one who is not. The former cannot steal by severing (unless he is a tenant and he severs a fixture: see exception (c), below). The latter can, but in respect of him a distinction is drawn between—

(ii)   Mushrooms and plants growing wild, and anything else "forming part of the land" (including cultivated plants). The latter can always be stolen by one not in possession of the land. As to "plants growing wild" the Act makes a third distinction:

(iii)   Severing and picking.[16] Uprooting a plant, even one growing wild, will be "severing"; if the plant belongs to anyone and the severing is dishonest, it will be theft. But taking individual blooms from a wild shrub or a basketful of wild berries or a quantity of wild holly will be mere "picking" and cannot be theft, subject to one final distinction:

(iv)   Commercial and non-commercial purpose. Even the picking of wild mushrooms or flowers, fruit or foliage from wild plants may be theft if done "for reward or for sale or other commercial purpose." So whether you steal when you pick wild flowers may depend on your motive: if you desire to decorate your house[17] or your lady-friend, it is not theft; if you are picking for pay or to sell in the market, it is.[18] This distinction is contrary to the general principle that theft does not depend upon motive, or even upon a view to gain (s. 1(2)). It may also present disproportionate problems of proof. The burden is on the prosecution to prove the commercial purpose; and this will no doubt usually be very hard to do—save, for instance, where a known market trader is caught in the act of amassing a large quantity of flowers, fruit or foliage.

(c)   The third exceptional case in which an appropriation of land or

---

[13] *McGill* v. *Shepherd* (1976: Victoria), unreported, cited by M.S. Weinberg and C.R. Williams, *The Australian Law of Theft*, p. 80.

[14] Includes any fungus.

[15] Includes any shrub or tree.

[16] The uprooting of any wild plant, or the picking, uprooting or destroying of a protected plant, may be a summary offence under s. 13 of the Wildlife and Countryside Act 1981 (or, until s. 13 is in force, under s. 4 or s. 5 of the Conservation of Wild Creatures and Wild Plants Act 1975).

[17] If you desire to decorate your shop-window for the sake of the aesthetic effect, this may be construed as a "commercial purpose." The phrase is very vague.

[18] So long as the other elements of theft are present: there must be someone to whom the wild plants belong, and your act must be dishonest.

things forming part thereof may be theft is that in which a tenant[19] in possession appropriates a fixture[20] or structure let to be used with the land (s. 4(2)(*c*)).

2–06 The following, in conclusion, are examples of cases in which appropriation of land or things forming part of land will not be theft:

(i) D is a lessee of land. He removes and sells ore or plants from the land. If he is "in possession of the land" (which he may not be; he may have sub-let it), he is not guilty of theft, for he is not within exception (b) above, and the thing taken is not a "fixture or structure" within exception (c).

(ii) D is in possession of land under a mere licence. He severs and appropriates a fixture. He is not within either exception (b) or exception (c) and so does not steal. It is odd perhaps that the licensee should have this advantage over the tenant.

(iii) D "squats" on P's land, or extends his fences so as to take in part of P's land, or forcibly turns P off his land. He does not steal, because exception (b) concerns only the severance of things forming part of the land.

Wild creatures

2–07 From the terms of section 4(4) it is clear that "a wild creature" means "a creature wild by nature." This was the language of the Larceny Act[21] and cases decided under the old law will therefore remain relevant for the classification of some creatures as wild or otherwise. The last of those cases amusingly illustrated the ambiguity of the word "wild." The case concerned mussels on the sea shore. The prosecution's concession that they were wild creatures was both inevitable and mildly incongruous.[22]

Wild creatures that have been tamed or are ordinarily kept in captivity can be stolen as readily as any other property.

As to creatures at liberty, the problem was whether by means of the law of theft to protect the owner of, or the person having sporting rights over, the land on which they may be taken or killed. More tersely: should poaching be theft? The Committee recommended[23] that it should be theft when done "for reward or for sale or other commercial purpose," and the Bill so provided. This would have been a substantial departure from the pre-existing law and would have rendered the offender liable to very much greater penalties than those provided under other statutes controlling poaching. In the end the relevant provision was excluded from the Bill during its passage.

2–08 The result is that if a wild creature is "not tamed nor ordinarily kept in captivity," it cannot normally be stolen. The rationale of this is that, although P may own the land on which the creature is and Q may have

[19] For the meaning of "tenancy" in this provision, see the text of s. 4(2) in Appendix 1.
[20] See note 4, above.
[21] Larceny Act 1916, s.1(3) proviso (*b*).
[22] *Howlett* [1968] Crim.L.R. 222.
[23] *Eighth Report*, para. 52.

sporting rights over the land, no one owns the creature until it is killed or taken.[24] But when it has been reduced into someone's possession (and so long as it has not subsequently been lost or abandoned), or when someone is in course of reducing it into possession, it can be treated as the proper subject of theft. Section 4(4) provides accordingly, treating a wild creature and the carcass of a wild creature in identical terms. So it is not theft to kill and take game on P's land, unless, for instance, the creature is taken from P's snares (even, it would seem, from another poacher's snares) or from a hut in which P has put the product of his own day's shooting.

Pending a general review of the various enactments dealing with poaching,[25] Schedule 1 to the Act preserves in a modified form certain provisions of the Larceny Act 1861 concerning the unlawful taking or destroying of fish in water which is private property or in which there is any private right of fishery. Other provisions, originally preserved by Schedule 1, relating to the taking or killing of deer, have been superseded by the Deer Act 1980, s.1. This creates summary offences of (1) entering any land, without the consent of the owner or occupier or other lawful authority, in search or pursuit of any deer with the intention of taking, killing or injuring it; (2) on any land, (a) intentionally taking, killing or injuring any deer (or attempting to do so), or (b) searching for or pursuing any deer with the intention of taking, killing or injuring it, or (c) removing the carcass of any deer, without the consent of the owner or occupier of the land or other lawful authority.

"Money"

"Money" is a very difficult word whose meaning varies greatly with context.[26] All that it plainly includes in the present context is current coins and bank notes (including, of course, foreign coins and notes).[27] It is tempting to give the word a wider meaning than this. After all, it is rightly observed in a different connection that according to "the ordinary language and usage of mankind, when a man says, 'I have so much money at my bankers,' he considers and treats it as his money"[28]; so that, even when a testator's reference to his "money" is to be interpreted in a "strict sense," it is allowed to include what he has on current and deposit account.[29] It is one thing, however, to permit a testamentary gift of "money" to pass the benefit of a bank account. It is quite another thing to suppose that a person's bank account is "money" in which he has a "proprietary right or interest" (so that it "belongs to" him as a potential victim of theft: s. 5(1)). The "property" in which a bank's customer can have such a right or interest is a thing in action—namely, the debt owed to

2–09

---

[24] See *Blades* v. *Higgs* (1865) 11 H.L.C. 621.
[25] See *Eighth Report*, para. 53.
[26] Mann, *The Legal Aspect of Money* (3rd ed.), pp. 3–5.
[27] That is, coins and notes issued by the authority of the law and currently capable of serving as universal means of exchange in their country of origin: adapting language of Mann, *op. cit.* p. 9.
[28] *Manning* v. *Purcell* (1855) 7 De G.M. & G. 55, *per* Turner L.J. at p. 67.
[29] *Re Collings* [1933] Ch. 920.

him by the bank when the account is in credit.[30] "Money at the bank" therefore appears not to be proper language for Theft Act purposes (though it is easily used and may occasionally lead to error[31]).

Despite the above, the word "money" must inevitably, for convenience, be used in a non-technical way from time to time throughout this book.

"Things in action and other intangible property"

2–10 (i) *Generally*. The phrase "things in action" brings within the scope of theft a great variety of types of property. According to conventional classification the category includes all property other than real property, leaseholds and things in possession (movable chattels, including money as defined above)[32]—that is, "all personal rights of property which can only be claimed or enforced by action and not by taking physical possession."[33] It therefore includes things as diverse as debts, rights under trusts and copyrights.[34] It appeared for some time to be so wide as to leave "other intangible property" possibly without content; but that phrase now covers patents and applications for patents, which are declared not to be things in action.[35]

An obligation owed in law by O to P, capable of being enforced by action, is a thing in action belonging to P and therefore "property" within the meaning of the Act.[36]

2–11 There are naturally serious limits to the ways in which things in action can in practice be appropriated with the necessary intention of permanent deprivation.[37] It is not possible to run away with a bank balance or physically to destroy a copyright. Nevertheless, any person having the power to dispose of any species of property is clearly capable of stealing it. He will do so, for instance, if he sells or assigns it dishonestly in breach of trusts or to defeat a co-owner.

2–12 (ii) *Bank accounts and overdraft facilities*. Where a person has a bank account which is in credit the bank stands to him in the relation of debtor to

---

[30] *Foley v. Hill* (1848) 2 H.L.C. 28; *cf. Davenport* [1954] 1 All E.R. 602, *per* Lord Goddard C.J. at p. 603, making the same point for Larceny Act purposes. The point is not inconsistent with the broader understanding of the term "money" in the action for money had and received—see, *e.g.* the discussion of the topic of following money into and through a bank account in Goode, "The Right to Trace and Its Impact in Commercial Transactions" (1976) 92 L.Q.R. 360 at p. 378. That action depends not upon establishing a "proprietary right or interest," but rather upon "[the defendant's] receipt of a fund to the use of [the plaintiff]": *ibid.* pp. 366, 390. As to "funds," see *ibid.* p. 384. Liability for theft by, in effect, a fund-holder may arise by virtue of s.5(3) if not by virtue of the existence of a trust: see below, § 2–24.
[31] It appears to have done so in *Pitchley* (1972) 57 Cr.App.R. 30: see below. § 13–16, n.44.
[32] *Colonial Bank* v. *Whinney* (1885) 30 Ch.D. 261, *per* Fry L.J. at p. 285; Crossley Vaines, *Personal Property* (5th ed.), pp. 11–13.
[33] *Torkington* v. *Magee* [1902] 2 K.B. 427, *per* Channell J. at p. 430; adopted in *Kohn* (1979) 69 Cr. App. R. 395.
[34] *Pace*, as to copyrights, Lord Fraser of Tullybelton in *Rank Film Distibutors Ltd.* v. *Video Information Centre* [1981] 2 W.L.R. 668 at p. 678, [1981] 2 All E.R. 76 at p. 83.
[35] Patents Act 1977, s. 30(1) (noticed by Smith, *Theft*, para. 100).
[36] See, *e.g.,* below, § 2–13, at n. 40.
[37] See further, below, § 2–69.

creditor.[38] The debt owed by the bank to the customer is property that can be stolen. So a trustee who dishonestly draws on a trust bank account for his own purposes is guilty of theft of the thing in action represented by the bank balance. And an employee (D) who has authority to draw on his employer's (P's) bank account and who dishonestly draws on it for unauthorised purposes also commits theft. He has in some manner appropriated the debt owed by the bank to P. Although nothing in the transaction operates as an assignment of that debt to D (or to E, in whose favour he draws the cheque), it would seem that D has appropriated the debt or part of it by causing P's credit balance to be diminished, or at the very least taking the risk of such diminution. The case is analogous to the theft of a chattel by destruction.[39]

The preceding paragraph assumes P's bank account to be sufficiently in **2–13** credit to meet the cheque drawn by D. If it is not P may nevertheless have an overdraft facility under which the bank is obliged to meet the cheque. That obligation is a thing in action which D steals by means of the cheque dishonestly drawn.[40] But where the bank is not obliged to meet the cheque, there is no theft (save of the cheque, as mentioned below), even if the cheque is in fact honoured by the bank as a matter of grace.[41]

(iii) *Cheques.* When D delivers to E a cheque dishonestly drawn in E's **2–14** favour on P's cheque form, he thereby at that time steals the cheque; it is immaterial whether the cheque is met, or whether it is drawn within the limits of P's credit or overdraft facility.[42] The courts regard the cheque not simply as a piece of paper but as a thing in action, on the ground that a cheque is an instrument embodying a right in the person entitled to it to receive payment of the amount for which it is drawn.[43] But this analysis, with respect, will not do. This is not simply because in a particular case E might acquire no right to payment against P. A more fundamental objection is that the property stolen[44] must be property belonging to P; and the thing in action created in the payee's favour by the transaction of drawing and delivering a cheque is not a thing that has ever belonged to the drawer. It is both simpler and more accurate to say that D has stolen P's cheque form—that is, a piece of paper. To charge such a theft is admittedly

---

[38] Above, text at n. 30 and cases cited there.
[39] *Kohn* (1979) 69 Cr. App. R. 395, upholding convictions where a company director improperly drew cheques on the company's account. The Court of Appeal approved the analysis in the text. But the words "or at the very least . . . diminution" should be disregarded if the court (at p. 407) was correct in treating theft as complete only when a cheque is met. Any other view would require an investigation of the state of the account at the moment of drawing, or possibly delivering, the cheque, which might be impossible. Yet the act of delivery seems to be an assumption of an owner's rights in the bank account, if then in credit, and therefore an appropriation (see s. 3(1)); *cf.* J. C. Smith [1979] Crim. L.R. at p. 676. The point does not seem to admit of a solution satisfying both in theory and in practice.
[40] *Kohn,* above, at pp. 406–407.
[41] *Ibid.* at p. 408.
[42] *Ibid.* at p. 410.
[43] *Ibid.* at pp. 409–410; *Duru* [1974] 1 W.L.R. 2 at p. 8; [1973] 3 All E.R. 715 at p. 720 (obtaining a cheque by deception contrary to s. 15).
[44] Or, as in *Duru,* above, obtained by deception.

artificial, as hardly expressing the *gravamen* of D's conduct. But it avoids difficulties involved in proving the state of P's account.[45]

Excluded or doubtful things

2–15   Although very wide, the scope of the definition of property is not without its difficulties. It is one of those definitions that defines the word to be defined in terms of itself: property "includes . . . all . . . property, . . . including . . . intangible property." This is unhelpful to the extent that there are some things whose status as "property" is uncertain. A few categories of things deserve separate consideration.

(i) *Electricity*. The fact that section 13 of the Act creates a separate offence of abstracting electricity suggests that electricity is not intended to be property for the purpose of theft. This has been confirmed by the Divisional Court in *Low* v. *Blease*.[46]

2–16   (ii) *The human body and its parts*. There could be no larceny of a corpse at common law; for there could be no property in a dead body.[47] The latter principle probably survives to limit the modern offence of theft. It is true that an executor, for instance, may have possession of a dead body, or a right to possession of it, until burial.[48] But he cannot be said to "own" it; and "property" within the Act is probably limited to that which is capable of ownership. If that is so, the theft sanction will not, without amendment of the Act, protect the possession of an executor or, for instance, that of a licensed anatomist receiving the body under the Anatomy Act 1832, s. 10. Nor can a buried corpse be stolen.[49] On the other hand, it has been argued (correctly, it is submitted) that modern medical advances make the body's "spare parts" important potential subjects of theft; that they should, once severed, be recognised as property; and that this result at least can be achieved without legislation.[50]

Products of the living body have been treated in practice as capable of theft—at least in the limited context of specimens provided to the police for laboratory examination.[51]

2–17   (ii) *Trade secrets and other confidential information*. It is probably a good guess that few of the people responsible for the Act contemplated

---

[45] See (ii), above. There is no difficulty about D's intention of permanently depriving P of the form: see below, § 2–74 (iv). *Quaere* whether there ought to be convictions in respect both of the cheque and of the bank account (when in credit), as there were in *Kohn*, above.

[46] [1975] Crim.L.R. 513.

[47] *Sharpe* (1857) Dears & Bell 160.

[48] Anatomy Act 1832, s. 7; Human Tissue Act 1961, s. 1; *Williams* v. *Williams* (1882) 20 Ch.D. 659.

[49] *Price* (1884) 12 Q.B.D. 247 at p. 252.

[50] A.T.H. Smith, "Stealing the Body and its Parts" [1976] Crim. L.R. 622. Blood banks and sperm banks must surely be protected by the law of theft. Interesting questions could arise as to the possible status as 'property' of an ovum removed from a woman's body for *in vitro* fertilisation or, until re-implantation, of an ovum fertilised *in vitro*: see B. M. Dickens, *Medico-Legal Aspects of Family Law*, p. 80. A dead body may apparently become property through the alteration of its condition by work lawfully done upon it: *Doodeward* v. *Spence* (1908) 6 C.L.R. 406.

[51] *Welsh* [1974] R.T.R. 478 (urine); *Rothery* [1976] Crim.L.R. 691 (blood).

trade secrets (secret industrial processes, for example) as "property" within the meaning of section 4(1) or as capable of being stolen. During the debates on the Bill, however, Lord Wilberforce took a wide view of the word "property" as including "things like business secrets."[52] He did not pursue in detail the analysis required to demonstrate that the law of theft has become an effective weapon against modern forms of industrial espionage. Probably it has not. One can in popular parlance describe a person who "bugs" a private conversation or photocopies a confidential document as "stealing" a secret. But to achieve that result in law would involve reading the Act in a very robust way for the purpose of producing a dramatic new offence not hinted at by the Committee. The Act is not in fact the appropriate instrument to deal with this specialised kind of mischief. The short way of disposing of an argument to the contrary is to deny that trade secrets are "property" within the Act. They should be treated in the same way as the confidential information contained in the proof copy of an examination paper; such information has been held to be incapable of being stolen because it is not "property."[53] But even if a secret were property, it would be peculiarly difficult to steal, for a reason that will be stated later in this chapter.[54]

4. "BELONGING TO ANOTHER"

Generally

In order that property may be stolen it must "belong to another" in the sense in which that phrase is defined in section 5.[55]   **2–18**

When D picks P's pocket and extracts money, or when he removes valuables from P's house, it is obvious that the *actus reus* of a theft has occurred; but even in such simple cases the property does not necessarily "belong" to P in the loosest sense of the word "belong." P may be carrying Q's money for him or have Q's valuables on loan or for safe keeping. Yet clearly D steals from P, and whether P owns the property or not it is necessary to regard the property, for the purpose of the law of theft, as belonging to P as well as to Q. Indeed the law of property and the remedies which protect property rights tend to be concerned less with absolute ownership than with grades and classes of possessory or proprietary interests (using "proprietary," as section 5(1) does, to include equitable interests, such as those which arise under a trust); and it is such interests, including as the most common case the interest of one in possession of property, that are protected by the law of theft.

Moreover, even in the many cases in which ownership can in practice be talked about and an owner accurately identified, experience under the old law showed that to exclude from the ambit of theft all cases in which D himself was already the owner of the property or became the owner by the

---

[52] H.L. Deb., Vol. 259, col. 1309.
[53] *Oxford* v. *Moss* (1978) 68 Cr.App.R. 183.
[54] Below, § 2–69. If a secret is written on a piece of paper and the paper is taken, a charge of theft naturally presents no difficulty.
[55] In *Edwards* v. *Ddin* [1976] 1 W.L.R. 942 at p. 945; [1976] 3 All E.R. 705 at p. 708, s. 5 was said to be "not definitive of" the expression "belonging to another." This statement was unexplained and is believed to be incorrect.

transaction alleged to involve a dishonest appropriation—to say that an owner could not steal, or that one could not both become owner and steal as a result of the same transaction—was unsatisfactory in a number of ways.[56]

The phrase "belonging to another" must therefore be given a meaning much wider than that which it bears in common speech. Section 5 provides accordingly.

Possession or control; proprietary right or interest

2–19   A very wide range of cases is covered by the provision in section 5(1) that property "shall be regarded as belonging to any person having possession or control of it, or having in it any proprietary right or interest (not being an equitable interest arising only from an agreement to transfer or grant an interest)."

(i) Possession or control

The word "possession" in English law is a veritable chameleon, changing its meaning with every change in the context in which it occurs. If it had been used alone in section 5(1) there might have been much room for argument as to its meaning in this context; whereas the addition of the words "or control" ensures that some cases doubtfully of possession are in fact to be treated as equivalent to cases of possession. For instance, if D seizes goods from the hands of P, a customer handling them in a shop, there is clearly a theft from P, who has control if not possession, and there is no need to discover whether P has yet acquired a proprietary right by purchase. If D scavenges on a golf-course for lost balls he can safely be treated as appropriating balls in the control of the club without reviving difficult arguments that formerly arose as to whether the club had possession of (or a "special property" in) the balls.[57] In *Woodman*[58] a company had sold all the scrap metal on the site of its disused factory but retained control of the site. The company did not know that the purchasers had left some of the metal on the site. One who entered the site and removed the metal was properly convicted on an indictment describing the metal as belonging to the company. The language of the judgment was cautious; a person in control of a site was described as "prima facie" having control of articles on it in "ordinary and straightforward cases."[59] Nevertheless it is submitted that P can always be treated as having control of property on land that he occupies.[60]

---

[56] It led among other things to multiplicity of offences (special provisions being made for some appropriations by owners); to artificial reasoning and impure doctrine (some owners being speciously treated as non-owners in order to secure convictions of larceny); and to the acquittal of a number of persons whom a law of theft should arguably catch.

[57] Cf. *Hibbert* v. *McKiernan* [1948] 2 K.B. 142.

[58] [1974] Q.B. 754.   [59] *Ibid.* at p. 758.

[60] This approach would substantially accord with that of Lord Goddard C.J. and perhaps of Humphreys J. in *Hibbert* v. *McKiernan* [1948] 2 K.B. 142, in avoiding difficult problems that arise in corresponding situations in civil cases. But it must be said that if certain much-debated civil decisions are correct (notably *Bridges* v. *Hawkesworth* (1852) 21 L.J.Q.B. 75 and *Hannah* v. *Peel* [1945] K.B. 509—though in the latter case the dispute was between a finder and a non-occupying owner of land) the approach suggested in the text could involve that a finder might steal property "belonging to" another while creating for himself, by his appropriation of the property, a title to it superior to that of the other.

One result of the protection of possession is that an owner can steal his **2–20** own property. D may, for instance, have pledged his goods with P; or he may have entrusted goods to P for repair so that P has acquired an artificer's lien entitling him to retain possession until the repair bill is paid. If in either of these cases, in order to defeat P's possessory rights, D dishonestly takes the goods from P's possession, he may be convicted of theft. The Court of Appeal has in fact gone further than this in *Turner* (*No.*2),[61] where P, having repaired D's car, left it in the road near his (P's) garage. D came and took the car away. The possible existence of a lien was disregarded. D was nevertheless held rightly convicted of theft if he acted dishonestly, for P had "possession or control" (presumably as a bailee at will). The decision goes very far and its correctness is not clear. Once P's possible lien is ignored, D did nothing in relation to the car that he was not perfectly entitled to do. Attention should perhaps have been concentrated, therefore, on the question whether D "appropriated" the car[62] rather than on the question whether it "belonged to" P. (And one may ask, incidentally, why the possibility that P had a lien was not explored. If he had, the case should have presented no difficulty.)

(ii) *Proprietary right or interest*

Something of the scope of theft is indicated by the inclusion among the **2–21** possible victims of the offence of "any person . . . having . . . any proprietary right or interest" in the property appropriated. The phrase clearly includes the owner of an estate in land or of any interest therein; a beneficiary under a trust; the owner of a thing in action (the creditor in respect of a debt, for instance); a partner in respect of partnership property; and so on. If D's act of appropriation is done with the intention of defeating P's right or interest in the property, it will properly be described as an appropriation of property "belonging to" P—even though other people may have other, and larger, rights in the same property. D himself may have a proprietary right or interest and still be guilty of theft: a part-owner or a partner, for example, may dishonestly appropriate property, as by selling it or by absconding with it, so as to defeat his co-owner or his partners[63]; and a dishonest sale by a trustee of trust property for his own purposes will be a theft of property belonging to the beneficiaries.

The range of persons to whom property belongs within the meaning of **2–22** section 1(1) is almost as wide as the number of different proprietary interests capable of subsisting in every kind of property. Almost as wide, but not quite: for "an equitable interest arising only from an agreement to transfer or grant an interest" is excluded. Since land cannot be stolen save in cases not material to this point, this exclusion will mainly affect dealings with shares and similar property. D contracts to transfer shares to P and

---

[61] [1971] 1 W.L.R. 901; [1971] 2 All E.R. 441.
[62] As to which, see below, § 2–42.
[63] *Bonner* [1970] 1 W.L.R. 838; [1970] 2 All E.R. 97n.

receives money from P; he then transfers them to Q; he does not steal the shares, for P has only an equitable interest arising from the agreement to transfer. There is difficulty also, on the same ground, in finding a theft from P in a third party's dishonest dealing with shares that P has contracted to buy from O.[64]

Trust property[65]

2–23   Section 5(2) makes special provision to ensure that where property is held on trust for a charitable object, a misappropriation of the property shall not fail to be theft merely because there is no particular person having a beneficial interest in the property. The property is to be regarded as belonging to "any person having a right to enforce the trust." Charitable trusts are enforced under the Charities Act 1960, s. 28, by (among others) the Attorney-General. The terms of subsection (2) are in fact wide enough to cover all trusts,[66] though most are already covered by subsection (1).

Property received from or on account of another
(i) *Introduction*

2–24   D may receive property (usually money) in circumstances in which he is bound, as between himself and another person, to deal with it in a particular way. It is desirable that a dishonest application of such property shall amount to theft. If the other person retains or acquires some proprietary interest in the property (as, most obviously, where D is a bailee or a trustee), the property "belongs to" him by virtue of section 5(1) and (2). Exhaustive examination of civil law principles might, in fact, reveal that the other person has a proprietary interest in any case in which use of the particular property is constrained in his favour.[67] If so, no further provision is strictly necessary to render such property capable of being stolen by D. The Act nevertheless makes such provision by section 5(3); and it is this provision, rather than the preceding subsections, that is in practice commonly referred to where an "obligation" such as it mentions exists:

> "Where a person receives property from or on account of another, and is under an obligation to the other to retain and deal with that property or its proceeds in a particular way, the property or proceeds shall be regarded (as against him) as belonging to the other."

The illustrative case offered by the Committee was that of the treasurer of a holiday fund; his misapplication of the fund or part of it is said to be theft, by virtue of section 5(3), from "the persons to whom he owes the

---

[64] See *per* Lord Keith of Kinkel in *Tarling* v. *Government of the Republic of Singapore* (1978) 70 Cr.App.R. 77 at p. 137. But see J. C. Smith [1979] Crim.L.R. at p. 225: there may be "property belonging to" P (an enforceable right against O: *cf.* above, § 2–10 at n. 36) other than an equitable interest in the shares.

[65] On the application of the Act generally to trustees, see Brazier (1975) 39 Conv. (N.S.) 29. As to constructive trustees, see A. T. H. Smith [1977] Crim.L.R. 395.

[66] But questions could, at least theoretically, arise as to the "right to enforce" non-charitable trusts for non-personal objects—so-called "trusts of imperfect obligation."

[67] See Williams, *Textbook*, pp. 713–723..

duty to retain and deal with the property as agreed."[68] Another situation undoubtedly contemplated is that where P deposits £50 with his employer, D, as security for his honesty, the sum to be returnable if P serves D honestly. If D is under an obligation to preserve the £50 and has not merely contracted a debt to P, the £50 is to be regarded as "belonging to" P.[69]

(ii) *To what kind of "obligation" does s. 5(3) refer?*

It must be stressed that it is not enough that D, when he receives money, **2–25** falls under some contractual obligation, or that a relationship of debtor and creditor is thereby created. D must be under an obligation which prescribes the application of *that* money or its proceeds. A debtor or contracting party has not normally so specific an obligation.

In *Hall*[70] D was a travel agent who had received deposits and payments from clients in respect of air trips to be arranged by him. He paid the sums into his firm's general trading account but arranged no trips and could not repay any of the money. His conviction of theft was quashed. On the facts—for each case must turn on its own facts—there was not established such a special arrangement between D and any of the clients as would give rise to an obligation within section 5(3).[71]

It would seem that section 5(3) will be satisfied where, having received money or other property from P or on account of Q, D has an obligation to P or to Q, as the case may be, to preserve a fund or corpus consisting of or representing[72] that money or other property, which fund or corpus is to be maintained except so far as it may or must be dealt with "in a particular way"—that is, in the manner agreed with P, or by transfer to or at the direction of Q, or as justified by an accounting with Q.

In *Hall*[73] the Court of Appeal seemed to say that where the transaction is **2–26** wholly in writing the question whether a relevant obligation existed may be one of law on which the jury must accept the judge's ruling, but that in any other case, if the judge decides that on some available view of the facts such an obligation can be found to have existed, the matter must be left explicitly for the jury's decision. This distinction between documentary and other transactions was not repeated in *Hayes*,[74] where the Court of Appeal

---

[68] *Eighth Report*, p. 127 (notes on draft Bill).
[69] *Cf. Smith* [1924] 2 K.B. 194 (fraudulent conversion).
[70] [1973] Q.B. 126.
[71] In any case the jury had received no direction upon the subsection. On the need for a "careful exposition," see [1973] Q.B. 126 at p. 131. But see below, § 2–26.
[72] The word "representing" is necessary because of the word "proceeds" in the subsection. "Proceeds" must be generously interpreted to include the case where D is at liberty to set aside money which is the equivalent in value of the money received; this commonplace situation cannot be intended to be excluded. Liberal interpretation may also be needed where D mixes in a cash box or a bank account sums received from various persons for a common purpose and is entitled to do so. If proprietary interests in mixed funds are ignored (that is, if, as usual, only s. 5(3) is alluded to, and not s. 5(1) and (2)), it may be necessary to regard the whole of the fund as the "proceeds" of each contribution. For otherwise (ignoring proprietary interests), who is the victim if D misappropriates a part only of the fund?
[73] [1973] Q.B. 126 at p. 133.
[74] (1976) 64 Cr. App. R. 82 (deposits paid to estate agent).

insisted that whether D had an obligation within section 5(3) was for the jury to decide. The court did not discuss the guidance that the jury might need in making such a decision. They surely need a good deal if, as must be strongly submitted, what has to be found is a *legal* obligation.

In the analogous context of section 5(4), considered below, the word "obligation" has been declared to refer to a legal obligation and not merely a moral one.[75] The same should be true in the case of section 5(3); and this should mean that the case is within the subsection only if at the time of the appropriation of property or its proceeds D was subject, by virtue of the principles of the civil law, to a relevant obligation, in relation to that property or its proceeds, which another person was entitled to enforce. But the case law contradicts this desirable principle.

2–27   First, the Court of Appeal decided in *Hayes* that the question whether an estate agent was, for the purposes of section 5(3), under an obligation to clients (vendors or purchasers) to retain and deal with deposits or their proceeds in a particular way was not concluded by the fact that in civil law he was under just such an obligation. This is quite remarkable; it leaves one without clues as to the meaning of the subsection and the scope of the criminal law.[76]

Secondly, there is the unsatisfactory case of *Meech*.[77] D agreed with P to cash a cheque that P had obtained from Q. He paid the cheque into his bank, intending to draw cash to pay P. He then learnt that P had obtained the cheque by fraud. He drew the appropriate sum from his account and, with help from E and F, contrived the appearance of a robbery so as to have an excuse for not being able to pay the money to P. The Court of Appeal held that D was guilty, at the time of the bogus robbery, of stealing the proceeds of property that he had received from P under an obligation within section 5(3). The argument that P could never have enforced the so-called "obligation"[78] was met by holding that the question was to be looked at from D's point of view. He had "assumed an 'obligation' " which he thought was a legally binding one, and was therefore "under an obligation" within the meaning of section 5(3).[79] This is hardly acceptable. It is contrary to principle that one should be guilty of an offence just because he believes an essential element of the offence to exist. D argued further that as at the time of the appropriation he knew the truth, he was not then under an "obligation." This argument was rejected. The court had in any case already stated that the crucial time is "the time of the creation or the acceptance of the obligation."[80] But it has been correctly

---

[75] *Gilks* [1972] 1 W.L.R. 1341; [1972] 3 All E.R. 280.

[76] The powerful attack on this case in Williams, *Textbook*, pp. 710–712, is respectfully adopted *in toto*. See now the Estate Agents Act 1979, s.13(1) (in force on May 3, 1982), under which estate agents will hold clients' money on trust, so that deposits will clearly "belong to" clients within the meaning of s. 5(1).

[77] [1974] Q.B. 549.

[78] Questioned by Glanville Williams [1977] Crim. L.R. at p. 337.

[79] [1974] Q.B. at p. 555. See also *Brewster* (1979) 69 Cr. App. R. 375, where insurance companies' rights and an agent's obligations in relation to premiums received by the agent were made to turn on whether the agent was dishonest at the time of the appropriation.

[80] [1974] Q.B. at p. 555. *Brewster* (above) appears not to be consistent with this.

objected that, reading sections 1(1) and 5(3) together, the obligation must plainly exist at the time of the appropriation.[81]

(iii) *Further examples of the application of section 5(3)*

    The following are some further cases within section 5(3):   **2–28**

    (a) D is under a duty to P to collect money and to account to P for the money less D's commission or other reward, the circumstances being such as to oblige D to maintain a distinct fund representing his receipts. D dishonestly pockets more than he is entitled to. He is guilty of theft of the excess.[82]

    (b) P employs D to carry out repairs to P's house and advances £50 to D, not simply on account of the total cost of the job but specifically for the purpose of buying necessary materials. If D has an obligation to use the money in that way,[83] a dishonest misuse of the £50, or any part of it, is an appropriation of property that is to be regarded, as against him, as belonging to P.[84]

    (c) P gives D goods to sell on P's behalf. D sells the goods but then absconds with the proceeds. If this is an isolated transaction, a jury may readily find an obligation to "retain" the proceeds, in which case D is guilty of theft. It may be quite otherwise with a continuing principal-agent relationship. (If D makes a dishonest sale of P's goods and misappropriates the proceeds, this seems to be theft of the proceeds on two grounds: the proceeds constitute a fund over which P has a proprietary claim[85] and which therefore "belongs to" him by virtue of section 5(1); and D receives the proceeds "on account of" P with a clear obligation to retain them for him.[86])

    (d) P sends D a cheque which goes astray in the post. D applies to P for a substitute payment, which is made on the understanding that if the cheque turns up it will be returned to P. D steals the cheque if, when it arrives, he dishonestly cashes it or pays it into his bank for collection.[87]

(iv) *Secret profits and bribes*

    A mere duty to account for an improper profit secretly made by D as P's   **2–29** servant or agent does not bring the property received within section 5(3). So, for example, a bargee who works his employer's barge for his own purposes has a duty to account to the employer for the money that he receives; but the money is not received "on account of" the employer

---

[81] J. C. Smith [1973] Crim. L.R. 774, and *Theft*, para. 69; Williams, *loc.cit.*, n. 78, above.

[82] *Cf.* the fraudulent conversion cases of *Lord* (1905) 60 J.P. 467 (debt collector) and *Messer* [1913] 2 K.B. 421 (taxi-driver). Contrast the case in which receipt of the money creates in the agent the obligation of a debtor only and no obligation to maintain a separate fund: *e.g. Stanley Robertson* [1977] Crim. L.R. 629.

[83] Or, at least, to preserve, and use in that way, an equivalent fund.

[84] *Cf. Hughes* [1956] Crim. L.R. 835 (fraudulent conversion); but, by contrast, *Jones* (1948) 33 Cr.App.R. 11 and *Bryce* (1955) 40 Cr. App.R. 62 show the need for great caution.

[85] See Goff and Jones, *The Law of Restitution* (2nd ed.), pp. 48–53.

[86] So also with money obtained by the fraudulent cashing of a cheque intended for P or drawn without authority on P's account: *cf. Gale* (1876) 2 Q.B.D. 141; *Davenport* [1954] 1 W.L.R. 569.

[87] *Wakeman* v. *Farrar* [1974] Crim. L.R. 136.

within the meaning of section 5(3).[88] Similarly, a bride received by D in the course of his employment has been held not to "belong to" his employer for theft purposes.[89]

Property "got" by another's mistake[90]

2–30   Section 5(4) provides:

> "Where a person gets property by another's mistake, and is under an obligation to make restoration (in whole or in part) of the property or its proceeds or of the value thereof, then to the extent of that obligation the property or proceeds shall be regarded (as against him) as belonging to the person entitled to restoration, and an intention not to make restoration shall be regarded accordingly as an intention to deprive that person of the property or proceeds."

The subsection is intended to cover a case like *Moynes* v. *Coopper*.[91] A wages clerk, not having been told that D had had an advance on his wages, gave D a wage packet containing his full wages without deduction. D was held not guilty of larceny when, opening the packet, he realised the error but kept the excess. Section 5(4) was passed primarily to reverse this result. If the wages clerk has authority to pay the full wages, ownership passes in the whole sum. But D "gets property" by his employer's mistake; he has an obligation to restore the value of part of the payment; to that extent the money paid is to be regarded as belonging to the employer.

2–31   The "obligation" referred to in section 5(4) is a legal obligation.[92] Where D decides to disregard a merely moral obligation to restore property got by P's mistake, the court has to resort to some other ground for holding that the property belonged to P if D is to be convicted. This was done in *Gilks*.[92] D, a punter, had won £10.62 by bets in P's betting shop. But P's manager paid D £117.25, wrongly thinking that D had backed one more winning horse than he had. D took the money knowing that he had been overpaid. His conviction of theft was upheld. If ownership in the amount overpaid (£106.63) passed to D, he had no legal obligation to make restoration, the overpayment having been made under a void wagering contract,[93] and he did not appropriate property belonging to another.[94]

---

[88] *Cf. Cullum* (1873) L.R. 2 C.C.R. 28. See *Eighth Report*, para. 57 (iii); *Kenatley* [1980] Crim. L.R. 505 (Judge Mendl).

[89] *Powell* v. *McRae* [1977] Crim. L.R. 571. But if D is a constructive trustee of the profit or bribe, it no doubt "belongs to" P by virtue of s. 5(1). The topic is controversial: see A.T.H. Smith, "Constructive Trusts in the Law of Theft" [1977] Crim. L.R. 395; Williams, *Textbook*, pp. 720–723; *Tarling* v. *Government of the Republic of Singapore* (1978) 70 Cr. App. R. 77, *per* Lord Wilberforce at p. 111 (on which see J. C. Smith [1979] Crim. L.R. at pp. 225–226).

[90] Glanville Williams, "Mistake in the Law of Theft" [1977] C.L.J. 62, for detailed discussion.

[91] [1956] 1 Q.B. 439.

[92] *Gilks* [1972] 1 W.L.R. 1341; [1972] 3 All E.R. 280.

[93] *Morgan* v. *Ashcroft* [1938] 1 K.B. 49 (though the case and its generally assumed consequence are both questioned by Williams, *loc. cit.*, n. 90, above, pp. 72–73).

[94] Even this is not quite certain in the light of *Lawrence* v. *Metropolitan Police Commissioner* [1972] A.C. 626, and *Turner (No.2)* [1971] 1 W.L.R. 901; [1971] 2 All E.R. 441 (see below, § 2–79).

But the Court of Appeal affirmed the trial judge's ruling that "the property in the £106.63 never passed to [D]."[95] On this basis D appropriated property belonging to P without recourse to section 5(4). This is not satisfactory. The court eschewed elaborate argument to defend its proposition that the mistake made by P (or rather his manager[96]) was of a kind to prevent property in the money from passing; they referred only to a long-doubted Larceny Act case that was readily distinguishable.[97] The better view, it is submitted, is that D did obtain ownership of all the money paid.[98] That is surely what would have been held if a quasi-contractual right to recover the overpayment had existed and section 5(4) could have applied.

The subsection presents difficulties of a number and degree that far outstrip its importance,[1] among them the following.　　**2–32**

First, although no doubt all quasi-contractual obligations at common law to repay money paid under a mistake of fact are covered by section 5(4), it is not satisfactory that the precise ambit of the subsection should depend upon anything as uncertain as the law of quasi-contract.[2] For instance, the quasi-contractual obligation may turn on difficult distinctions between mistakes of fact and mistakes of law, the former founding a claim to restoration, the latter not. Whether such distinctions should be relevant to criminal liability may be doubted.

Secondly, section 5(4) is not necessarily limited to *common law* obligations to restore money paid by mistake. It is possible, for instance, that D is guilty of theft if he knows that money has been wrongly paid to him under a will (whether the mistake is one of fact or of law) and decides against repaying it. If there is here "an obligation to make restoration" within the meaning of section 5(4), the "person entitled to restoration" may not be the same as the person who paid the money in error; but the subsection does not require that he should be. The difficult problems attending claims in equity in respect of money paid under a mistake[3] may thus infect the law of theft.[4]

Thirdly, there has been controversy as to whether the effect of section　**2–33** 5(4) may be to make guilty of theft (as well as of obtaining property by

---

[95] [1972] 1 W.L.R. 1341 at p. 1344; [1972] 3 All E.R. 280 at p. 282.
[96] It would be unsatisfactory if the case turned upon a want of authority in the manager to make an overpayment. The manager should be equated with P.
[97] *Middleton* (1873) L.R. 2 C.C.R. 38: 10s. due to D from post office; clerk, consulting document referring to E, handed D £8 odd; held, property did not pass (*sed quaere*).
[98] See also Williams, *loc.cit.*; Smith, *Theft*, para. 79; Heaton, "Belonging to Another" [1973] Crim L.R. 736 at p. 739.
[1] For a critical discussion, see Stuart, "Law Reform and the Reform of the Law of Theft" (1967) 30 M.L.R. 609, especially at pp. 622–623.
[2] See Goff and Jones, *The Law of Restitution* (2nd ed.), Chap. 3. Note that the subsection speaks of "property," not of "money." There may be cases in which an obligation arises to restore chattels or other property transferred under a mistake, or to restore the value of such property, even where ownership in the property has passed. As to restitution in respect of chattels transferred under a mistake, see Goff and Jones, *op. cit.* pp. 116–117.
[3] See Goff and Jones, *op. cit.* pp. 450–453.
[4] If the claimant has a proprietary claim, such problems would appear to be imported via s. 5(1): property "belongs to" anyone having any "proprietary . . . interest" in it.

deception) a person who induces another by deception to transfer ownership of property to him and who appropriates that property, intending not to restore it or its value.[5] Such a person, it would seem, "gets property by another's mistake."

Where D by deception induces P to make a payment in circumstances giving P a quasi-contractual right to recover money paid under a mistake of fact, there should be no difficulty. If, for example, D falsely stated facts which would have the effect that money was due under an existing contract, and P paid that money, the money would no doubt be "got" by mistake and a duty to make restoration of it would exist; section 5(4) would apply. The terms of the subsection will also be satisfied where a payment by P to D does not transfer ownership in the money concerned because it is made under a contract *void* for fundamental mistake induced by D's fraud; though in such a case the money "belongs to" P without resort to section 5(4).[6] But where P pays money or delivers property under a contract (say, for the sale of goods) which is itself *voidable* because of D's fraud, it is said that D has no obligation to make restoration unless and until the contract is avoided by a disaffirming act on P's part, and that on that ground section 5(4) does not apply to such a case.[7] It is odd, if it be the case, that D is not under an obligation to restore what he has obtained by fraud until the fraud is discovered. Nevertheless, to reject this view would involve giving an unduly wide effect to a provision with a limited purpose or would require a very artificial reading of the subsection in order to avoid that result.[8]

Corporations sole

2–34   Property belonging to a corporation sole is to be regarded as belonging to the corporation notwithstanding a vacancy in the corporation (s. 5(5)).

"Belonging to another" at the time of the appropriation

2–35   The property must still have belonged to P (in some sense within s. 5) at the time of D's alleged act of theft. It is not always easy to decide whether this was the case. The point may require application of principles of the law of agency, contract and sale. It may be illustrated by reference to simple retail transactions.

(i) *Shops*.[9] Ownership (the "property") in goods passes to a buyer at the time the parties intend it to pass.[10] In the case of a supermarket or cash and

---

[5] The controversy may be academic; the case may be one of theft without resort to s. 5(4); see below, §§ 2–63.

[6] As in *Williams* [1980] Crim. L.R. 589 (but see commentator's note as to the court's remarkable view that the contract was void).

[7] Smith, *Theft*, para. 80. *Kaur v. Chief Constable for Hampshire* [1981] 1 W.L.R. 578; [1981] 2 All E.R. 430, is consistent with this view. (Williams [1981] Crim.L.R. at p. 676 asserts the contrary as to money, but without citing authority. *Sed quaere*; see Chitty on *Contracts* (24th ed.), para. 1827).

[8] Williams [1977] C.L.J. at pp. 70 and 79, suggests that D's liability to pay damages for deceit brings a case of fraud within s. 5(4). But this, with respect, is a curious, and surely unintended, meaning to give to the phrase "obligation to make restoration of the property . . . or of the value thereof."

[9] For a general treatment of theft from shops, see A.T.H. Smith, "Shoplifting and the Theft Acts" [1981] Crim. L.R. 586.

[10] Sale of Goods Act 1979, s. 17.

carry store the courts attribute to the parties the intention that ownership shall pass only upon payment. This applies no less to goods (such as meat and vegetables) wrapped and priced by an assistant within the store, but to be paid for at the check-out, than to goods with which the customer serves himself from the shelves. Accordingly, where a customer leaves the store without paying for goods so wrapped and priced, he removes goods that still "belong to" the store.[11]

Conversely, once ownership in the goods has passed under a valid contract and the buyer has taken delivery, there is no question of theft by any further act of the buyer. A diner who decides at the end of the meal not to pay for it cannot steal the food in his stomach—as the Divisional Court had once solemnly to hold.[12] Of course there may be a question as to the validity of a contract of sale and therefore as to whether ownership passed. In *Kaur* v. *Chief Constable for Hampshire*[13] a supermarket cashier mistook the price of goods and undercharged D (who knew the correct price). But the mistake was not such as to render the contract a nullity or to destroy the cashier's authority. Ownership passed on payment by D, who, despite her dishonesty, did not steal the goods when she took them from the shop.

(ii) *Garages.* If D puts petrol in his car at a self-service garage and drives **2–36** off without paying, two cases must be distinguished.

(a) If his decision not to pay is made only after he has put the petrol into the tank, driving away cannot be an appropriation of the petrol as property belonging to another; property in the petrol will have passed to him under the sale transaction.[14] (It is submitted that this is true even if there is a notice at the garage declaring that ownership in petrol is not to pass until it is paid for. Considering the nature of the transaction, such a notice can hardly represent a serious intention as to the time of the passing of property; its sole purpose is to try to keep the bilking motorist within the law of theft.[15])

(b) If D intends from the outset not to pay for the petrol, he should be guilty of theft,[16] for what he takes belongs to another at the time he dishonestly takes it. This seems certainly to be true in a case where P is unaware that D is helping himself to the petrol. A possible argument to the contrary based on P's consent to the taking is met by the commonsense point that P's invitation to people at large to help themselves to petrol must be understood as limited to those who intend to pay for it.[17] The case

[11] *Davies* v. *Leighton* (1978) 68 Cr. App. R. 4.
[12] *Corcoran* v. *Whent* [1977] Crim. L.R. 52.
[13] [1981] 1 W.L.R. 578; [1981] 2 All E.R. 430 (pair of shoes, each with a different price label; cashier chose the lower price). For a doubt about the reasoning in this case, see below, § 2–65. For discussion of the case and its implications, see J.C. Smith at [1981] Crim. L.R. 259; Williams, "Theft and Voidable Title" [1981] Crim. L.R. 666 (with a reply by Smith at p. 677).
[14] *Edwards* v. *Ddin* [1976] 1 W.L.R. 942; [1976] 3 All E.R. 705 (in fact a case of pump-attendant service); Sale of Goods Act 1979, s.18, r. 5(1).
[15] *Cf. Edwards* v. *Ddin* [1976] 1 W.L.R. 942 at p. 945; [1976] 3 All E.R. 705 at p. 708; *contra*, Williams, *Textbook*, p. 692, n. 5.
[16] Apparently so assumed in *Greenberg* [1972] Crim. L.R. 331, and *McHugh* [1977] Crim.L.R. 174.
[17] Smith, *Theft*, para. 32, and [1977] Crim. L.R. at p. 175.

would be like one in which D syphons petrol from P's car as it stands outside P's house. But if, to avoid suspicion, D has pressed the red button on the pump and attracted the cashier's attention, it can be argued that a contractual situation arises, and ownership in the petrol may pass as under any other contract rendered voidable by fraud. The petrol has been obtained by deception and an offence under section 15 can be charged. The question whether theft is also committed when ownership is obtained by deception is discussed below.[18] One problem that arises in that connection also is that of the time at which the property ceases to "belong to" the victim.

5. "APPROPRIATES"

General and theoretical
The statutory definition; general tendency of the cases

2–37   Section 3(1) declares that

> "Any assumption by a person of the rights of an owner amounts to an appropriation . . . ."

Although this "partial definition"[19] must be constantly borne in mind, it does not go far to solve the problems that arise in determining what conduct can amount to theft. It provokes the obvious question: in what circumstances is a person to be regarded as assuming the rights of an owner? This question, which will arise in a wide range of factual situations and in relation to all kinds of property, is hardly susceptible of a ready comprehensive answer. There is a good deal of work for the courts to do in elucidating the essential element of appropriation. Unhappily, the problems presented by the terse statutory text have not been seriously faced in the case law; rationalisation and consistency seem not to have high priority as judicial objectives in this context.[20] In consequence the law is difficult to state with either confidence or satisfaction.

2–38   It is nevertheless possible to express the main tendency of the case law in two broad generalisations that may be found helpful before the topic is examined in detail. (1) The courts have insisted on the need for some act (or, perhaps, omission[21]) inconsistent with the rights of the alleged

---

[18] § 2–63.

[19] *Eighth Report*, para. 34. But s. 3(1) is consistently described by the courts as providing a "definition" of "appropriation": see, *e.g. Bonner* [1970] 1 W.L.R. 838; [1970] 2 All E.R. 97n.; *Stapylton* v. *O'Callaghan* [1973] 2 All E.R. 782; *Pitham and Hehl* (1976) 65 Cr. App. R. 45. The generality of the opening words of s. 3(1) is not limited by the following passage, which provides that there may be an appropriation in some cases in which a person has originally "come by" property without stealing it (see below, § 2–53). Appropriation does not require something amounting to a "coming by" the property: *Pitham and Hehl*, above.

[20] A statement by Roskill L.J. in *Anderton* v. *Wish* (1980) 72 Cr.App.R. 23 at p. 25, seems characteristic of the judicial approach: "We have had cited to us a large number of authorities on appropriation. I do not propose to go through them or consider whether one authority is precisely in line with another; all these cases turn upon their own facts."

[21] See below, § 2–46.

victim—the person to whom the property "belongs."[22] In cases where D, albeit intending to deprive P permanently of property, has acted only in a manner permitted by P, the existence of an appropriation has been denied.[23] (2) Conversely, the courts appear to be treating the phrase "any assumption of the rights of an owner" in section 3(1) as meaning, in effect, any act inconsistent with one or more of the rights of a person to whom the property "belongs." The following pages will contain the evidence for this generalisation, will reveal what a wide range of conduct it embraces, and will refer to one or two cases that may be thought to go even further.[24] Subject to proposition (1) above, the appellate courts have very rarely failed to find an appropriation in the conduct of a plainly dishonest person in relation to property "belonging to another."

Appropriation and conversion

"The expression 'dishonestly appropriates' . . . means the same as 'fraudulently converts to his own use or benefit, or the use or benefit of any other person' " in the Larceny Act 1916, s. 20(1)(iv), the word "appropriates" being preferred as a shorter expression and as less of a "lawyers' word."[25] The Committee referred to appropriation as "the familiar concept of conversion."[26] But the *word* "conversion," though long used both in criminal law[27] and in the law of tort, does not represent a single *concept* of settled meaning. The Committee expressed the hope and belief "that the concept of 'dishonest appropriation' will easily be understood even without the aid of further definition."[28] Yet it was clear from the outset that such understanding could not be achieved simply by relying upon the meaning of conversion in either of the contexts in which it had become familiar. **2–39**

The earlier criminal context can be shortly disposed of. The offences of larceny as a bailee and fraudulent conversion covered only part of the ground now covered by theft. They were concerned with misappropriations by those lawfully in possession of property with the consent of the owner, or entrusted with ownership or possession of property for particular purposes. What is more, the meaning of conversion in relation to them was never fully worked out.[29] **2–40**

On the other hand, appropriation in criminal law appears not to be a replica of its tort counterpart. In *Rogers* v. *Arnott*,[30] decided under the Larceny Act, the act of a bailee in attempting to sell a borrowed tape recorder was held to be a criminal conversion although it would not in itself

---

[22] In practice called "the owner" by the courts, reflecting the reality of most cases.
[23] See below, §§ 2–58, 2–61.
[24] See §§ 2–42, 2–47.
[25] *Eighth Report*, para. 35.
[26] *Eighth Report*, para. 34.
[27] Larceny Act 1916, ss. 1(1) proviso, 20(1)(i) and (iv), 21 ("converts or appropriates"!).
[28] *Eighth Report*, para. 34.
[29] See Smith and Hogan, *Criminal Law* (1st ed.), pp. 358–360; *Russell on Crime* (12th ed.), pp. 966–969.
[30] [1960] 2 Q.B. 244.

have founded liability in tort; and in *Bonner*[31] the Court of Appeal had no doubt that a partner who absconds with partnership property must be held to "appropriate" that property even if in the circumstances he would not be liable to his co-partner in tort.[32] It is submitted that this refusal to equate conversion in crime and in tort is right and inevitable.

Consistency between civil and criminal law

2–41   Notwithstanding the broad terms of section 3(1), Professor Glanville Williams has powerfully urged that theft cannot be committed (a) "by a person who has or obtains an indefeasible title to the property when he commits the act charged as an appropriation" or (b) "by an act that is not wrongful (under the general law) against the person to whom the property belongs."[33] His arguments in favour of consistency between, on the one hand, what is permitted by the civil law and achieved by its transactions and, on the other hand, what may be done and enjoyed without attracting the sanctions of the criminal law are recommended for careful study. It is thought that his general thesis ought to be found persuasive in principle, although disagreement over particular applications of it will be expressed in the ensuing paragraphs—especially as to what can be regarded as "wrongful (under the general law)" for the purpose of his second principle.

2–42   Professor Williams refers to decisions which are, or are possibly, against his thesis. Three such decisions have appeared earlier in this chapter and may conveniently be mentioned again here. The conviction in *Turner* (*No.2*)[34] seems to have rested solely on a finding that D did not, as he claimed, believe that he was entitled to repossess his own car from outside the garage where it had been repaired. But if he was so entitled, the repossession should probably have been held to be no appropriation.[35] When *Gilks*[36] took up from the betting shop counter the excessive sum he was paid as winnings, he took what, according to civil law, could not be recovered from him. It seems odd, then, that his taking of it was theft. The oddity is made possible by the even odder view, criticised above, that although Gilks could keep the money he did not become owner of it. The judgment in *Turner* (*No.2*) is very obscure and *Gilks* has been demons-

---

[31] [1970] 1 W.L.R. 838; [1970] 2 All E.R. 97n.
[32] Co-ownership is a defence to an action founded on conversion except as specified in the Torts (Interference with Goods) Act 1977, s. 10(1). S. 10(1)(*a*) restates the only pre-existing exceptions as understood by the court in *Bonner*. Para. (*b*) adds a further significant exception. The same Act makes other modifications of the scope of conversion as a tort: see ss. 2(2), 8(1), 11(2). It can hardly be the case that it has also casually modified the scope of theft.
[33] "Theft, Consent and Illegality" [1977] Crim. L.R. 127 and 205; "Theft, Consent and Illegality: Some Problems" [1977] Crim L.R. 327; *Textbook*, Chap. 34.
[34] Above, § 2–20. See on this case Smith, *Theft*, para. 58, and "Civil Law Concepts in the Criminal Law" [1972B] C.L.J. 197, at pp. 215–217; Williams, *Textbook*, pp. 706–709.
[35] See *Meredith* [1973] Crim. L.R. 253 (Judge da Cunha), where D, without reference to the police, removed his car from a police pound; a charge of theft was said to be improper (possibly overlooking *Turner*, but to satisfactory effect).
[36] Above, § 2–31.

trated to be unsatisfactory in a number of ways.[37] So these cases (in neither of which was the word "appropriates" discussed) do not contribute convincingly to a denial of Williams' suggested principles. And it is submitted that *Bonner*,[38] where it was held that a partner's dishonest taking for himself of partnership property would be theft although not conversion, presents no problem; for the act seems plainly "wrongful" as a breach of the statutory obligation to hold and apply partnership property exclusively for the purposes of the partnership.[39]

Appropriation and intention

In an analysis of the basic definition of theft it is inevitable that attention **2–43** should be given separately to the element of appropriation and to the required intention. But a separation that is convenient for purposes of exposition will be misleading if it suggests a total divorce in reality. Appropriation and intention are inextricably bound together.

An act will often be in itself neutral; it will or will not be an appropriation according to the actor's state of mind.[40] For instance, if D is in possession of P's goods, a merely negligent destruction by him of the goods will not be an appropriation, while an intentional destruction will amount to the deliberate assertion of dominion over the goods—to an "assumption of the rights of an owner"—and therefore to an appropriation.[41] Again, when D removes P's goods from one place to another, his act will be an appropriation if he takes them for use or to prevent P from recovering them, but not if his act is innocent of any assertion of dominion, as when he moves P's goods in order to get at his own. And an intention to steal has been treated in some cases as converting preliminary and even quite unsuccessful acts in relation to property into complete theft. Although an appropriation and an intention of depriving P are separate elements in the definition of theft, it is clear that the existence of the former will often depend upon the existence of the latter.

On the other hand, the required element of permanence in the intended **2–44** deprivation of the person to whom the property belongs does seem to be additional to the element of appropriation itself. It was certainly so understood when, during the passage of the Bill, the word "permanently" was for a time deleted by amendment from section 1(1); it was assumed that without this qualifying word theft would be constituted by a mere unauthorised borrowing.

This understanding is reflected in the language of the judgment in the

---

[37] See Williams [1977] Crim. L.R. at pp. 205–207, and "Mistake in the Law of Theft" [1977] C.L.J. 62 at pp. 72–73; Smith, *Theft*, para. 79, and [1972] Crim. L.R. 586–590.

[38] Above, § 2–40.

[39] Partnership Act 1890, s. 20(1); and see now the Torts (Interference with Goods) Act 1977, s. 10(1)(*b*).

[40] As to directing a jury on the determining of the defendant's state of mind, see *Ingram* [1975] Crim. L.R. 457.

[41] Many cases of unlawful damage under the Criminal Damage Act 1971 are therefore also cases of theft, and some are charged as such: see J. N. Spencer (1978) 42 J. Cr. L. 125 at p. 126.

instructive case of *Easom*.[42] D took up P's handbag as it lay beside her in the cinema, examined its contents, replaced them all and left the handbag behind P's seat. The Court of Appeal held that he was not guilty of stealing the bag or its contents, although he no doubt intended to steal from the bag if he found anything in it worth taking. "What may loosely be described as a 'conditional' appropriation," it was said, "will not do."[43] The decisive circumstance was the absence of a formed intention to deprive P permanently of the property named in the indictment; but the court does appear to hold that D did, however temporarily, appropriate that property. It is thought, with respect, that this is the correct analysis.

Duration of appropriation; successive appropriations[44]

2-45   Is theft over as soon as anything has been done that qualifies as an appropriation? Or does the activity of stealing last beyond the first moment of appropriation? The answer given in the context of robbery, where it may be necessary to decide whether force was used "at the time of" the stealing, is that an appropriation is not a merely momentary event.[45] This answer gives the law of theft a necessary flexibility for a number of purposes.[46] No formula, of course, can express for all types of case how long an appropriation lasts. This must depend upon nature of the property, the mode of appropriation and all the circumstances.

It is clear that a person may appropriate the same property more than once. He may, for instance, find goods and keep them, thinking the owner untraceable (this is an appropriation but not dishonest, according to s. 2(1)), and when he learns who the owner is, steal by a subsequent appropriation (as s. 3(1) confirms).[47] But this does not mean that one can steal the same property more than once as principal offender. So where D bought stolen goods in France and conveyed them to England, his only theft was committed outside the jurisdiction and he could not be convicted here.[48] His original appropriation of the goods, however long exactly it lasted, was certainly over before he arrived within the jurisdiction.

Omissions and inchoate transactions

Omission to act as appropriation

2-46   There are cases in which an omission to do something that should be done is all that can be identified as an appropriation.

Suppose, for instance, that D finds goods. Thinking the owner is not traceable, he keeps them. This is not theft.[49] He then hears who the owner

---

[42] [1971] 2 Q.B. 315.
[43] *Ibid.* at p. 319, *per* Edmund-Davies L.J. D may be guilty of attempted theft: see *ibid.* at p. 321; below, § 2–78.
[44] Williams, "Appropriation: A Single or Continuous Act?" [1978] Crim. L.R. 69; Smith, *Theft*, para. 48.
[45] *Hale* (1978) 68 Cr.App.R. 415, below, § 3–08. But see also, § 13–28, for possibly inconsistent authority on the meaning of "the course of the stealing" in s. 22(1) (handling).
[46] *e.g.* powers of arrest: see Tunkel [1978] Crim. L.R. 313. As to the pleading notion of one "continuous" theft by successive appropriations of different things, see below, § 2–94.
[47] See below, § 2–53.
[48] *Figures* [1976] Crim. L.R. 744.
[49] s. 2(1)(*c*).

is, but he decides not to give them up. His keeping them is then theft.[50] No doubt in practice D's theft will be revealed when he deals with the property in some active way or expressly refuses to give it up; but in a case like this it seems that the theft is, strictly speaking, complete on the occurrence of a dishonest non-restoration (assuming that D has an opportunity to restore).

A strong case of theft by omission is that of a shop-assistant's dishonest **2–47** omission to ring up money on the till. What was actually done in *Monaghan*[51] was what the defendant cashier was supposed to do: she received £3.99 from a customer and put it in her till. She did not ring the sum up because she had a proved intention to remove an equivalent sum; but she was arrested before proceeding further. Her conviction of stealing the sum of £3.99[52] was upheld on appeal. It is submitted that this goes too far. It cannot be known whether in the end the defendant would have removed any money. She had not yet got as far as attempting to do so within the meaning of a general law of attempt which provides ample opportunity for a late change of mind. Her conviction denies her that opportunity. Nor was it necessary, as the Court of Appeal implied, to charge her with theft in order to avoid keeping observation on her until she removed money; for she might have been charged, on the strength of her guilty omission, with false accounting contrary to section 17 of the Act.

Inchoate transactions as complete thefts

Conduct falling short of theft may, of course, amount to an attempt to **2–48** commit theft. This will require "an act which is more than merely preparatory to the commission of" an intended theft.[53] But a relatively limited function is accorded to attempted theft. For the wide terms of section 3(1), and the omission from the definition of theft of anything equivalent to the old larceny requirement of a "carrying away" (that is, some "asportation" or movement) of property, combine to ensure that many essentially inchoate transactions are complete thefts. This is not in itself objectionable. However, the field is divided up between attempt and the full offence, there is no question of confining the latter to cases where the criminal activity is in a real sense successful. A thief caught in possession of property a few seconds after seizing it has stolen and not merely attempted to steal. And there is no reason why the same should not be true of one who has gripped property so as to achieve effective control of it, but has not got as far as moving it. The word "appropriates" as elaborated by section 3(1) is capable of achieving this result.

It seems that the courts will go as far as possible along this path. A **2–49** dictum in one case assumes that the theft of a car occurs as soon as the thief

[50] See below, § 2–53. Similarly with the non-restoration of property got under a mistake: see above, § 2–30.
[51] [1979] Crim. L.R. 673; C.A. No. 1251/C/78.
[52] What "sum of £3.99," it may be asked? It is hardly likely that she would have removed the very money she put in the till. The point is admittedly technical and unmeritorious. Perhaps what is meant is that the defendant assumed rights in all the money in the till and that this greater sum included the lesser (£3.99).
[53] Criminal Attempts Act 1981, s. 1(1).

opens the car door.[54] And a youth was held guilty of robbery (which involves theft) when he was party to an attack on a lady in which her handbag was wrested from her grasp—even though the bag fell to the ground and was never in his or his companion's control.[55] The decisive circumstance may have been that the lady was made to lose control, if only momentarily. This, it is suggested, rendered the case a borderline one and possibly justified the court in finding a complete appropriation. On the other hand, merely grasping property in an unsuccessful effort to loosen it from P's control, or to part it from something to which it is attached, should probably be regarded as a mere attempt.[56] And it is surely not necessary to hold that the mysterious phrase "any assumption of the rights of an owner" is satisfied by the exercise of so trivial a proprietary privilege as merely touching the property.

2–50   Theft has been held to be complete at relatively early stages of the intended transaction in at least four other kinds of case. The following events have been held to suffice:

(i) D picked up goods in a self-service shop and put them in her shopping bag, intending to take them from the shop without paying for them.[57]

(ii) (a) D placed over the price ticket on an article exposed for sale a ticket showing a lower price, intending to deceive the cashier into selling the article for the lower price.[58]

(b) D, a supermarket assistant, in league with E, a customer, wrapped goods and understated their price on the wrapper, so that E would be charged too little at the check-out.[59]

(iii) D, a cashier employed by P, failed to ring up money received into her till, intending later to withdraw an equivalent sum.[60]

(iv) D offered P's goods to E for sale.[61]

---

[54] *Hale* (1978) 68 Cr. App. R. 415 at p. 418.

[55] *Corcoran* v. *Anderton* (1980) 71 Cr. App. R. 104.

[56] Watkins J., giving the main judgment in *Corcoran* v. *Anderton*, did not express a clear opinion on this subject; but Eveleigh L.J.'s supporting judgment (at p. 108) regards D's "*seeking* to overcome [P's] efforts to retain [the bag]" as an appropriation. (Italics supplied.)

[57] *McPherson* [1973] Crim. L.R. 191. (Contrast the case where the shopper bent on theft places goods in the wire basket provided: *Eddy* v. *Niman* [1981] Crim. L.R. 502, below, § 2–58.)

[58] *Anderton* v. *Wish* (1980) 72 Cr.App. R. 23n.; followed in *Oxford* v. *Peers*, *ibid.* 19. See next note.

[59] *Pilgram* v. *Rice-Smith* [1977] 1 W.L.R. 671; [1977] 2 All E.R. 658. In this case and in *Anderton* v. *Wish* D's act in reality deprived P of control of the goods, for all that was of interest to P was the sale price. It is thought that there was indeed: (i) an appropriation—which cannot require an assumption of *all* the rights of an owner (an owner himself can steal) and is not incompatible with recognition that P is owner (*cf.* as to conversion, *Howard E. Perry Ltd.* v. *British Railways Board* [1980] 1 W.L.R. 1375; [1980] 2 All E.R. 579); and (ii) the intention required by s. 1(1). See *contra* on both points, J. C. Smith at [1978] Crim. L.R. 577; [1980] Crim. L.R. 320.

[60] *Monaghan* [1979] Crim. L.R. 673 (discussed above, § 2–47).

[61] *Pitham and Hehl* (1976) 65 Cr. App. R. 45; *cf. Rogers* v. *Arnott* [1960] 2 Q.B. 244 (larceny as a bailee). Williams objects, observing that the offer itself is not a conversion of the goods: [1977] Crim. L.R. at pp. 131–132; *Textbook*, pp. 730–733. But this objection would tie theft too closely to the technicalities of conversion: *cf.* § 2–40, above. D's act can be regarded as "wrongful" within Professor Williams' own requirements for an act of theft: see above, § 2–41, at n. 33.

Theft by taking possession; theft by possessors; theft without possession
Appropriation by taking possession or control

In cases of theft D appropriates property by taking possession of it. Any **2–51** assumption—or at any rate, any wrongful assumption—of possession is an appropriation. What, if any, physical interference with property short of taking possession should suffice has been discussed above.[62]

The exclusion of P from possession without D's actually getting his hands on the property could be theft, as where P is looking for his property and D, knowing where it is and intending to steal it, misdirects P so that he will not find it.[63]

One kind of property requires a particular kind of acquisitive conduct: in order to steal something forming part of the land, one not in possession of the land must sever it or cause it to be severed.[64]

A person may take possession of something when he finds it lying lost **2–52** and takes it up. Whether this is an appropriation depends upon his state of mind. If he intends to seek the owner, there is no appropriation: he has not assumed possession for himself. If he decides to keep the thing for himself, there is an appropriation (which may or may not be dishonest).[65] The same possibilities exist where goods belonging to P are brought to D by a third party and D assumes possession. It does not matter whether the third party is guilty or innocent of any offence in relation to the goods. D's receipt of them is an appropriation unless he intends to restore them to P. If he dishonestly does not intend to do so, he commits theft[66]—and if the goods are stolen and D knows or believes this, he is also guilty of handling.[67]

Appropriation by one in possession: finders, etc.; and bona fide purchasers
Section 3(1) is at pains to provide that where a person **2–53**

"has come by . . . property (innocently or not) without stealing it, any later assumption of a right to it by keeping or dealing with it as owner"

is an appropriation. This makes clear that certain gaps that existed under the old law are filled. The primary object of the provision is the person who finds property and takes possession of it, but is not then guilty of theft either (i) because he intends to restore it to its owner or (ii) because he does not believe that the owner can be found,[68] and who subsequently decides (i) not to restore the property to its owner or (ii) to hold on to the property although the owner turns out to be known or traceable. Such a person is within the reach of the law of theft, as is he who receives stolen goods intending to take them to the victim or the police but who changes his mind.

---

[62] §§ 2–48 to 2–50.
[63] Williams, *Textbook*, p. 730, thinks this would not be theft.
[64] s. 4(2)(*b*).
[65] s. 2(1)(*c*). See below, § 2–84.
[66] *Stapylton* v. *O'Callaghan* [1973] 2 All E.R. 782; *Sainthouse* [1980] Crim. L.R. 506.
[67] s. 22. See below, § 13–30.
[68] See s. 2(1)(*c*).

So too is one who takes property when too drunk to steal and who when sober decides to deal with it as his own; and the person who has "come by" property as a result of an error and, discovering some time later the fact that he has it or that it was not intended for him or is not what he was intended to have, decides nevertheless to keep it.

2-54   One person who is clearly within section 3(1) is nevertheless expressly saved from liability for theft by section 3(2). This is the bona fide transferee for value of property who discovers after the transfer that his tranferor's title was defective and nevertheless keeps or deals with the property. C steals property from P and sells it to D, who neither knows nor suspects that it is stolen. He later learns the truth. But he does not restore the property to P. Indeed, he deals with it as his own. This is not theft.

Appropriation by one in possession: bailees and custodians

2-55   The coal merchant's employee who takes a sack of coal from the coal lorry for his own use; the hirer of a camera who sells it as his own; the borrower of a library book who gives it as a birthday gift to his friend; the cashier at the supermarket check-out who deliberately rings up too low a price for goods on the till and "sells" them to a customer for the reduced price[69]: each of these people, having lawful possession or custody of the property of another, appropriates it by assuming in it the rights of an owner—in the language of the second part of section 3(1), having "come by . . . property . . . without stealing it," he commits a "later assumption of a right to it by . . . dealing with it as owner." Such cases present no difficulty.

In some other kinds of situation it may be less clear whether the conduct of the possessor amounts to an appropriation. It will be helpful to remember that the question to be resolved is whether there is sufficient evidence of some exercise by D of dominion over the property. That evidence must almost inevitably include evidence of a departure from the terms on which, as bailee or otherwise, D holds the property.[70] But evidence of such a departure will not always be enough. For instance, if D has P's authority only to receive offers for goods in his hands, his actual sale of the goods will not be an appropriation if he misunderstood the extent of his authority and was selling on P's behalf. Similarly, an unjustified refusal by D to return the goods bailed to P, his bailor, may be an appropriation[71] but is not necessarily one; D may believe that someone other than P is entitled to possession. These are cases in which *actus reus* and *mens rea* become hopelessly entangled.

---

[69] As to this example, cf. *Bhachu* (1976) 65 Cr. App. R. 261, where, however, the only appropriation identified by the Court of Appeal was that of the shopper (to which the cashier was naturally held to be a party) in taking the goods from the shop.
[70] It is submitted (supporting Smith and Hogan, *Criminal Law* (4th ed.), p. 492) that a departure from the terms of the bailment may be evidence of appropriation even where D's only use of the chattel is of a kind contemplated by the bailment.
[71] Cf. *Wakeman* (1912) 8 Cr. App. R. 18.

Appropriation without possession

In *Pitham and Hehl*[72] D was a complete stranger to the property, which   **2–56**
was the furniture of P, a man in prison. D offered to sell the furniture to E.
The offer was an appropriation and E's purchase of the furniture was a
handling of stolen goods. There was no difficulty in treating the offer to sell
as an appropriation, since D fully intended to deprive P of the property if E
should decide to buy and he was clearly assuming the rights of an owner.
The position is less clear, however, when D purports to sell P's property
merely for the sake of inducing E to pay for it and without any intention of
taking steps to deliver it. It is submitted that in such a case there is no theft.
A sufficient justification for this view, surely, is that there is no intention of
permanent deprivation.[73] But in case this is wrong, it is necessary to argue
that there is no appropriation. D's reference to the property is a mere
device to support the deception practised on his purchaser. If D and E are
not in the presence of any property when they conclude their bargain, it
would seem to be all one whether the property referred to is actual or
fictitious. It should surely make no difference if the fraud is given an air of
verisimilitude by the rogue's being able to point at P's property and say,
"That is what I am selling you."[74] (It would indeed seem, by parity of
reasoning, that even a bailee who uses his possession merely as a device to
defraud a dupe will not appropriate—save in a rare case such as that where
the victim acquires title by the transaction, as on a contract to sell specific
goods in market overt.)

Victim's consent or authority; consent obtained by deception etc.

Absence of consent not an additional element in theft

Theft requires a dishonest appropriation of property belonging to   **2–57**
another with the intent stated in section 1(1). It does not in addition
require the absence of the victim's consent. The omission from section 1(1)
of words equivalent to the phrase "without the consent of the owner" in
the repealed definition of larceny[75] was deliberate. This was asserted by
the House of Lords in *Lawrence* v. *Metropolitan Police Commissioner*.[76]

P was an Italian newly arrived in England, who hired D, a taxi-driver, to
drive him from Victoria to Ladbroke Grove. The lawful fare for the
journey was 10s. 6d. D said that it was very far and very expensive. P gave
D a £1 note, but D said that this was not enough and himself took £6 more
from P's open wallet. P offered no resistance to this act. D drove to

---

[72] (1976) 65 Cr. App. R. 45.
[73] As to the intention of permanently depriving, see below, § 2–76.
[74] *Cf. Bloxham* (1943) 29 Cr. App. R. 37, where D was not guilty of attempted larceny, for
    there was no attempted removal (asportation) of the property. He would, of course, now
    be guilty of obtaining (or attempting to obtain) the price of the property from his purchaser
    by deception, if the fraud has progressed far enough. But Smith, *Theft*, para. 27, thinks that
    he is also guilty of theft and rejects the argument advanced in the text.
[75] Larceny required a taking and carrying away of goods "without the consent of the owner":
    Larceny Act 1916, s. 1(1).
[76] [1972] A.C. 626.

Ladbroke Grove. D was charged with theft of the approximate sum of £6 and convicted. It was conceded on D's behalf, and regarded as clear by the House of Lords, that there had been an appropriation of the £6. An appropriation may occur "even though the owner has permitted or consented to the property being taken." The prosecution need not prove "that the taking was without the owner's consent."[77] The passage from which these quotations are taken seems to confuse two propositions: (i) P's consent to D's *act* (a "taking") need not prevent that act from being an appropriation. (This proposition is closer to the actual language of the passage.) (ii) P's consent to D's *appropriation* (the "taking"?) does not prevent that appropriation from being theft. This would be consistent with their lordships' confidence (and D's concession) that there was an appropriation and with their observation on the deliberate omission of absence of consent from a formula in which the word "appropriates" occurs. Proposition (ii) is uncontroversial, and it is easy to reconcile with the principle that what is rightful in the civil law should not be held wrongful by the criminal law. Proposition (i), if intended by the House of Lords, has had little effect on other courts, as the cases next to be mentioned show.

Consent or authority as preventing appropriation

2–58   A number of cases deny the possibility of an appropriation until D does "some overt act . . . inconsistent with the true owner's rights"[78]—which seems to mean something done without P's consent or authority.

The case of *Meech*[79] has already been discussed. It was said that when D withdrew from his bank the proceeds of the cheque received from P, he did not thereby appropriate the proceeds, even though he withdrew the money dishonestly intending to deprive P of it.[80] This must be because the withdrawal was an act authorised by P. And in *Eddy* v. *Niman*[81] intending shoplifters were held not guilty of theft on the strength only of the act of placing the goods to be stolen in a wire basket or trolley provided by the store for self-service customers.

What is more, reference must be made below[82] to cases in which D, intending to deprive P permanently of goods, has deceived P into parting with possession of them, but in which the Court of Appeal (wrongly, it will

---

[77] [1972] A.C. at p. 632. Note "taking" and "owner." Probably what was meant was "appropriation" and "person to whom the property belonged" (see text immediately following). But "takes" and "owner" were terms in the definition of larceny. Old habits, dying hard, have contributed to the obscurity of the modern case law.

[78] *Eddy* v. *Niman* [1981] Crim. L.R. 502.

[79] [1974] Q.B. 549; above, § 2–27.

[80] This aspect of *Meech* appears to have been doubted in *Anderton* v. *Wish*, as reported at [1980] Crim. L.R. 320. But the approved judgment, reported at 72 Cr. App. R. 23, does not contain the relevant passage. Perhaps there were second thoughts.

[81] [1981] Crim. L.R. 502, distinguishing *McPherson* [1973] Crim. L.R. 191 (above, § 2–50), where the intending shoplifter used her own shopping basket. See also *Grundy (Teddington) Ltd.* v. *Fulton, The Times*, July 2, 1981.

[82] § 2–61.

be submitted) has regarded D as not appropriating the goods when receiving possession.

Consent and facilitation[83]

A case where P's acquiescence in D's act should not prevent that act **2–59** from being an appropriation is that where P learns that D proposes to steal his goods and instructs Q to "assist" D by facilitating his access to the goods or by handing them to him in the guise of an accomplice. Suppose that D comes and takes the goods and is promptly arrested. Whether he appropriates them when he takes possession should not, it is submitted, turn on the nature of the "assistance" given to him. If he is simply afforded easy access to the goods, it would seem that he steals when he takes them.[84] So too, it is thought—though this is more controversial—if Q actually hands them to him on P's instructions. P may be said to consent to D's receipt of the goods; but D can hardly claim a gift, or a bailment for any definable purpose. P consents to the bare receipt only; and D's state of mind, it is submitted, makes that receipt an appropriation.[85]

Consent obtained by fraud—theft and obtaining by deception[86]

Another situation in which P's consent to D's acquisition ought not to **2–60** prevent that acquisition from being an appropriation is that in which the consent is obtained by fraud. In *Lawrence* (the facts of which have already been mentioned)[87] the Court of Appeal regarded the £6 taken by D from P's wallet as having been obtained by deception. D had also appropriated the money, as the House of Lords agreed. The Court of Appeal went so far as to say "that in any case where the facts would establish a charge under section 15(1) they would also establish a charge under section 1(1)."[88] Yet in subsequent cases in which property has been obtained by deception, the court has regarded theft as committed only at some later time although from the outset D had the intention necessary for theft. It will be convenient to refer to these cases under the heading "obtaining *possession* by deception" and then to return to *Lawrence* to discuss "obtaining *ownership* by deception."

---

[83] For a detailed treatment, see Williams [1977] Crim. L.R. at pp. 330–335, taking a very different view from that offered here. And see I.D. Elliott (1977) 26 I.C.L.Q. at pp. 121 *et seq.* and 144 *et seq.*

[84] *Cf. Greater London Metropolitan Police Commissioner* v. *Streeter* (1980) 71 Cr. App. R. 113, *per* Ackner L.J. at p. 119.

[85] The point is of reduced importance now that D's receipt of the goods plainly amounts at least to an attempt to steal: see Criminal Attempts Act 1981, s. 1(1)(3).

[86] See Smith, *Theft*, paras. 33 *et seq.*; Williams [1977] Crim. L.R. at pp. 133 *et seq.*, 207 *et seq.*; *Textbook*, pp. 762 *et seq.*; and for controversy between these writers, see Williams, "Theft and Voidable Title" [1981] Crim. L.R. 666, and a reply by Smith at p. 677.

[87] Above, § 2–57.

[88] [1971] 1 Q.B. 373 at p. 378. A person is guilty of an offence under s. 15(1) if by deception he dishonestly obtains ownership, possession or control of property belonging to another with the intention of permanently depriving the other of it.

2–61 (i) *Obtaining possession by deception.* In *Skipp*[89] D established the outward appearance of a haulage business. He secured instructions from P to collect three consignments of oranges and onions and to carry them from London to customers in Leicester. He loaded the goods on to his lorry at three different places in London and set off—but not for Leicester. He had intended all along to steal the goods. He was charged in one count of an indictment with theft of all the goods; and it was argued that the count was bad for duplicity as it concerned three appropriations at different times and places. The Court of Appeal (without referring to *Lawrence*) rejected this argument on the ground that, until all the loading was completed, and probably until D diverted from the route to Leicester, he had "not . . . got to the point of assuming the rights of the[90] owner by doing something inconsistent with those rights." And in *Hircock*[91] a person who took a car on hire-purchase with the fraudulent intention from the outset of selling it as his own was held not to have stolen the car until he sold it. Both these cases are inconsistent with the decision of the Court of Appeal in *Lawrence*, possibly also with that of the House of Lords.

2–62 If there was an appropriation in *Lawrence* when P was deceived into letting D take the extra £6, it is difficult to see why there was not an appropriation in *Skipp* each time D collected a load of greengrocery or in *Hircock* when D received possession of the car. In each case delivery was obtained by deception and an offence under section 15 was committed at that time. Why should the offence of theft be postponed to a later stage? Under the old law, if D induced P by fraud to deliver property to him, he was regarded as "taking" the property "without the consent of the owner" so long as P intended to part with possession only. He was guilty of "larceny by a trick" if he intended to deprive P permanently. Under the Theft Act, where the absence of P's consent is said not to be an element of theft, liability should be even clearer. Yet according to *Skipp* and *Hircock* the larceny by a trick situation is not one of theft. This is very puzzling. It is certain that the Committee assumed that what used to be larceny by a trick would be an offence under both section 1 and section 15.[92] So it is firmly submitted that *Skipp* and *Hircock* are wrong as to the time at which theft is committed when possession is obtained by fraud.

---

[89] [1975] Crim. L.R. 114. The report is very brief. References in the text are to the transcript of the judgment (No. 985/B/74) kindly supplied by the Criminal Appeal Office. Smith, *Theft*, para. 31, n. 8, appears to treat *Peter Jackson Pty. Ltd.* v. *Consolidated Insurance of Australia Ltd.* [1975] V.R. 781 as supporting *Skipp*. But that case was decided under the old law of larceny and was not concerned with "appropriation" in the modern law of theft (adopted by the State of Victoria in the Crimes (Theft) Act 1973). In case the decision is thought to be relevant, however, it is submitted that the powerful judgment of Gillard J., dissenting , should be preferred to that of the majority.

[90] *Sic.* The "the" (repeated later in the judgment) is calculated to conceal error. s. 3(1) refers to an "assumption of the rights of *an* owner," which is a very general (and vague) conception having nothing to do with the particular "rights" of the person (owner or not) to whom the property "belongs."

[91] (1978) 67 Cr. App. R. 278; criticised in more detail at [1979] Crim. L.R. 292.

[92] *Eighth Report*, para. 90.

(ii) *Obtaining ownership by deception (as well as possession).* It is clear   **2–63**
that in *Lawrence* the Court of Appeal regarded D as having obtained
ownership in the £6 by fraud. This appears from their having taken the
view[93] that under the old law D's offence would have been obtaining by
false pretences, which occurred where, under the influence of D's fraud, P
intended to part with ownership of property. Such a case could not be one
of larceny, and the offence of false pretences was created by statute
precisely because of the impotence of the law of larceny in this respect. The
problem, on the Court of Appeal's view of the facts in *Lawrence*, was not
so much whether D appropriated the £6 as whether when he did so it was
property belonging to another.

It is clear that it had not been the intention of the Committee that every
case of obtaining property by deception should also be a case of theft.[94]
And it was the general understanding of early commentators on the Act
that when by deception I obtain *ownership* of property, my appropriation
is of property which, by virtue of the transaction so induced, has come to
belong not to my victim—he retains no "proprietary right or interest" in
it—but to me; and according to that understanding the case is not one of
theft. This view was never without its difficulties, however. Suppose (to
take facts less ambiguous than those in *Lawrence*) that D deceives P into
making him a gift of money, which P does by placing cash in D's hands.
The transfer of ownership here[95] is of course effected by the transfer of
possession. To say in this case that D has committed an offence under
section 15 but not under section 1 is, in effect, to say (i) that what is
"obtained" by the transaction of gift is property that at the crucial moment
is owned or possessed by P ("belonging to" P), but (ii) that what is
"appropriated" by the closing of D's hands around the notes or coins is
property that P has already ceased either to own or to possess (not
"belonging to" P). To say this permits the degree of separation between
the two offences that the Committee envisaged. But it involves some
strain.

Just such an argument was unsuccessfully advanced for the appellant in   **2–64**
Lawrence. The Court of Appeal, as seen above, treated ownership in the
money as having passed and offences under both section 1 and section 15 as
having being committed. The view of the House of Lords, in the opinion of
Viscount Dilhorne, is less easy to interpret. His lordship stated that it had
not been established at the trial that P had consented "to the acquisition by
[D] of the £6" or "to the taking of the £6."[96] If he meant, expressing the
burden of proof correctly, that an absence of consent had been established,
this was in any view enough to dispose of D's appeal. D's counsel in his

---

[93] [1971] 1 Q.B. 373 at p. 378.
[94] *Eighth Report*, paras. 38, 90. (A case involving land must in any case be an exception.)
[95] It is assumed that the deception does not induce a mistake so fundamental as to prevent a
transfer of ownership. *Cf. Williams* [1980] Crim. L.R. 589; *Davies, The Times*, November
7, 1981.
[96] [1972] A.C. at p. 631.

argument had correctly stressed that if ownership in the £6 did not pass, that was the end of the matter. In fact Viscount Dilhorne went on to deal with the argument in this way:

> "Mr. Back Q.C. . . . contended that if Mr. Occhi consented to the appellant taking the £6, he consented to the property in the money passing from him to the appellant and that the appellant had not, therefore, appropriated property belonging to another. He argued that the old distinction between the offence of false pretences and larceny had been preserved. I am unable to agree with this."[97]

"This" must surely mean "this argument as a whole." Viscount Dilhorne's opinion, itself read as a whole, seems to mean: "It does not appear that ownership in the £6 passed; but even if it did, the conviction stands." This appears to be confirmed by the fact that his lordship went on at once (irrelevantly, if the view advanced here is wrong) to remark on the occurrence of the words "belonging to another" in both section 1(1) and section 15(1) and to express the view that in both contexts the phrase

> "signifies no more than that, at the time of the appropriation or the obtaining, the property belonged to another . . . . The short answer to [D's contention] is that the money in the wallet which he appropriated belonged to another, to [P]."[97]

It has been suggested[98] that the decision of the House of Lords leaves open the question whether theft is committed where D by deception obtains ownership as well as possession. That is certainly one available interpretation of the decision. A more positive reading of the decision has been offered here—namely, in effect, that the House of Lords has in fact rejected the subtlety that would be involved in finding some theoretical difference in time between the obtaining and the appropriation in a case of the old false pretences type.

2–65   (iii) *Obtaining of ownership followed by delivery.* Suppose that D, by fraud, induces P to sell him an article for much less than its real value and that D pays there and then for the article but does not yet take delivery. There is here an obtaining of ownership by deception and thus an offence under section 15, but probably no appropriation.[99] If there is an appropriation when, perhaps a very short time afterwards, D does take delivery, there may now be a theft. But this time the two offences have been constituted by different transactions[1]; there is a real and not merely a

---

[97] *Ibid.* at p. 632.
[98] Smith, *Theft*, para. 36; Cross and Jones, *Introduction to Criminal Law* (9th ed.), p. 229. See also for another treatment of the case, Smith and Hogan, *Criminal Law* (4th ed.), pp.512–515, 561.
[99] *Contra*, Williams [1977] Crim. L.R. at p.136.
[1] Where the two offences occur at different times, though in respect of the same property, D may be convicted of both: *Hircock* (1978) 67 Cr. App. R. 278. But it is submitted that this should be avoided if possible, *e.g.* by not requiring a verdict on the count charging the later offence.

fictitious interval between the obtaining and the appropriation. It ought indeed to be possible to say that, taking delivery while the fraud still influences P, D appropriates property that then "belongs to" P as possessor.[2] This is by analogy with *Lawrence*, if that case has been correctly understood. But in one case[3] where ownership passed before delivery the fact that the goods "belonged to" P as possessor until delivery seems to have escaped attention. No deception was found in that case; it might therefore have been better to say that there was therefore no appropriation rather than to deny that D took delivery of goods "belonging to" P.

Theft and obtaining by deception—the choice of charge
It must be plainly said that the decision in *Lawrence's* case, if correctly   **2-66**
understood above, is strikingly at variance with the intention of the Committee; and, for what it is worth, it does some violence to the popular conception of theft. On the other hand, it may be said to avoid artificial and over-subtle reading of the statute and unmeritorious acquittals deriving simply from ineptness in the formulation of the charge.[4]

But it would be a mistake to be dogmatic about either the scope or the meaning of the decision. The facts of the case were hardly an ideal peg on which to hang a fully-developed doctrine of maximum overlap between sections 1 and 15 (D helped himself to money in P's wallet—it is not quite like a case where P hands money over after D has lied to him); and neither the judgment of Megaw L.J. for the Court of Appeal nor the opinion of Viscount Dilhorne in the House of Lords is remarkable for clarity or analytical completeness. The matter, therefore, continues to be affected with uncertainty.

Moreover, even in a case where possession only is obtained by deception, *Skipp* and *Hircock*[5] are unequivocal Court of Appeal authorities, however weak, against a conviction of theft based on that obtaining.

So it is doubly clear that whenever property has plainly been obtained by deception, it will be a prosecutor's course of prudence to proceed under section 15 rather than under section 1. Under section 15 it is immaterial whether it is ownership or possession that was obtained.

Some other voidable transactions: agent for sale; sale or return; duress
The doctrine that in some circumstances one may steal property in the   **2-67**
very act even of obtaining ownership of it (the Court of Appeal decision in *Lawrence* is certainly authority for this and it has been suggested above that the House of Lords decision is also) should contribute to a conviction of theft in a number of situations. The following are some examples:
(i) P owns a motor-car. D induces P to put the car in his hands for sale,

[2] By virtue of s.5(1).
[3] *Kaur* v. *Chief Constable for Hampshire* [1981] 1 W.L.R. 578; [1981] 2 All E.R. 430.
[4] The Act does not permit a conviction under either s. 1 or s. 15 when the indictment charges one offence and the evidence discloses the other; contrast Larceny Act 1916, s. 44(3)(4). See above, § 1–11.
[5] Above, § 2–61.

intending from the outset to sell the car for his own profit and to pocket the proceeds. This should be theft when D receives the car[6]—even though D may subsequently sell the car within the terms of his authority.

(ii) P delivers goods to D "on sale or return."[7] When D receives them he intends neither to return them nor to pay for them. This, again, should be a clear case of theft in the light of the above doctrine.

(iii) D compels P to part with property by duress (*e.g.* by physical violence or the threat of it, by imprisonment, or by a threat to prosecute for some actual or pretended crime). Where P, thus coerced, gives up possession only, D should be guilty of theft (and of robbery in a case of violence) if he intends to deprive P permanently. In some cases, however, the duress may induce a voidable contract under which ownership passes and not mere possession. Even if this should occur, the doctrine derived from *Lawrence's* case would support a conviction of theft.[8]

Common to these examples of fraud and duress, as to other cases of fraud discussed above, is the fact that D's title or his authority to deal with the property is at best voidable. Such title or authority should not prevent the act by which it is obtained from amounting to an appropriation.

Theft of "things in action and other intangible property"

2–68   The Act provides that any kind of property can be the subject of theft. But the ways in which various kinds of intangible property can be stolen are obviously very limited—either by the lack of available modes of appropriation, or by the difficulty of depriving of the property the person to whom it belongs. Although the problem does not simply concern the word "appropriates," the subject is dealt with here in a general way as a matter of convenience.

Two relevant points have already been made:

(i) Anyone—such as a trustee or co-owner—who has the power to dispose of property can steal that property by a disposition intended to defeat the interests of others to whom the property belongs.[9] Clearly such a person can as readily steal debts, shares and other forms of intangible property, by assignment or transfer, as he can, for instance, steal land by sale or goods by sale or consumption.

(ii) A dishonest unauthorised drawing upon another person's bank account is a theft of the bank balance or part of it if the account is in credit.[10] So is a dishonest drawing upon an account in the accused's own name if he holds the account in a fiduciary capacity.

2–69   Theft is more difficult, however, for one who has no existing power to dispose of the property or to control its disposition. How, if at all, can a

---

[6] *Cf.* Williams [1977] Crim. L.R. at p. 135. But *Hircock* (above, § 2–61) stands in the way.
[7] For the effect of such a transaction, see the Sale of Goods Act 1979, s. 18, r.4.
[8] For a case of theft by duress, see *Chapman* [1974] Crim. L.R. 488.
[9] Above, § 2–21.
[10] Above, § 2–12. See also, as to the money drawn, above, § 2–28, n.86.

stranger steal, for instance, shares, trade marks, copyright or trade secrets? We may take these kinds of property as examples of the problem and discuss each briefly:

(i) *Shares*. The theft of shares by a stranger seems bound to involve theft of the share certificates. No doubt, however, if such a theft occurred, it could now be charged as a theft of the shares themselves and not just as a theft of the certificates, which under the old law were the only relevant property "capable of being stolen."

(ii) *Trade marks*. The obvious case to be considered is the dishonest infringement of a trade mark, as by using the mark upon goods of the same description as that to which it applies. This may be an appropriation—an assumption of the rights of the owner in the trade mark. Yet there can hardly be said to be an intention to deprive the owner of the trade mark itself.[11] The infringement is therefore no theft.

(iii) *Copyright* is the exclusive right to do and to authorise certain acts in relation to, *e.g.* a literary work—for instance, to reproduce or publish the work.[12] If D copies and publishes P's work, he may popularly be said to "steal" the benefit of P's skill and labour. He may also be said to appropriate the copyright—by assuming the rights of an owner in the *right of reproduction* (the relevant property). But he does not do so with the effect of depriving P of that right[13] and so does not steal.[14]

(iv) *Trade secrets*. The suggestion that trade secrets might be a species of "property" within the meaning of section 4(1) and might therefore be capable of being stolen was mentioned earlier in this chapter, where it was seen that the suggestion must be rejected.[15] But even if they were property, trade secrets would be difficult to steal. No doubt we may say that D "appropriates" P's secret if he dishonestly acquires the knowledge that P has a right to preserve to himself or makes use of the knowledge that P alone has the right to use. But D does not thereby *deprive* P of his knowledge: he deprives him only of an advantage attaching to it—its exclusiveness. On that analysis the thing appropriated is not the same as that of which P is deprived; but the basic definition of theft requires that it shall be ("appropriates property . . . with the intention of depriving [P] of it"). The conclusion must be that trade secrets, even if "property," could not in general be stolen. But exceptional situations might be envisaged: for instance, D seduces from P's employment a chemist, Q, who alone knows a formula developed by Q for P; and D elicits from Q both the formula and the promise to keep it secret from P. This (if secrets were property) would satisfy the definition of theft, as might some other even more fanciful situations.

---

[11] There is no intention in D "to treat the thing as his own *to dispose of*"; so s. 6(1) does not affect this case: see below, § 2–74.
[12] Copyright Act 1956, ss. 1(1), 2 (5).
[13] See n.11, above.
[14] He may be guilty of a summary offence under the Copyright Act 1956, s. 21.
[15] Above, § 2–17.

Appropriation by handling

2–70   A person guilty of handling stolen goods under section 22 will usually be guilty of theft also.[16] The reader is at this point merely referred to the definition of handling in section 22(1) in order to see that many acts within that definition are acts of appropriation. Fuller treatment of the overlap between the two offences is best deferred to the chapter on handling.[17]

6. "With the Intention of Permanently Depriving the Other of it"

The basic rule

2–71   The Committee recommended that an intention to deprive P permanently of the property should be a necessary element in theft, as it was in larceny. They recognised that temporary deprivation can sometimes occasion great loss or hardship and that an intention to cause such deprivation "may involve dishonesty comparable with that. involved in theft." But they considered that where there is an intention to return the property, the conduct is "essentially different from stealing" and that either the inclusion in theft of all dishonest borrowing or the creation of a general offence of temporary deprivation would be "a considerable extension of the criminal law [not] called for by any existing serious social evil."[18] Despite much controversy while the Bill was before Parliament, this view finally prevailed.[19]

So the general rule is that dishonest borrowing is not theft. If D takes P's property he is not normally guilty of stealing it if he intends in due course to return it or at least that P shall recover it. It is necessary to describe this as "the general rule" because section 6 is at pains to provide expressly that one who intends a borrowing that is "equivalent to an outright taking" is to be regarded as intending to deprive permanently. Subject to this obscure provision, which is dealt with below, it is immaterial for how long D can be shown to have intended to enjoy possession of the property or for how long P is actually deprived of it. Immaterial, that is, as a matter of law. As a matter of common sense, of course, the longer the period is, the less plausible will be D's claim that he intended P to have the property back. But if that claim appeals to the court as a reasonable possibility, he will be entitled to an acquittal.

2–72   The word "permanently" must, of course, be understood in the light of P's particular interest in the property. If P merely has temporary "possession or control" of the property, it nevertheless belongs to him for the purpose of his being a victim of theft (s. 5(1)), and he can be "permanently" deprived by D's appropriation although he might have had to relinquish the property very shortly in any event.

---

[16] See, *e.g. Stapylton* v. *O'Callaghan* [1973] 2 All E.R. 782; *Stainhouse* [1980] Crim.L.R. 506.
[17] See below, §§ 13–27 to 13–30.
[18] *Eighth Report*, para. 56.
[19] For full argument of the contrary view, see Glanville Williams, "Temporary Appropriation Should be Theft" [1981] Crim. L.R. 129.

It does not matter when the intention to deprive P permanently is formed. If D takes P's property, intending at first to borrow it, he has "come by the property . . . without stealing it"; if he later decides to keep it for good or to sell it, this is a "later assumption of a right to it by keeping or dealing with it as owner" and a fresh appropriation (s. 3(1)). Theft occurs at this point.

A preface to section 6

Section 6 provides a partial definition of the phrase "with the intention **2–73** of permanently depriving the other of it."

The draft Bill had no clause corresponding to section 6. The Committee described "cases where the offender intends to do something with the property which for practical purposes is equivalent to permanent deprivation" and thought that these cases would be treated as theft without the need for special provision.[20] It was made clear in the House of Commons that the section was drafted largely with the same cases in mind. In *Warner*[21] the Court of Appeal said that the section was intended merely to "clarify" the meaning of the words "intention of permanently depriving" and not to enlarge[22] the definition of theft.

The section was an unsatisfactory late amendment to the Bill.[23] It is badly drafted and employs language new to this branch of the law. For instance, a curious distinction is taken between "property" and "the thing itself"; yet as between subsections (1) and (2) the two phrases are used indifferently in precisely the same context: subsection (1) talks of D's treating "the thing" and subsection (2) of his treating "the property" as "his own to dispose of regardless of [P's] rights." In subsection (1) the phrases "having the intention" and "meaning" are both used, with no clear difference in meaning or intention. Subsection (1) ends with the obscure expression "equivalent to an outright taking or disposal." A provision inserted for clarification can rarely have contributed more obscurity.

The moral is clear. *Section 6 should be referred to in exceptional cases only.* The impression of some students to the contrary prompts this cautionary statement, as does the strange use to which the section has been put at first instance in some cases.[24]

Section 6(1)

"A person appropriating property belonging to another without **2–74** meaning the other permanently to lose the thing itself is nevertheless

---

[20] *Eighth Report*, para. 58.
[21] (1970) 55 Cr.App.R. 93.
[22] Edmund-Davies L.J., at p. 97, actually said "cut down," but he presumably meant "enlarge."
[23] For the illuminating, and remarkable, parliamentary history of the section, see Spencer, "The Metamorphosis of Section 6 of the Theft Act" [1977] Crim.L.R. 653.
[24] See *Warner* (1970) 55 Cr.App.R. 93; *Halstead* v. *Patel* [1972] 1 W.L.R. 661; [1972] 2 All E.R. 147; *Cocks* (1976) 63 Cr.App.R. 79. Stannard, "Fools Rush In—The Meaning of Section 6 of the Theft Act" (1979) 30 N.I.L.Q. 225, valiantly attempts to make sense of the section. He treats the passage in the text as intended to deter such endeavours. Its point, however, is rather that s. 6 is not a definition of the relevant part of s. 1(1) but is concerned only with fringe cases, so that happily it rarely needs consideration.

to be regarded as having the intention of permanently depriving the other of it if his intention is to treat the thing as his own to dispose of regardless of the other's rights; and a borrowing or lending of it may amount to so treating it if, but only if, the borrowing or lending is for a period and in circumstances making it equivalent to an outright taking or disposal."

The following are some situations apparently within section 6(1).

(i) D takes P's chattel. His intention is to pretend that it is his own and to induce P to "buy" it. Thus P will not permanently "lose the thing itself." But D will be treating the chattel as his own to dispose of regardless of P's rights. This is theft.

(ii) D takes an exhibit from an exhibition and holds it to ransom: he will return it only if the exhibitor fulfils some condition named by D. This is identical with situation (i) save that there is no deception.

(iii) D takes P's gold watch, intending to pawn it and to send the pawn ticket to P. He intends, that is to say, to treat the watch as his own to dispose of, although he hopes that P will recover the watch by redeeming it. (Even if D does not get as far as pawning the watch, his intention to do so is, of course, enough.)

(iv) P has written a cheque in favour of D but will deliver it only on performance of some act by D, *e.g.* the delivery of goods. D comes and takes the cheque without performing the required act; he intends to pay the cheque into his bank for collection. The taking is with the intention of treating the thing as his own to dispose of. Although the cheque as a piece of paper will in due course return to P (or at least will return to his bank and thus be available to him), as a cancelled cheque its character will have completely changed.[25]

(v) D takes from P's ticket office a train ticket or a ticket giving access to a place. He cannot say this was not theft merely because he meant to surrender the ticket at the end of the journey or on entering the place and because thereby the ticket would return to P.[26]

(vi) D takes P's railway season ticket, intending to use it for as long as he may wish to do so, possibly for as long as it is valid. This is theft. It is no use D's saying that he meant in any event to return the ticket to P at some future date. It might have been worthless by the time it was returned.[27] (But if he intends to keep the ticket for a limited time substantially shorter than the unexpired period of the ticket's validity, the case would seem to be outside the section: it will not be a borrowing "for a period and in

---

[25] *Cf. Kohn* (1979) 69 Cr.App.R. 395; *Duru* [1974] 1 W.L.R. 2; [1973] 3 All E.R. 715, decided under s.15.

[26] Williams, *Textbook*, pp. 648 *et seq.*, would seem to regard situations (i) to (v) as being all "borrowings" within the meaning of the second limb of s. 6(1), leaving the first limb almost without function. It is suggested, however, that "borrowing" refers to a case where D assumes possession of property without deciding never to return it to P but, equally, without having in mind a use or dealing (such as sale, ransom, pledge) that would be inconsistent with a borrowing legitimately so called.

[27] This example has been rewritten in the light of just criticism by Williams, *Textbook*, p. 650, n.7.

circumstances making it equivalent to an outright taking." The section's obscurities may be illustrated, however, by asking what the effect will be of D's intending to return the ticket (say, a quarterly season ticket) a very short time before its expiry—two weeks, a week, a day. At what point does a borrowing become "equivalent to an outright taking"?)

(vii) D takes P's chattel, uses it for a time and then abandons it. This **2–75** situation must be subdivided. (a) If the circumstances of the abandonment show that D, though content that P should recover the chattel, must have realised that P was extremely unlikely to do so, the case is certainly intended to be caught by the section and no doubt is. (b) At the other extreme, if D leaves the chattel in such a place that he can be virtually regarded as returning it to P (*e.g.* leaves a book with P's name in it in the office where P works), he will not be regarded as treating it as his own to dispose of. (c) Intermediate cases will involve different degrees of recklessness as to P's chances of recovering the chattel. It is to be hoped that in dealing with these cases the courts will not treat borrowing-plus-abandonment simply as borrowing. If they do they will become enmeshed in the obscurities of the statement that a *borrowing* may amount to treating the thing as one's own to dispose of "if, but only if, [it] is for a period and in circumstances making it equivalent to an outright taking . . . " There is no need in this situation to ask what is "equivalent to an outright taking." The correct course, it is submitted, is to concentrate on the *abandonment*: if the facts of the abandonment show D to be indifferent whether P recovers the chattel or not, he can be regarded as thereby, if not before, appropriating it "by . . . dealing with it as owner" (s. 3(1)), having then the intention to treat the thing as his own to dispose of.

(viii) D is a bailee of P's chattel. He lends the chattel to E, telling E that he may keep and use it for as long as he likes. The circumstances, to D's knowledge, are such that the chattel may never be returned (*e.g.* E is going abroad) or that when it is returned it may be of little or no use to P (*e.g.* the chattel is a ticket for a series of concerts and E may keep the ticket for the whole or the greater part of the series). In either case there appears to be a "lending . . . for a period and in circumstances making it equivalent to an outright . . . disposal." D is not protected by his claim that he did not mean P permanently to lose "the thing itself."

Section 6(1) was expressly regarded as having no application in *Easom*.[28] **2–76** D took up P's handbag and looked into it to see whether there was anything worth stealing. There was not; so in effect he returned the bag to P. By quashing D's conviction of theft with section 6 in mind, the Court of Appeal clearly—and, with respect, rightly—declined to say that D intended, while he looked through the handbag, to treat the contents "as his own to dispose of" or that his conduct was "equivalent to an outright taking." The decision reinforces the warning given above against making too much of the section.

[28] [1971] 2 Q.B. 315.

One further situation must be considered as a possible candidate for the application of section 6(1)—namely, that in which D pretends to E that P's property is his (D's) own, in order to induce E to pay for it, but in which D does not intend to secure a transfer of the property to E. It was suggested earlier[29] that in such a case D does not appropriate the property. If that is right, *cadit quaestio*—there is no theft. But if that suggestion is wrong, the question arises whether D has the necessary intention of permanently depriving P. In the absence of section 6(1) one would confidently have argued that he has not. Such confidence evaporates in the face of the subsection. If the fictitious bargain is regarded as an appropriation, it may be only consistent to say that D intends "to treat the thing as his own to dispose of . . . " and that he therefore has the *mens rea* of theft. Anyone who shares the writer's instinctive sense that the situation is not one of theft may in the last resort be prepared to argue that the phrase "to dispose of" is, like so much in section 6, imprecise and should be given a narrower rather than a liberal interpretation.

Section 6(2)

2–77   One kind of case is specifically mentioned by section 6(2) as being within section 6(1). Where D, "having possession or control (lawfully or not) of [P's property], parts with the property under a condition as to its return which he may not be able to perform, this . . . amounts to treating the property as his own to dispose of regardless of [P's] rights" if it is done for D's purposes and without P's authority.

An obvious case is that where D, a bailee of P's property, pledges the property with E as security for a loan by E to himself, intending to redeem it and to return it to P. There are two possible views of this situation. One is that D is guilty of theft only if he realises that he may be unable to redeem; the other is that the case must be within the subsection, as it can be asserted of every pledgor, life being full of uncertainties, that he *may* not be able to redeem his security. The former view is doctrinally the purer; the latter is more readily suggested by the terms of the poorly drafted section.

"Conditional intention to steal"

2–78   In *Easom*, referred to above,[30] it was held that D's "conditional appropriation" of the handbag and its contents did not suffice to establish theft of those things. *Easom* came in due course to be seen[31] as the source of a doctrine that a "conditional intention to steal"—an intention, for example, to steal if there should prove to be anything worth stealing—was no intention to steal for the purpose of an offence requiring that ingredient. The doctrine itself, with which English law briefly flirted, has been renounced and no longer troubles the law of burglary or attempted

---

[29] Above, § 2–56.
[30] § 2–76; also § 2–44.
[31] Koffman, "Conditional Intention to Steal" [1980] Crim.L.R. 463. Parry, [1981] Crim.L.R. 6, correctly demonstrates that *Easom* is not, as Koffman argues, inconsistent with other theft cases.

theft.[32] As to theft, what section 1(1) requires in terms is not an "intention to steal" but a more specific "intention of permanently depriving [P] of [the property appropriated]." It is productive of error to argue (as has been done) that what was "conditional" was not Easom's appropriation but his intention. He had *no* intention to deprive P permanently of the particular things he found. It is thought that the attribution to *Easom* of a so-called "doctrine of conditional intention" is misconceived.

It was hinted in *Easom* itself that the appellant, who was plainly looking for something to steal, could have been convicted of attempted theft on a charge framed in the right manner.[33] Within a few years of *Easom*, however, such a conviction became problematical because of a short-lived aberration of the law relating to "impossible attempts."[34] But impossibility of success has now ceased to be a bar to a conviction of attempt.[35]

It has been suggested that one who appropriates another's property with the intention of keeping it if on examining it he should think it worth keeping ought without more to be guilty of theft.[36] But it is doubtful whether legislation to bring this about, such as would surely be needed, would be justified. The law of attempt now adequately deals with cases that are not at present complete thefts.

7. "Dishonestly"

Some of the cases considered above can be read as according to dishonesty a very powerful function as an element in the definition of theft. For if it is the case that D "appropriates property belonging to" P when he accepts from P the latter's entire interest in the property (one reading of *Lawrence* v. *Metropolitan Police Commissioner*[37]), or when he removes from P's control goods that he is entitled to remove according to the principles of the civil law (which appears to be implied by *Turner (No.2)*[38]), D may be convicted of theft simply because of a dishonest state of mind with which he acts and not because he has done anything otherwise wrongful. This, it has been persuasively urged, is to give dishonesty too positive a role and to extend the offence of theft too far.[39] The way to avoid this error is probably to subdue the notion of "appropriation" by limiting it to activities that are wrongful in relation to the property involved.[40] So, for instance, the broad principle derived from *Lawrence* must at least be limited to the case where D acquires P's interest in

---

[32] As to burglary, see below, § 4–25; as to attempted theft, *Scudder* v. *Barrett* [1980] Q.B. 195n.; *Bayley and Easterbrook* [1980] Crim. L.R. 503.
[33] [1971] 2 Q.B. at p. 321; and see cases cited in n.32.
[34] *Haughton* v. *Smith* [1975] A.C. 476; *Partington* v. *Williams* (1975) 62 Cr.App. R. 220. (The difficulty was overlooked or ignored in *Bayley and Easterbrook*, above.)
[35] Criminal Attempts Act 1981, s. 1(2).
[36] Williams, *Textbook*, pp. 651–652; "Three Rogues' Charters" [1980] Crim. L.R. 263 at pp. 264–265.
[37] Above, §§ 2–60 *et seq.*
[38] Above, §§ 2–20, 2–42.
[39] Glazebrook [1971] C.L.J. 186; I. D. Elliott (1974) 9 Melbourne U.L.Rev. at p. 452; Williams [1977] Crim. L.R. at p. 129.

property only voidably; and *Turner* (*No.2*) must be regretted as a wrong, or at best an obscure, decision.

2–80   Discussion of the element of dishonesty in theft is better, and more commonly, conducted from a negative point of view. The question to be considered is: When may D claim that he was *not* dishonest and therefore not guilty of theft? Section 2 of the Act contributes to an answer to this question. As we turn to examine that section, there are two elementary points to bear in mind. First, the question is whether D was dishonest at the time of the appropriation. The Court of Appeal has several times had occasion to emphasise this point, notably in relation to the prosecution's difficult task of establishing theft of property to which section 5(3) applies.[41] Secondly, it is for the prosecution to prove that the appropriation was dishonest, not for D to prove the contrary. No doubt D will commonly need to ensure that the question of the honesty or otherwise of his conduct is a live issue, as by giving evidence that he acted with one of the beliefs mentioned in section 2(1). But the burden of proof on the issue remains with the prosecution.[42]

Belief in a right to deprive
2–81   The appropriator who believes "that he has in law the right to deprive" of the property the person to whom it belongs is not guilty of theft, for his appropriation is not to be regarded as dishonest (s. 2(1)(*a*)). This belief corresponds to the "claim of right made in good faith" the absence of which was formerly an ingredient of larceny. D's belief that he has a right to deprive P[43] will protect him however mistaken or unreasonable it is, even though it is the result of self-induced intoxication,[44] and even though the claim he makes is of a kind completely unknown to the law.[45] The less plausible the claim, the less likely it is, of course, that anyone will believe that it was entertained. But it is sufficient for D to raise a reasonable doubt as to his having had the belief in question; the prosecution must prove that the appropriation was dishonest.

Unless D knows that the property in question is or may be property belonging to another (within the wide meaning given to that phrase by s.5), he cannot strictly be said to intend to deprive the other of the property. So where, for example, D takes P's umbrella from a stand, mistaking it for his own, or where D has got property by another's mistake and is under an obligation to restore it or its value to P, but D is unaware of the mistake and believes the property was intended for him, his taking in the former case and his retention of the property in the latter case[46] do not need to be

[40] See above, § 2–41.
[41] *Hall* [1973] Q.B. 126; *Hayes* (1976) 64 Cr.App.R. 82; as to s.5(3), see above, § 2–24.
[42] *Falconer-Atlee* (1973) 58 Cr. App. R. 348, which illustrates the importance of a direction to the jury on a part of s. 2(1) rendered relevant by the evidence.
[43] Whether on behalf of himself or of another: s. 2(1)(*a*); *cf. Williams* [1962] Crim. L.R. 111.
[44] *Cf. Jaggard* v. *Dickinson* [1981] 2 W.L.R. 118; [1980] 3 All E.R. 716 (Criminal Damage Act 1971, s.5(2)).
[45] See Williams, *Criminal Law—The General Part* (2nd ed.), pp. 321–325; *Russell on Crime* (12th ed.), pp. 1023–1025.
[46] See s. 5(4).

defended by resort to section 2(1)(*a*); D does not intend to deprive P, let alone believe that he has a right to do so.

Occasionally section 2(1)(*a*) may be the ground of D's immunity when he takes or retains property to which, because of a legal error, he makes a specific claim. For example, D, wrongly believing that ownership in certain goods has passed to him by virtue of a transaction, takes them from P's possession. The goods "belong to" P not only in the loose sense of the term, but as possessor under section 5(1). But D believes he has the right to deprive P.[47] D may have a similar belief where he has himself sold and delivered goods to P and repossesses them because of P's failure to pay the full price. Or D may find money whose owner he knows to be traceable, but appropriate the money because he believes "findings is keepings." In each of these cases section 2 (1)(*a*) will protect D from liability for theft. **2–82**

Reliance on section 2(1)(*a*) will more often be required where D knew that the particular property (usually money) was P's, but alleges that he believed P owed him or a third person a sum equivalent in value to what he took. If with such a belief D removed the sum in question from the pocket of P's coat as it hung on a peg in their office, he will clearly not be guilty of theft. But it is important to notice that that belief would also suffice to acquit him if he chose some less acceptable and even, in other respects, seriously criminal method of debt-collecting. In *Robinson*[48] it was alleged that D brandished a knife and used force to get from P money that he said P owed him. His conviction of theft was quashed because the jury had been directed that D could rely on section 2(1)(*a*) only if he believed that he was entitled to get his money in the way he did. This was a misdirection. Similarly, if D believes that she is legally entitled to £20 promised to her by P as a reward for sexual favours, she is not guilty of theft whether she takes that sum by stealth or force or extorts it by threatening to reveal P's indiscretions if he does not pay.[49]

Belief that the victim would consent

Section 2(1)(*b*) protects one who appropriates property in the belief that, if the person to whom it belongs "knew of the appropriation and the circumstances of it," that person would consent.[50] A typical case is that of the housewife who "borrows" a bag of sugar from a neighbour to whom **2–83**

[47] The summary jurisdiction of justices is not ousted by such an assertion of belief in title to personal property: *Eagling* v. *Wheatley* [1977] Crim.L.R. 165 (and see commentary at p. 166, pointing out that even if the case concerned real property, the justices would not be called upon to decide a question of title, but only a question as to D's state of mind, and their jurisdiction should be unaffected).
[48] [1977] Crim.L.R. 173; *cf. Skivington* [1968] 1 Q.B. 166 (acquitted of robbery, of which larceny was, and theft now is, an essential ingredient, but convicted of offences against the person; might now also be convicted of blackmail).
[49] But in the latter case she might now be convicted of blackmail; see discussion of *Bernhard* [1938] 2 K.B. 264, below, § 12–29.
[50] "*A fortiori*, a person is not to be regarded as acting dishonestly if he appropriates another's property believing that with full knowledge of the circumstances that other person has in fact agreed to the appropriation." *Per* Viscount Dilhorne in *Lawrence* v. *Metropolitan Police Commissioner* [1972] A.C. 626 at p. 632.

she mistakenly attributes a spirit of local co-operation. She intends to deprive her neighbour permanently of the sugar she takes, though she may intend to offer later an equivalent quantity in return. So also with the man who borrows money from his colleague's wallet or his employer's till. He, like the housewife, if charged with theft, must succeed on the issue of dishonesty if he is to escape a conviction. Either of two pleas may yield that success. The first—"I thought P wouldn't mind"—is provided by section 2(1)(*b*). The second—"I intended to repay"—may co-exist with the first. As a separate plea it is referred to below.[51]

Belief that the owner cannot be discovered

2–84   If one appropriates property "in the belief that the person to whom [it] belongs cannot be discovered by taking reasonable steps," the appropriation is not to be regarded as dishonest—save in the case of the appropriator to whom the property came as trustee or personal representative (s. 2(1)(*c*)).

The obvious example is the finder of lost property. Factors such as the place where the thing is found, its apparent value and the existence of any distinguishing marks or features will determine whether it seems worth while handing the thing to the police, advertising for the owner or taking other steps. For the purpose of the law of theft the finder may make his own assessment (i) of the likely outcome of the steps he might take, and (ii) (it is suggested[52]) of the reasonableness in the circumstances of his being required to take them. As to (i), the law seems strict in requiring a belief that the owner *cannot* be discovered rather than that he is unlikely to be. As to (ii), the law (if the suggestion here is correct) is both generous, in that liability for theft depends to this extent on the accused's own moral standard, and paradoxical, in that the less natural it is to him to put himself out for his neighbour, the less likely is his appropriation of his neighbour's goods to be dishonest.

Other cases besides those of finders fall within section 2(1)(*c*)—for instance, that of the person who gets property by another's mistake but does not know how by reasonable steps to identify or trace the person to whom he should make restoration.

A willingness to pay for the property

2–85   If D knows that P is unwilling to sell property to him, D cannot claim that his appropriation of the property was necessarily honest just because he was prepared to pay for it or, indeed, because he actually paid P's asking price or a reasonable price for the property. A provision designed to exclude an argument to the contrary is contained in section 2(2).

The residual function of "dishonestly": the Feely principle

2–86   For some time after the passing of the Act two questions remained unanswered. First, does section 2 provide, albeit in negative terms, a

---

[51] § 2–87.
[52] *Contra*, Williams, *Textbook*, p. 664.

partial or a comprehensive definition of dishonesty? Are there other situations, apart from those referred to in section 2(1), in which D will be or may be regarded as not appropriating dishonestly? Secondly, if there are such situations, is the residual meaning of "dishonestly," left unexpressed by section 2, a matter of law for the court or of fact for the jury?

The Committee regarded section 2 as providing only a "partial definition" of dishonesty.[53] Some doubt existed, however, as to whether this interpretation would prove to be correct, because of cases[54] on the corresponding word "fraudulently" in the definition of stealing in the Larceny Act 1916. The reasoning of these cases, if held to apply to the Theft Act, would apparently allow the word "dishonestly" in section 1(1) no function not already covered by section 2(1). And early decisions on the Theft Act seemed to treat those cases, indeed, as authoritative for the purposes of the Act.[55]

Even if some situations not within section 2(1) might justify an acquittal for lack of the element of dishonesty, the same larceny cases suggested that the residual meaning of "dishonestly," whatever it was, was a matter of law, though the case law as a whole was equivocal on the question whether the jury has any (and, if any, what) function in relation to the issue of dishonesty.[56]

These uncertainties were, in general, resolved by the controversial **2–87** decision of a full court of the Court of Appeal in *Feely*.[57] Simply summarised, this case decides that section 2(1) is not exhaustive of the situations in which D's appropriation of P's property may be regarded as not dishonest, and that, in cases not within section 2(1), the decision on the question of dishonesty is one for the jury. D, the manager of a betting shop, took about £30 from his employers' safe. He left no IOU or other record of the transaction and did not tell his employers. His defence, when charged with theft, was that he would have repaid the money.[58] On the strength of the larceny cases, the trial judge directed the jury in effect that there was no issue as to dishonesty for them to decide; if D did not believe that his employers would have consented to his taking the money (and they had in fact prohibited the practice of borrowing from the till), he was guilty

---

[53] *Eighth Report*, para. 39.
[54] *Williams* [1953] 1 Q.B. 660; *Cockburn* [1968] 1 W.L.R. 281; [1968] 1 All E.R. 466.
[55] *Halstead* v. *Patel* [1972] 1 W.L.R. 661; [1972] 2 All E.R. 147; *Rao* [1972] Crim.L.R. 451.
[56] In addition to the cases cited in nn. 54 and 55, see especially *Potger* (1970) 55 Cr.App.R. 42. For an incisive treatment of the problem of "Dishonesty under the Theft Act" just before the decision of *Feely*, below, see D. W.Elliott [1972] Crim.L.R. 625.
[57] [1973] Q.B. 530. The case has been severely criticised: see Smith, *Theft*, para. 116; I. D. Elliott, "Three Problems in the Law of Theft" (1974) 9 Melbourne U.L.Rev. 448 at pp. 466 *et seq.*; D. W. Elliott, "Law and Fact in Theft Act Cases" [1976] Crim. L.R. 707; Griew, *Dishonesty and the Jury* (Leicester U.P., 1974); *Salvo* [1980] V.R. 401, *per* Fullagar and Murphy JJ. (on which see C.R. Williams, "The Concept of Dishonesty" (1980) 54 Law Institute Journal 567; I.D. Elliott, "Dishonesty in Victoria" [1980] Crim.L.J. 149).
[58] When D was transferred to another branch of the employers' business a few days after taking the money, he was owed some £60 wages. Although at that time D told the police that the employers could repay themselves the £30 he had taken by deduction from what they owed him, it is not clear the he claimed to have been aware *at the time he took the £30* that he was owed a greater sum (if indeed at that time he was—the facts as to this are not quite clear). Williams, *Textbook*, p.666, n.3, has a different interpretation.

of theft even if he intended to repay, however soon, and had the means to do so.[59]

The Court of Appeal quashed the conviction, the jury having been misdirected. They held that it can be "a defence *in law* for a man charged with theft and proved to have taken money, to say that when he took the money he intended to repay it and had reasonable grounds for believing and did believe that he would be able to do so."[60] Whether in a particular case he falls to be convicted or acquitted depends on the finding of the jury as to whether when he took the money he acted "dishonestly." This is a question of fact. The judge should not define for the jury what "dishonestly" means, for this is "an ordinary word of the English language" and its meaning is not a question of law. In deciding whether an appropriation was dishonest the jury "should apply the current standards of ordinary decent people." This the jury in *Feely* had not been allowed to do.[61]

Feely explained; D's "state of mind" and the jury's or magistrates' "standards"

2–88   It is one thing to refer to the tribunal of fact the question whether the defendant's conduct was dishonest and therefore theft, rather than resolving the question as a matter of law. It would be quite another thing to refer the question to the defendant himself! Yet for a time it appeared that the courts were flirting even with this approach. In *Boggeln* v. *Williams*,[62] where D had used electricity without the consent of the Electricity Board, it was asserted by Lloyd J. that a finding that D "did believe that . . . he was not acting dishonestly" was "not only relevant, but crucial." In *Landy*,[63] a case of alleged conspiracy to defraud, Lawton L.J. on behalf of the Court of Appeal purported to explain "the way *R.* v. *Feely* should be applied in cases where the issue of dishonesty arises." He said that "if the jury, applying their own notions of what is honest and what is not, conclude that [the defendant] could not have believed that he was acting honestly, then the element of dishonesty will have been established." But only then, it seemed. These statements suggested that a defendant's "belief that he was acting honestly" (whatever that might mean) could be decisive

---

[59] Note that the problem in a case of this kind arises from the fact that although D intends to return the equivalent in value of the cash he takes, he intends to deprive P permanently of *those* notes and coins. The artificiality of the distinction between such a case (assuming a power to repay) and that where the thing is a chattel that will be specifically returned is frequently a source of comment.

[60] [1973] Q.B. 530 at p. 535. The italics, repeated a few lines later, seem to mean that the defence is *legally available*, however rarely realistic on the facts.

[61] [1973] 1 Q.B. 530 at p. 538, citing in support Lord Reid in *Brutus* v. *Cozens* [1973] A.C. 854 at p. 861: "The meaning of an ordinary word of the English language is not a question of law." As to this use (or misuse) of the notion of "dishonestly" as "an ordinary word," see Griew, *op.cit.* pp. 21–22. There is a substantial literature on the dishonesty of "ordinary decent people": see *e.g.* J. Ditton, *Part-Time Crime*; S. Henry, *The Hidden Economy*.

[62] [1978] 1 W.L.R. 873 at pp. 876–877; [1978] 2 All E.R. 1061 at p. 1065 (a charge under s.13: see below, § 2–98). Compare, pre-*Feely*, a dictum in *Gilks* [1972] 1 W.L.R. 1341 at p. 1345; [1972] 3 All E.R. 280 at p. 283.

[63] [1981] 1 W.L.R. 355 at p. 365; [1981] 1 All E.R. 1172 at p. 1181.

in his favour. This would occur if his view, as found by the tribunal of fact, differed from that of the tribunal itself. Juries and magistrates therefore seemed to be required to prefer the defendant's code of conduct to their own.

These statements were widely regarded as remarkable and as unsupportable in principle. Perhaps they were merely badly expressed. At all events the Court of Appeal has subsequently attempted, in *McIvor*,[64] to ensure that they no longer embarrass the law of theft. *Boggeln* v. *Williams* is interpreted, despite the passage quoted above, as depending entirely on a finding that D believed he would be able to pay, and intended to pay, for the electricity he used; the case, "properly understood," is declared not to be in conflict with *Feely*, as to many it seemed to be. *Landy* is explained as not relating to charges of theft. In a case of theft the jury "may . . . be directed" (as they were in *McIvor*) "that they should apply their own standards to the meaning of dishonesty." They surely *should* be so directed if they might be in doubt on the point.[65]

Feely and *McIvor* are less clear than they might be because of statements **2–88a** in both cases to the following effect: the word "dishonestly" relates to a state of mind; whether D has a certain state of mind is a question of fact; the question whether D was dishonest is therefore a question for the tribunal of fact.[66] This kind of reasoning suggests that under the *Feely* principle the jury or magistrates have only one question to decide, and that that question concerns a "state of mind" in only one sense of the phrase. But this cannot be true. Dishonesty is not a "state of mind" in the same sense that belief as to a fact or intention as to future action is a "state of mind"; yet on the issue of dishonesty it may be in dispute whether D had a particular belief or intention.

The fact is that there are two questions for decision. (i) It must first be found whether D, when he appropriated the property, may have believed that he could repay P, or intended that P should suffer no loss, or expected a third party to compensate P—or whatever else he has claimed in his defence. To determine D's "state of mind" in this sense is simply to find the facts of the case. (ii) The application of section 1 to those facts then requires an answer to the second question: was it "dishonest" to do what D did (that is, appropriate the property), having that state of mind? This is a question, not as to what state of mind he had, but as to how the found state of mind is to be characterised. It is this question that *Feely* assigns to the jury or the magistrates; and in the decision of this question they are to apply their own standards as representatives of the "decent" community.

---

[64] *The Times*, November 18, 1981; C.A. No. 3488/A/80.
[65] *Cf.* the explicit direction already approved by the Court of Appeal in *Greenstein* [1975] 1 W.L.R. 1353 at p. 1359; [1976] 1 All E.R. 1 at p. 6 (obtaining property by deception; below, § 6–48) that on the issue of dishonesty the jury were to apply their own standards and not those of the defendants.
[66] For the relevant passage in *Feely*, see [1973] Q.B. at p. 537.

It is submitted that a jury should be advised to approach an issue of dishonesty in these two stages.[66a]

Lawton L.J. in *McIvor* claimed that in *Feely* a "clear distinction was . . . drawn between the meaning of the word 'dishonestly' which the jury had to derive from current standards, and their need also to decide upon the actual state of mind of the defendant at the time of the offence alleged." But the way his lordship used the phrase "state of mind" in *Feely*, in *Landy*,[66b] and elsewhere in *McIvor*, makes even this passage less clear than it should be. It must be hoped that at this point at least the phrase refers only to a state of mind of the kind relevant to the first question identified above.

Scope of the Feely principle

2–89   How thoroughgoing is the principle that in cases not covered by section 2(1) it is a question for the tribunal of fact whether the conduct charged as theft was dishonest?

(i) *Indications in the judgment*

The judgment in *Feely* itself suggests that there are some limits to this principle. The case is put of an employee acting in a way "to which no one would, or could reasonably, attach moral obloquy."[67] To hold the case to be theft, it is said, "would tend to bring the law into contempt." The point is generalised: "a taking to which no moral obloquy can reasonably attach is not within the concept of stealing . . . under the Theft Act 1968."[68] The meaning of "dishonestly" is limited to this extent as a matter of law. And a direction to the jury to acquit is surely contemplated in the case put.

There is also a passage at the end of the judgment where the court exhibits some ambivalence, if not inconsistency, in its approach to facts like those of *Feely* itself. It appears to be asserted that "a man who takes money from a till intending to put it back and genuinely believing on reasonable grounds[69] that he will be able to do so" is not guilty of theft,

---

[66a] Unless the defendant is found to have one of the beliefs mentioned in s. 2(1), in which case that subsection determines the second question in the defendant's favour as a matter of law; or unless the facts as to the defendant's state of mind are agreed, in which case only the second question arises.

[66b] [1981] 1 W.L.R. at p. 365; [1981] 1 All E.R. at p. 1181: "An assertion by a defendant that throughout a transaction he acted honestly . . . has to be weighed like any piece of evidence. If that was the defendant's state of mind, or may have been, he is entitled to be acquitted." The language of this passage is unhappily echoed at the end of the judgment in *McIvor*, where it is said that the jury must give appropriate weight to D's evidence about his state of mind. If this were taken to mean that the jury should have regard to an assertion by D about his honesty, the retreat from *Boggeln* and *Landy* would not after all have been quite completed.

[67] The case is "that of a manager of a shop who, having been told that under no circumstances was he to take money from the till for his own purposes, took 40p from it, having no small change himself, to pay for a taxi hired by his wife who had arrived at the shop saying that she only had a £5 note which the cabby could not change."

[68] [1973] Q.B. 530 at p. 539.

[69] The requirement that D's belief in his ability to pay be held "on reasonable grounds" is inconsistent with *Waterfall* [1970] 1 Q.B. 148, and is corrected by *Lewis* (1975) 62 Cr.App.R. 206.

just as "a man who obtains cash by passing a cheque on an account which has no funds . . . *is deemed in law not to act dishonestly*[70] if he genuinely believes . . . [71] that when it is presented to the paying bank there will be funds to meet it."[72] This passage lends the judgment a certain overall obscurity. The main burden of the decision is that the jury should have been left to decide whether D's conduct was dishonest. The passage quoted suggests that they should have been told that, if they believed what he said about his state of mind, they could only say that he was not dishonest—the case would not be one of theft. It is true that the passage ends with a reaffirmation of its being for the jury to decide whether persons have acted dishonestly who do not by pleading guilty admit that they are thieves. But this statement is ambiguous. It may be a return to the general principle of the decision, in which case it sits ill with the immediately preceding passage. Or it may refer simply to the jury's function of finding the primary facts—what *was* D's intention?

(ii) *Rulings in favour of the defence*

Whatever the correct reading of these two passages in the *Feely* **2–90** judgment, it is submitted that the court must be involved to some extent in determining the breadth of the concept of dishonesty. The court is entitled to rule in respect of any element of an offence that no reasonable jury could find that element proved on the evidence. The element of dishonesty in theft should be no exception. Of course the jury must find what D's state of mind was, if there is any contest on that point. But the judge must be able to control improper extension of the offence of theft at least to the extent of ruling, if necessary, that a particular state of mind cannot on any reasonable view be said to be a dishonest one. And if that is right, dishonesty is to that extent at least a question of law.

(iii) *Laudable motive; necessity*

A person charged with theft may claim that he acted with a laudable **2–91** motive—perhaps in the interests of a moral or political crusade. But his own view of the justifiability of his conduct cannot secure an acquittal— even if it is expressed as a view that the conduct, being high-minded, was not dishonest.[73]

What if the jury themselves take the view that D's motive was morally praiseworthy, or that it so far justified his act that it ought not to be a crime? Motive is in principle irrelevant[74] and ought not to be allowed in simply by permitting the limiting adverb "dishonestly" an unlimited function. It should to be open to the court to say that a particular motive

---

[70] Italics supplied. It is not suggested in *Feely* that the meaning of "dishonesty" is more a matter of law in s. 15 than it is in s. 1. See below, §§ 6–47, 6–48.

[71] The words "on reasonable grounds" are omitted in the text in the light of *Lewis*, above.

[72] [1973] Q.B. 530 at p. 541, citing *Halstead* v. *Patel* [1972] 1 W.L.R. 661 at p. 666; [1972] 2 All E.R. 147 at p. 152.

[73] See above, §§ 2–88, 2–88a.

[74] The Act's express reference to motive in s. 1(2) may in fact have been unnecessary: "It is immaterial whether the appropriation is made with a view to gain, or is made for the thief's own benefit."

said to have inspired D's conduct cannot protect it from the label "dishonest." *Feely* decided more than it needed to if it decided the contrary. Even a claim to have acted from necessity (to save human life, perhaps) is not, it is thought, properly to be classified as a claim to have acted honestly.[75] If it were, the consequence of a wide interpretation of *Feely* would be to entrust to the jury the surprising power of allowing a necessity defence of unlimited scope—but necessity disguised under a different name. If necessity is to be available as a defence to theft, it should remain under firm judicial control.[76]

8.   INFORMATIONS AND INDICTMENTS

The procedural rules

2–92   Rule 1(2) of the Indictment Rules 1971 provides:

> "Where more than one offence is charged in an indictment, the statement and particulars of each offence shall be set out in a separate paragraph called a count."

Rule 12 of the Magistrates' Courts Rules 1981 provides that "a magistrates' court shall not proceed to the trial of an information that charges more than one offence." Moreover, a defendant must be expressly asked whether he consents to simultaneous summary trial of two or more informations; and if he does not consent, the informations must be tried separately.[77]

Problems can arise in applying these rules where a person is alleged to have stolen a number of things on different occasions, or at different times and places on the same occasion; or where he is alleged to have stolen an amount of money or a number of items during a certain period, but the time or times at which he stole this or that amount or item cannot be demonstrated. It is clear that too narrow or technical a conception of an "offence" for the purpose of the rules quoted above could have serious consequences for the efficient prosecution of such cases. The courts have in fact avoided a restrictive view. They have tended rather to facilitate prosecution and conviction by the use of a number of concepts and devices.

---

[75] Contrast D's claim that he believed that P would have consented if he had known of the necessity: see s. 2(1)(*b*), above, § 2–83. But the Law Commission, in *Report on Defences of General Application* (Law Com. No. 83), para. 4.5, contemplate that "proof of dishonesty in theft may perhaps be negatived if, although the defendant knows an appropriation is without the owner's consent, he takes the property to avoid a greater evil, for example, to save life." The tentativeness in this statement disappears in para. 4.17: "Discussion of the defence [*sc.* of necessity] in the context of theft has now been settled by the terms of the Theft Act 1968." It is thought, with respect, that it is far from settled and that the point needs more argument than the Law Commission accord it.

[76] For relevant dicta inhospitable to the defence, see *Southwark L.B.C.* v. *Williams* [1971] Ch. 734.

[77] *Brangwynne* v. *Evans* [1962] 1 W.L.R. 267; [1962] 1 All E.R. 446 (informations charging thefts from three shops in Neath on the same day). For an exception, see Criminal Attempts Act 1981, s.4(2) (summary trial for full offence and for attempt).

One charge for a single "activity"

In *Wilson*[78] an indictment for shoplifting contained two counts, among   **2–93**
others, each of which related to D's conduct in a different store. In one
count he was alleged to have stolen records and after-shave lotion from
Boots; in the other clothes of various kinds, electrical switches and a
cassette tape from Debenhams. The evidence showed that in each of these
stores the articles came from different "departments." The Court of
Appeal applied a principle recently stated in the Divisional Court in
relation to informations,[79] subsequently applied to indictments by the
Court of Appeal,[80] and approved in the House of Lords in these terms: "it
will often be legitimate to bring a single charge in respect of . . . one
activity even though that activity may involve more than one act."[81] The
question whether the charge relates to one offence or to more than one is
to be determined "by applying common sense and by deciding what is fair
in the circumstances"[82]; it is "a question of fact and degree."[83] D's
convictions on the two counts were upheld. Neither count, in the Court of
Appeal's view, charged more than one offence, either on its face or in the
light of the evidence. The decision may be felt to be a generous but realistic
application of the notion of a single "activity."[84] In another case the court
would even have been prepared if necessary to apply the "activity" test to
sanction a single theft charge where a bogus haulage contractor loaded
greengrocery in three different parts of London for carriage on the
instructions of the same principal.[85]

One charge for a "continuous" offence

A number of cases decided before the Indictments Act 1915 concerned,   **2–94**
respectively, mining operations conducted continuously over four years,
involving the taking of coal belonging to many persons[86]; the cutting of
eight trees with intent to steal them during a tree-felling operation carried
out in a particular season[87]; the abstraction of gas from a main, by-passing
the meter, day after day for several years[88]; and pilfering identified articles
from an employer, the articles being found in the accused's possession on
the day named in the indictment as that of the offence.[89] In each of these

---

[78] (1979) 69 Cr. App.R. 83.
[79] *Jemmison* v. *Priddle* [1972] 1 Q.B. 489, *per* Lord Widgery C.J. at p. 495.
[80] *Jones* (1974) 59 Cr. App. R. 120.
[81] *D.P.P.* v. *Merriman* [1973] A.C. 584, *per* Lord Morris of Borth-y-Gest at p. 593 (and see
   per Lord Diplock at p. 607).
[82] *Ibid.*
[83] (1979) 69 Cr. App. R. at p. 88.
[84] The court found "not clear at all" the facts of *Ballysingh* (1953) 37 Cr. App. R. 28, where a
   count charging theft from (as the evidence showed) several "departments" of a store was
   regarded as defective. They appeared to contemplate that thefts from different
   departments of a large store like Harrods might not necessarily constitute a single activity
   (69 Cr. App. R. at p. 88). The size and layout of the stores in *Wilson* itself are not clear
   from the report.
[85] *Skipp* [1975] Crim. L.R. 114.
[86] *Bleasdale* (1848) 2 Car. & K. 765.
[87] *Shepherd* (1868) L.R. 1 C.C.R. 118.
[88] *Firth* (1869) L.R. 1 C.C.R. 173.
[89] *Henwood* (1870) 11 Cox 526.

cases the course of conduct was held to constitute a "continuous taking." There is no reason to doubt that a correspondingly broad view would now be taken of similar facts, so as to permit the charging of a simple "continuous" offence.

One charge for a "general deficiency"

2–95 A single count is convenient (indeed often unavoidable) in another familiar kind of case—namely, where a servant or agent, liable to account to his principal for money received or held for the principal, is found to have less of the principal's money in his hands than he should have, but where the dishonest appropriations causing the deficiency cannot be individually demonstrated. In such cases it was held under the Larceny Act 1916 that a count charging theft, embezzlement or fraudulent conversion of a general deficiency might be framed—that is, a count alleging that on a day between specified dates, D stole (etc.) £x (*i.e.* the total amount of the deficiency). A conviction on such a count was justified by evidence satisfying the jury that on some unknown day between the specified dates D did steal (etc.) some part at least of the deficiency.[90] There can be no doubt that a similar count charging theft of a general deficiency is proper today.

Amendment; election; applying the proviso

2–96 An indictment defective for duplicity may be amended so that no count charges more than one offence; and the amendment may include the addition of counts so that no allegations are in fact lost. Amendment cannot achieve so much in the case of summary trial (at least in the absence of the defendant's consent); so the prosecutor with a defective information may be obliged to elect upon what single offence to proceed.

If an information is successfully attacked for duplicity after summary conviction, the conviction must be quashed; the magistrates' court had no jurisdiction to try the information.[91] But on appeal against conviction on indictment it may be held that, although strictly the indictment was defective, no miscarriage of justice has occurred—the defendant not having been prejudiced in his defence by the form of the indictment[92] or his counsel having refrained from objection at the trial.[93] The proviso to section 2(1) of the Criminal Appeal Act 1968 may be applied and the appeal dismissed.

Theft of part or whole of a collection or quantity

2–97 On a charge of stealing several specific items there may be a conviction of stealing some of them if theft of them all is not proved.[94] The same principle should apply if what is charged is theft of an undifferentiated

---

[90] The modern cases were *Lawson* (1952) 36 Cr. App. R. 30; *Tomlin* [1954] 2 Q.B. 274; *Wilson* v. *Read* [1956] Crim. L.R. 418. See also *Balls* (1871) L.R. 1 C.C.R. 328.
[91] See the terms of rule 12 (above, § 2–92).
[92] *Thompson* [1914] 2 K.B. 99.
[93] *Ballysingh* (1953) 37 Cr. App. R. 28.
[94] *Machent* v. *Quinn* [1970] 2 All E.R. 255.

whole and theft of part only is proved. For theft of part of such a larger quantity is perfectly possible.[95] In *Gilks*,[96] for instance, P paid D £117.25 in cash when, as D realised, he should have paid £10.62. It was held that D was guilty of theft of £106.63.

If D is charged with stealing a part of a larger unit of property, he can be convicted as charged although it is proved that he stole the whole unit. Thus, in *Pilgram* v. *Rice-Smith*[97] D, a shop assistant, "sold" corned beef and bacon to her friend at 83½p below the proper price. This was theft of all the meat, not merely, as the information alleged, of meat to the value of 83½p. It was held that that fact would not prevent a conviction on the information as laid.

9. ABSTRACTING OF ELECTRICITY; DISHONEST USE OF PUBLIC TELEPHONE OR TELEX SYSTEM

The peculiar nature of electricity necessitates special provision for its dishonest use.[98] Section 13 provides: **2–98**

> "A person who dishonestly uses without due authority, or dishonestly causes to be wasted or diverted, any electricity shall on conviction on indictment be liable to imprisonment for a term not exceeding five years."

The partial definition of "dishonestly" in section 2 is not made to apply for the purposes of this section (s. 1(3)), but there can be no doubt that belief in a right to use or a belief that the supplier or consumer concerned would consent if he knew will exclude dishonesty (compare s. 2(1)(*a*) and (*b*)).[99] Reference should be made to the discussion of the general function of the word "dishonestly" in the definition of theft; the same principles apply for the purposes of both offences.[1]

A new offence under the Post Office Act 1953 of dishonestly using a public telephone or telex system with intent to avoid payment is created by Schedule 2, Part I, paragraph 8.

---

[95] Smith, *Theft,* para. 102, citing *Tideswell* [1905] 2 K.B. 273.
[96] [1972] 1 W.L.R. 1341; [1972] 3 All E.R. 280. *Cf. Levene* v. *Pearcey* [1976] Crim.L.R. 63 (below, § 6–09).
[97] [1977] 1 W.L.R. 671; [1977] 2 All E.R. 658.
[98] Electricity is not "property" and cannot be stolen: *Low* v. *Blease* [1975] Crim.L.R. 513.
[99] See above, §§ 2–81 to 2–83.
[1] Above, §§ 2–86 to 2–91. In *Boggeln* v. *Williams* [1978] 1 W.L.R. 73; [1978] 2 All E.R. 1061, D's electricity supply was cut off for non-payment. He reconnected it himself, intending to pay for future use and believing in his ability to do so. *Held,* that it was open to the tribunal of fact to find that he had not used electricity dishonestly (applying *Feely* [1973] Q.B. 530).

CHAPTER 3

ROBBERY

1. DEFINITION

3–01   THE Larceny Act 1916 provided different maximum penalties for a number of offences of robbery and aggravated robbery. There was no statutory definition of robbery and its meaning at common law was neither clear in all respects nor very satisfactory. The present Act preserves robbery as the only aggravated form of theft. The various degrees of robbery are eliminated. Robbery and assault with intent to rob are both made punishable on conviction on indictment with life imprisonment (s. 8(2)). They are not triable summarily.[1]

Robbery is defined in section 8(1):

> "A person is guilty of robbery if he steals, and immediately before or at the time of doing so, and in order to do so, he uses force on any person or puts or seeks to put any person in fear of being then and there subjected to force."

This definition preserves the essence of the traditional offence but avoids some undesirable features of the common law definition. Although the language of the new definition contains pronounced echoes of the old (in the references to force and to putting in fear), it would be an error to seek to elaborate the statutory language by resort to the old cases.[2] Pre-1969 cases are accordingly banished from the rest of this chapter, with the exception of one late decision, to be mentioned immediately, which is clearly exempt from the ban.

2. THE DETAILS OF THE OFFENCE

"Steals"

3–02   A person is guilty of robbery only if he steals (or of an assault with intent to rob only if he intends to steal). Proof of a robbery therefore requires proof of all the elements of theft.[3] In particular there can be no robbery if D believes that he has in law the right to deprive P of the property in question.[4] The Act preserves the effect of *Skivington*.[5] In that case D went to the offices of the firm which employed him and his wife and demanded his wife's wages at the point of a knife. Two wage packets were handed to

---

[1] Magistrates' Courts Act 1980, Sched. 1, para. 28(a).
[2] Compare *Dawson* (1976) 64 Cr. App. R. 170 (below, § 3–04), where the Court of Appeal declined to flirt with "the old technicalities." But the court seems to prefer to leave the jury to interpret the statutory language.
[3] See Andrews, "Robbery" [1966] Crim.L.R. 524 at p. 527 (in an article on the draft bill), on the association of robbery with a wide offence of theft.
[4] See s. 2(1)(*a*): discussed above, §§ 2–81, 2–82.
[5] [1968] 1 Q.B. 166.

him. It was held by the Court of Appeal that to avoid a conviction of robbery it was necessary only that D should believe, as he asserted he did, that he had a right to the money. It was not necessary that he should also believe that he was entitled to take the money in the way that he did.[6] So, now, under section 8, D need not allege a belief in a right to use force.[7]

Where D has used force on P in order to steal from him but has failed to   **3–03**
make himself master of P's property, it may be a nice question whether D has committed a robbery or only an assault with intent to rob. This depends on whether D's acts have amounted to an appropriation of any property or only to an attempted appropriation. This distinction has been discussed in the preceding chapter.[8] It was seen that the courts will not be slow to find a complete appropriation. But in any case in which appropriation is at all doubtful the safer charge will be assault with intent to rob (assuming the assault can be proved) or attempted theft (if not). This has been explained above.[9]

"Uses force on" a person

The element of force in robbery, though expressed in simple language,   **3–04**
involves questions that may be expected to call for judicial solution. It is submitted that the Court of Appeal was insufficiently decisive in the only reported case on this aspect of section 8. In *Dawson*,[10] two men nudged P so that he lost his balance, and while he was off balance a third man stole his wallet. The Court of Appeal appears to have approved of the approach of the trial judge in leaving it to the jury to decide whether jostling having such an unbalancing effect amounted to the use of force. It is submitted[11] that the question is one for uniform decision and that the court should have offered a plain affirmative ruling on the question as a matter of law. More broadly, it is suggested that force can properly be said to be used on a person whenever he himself is an object of any force, however slight, used as a means of parting the property from him or overcoming or preventing his resistance to the theft or his interference with its accomplishment. The scope of robbery is adequately limited by the requirements that the force be used "in order to [steal]" and that it be used "on" a person.

Because the section speaks of the use of force "on any person" it is not sufficient if the force is used merely against, or in order to obtain, the property. There is a difference between, on the one hand, being struck or knocked down or tied up and, on the one hand, noticing the effect of force that is not directed against oneself but is used to detach property from one's hand or person. But the dividing line between the two types of case is not easy to draw.

[6] See also *Robinson* [1977] Crim.L.R. 173 (above, § 2–82).
[7] But he would have to allege something very similar in order to avoid a conviction of blackmail under s. 21. See Chap. 12.
[8] See §§ 2–48, 2–49, (including discussion of *Corcoran* v. *Anderton* (1980) 71 Cr. App. R. 104, a robbery case).
[9] See §§ 1–09, 1–10.
[10] (1976) 64 Cr.App.R. 170.
[11] Agreeing with the comment of Professor J. C. Smith in [1976] Crim.L.R. 693.

3–05 The Committee said on this point:

> "We should not regard mere snatching of property, such as a handbag, from an unresisting owner, as using force for the purpose of the definition, though it might be so if the owner resisted."[12]

This observation provides a helpful illustration of the intended distinction, but leaves some questions unanswered. The effect of the owner's resisting may merely be to increase the effort required to detach her handbag from her. If that effort continued to be directed against the handbag (harder pulling) and not unequivocally against the owner (striking or twisting an arm), it is not clear that the effort would even then necessarily be force used "on" her. Yet if, as a result of violent pulling, she fell and was hurt, the temptation to say that force had been used on her would be great. Nor, presumably, need that temptation be resisted. One difficulty, however, is that a sudden unexpected snatching might make even an unresisting owner fall or in some other way be incidentally hurt. This case makes the distinction between the resisting and the unresisting owners look inadequate. A happier distinction would perhaps be that between cases in which the thief does and does not consciously submit the victim to the risk of being physically affected by the use of the violence employed to obtain the property. If it is clear from the circumstances that the thief must have foreseen that risk, it would surely be proper to say that force had been used "on" the victim even though it was primarily directed against the property. But such a test, even if acceptable, would apply only to cases in which the physical separation of the property from the victim was the object of the violence. It would not work for other cases: the use of an explosive to blow a safe might well be seen to carry the risk of injury to the owners in an adjoining room, but such injury, if it occurred, would not be the result of force used "on" him in order to steal.

"Puts or seeks to put . . . in fear"

3–06 It is sufficient if the thief "puts or seeks to put any person in fear of being then and there subjected to force."

Although a threat of future force will not suffice for robbery, one who obtains property by such a threat will normally be guilty both of theft and of blackmail, the essence of which is the making of an unwarranted demand with menaces.[13]

The putting in fear must be "in order to [steal]." The fact that P is in fact put in fear will therefore not suffice if D did not intend or (probably) foresee that he would be.

The words "or seeks to put . . . in fear" cover the case in which D intends to use the threat of force as a means of accomplishing his theft, but in which P remains either unconscious of the threat or unmoved by it. If there is no question but that D intended P to be fearful of the imminent use of force, there is no need for P to say, on D's trial, whether he was actually frightened—except as a matter possibly relevant to sentence.

---

[12] *Eighth Report,* para. 65.
[13] s. 21. See Chap. 12.

"Any person"

There must of course be a victim of the theft (or, in the case of an assault   **3–07**
with intent to rob, somebody who would be the victim of the theft
proposed). But the victim of the use of force or of the putting or seeking to
put in fear may be "any person"; he need not be the owner, possessor or
custodian of the property (the person to whom the property "belongs"). D
may use force on P, or put P in fear, in order to steal from P or from Q.

It follows that the force need not be used at the scene of the theft, so
long as it is used immediately before or at the time of stealing and in order
to do so. The Committee gives a clear example: "If . . . the only force used
at the time of the Aylesbury train robbery in 1963 had been on a
signalman, this would under [section 8] have been sufficient."[14]

"Immediately before or at the time of" the stealing

The force, or the threat of force, must be used "immediately before or at   **3–08**
the time of" the stealing.

It was held in *Hale*[15] that a theft is not over and done with the very
moment the thief lays hands on the property. Appropriation is a
"continuous," not a momentary, act. Having already taken possession of a
jewellery box in P's house, the accused men tied P up in order to ensure
their escape; they thereby used force "at the time of" the theft and were
guilty of robbery. It is in general, according to the Court of Appeal, a
question for the jury whether the appropriation was finished before the
force was used; but in *Hale* itself it was "a matter of common sense" that it
was not. This decision goes far (happily, it is submitted) to undo the effect
of the deliberate omission from section 8 of a reference to force, or the
threat of force, used "immediately after" the stealing.[16]

Cases could arise in which it would be desirable to entertain a generous   **3–09**
conception of the period "immediately before" the stealing. Force might
be used on a signalman or security guard some while before theft from a
train or a warehouse actually takes place. It is thought that, if the force can
realistically be regarded as an aspect of the physical accomplishment of the
theft on the occasion of its occurrence, the court—or perhaps, in the light
of *Hale*, the jury—will be justified in treating it as occurring "immediately
before" the stealing.

"In order to" steal

The act of using force or of putting or seeking to put P in fear must be   **3–10**
done "in order to" steal. The mere fact that violence and theft occur as
ingredients of the same transaction does not justify a conviction of
robbery.[17] D may, for instance, attack P and steal from him a wallet that is

---

[14] *Eighth Report,* para. 65.
[15] (1978) 68 Cr. App.R. 415.
[16] *Eighth Report,* para. 65. The words "or immediately after" appeared in the corresponding
phrase in the old offence of robbery with violence: Larceny Act 1916, s. 23(1)(*b*).
[17] See, *e.g. Shendley* [1970] Crim.L.R. 49; *Donaghy and Marshall* [1981] Crim.L.R. 644.

shaken from his pocket by the violence. If the attack was not made for the purpose of theft, D cannot be convicted of robbery.[18]

In other respects the words "in order to do so" will be read fairly liberally as meaning not only "in order to accomplish the theft" but also "in order to do so more safely, more expeditiously," and so on. It will thus be robbery if force is used upon someone who might discover the theft and give the alarm.[19] So if D, immediately before or at the time of the theft, uses force on a jeweller at his home, to prevent him going to his shop where he would find D's confederates opening the safe, D and any confederates who are parties to this use of force will, it is submitted, be guilty of robbery if they succeed in stealing from the safe and of an assault with intent to rob if they do not.

[18] On an indictment for robbery, D may be convicted of theft if force is not used, or not used at the appropriate time or in order to steal: see above, § 1–09.
[19] The point passed without comment in *Hale* (1978) 68 Cr. App. R. 415 (above, § 3–08).

CHAPTER 4

BURGLARY AND AGGRAVATED BURGLARY

1. INTRODUCTION

SECTIONS 24 to 27 of the Larceny Act 1916, as amended by the Criminal **4–01**
Law Act 1967, provided a bewildering battery of offences involving
breaking and entering, or entering or breaking out of, different kinds of
buildings, in which the accused intended to commit, committed or had
before breaking out committed an arrestable offence. Further, section 28
included an offence of being found by night in any building with intent to
commit an arrestable offence therein. The scheme of offences was
impossible to justify. They applied variously to places of divine worship
only, to dwelling-houses only, or to a wide but not comprehensive range of
buildings. Some could be committed only at night, others at any time. The
expressions "dwelling-house," "breaks" and "enters" had highly technical
meanings: guilt or innocence of any particular offence, or of any offence at
all, could turn on circumstances of absolutely no moral significance.

For the provisions described above, the Theft Act substituted two
offences, one of which is merely an aggravated form of the other.

2. BURGLARY

Definition; mode of trial

Burglary is defined by section 9. It is committed by one who— **4–02**

   (i) enters any building or part of a building as a trespasser and with
   intent to commit therein[1] an offence of theft, inflicting grievous
   bodily harm, rape or unlawful damage (subss. (1)(*a*), (2)); or
   (ii) having entered any building as a trespasser, steals or attempts to
   steal anything therein or inflicts or attempts to inflict grievous bodily
   harm therein (subs. (1)(*b*)).

The section applies to an inhabited vehicle or vessel as it does to a
building (subs. (3)).

The maximum penalty for burglary is 14 years' imprisonment (s. 9(4));
for aggravated burglary, considered below, it is life imprisonment
(s. 10(2)).

Any (non-aggravated) burglary is triable either way *except* the **4–03**
following[2]:

   (i) "burglary comprising the commission of, or an intention to commit,
an offence which is triable only on indictment." The relevant offences
triable only on indictment are rape (Sexual Offences Act 1956, s. 1) and

---

[1] In one minor respect this word is inaccurate: see below, § 4–23 at n.46.
[2] Magistrates' Courts Act 1980, Sched.1, para. 28(*b*)(*c*).

causing grievous bodily harm with intent (Offences against the Person Act 1861, s. 18). So any burglary involving (a) entry with intent to rape, (b) entry with intent to inflict (and therefore cause) grievous bodily harm, or (c) entry and attempting to inflict (which must involve an intention[3] to cause) grievous bodily harm, is triable only on indictment. But burglary in the form of entering as a trespasser and actually committing an offence under section 20 of the Offences against the Person Act 1861—that is, maliciously inflicting grievous bodily harm—is triable either way, the section 20 offence being itself so triable.

(ii) "burglary in a dwelling if any person in the dwelling was subjected to violence or the threat of violence." Some other cases of "burglary in a dwelling," now triable either way, were originally triable only on indictment.[4] Their description included the phrase "building containing the dwelling," language which confirmed that where a "dwelling" is part of a larger building, burglarious entry into some other part of that building is not "burglary in a dwelling."[5]

Entry as a trespasser

4–04   Burglary depends upon entry as a trespasser and therefore in part upon the civil law of trespass to land. For the purpose of burglary, to enter as a trespasser may be defined as to intrude into a building or part of a building in the possession of another without a right, by law or licence, to do so. In most cases it will be easy to see that the accused had done just this. But there may be exceptional cases in which the application of the civil law will not be a straightforward matter or on which the precise rules of the civil law are not appropriate to the policy of the criminal law.[6] One possible case is that in which D enters P's house upon the invitation of Q, a member of P's household. If Q has no authority to permit D's entry, D will be a trespasser for the purposes of the law of tort. It was said in *Collins*[7] that such a result would be "unthinkable" in the criminal law. But would it be unthinkable? If D does not doubt Q's authority, he is innocent of burglary on another ground, established in *Collins* itself.[8] On the other hand, D may know or suspect that Q's pretended permission gives him no right to enter. Why then should it not be burglary if he enters with intent to steal (Q might, after all, be a party to that intent)? The context in *Collins* was a special one; Q was herself the intended victim of rape. Perhaps D needs the licence of the occupier (or of one acting with the occupier's authority) *or* of the intended victim of the ulterior offence.

4–05   Trespass is a wrong committed against another's possession of land. If no one else has a possession that excludes the entrant, there is no trespass. This platitude becomes of obvious importance when it is necessary to

---

[3] Criminal Attempts Act 1981, s. 1(1).
[4] s. 29(2) (repealed).
[5] Smith, *The Law of Theft* (3rd ed.), para. 447.
[6] See especially "Trespass and *mens rea*," below, § 4–10.
[7] [1973] Q.B. 100 at p. 107.
[8] See below, § 4–11.

consider, for instance, the liability for burglary of a person entering, in his own house, the room of a tenant or lodger, with intent to steal therein. If D himself has granted P a right to occupy premises, when does that right amount to exclusive possession as against D and when is it a mere right of occupation and enjoyment? If P occupies part of D's house as a tenant, D requires P's permission to enter that part if he is to enter without trespassing. When he enters to steal P's property, he commits burglary. On the other hand, if P occupies part of D's house as a lodger he will not usually have exclusive possession, so that when D enters to steal P's property he will not commit burglary.[9] The distinction is not an obviously happy one from a policy standpoint. The law of burglary should protect the security of the individual within the premises he occupies, irrespective of the precise terms upon which he does so.

A person may be entitled to enter a building by virtue of a *right granted* **4-06** *by the law.* A constable, for instance, does not trespass when he enters a building to execute a search warrant. But if, armed with a search warrant, he enters the premises intending to steal therein and not to search, it is clear that he trespasses. It is otherwise if he enters to execute the warrant and after entry steals; for in such a case his entry can only be treated as trespassory by application of the doctrine of trespass *ab initio,* which does not apply to burglary.[10]

What of a person who, having a *licence* to enter premises, enters with **4-07** intent to commit a relevant offence? Does he enter as a trespasser for the purpose of burglary? It was presumably the notion of an entry not covered by an admitted licence that was intended to be conveyed by James L.J. in *Jones and Smith*[11] in his rather oddly-worded reference to entry "in excess of" a permission to enter. The court in this case upheld the convictions of the two appellants who had entered the house of Smith's father (which he had a general licence to enter at any time) for the purpose of stealing. It was held that a licence to enter does not protect against liability for burglary a person who, when he enters, knows that his entry (or is reckless whether his entry) is "in excess of the permission that has been given to him." The decision can be applied to familiar situations in which people in general are invited to enter buildings or parts of buildings. A person entering a shop during business hours[12] or entering a museum that is open to the public free of charge is (on the strength of *Jones and Smith*) guilty of burglary if he enters with intent to steal, for he enters as a trespasser.

---

[9] For the distinction between lease and licence, which no longer turns simply on the question of exclusive possession, see Woodfall, *Landlord and Tenant* (28th ed.) paras. 1–0016 *et seq.*; as to lodgers, para.1–0021.
[10] *Collins* [1973] Q.B. 100 at p. 107.
[11] [1976] 1 W.L.R. 672; [1976] 3 All E.R. 54 at p. 59; applying *Hillen and Pettigrew* v. *I.C.I.(Alkali) Ltd.* [1936] A.C. 65, and distinguishing *Byrne* v. *Kinematograph Renters Society Ltd.* [1958] 1 W.L.R. 762; [1958] 2 All E.R. 579.
[12] See Smith, *Theft*, para. 340.

4–08   *Jones and Smith* has been vigorously criticised by Professor Williams.[13] His main objections to the decision appear to be these:

(i) That it is not well-founded in the tort authority relied on by the court. This objection is no doubt technically sound but does not demonstrate that the decision is incorrect.

(ii) That it takes inadequate account of the language of section 9, even to the point of rendering redundant the words "as a trespasser" in section 9(1)(*a*). For according to the decision an intent to commit a relevant ulterior offence suffices to make the entry trespassory; yet such an intent is itself an independent requirement under paragraph (*a*). This objection, again, has a technical flavour. And it is respectfully suggested that it is not sound. If the intent is to commit an offence against someone other than the occupier, the entry will not necessarily be trespassory; the occupier may license the entry, acquiescing in or being indifferent to the proposed offence. Thus the phrase "as a trespasser" does have a function independent of the ulterior intent.

(iii) That it is inconsistent with the case of *Collins*.[14] This will be explained and discussed below.[15]

(iv) That it is contrary to the purpose of the law of burglary. Burglary is aimed at the unwelcome intruder. It is not intended to deal with the entrant whose presence is expected, even welcome—such as the occupier's son (as in *Jones and Smith*), or his customer, guest or employee. The decision rests burglary on the entrant's state of mind, not on the "objective illegality" of his entry. This objection has considerable force. Burglary is a traditional category of crime protecting premises and their occupants against invasion, against entry that is "manifestly suspicious."[16] Its maximum penalty is set very high. These considerations may in due course lead to a review of the *Jones and Smith* decision.[17]

4–09   D may obtain permission to enter a building by pretending to be someone he is not or by falsely claiming to have a valid reason for entering. He may, for instance, pretend to be the gas man come to read the meter. His entry is surely a trespass, either because the fraud vitiates the apparent consent to his entry (a sufficient explanation in cases like that of the bogus gas man) or because the permission to enter, properly understood, does not extend to an entry made for D's secret nefarious purpose. One who obtains his licence to enter by fraud can hardly be in a better position than one who abuses a licence legitimately obtained.[18]

A licence to enter a building may extend to part of the building only. If

---

[13] Williams, *Textbook,* pp. 812–815.
[14] [1973] Q.B. 100 (below, § 4–11).
[15] § 4–13.
[16] G. Fletcher, *Rethinking Criminal Law,* p. 128.
[17] *Cf.* M.S. Weinberg and C.R. Williams, *The Australian Law of Theft,* p. 256. Professor Williams suggests that the decision can stand on the narrow ground that Smith's licence from his father did not entitle him to authorise Jones's entry, to which he was a party: *Textbook,* p. 815. But it is clear that the court had no such *ratio* in mind.
[18] "Entry under false pretences" is more fully discussed by Smith, *Theft,* paras. 338, 339.

so, the licensee will trespass if he enters some other part not within the scope of the licence. To do so with intent to commit in that other part one of the specified offences, or to do so and then to commit or attempt to commit one of those offences therein, will be burglary.

Trespass and mens rea

What if D wrongly believes that he is not trespassing? His belief may rest **4–10** on facts which, if true, would mean that he was not trespassing: for instance, he may enter a building by mistake, thinking that it is the one he has been invited to enter. Or his belief may be based on a false view of the legal effect of the known facts: for instance, he may misunderstand the effect of a contract granting him a right of passage through a building. Neither kind of mistake will protect him from tort liability for trespass. In either case, then, D satisfies the literal terms of section 9(1): he "enters . . . as a trespasser." But for the purpose of criminal liability a man should be judged on the basis of the facts as he believed them to be, and this should include making allowances for a mistake as to rights under the civil law. This is another way of saying that a serious offence like burglary should be held to require *mens rea* in the fullest sense of the phrase: D should be liable for burglary only if he knowingly trespasses or is reckless as to whether he trespasses or not. Unhappily it is common for Parliament to omit to make clear whether *mens rea* is intended to be an element in a statutory offence. It is also, though not equally, common for the courts to supply the mental element by construction of the statute.

In the present context, the Court of Appeal, accepting the view stated **4–11** above, has supplied the mental element in the remarkable case of *Collins.*[19] D stripped off his clothes and climbed to the window-sill of P's bedroom, intending to enter and to have intercourse with her, by force if necessary. P mistook him for her boyfriend. She beckoned or assisted him into the room and intercourse took place. The Court of Appeal quashed D's conviction of burglary, holding that

> "there cannot be a conviction for entering premises 'as a trespas- ser' . . . unless the person entering does so knowing that he is a trespasser and nevertheless deliberately enters, or, at the very least, is reckless as to whether or not he is entering the premises of another without the other party's consent."[20]

D may not have satisfied this test, for it was not clear on the evidence "where exactly [D] was at the moment when, according to him, [P] manifested that she was welcoming him . . . . It was a crucial matter."[21] At the moment of entering the room he may have believed, ignorant of her mistake, that she was consenting to his entry.

[19] [1973] Q.B. 100 ("about as extraordinary a case," according to Edmund Davies L.J., "as my brethren or I have ever heard either on the Bench or while at the Bar").
[20] At p. 105.
[21] At pp. 103–104. The decisive point in the case was therefore "a narrow one, as narrow maybe as the window-sill" (p. 106).

4–12   Edmund Davies L.J., giving the judgment of the court in *Collins*, was probably using the word "reckless" in a restricted sense according to which D will be reckless as to whether he is entering premises without consent only if he realises that he may not have consent. This is suggested by the terms of his lordship's speech in the later case of *Caldwell*,[22] in which he strongly dissented from the attribution of a wider meaning to the same word in another context. It is true that in *Collins* he hinted that a belief on D's part that P consented to his entry must be a reasonable one if it is to protect D from conviction of burglary.[23] But this is explained by the view his lordship then held of the weight of the authorities on the defence of mistake: see his dissenting speech in *D.P.P.* v. *Morgan*[24] three years later. By analogy with the decision in *Morgan*, D's belief that he has consent to enter is in fact inconsistent with recklessness on that issue (in the supposed *Collins* sense), whether that belief is reasonable or not.

But D's failure to realise that he is trespassing, or his belief that he is not, may be the result of intoxication. It seems that in such a case he does enter as a trespasser if the truth would have been obvious to him had he been sober.[25]

Is Jones and Smith inconsistent with Collins?

4–13   Professor Williams suggests[26] that *Jones and Smith*[27] is inconsistent with *Collins*. Collins may have believed that the girl was inviting him to enter the house. The jury's verdict nevertheless involves a finding that when he entered he intended to rape her if necessary. Entry with this intention (the argument runs) was surely entry "in excess of" the permission apparently given to him to enter. Yet his conviction was quashed. This implies that entry with a relevant criminal intention outside the terms of the licence granted does not negative that licence. Yet *Jones and Smith* holds that it does.

Two answers are available.[28] First, a distinction might be taken between an unqualified intention (that of Jones and Smith to steal) and a conditional one (that of Collins to have intercourse by force if necessary). Collins may fulfil his purpose of having intercourse without exceeding the licensor's purpose in admitting him; not so with Smith. This is a real distinction, but hardly a satisfying one. The second answer is simply that, for all that appears, the court in *Collins* did not advert to the effect upon the (supposed) licence of the ulterior intent. It may be *Collins* that is

---

[22] [1981] 2 W.L.R. 509; [1981] 1 All E.R. 961.
[23] [1973] Q.B. at p. 106.
[24] [1976] A.C. 182 at pp. 230 *et seq.* The case concerned the analogous problem of mistake as to the victim's consent in rape.
[25] *Cf. Caldwell* [1981] 2 W.L.R. 509; [1981] 1 All E.R. 961.
[26] Williams, *Textbook*, pp. 813, 814.
[27] [1976] 1 W.L.R. 672; [1976] 3 All E.R. 54; above § 4–07.
[28] Smith, *Theft*, para. 336, and Weinberg and Williams, *op.cit.* p. 255, in effect propose a third—namely, that by the time he entered (see text below) Collins may have felt assured of voluntary intercourse and so lost the intent to rape. But there is no hint that the Court of Appeal was dissatisfied with the trial judge's direction on the issue of intent to rape or with the jury's finding of that intent at the time of entry.

defective on this point. On the other hand, the possible conflict that Professor Williams has pointed out is certainly a further basis upon which *Jones and Smith* may in future be reviewed.

Entry

Under the old law, the intrusion into the building of part of the body, **4-14** however small, satisfied the requirement of an entry.[29] If that rule survives for the purpose of section 9, the Court of Appeal in *Collins* might have been expected to regard as crucial the question whether any part of D's body was within the room before P made her welcoming signs. But the test adopted by Edmund Davies L.J., in an *extempore* judgment, was whether before that time D had made "an effective and substantial entry."[30] It may be that that was simply a realistic formula in the peculiar circumstances of the case, having regard to the uncertainty in the evidence. That view is suggested by the absence of any elaboration of the point in the judgment. A second possibility is that a general modification of the old rule is intended, to the extent of excluding cases of minimal entry, as when D's toes protrude onto an inner sill and his fingers clutch the window frame. It is not likely that the Court of Appeal intended, in so casual a manner, to change the law even more drastically, as would be the case if the test of "effective and substantial entry" were regarded as excluding from the scope of burglary the act of the smash-and-grab raider who puts part of his arm through the jeweller's window and steals a ring. This would be an unexpected and probably unacceptable result. Further decisions must be awaited before the position is clearer.

There is no decision on the question whether D "enters . . . as a **4-15** trespasser" within the meaning of section 9(1) when he does not himself physically enter but trespasses through the instrumentality of an innocent agent (a child under 10, an adult without *mens rea*[31] or a well trained animal). It should be held that he is within the statutory wording in such a case. Burglary should be no exception to the general rule that crimes can be committed through innocent agents.[32]

There is a third category of problem cases on the meaning of entry. D **4-16** may insert an instrument into the building without any part of his own body intruding. Under the old law this was an entry if the instrument was inserted for the purpose of committing a relevant ulterior offence (*e.g.*

---

[29] *Davies* (1823) R. & R. 499.
[30] [1973] Q.B. 100 at p. 106.
[31] In *Paterson* [1976] 2 N.Z.L.R. 394, D asked E to fetch a television set from a flat which he described as his own; in fact the flat and the set were P's. E did as he was asked. D's conviction of burglary (depending on "breaking and entering") was upheld by the New Zealand Court of Appeal. *Cf.* Hale, 1 *Pleas of the Crown*, pp. 555–556.
[32] Williams, *Criminal Law—General Part* (2nd ed.), pp. 349 *et seq.* Authority under the Game Act 1831, s. 30 ("commit any trespass by entering or being upon any land") is to the contrary effect: *Pratt* (1855) 4 E. & B. 860 at pp. 864, 868; *Martin* [1911] 2 K.B. 90; but "he would be a bold lawyer who would argue from the Game Acts to any general principle of law": Williams, *op. cit.* p. 329.

theft or causing grievous bodily harm), but not if it was inserted merely to facilitate access to the premises. The view was expressed in the first edition of this book that such a distinction "would be discreditable under the present Act, which is intended to simplify and rationalise the law." Further reflection, however, assisted by the Court of Appeal's criterion of "effective and substantial entry,"[33] suggests that such a distinction, slightly adapted, may be perfectly respectable. The insertion of an instrument simply as a means of access need not be regarded as an entry. D is not, by that insertion, "effectively" in the building. His act seems to be described more convincingly as an attempt to enter the building than as an actual entry by him, and attempted burglary can be charged if nothing further occurs. On the other hand, when D inserts an instrument into the air-space of the building he certainly does trespass; the instrument can readily be regarded as an extension of his person,[34] and if by the instrument so inserted he commits or attempts to commit one of the specified offences without intrusion of his own body, he has made as effective and substantial an entry as he intends, and it will be proper to convict him of burglary. But should the hooked object, by which D proposed to steal, or the gun, with which he seeks to cause grievous bodily harm, enter only slightly and not far enough for the ulterior purpose to be effected, the case would again, it is submitted, be adequately treated as attempted burglary.

Buildings and parts of buildings

4-17   "The imperfection of human language renders it not only difficult, but absolutely impossible, to define the word 'building' with any approach to accuracy. One may say of this or that structure, this or that is not a building; but no general definition can be given . . . "[35]

The Act attempts no definition; nor need we. There must be a structure capable of being entered; it must presumably be a fairly permanent affair[36]; and further than this it is probably not safe to go. Difficulty will occur infrequently, but eventually the courts will no doubt have to decide whether a kiosk is a building; or a potting-shed; or a bandstand; and so on.[37] There is little point in trying to anticipate their decisions. Nor would it be wise to base any predictions upon decisions given on various structures under the numerous statutes in which the word "building" is used, for what is denoted by a word of this kind in a particular statute depends so much on the subject and purpose of the legislation.

The word "building" and the distinction taken by the Act between

---

[33] Above, § 4–14.
[34] It is submitted that this consideration, if any be needed, is sufficient to distinguish the case of the hand-held instrument from that of the projected missile. *Cf.* Smith, *Theft,* para. 334.
[35] *Per* Byles J. in *Stevens* v. *Gourley* (1859) 7 C.B. (N.S.) 99 at p. 112.
[36] It is clear that a tent is not a building. The Committee were against giving tent-dwellers the protection of the law of burglary on the not very satisfying ground that "a tent seems too open a structure to be naturally regarded as the subject of burglary": *Eighth Report,* para.78.
[37] A large freezer container standing in a farmyard, without foundations, has been ruled to be a "building" : *B. and S* v. *Leathley* [1979] Crim. L.R. 314 (Crown Court appeal).

buildings and parts of buildings give rise to some tantalising problems.[38] In considering the illustrations and explanations that follow, it must be remembered that burglary is committed if D intends to commit one of a number of offences either (a) in a *building* that he enters as a trespasser, or (b) in part of a building, that *part* being entered by him as a trespasser.

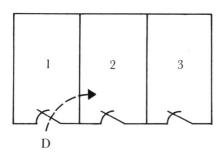

4–18

Premises 1, 2 and 3 are contiguous. If D enters 1, intending to pass from it into 2 or 3, there to steal, he is guilty of burglary if 1 and 2 or (as the case may be) 1, 2 and 3 constitute one "building."[39] This must depend on detailed facts as to structure and, perhaps, occupancy. A block of offices is surely one building. A row of terraced houses almost as surely is not; but it is possible to conceive of doubtful cases, such as that in which one large building has been converted into a row of residences with a common roof.

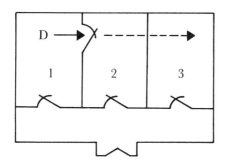

4–19

Here is a block of flats. D is lawfully in 1. He enters 2, intending to pass from it into 3 and to steal in 3. Assuming that the block of flats is one "building," do 2 and 3 constitute one "part," so that D enters that part as a trespasser with intent to steal therein? It is thought not.[40] In such a case, the relevant component portions of the building are clearly distinguishable; in other cases the meaning of "part" may seem less clear.

---

[38] For a valuable and ingenious discussion, see Smith, *Theft*, paras. 345–353.

[39] He is also guilty of burglary if, when entering 1, he intends to do damage to 1 by damaging the wall between 1 and 2. I am indebted for this observation to Collins [1968] Crim.L.R. at pp. 643–644. A similar point affects the next illustration.

[40] *Contra*, it seems, Smith, *Theft*, paras. 349, 352, who argues that for the purpose of s. 9 a building has only two parts; that where D may lawfully go, and the remainder. *Sed quaere?* The reading is desirable but strained.

4-20

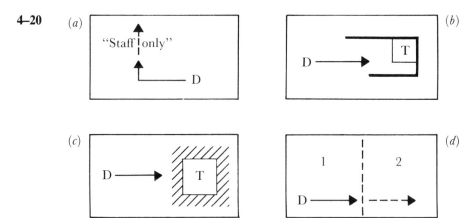

Each of these diagrams represents a floor of a shop. D is a customer, lawfully present in the shop.

   (a) Here the prohibition imposed by the notice and the area to which it relates are clear. That area is a "part" of the building which D enters as a trespasser.

   (b) A counter area is formed by three movable counters, with a till in one corner. D moves into the counter area in order to steal from the till. The jury are entitled to find that the area is a "part" of the building which members of the public are, to D's knowledge, impliedly prohibited from entering.[41] It seems that the area may be a "part" for this purpose although its boundaries cannot be exactly defined.

   (c) There is "a single table" (with, say, a till on it) "in the middle of the store, which it would be difficult for any jury to find properly was a part of the building in which the licensor prohibited customers from moving."[42] A customer is not plainly prohibited from standing right by the table. So the dictum perhaps concerns the difficulty of identifying a prohibition rather than the question whether the ill-defined area round the table could constitute a "part."

   (d) D has the licence that all customers have in a shop to move from counter to counter. He has lawfully entered the shop and bought something from counter 1. He now moves to counter 2, intending to steal at it. If in doing so he is entering a different "part" of the shop, he may be guilty of burglary, for entry for a purpose other than that for which a licence to enter is granted is a trespassory entry.[43] But it does not seem likely that the courts will be hasty to divide buildings artificially into "parts" in the way that would be necessary to make a case of burglary out of the situation presented here.

[41] *Walkington* [1979] 1 W.L.R. 1169; [1979] 2 All E.R. 716.
[42] *Ibid.* at pp. 1175–1176 and p. 721 respectively.
[43] See above, § 4–07.

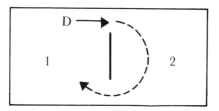

1 and 2 are distinct "parts" of a building. D is lawfully in 1 as a customer, guest, etc. He trespasses in 2 but commits no offence there. Later he comes back into 1, intending to steal therein. When he re-emerges into 1, does he enter that part as a trespasser? Probably he does. Although originally he lawfully entered the *Building* and has not yet left it, his licence to enter even part 1 is limited to permitted purposes. He now re-enters that *part* for another purpose and is to be regarded as trespassing when he does so.[43]

Inhabited vehicles and vessels

An inhabited vehicle or vessel, whether or not "the person having a habitation in it" is there at the time of the offence, is given the same protection as a building by section 9(3). Moreover, the law of burglary applies as between the parts of, *e.g.* an ocean liner as it does between the parts of a building.

Clearly a person ordinarily living in, or for the time being spending a holiday in, a caravan or a house-boat has a habitation in it; and the subsection does not cease to apply because he goes away for a few hours or days. It is not, however, so clear, for instance, whether during the winter a caravan left fully equipped on a caravan site for the purpose of occasional visits during the summer is an "inhabited vehicle" within the meaning of the subsection. It is tentatively suggested that it is not; that the phrases "inhabited" and "having a habitation in it" should be understood as referring to active or regular residential use in the period in which the alleged burglary occurs; and that in each case it must be a question of degree whether P currently has a habitation in the vehicle or vessel (whether it is *then* "inhabited"). It is easy to see the force of a contrary argument according to which, if the primary use of the vehicle or vessel is residential, one has a habitation in it so long as it is available (and equipped?) for use as an occasional home, no matter how long the gaps between visits. But this argument seems to give insufficient force to the word "inhabited." The language of the subsection is lamentably imprecise.

Nor is it clear to what use one must put a vehicle or vessel for it to be inhabited. Its mere casual use for sleep on an isolated occasion is presumably not enough. On the other hand, must it serve as a self-sufficient home? At first sight one would suppose not; but if not, a vehicle fitted out for sleeping and for no other non-vehicular purpose might be "inhabited" and within the protection of the law of burglary when its tourist occupants are taking a meal elsewhere. There seems little need for such special protection.

Two modes of burglary: entry with intent; offence after entry

4–23   It must be proved *either* that D intended when he entered the building or part to commit one of the offences mentioned in section 9(2) (s. 9(1)(*a*)), *or* that after entry he actually stole or inflicted grievous bodily harm on any person or attempted to do either (s. 9(1)(*b*)). On the one hand, the only justification for the alternative provided by section 9(1)(*b*) is that it meets the case where the relevant guilty intention at the time of entry cannot be proved; there is no wider ground for making an offence more serious merely because it is committed by a trespasser.[44] On the other hand, limbs (*a*) and (*b*) of section 9(1) create distinct offences of burglary. The charge or indictment must clearly specify which mode of burglary is alleged; and if only one mode is alleged, a conviction cannot be sustained upon proof only of the other.[45]

Where the ulterior offence in question is theft, inflicting grievous bodily harm or rape, it must be proved that that offence was intended to be committed, or was committed or attempted, in the very building that D entered as a trespasser, or, as the case may be, in the very part that he entered as a trespasser, and not elsewhere. Where D intends to do unlawful damage, the damage must be intended to the building or to something therein, but here there is no limitation to the part trespassed in if D's presence in the building itself was lawful.[46]

The specified offences

4–24   Four offences are mentioned in section 9(2). The first two, and attempts to commit them, appear also, in substance, in section 9(1)(*b*). The four offences are those—

(i) *"of stealing anything in the building or part of a building in question"* There can be no intent to steal unless the accused would be guilty of theft if the intended appropriation took place. So, for example, his belief that he has a right to deprive of the property the person to whom it belongs will exclude burglary as it will exclude theft.[47] Again, theft depends upon an appropriation of "property"; and as electricity is not "property," burglary is not committed by entering a building as a trespasser and abstracting electricity therein (or entering with intent to do so).[48]

---

[44] Paragraphs (*a*) and (*b*) of s. 9(1) are not, of course, mutually exclusive: *Taylor* [1979] Crim. L.R. 649. So in practice the existence of s. 9(1)(*b*) enables the normal case of entry (with intent) plus theft to be charged as a single offence, instead of as two offences under s.9 (1)(*a*) and s. 1. Paradoxically, therefore, s. 9(1)(*b*), justified by the exceptional (and probably bogus) defence, "I did not at the time of entering intend to steal; prove that I did," is used for the vast majority of burglaries.

[45] *Hollis* [1971] Crim. L.R. 525. The Criminal Law Act 1967, s. 6(3) (see above, § 1–08), does not help. A charge of entry as a trespasser and theft after entry does not imply entry with intent to steal; and similarly with the converse case.

[46] See the precise terms of s. 9 (1)(*b*), (2).

[47] See above, § 2–81.

[48] *Low* v. *Blease* [1975] Crim.L.R. 513.

A charge under section 9(1)(*a*) of entering a building or part of a   **4–25**
building as a trespasser "with intent to steal therein," without reference to
particular property, is permissible.[49] On such a charge it is not necessary to
prove either that D entered with intent to steal any specific thing,[50] or that
anything, or anything such as he was seeking, was present in the building or
part of a building in question.[51] "An intention to steal can exist even
though, unknown to the accused, there is nothing to steal . . . ,"[52] and
even though his only intention is to steal anything that he might find worth
stealing.[53] It follows that one who attempts to enter a building with such an
intention can be convicted of attempted burglary.[54]

(ii) "*of inflicting on any person therein any grievous bodily harm*"[55]   **4–26**
A distinction must be drawn between entry with intent and the infliction of
the harm after entry. It is submitted that a person charged with entering
with intent to commit an offence under this head must be proved to have
had in mind the infliction of, specifically, *grievous* bodily harm.[56] But the
Act is obscure as to the *mens rea* required for burglary committed by
entering and actually inflicting grievous bodily harm. Section 9(1)(*b*) does
not in terms require the commission of any *offence*,[57] and on a literal
reading a trespasser could commit burglary by accident. On principle,
however, *mens rea* should be—and presumably will be—required, in the
form of intention or recklessness as to the kind of harm done.[58] But so long
as grievous bodily harm is in fact inflicted, the fact that the trespasser
foresaw that his act might cause bodily harm even "of a minor character"
would appear to be enough, for such foresight satisfies the requirement of
malice for the purpose of the offence of maliciously inflicting grievous
bodily harm under section 20 of the Offences against the Person Act
1861.[59] Thus: D trespasses in P's premises; P uses reasonable force to eject
him; D resists P's force by a blow that D realises may cause a slight wound;
in fact the blow unexpectedly causes severe injury; D is guilty of burglary.

(iii) "*of raping any woman therein*"   **4–27**
The offence of rape is defined by section 1(1) of the Sexual Offences
(Amendment) Act 1976. For a conviction of burglary it is sufficient if, at

---

[49] *Attorney-General's References (Nos. 1 and 2 of 1979)* [1980] Q.B. 180, approving the
indictment in *Walkington* [1979] 1 W.L.R. 1169; [1979] 2 All E.R. 716.
[50] *Attorney-General's References,* above.
[51] *Walkington,* above; *Attorney-General's References,* above.
[52] *Per* Lord Scarman in *D.P.P.* v. *Nock* [1978] A.C. 979 at p. 1000; *Attorney-General's
References,* above, at p. 194.
[53] These obvious propositions needed to be established because a doctrine to the contrary was
in vogue, based on an unsatisfactory dictum in *Husseyn* (1977) 67 Cr.App.R. 131, on
attempted theft. Crown Court rulings in *Bozickovic* [1978] Crim.L.R. 686, and *Greenhoff*
[1979] Crim.L.R. 108, justified the impression that the law had for a time "taken leave of
its senses": *per* Geoffrey Lane L.J. in *Walkington,* above, at p. 1179 and p. 724
respectively.
[54] This was the specific point in the second of the *Attorney-General's References,* above.
[55] Grievous bodily harm is "really serious bodily harm": *Metharam* (1961) 45 Cr.App. 304.
[56] The point is even clearer in the case of an entry followed by an alleged *attempt*.
[57] The drafting (the result of an amendment) is defective: "having entered . . . as a trespasser
he . . . inflicts . . . any grievous bodily harm."
[58] That is, harm to the person: see *Cunningham* [1957] 2 Q.B. 396.
[59] *Mowatt* [1968] 1 Q.B. 421.

the time of entering the building or, for example, P's room, as a trespasser, D intends to have intercourse with P whether she consents or not.[60] If in the event she consents, or D believes that she does, no rape or attempted rape is committed, but liability for the burglary would strictly be unaffected.[61]

(iv) *"of doing unlawful damage to the building or anything therein"*
The question will be whether what D intended would have been an offence under section 1 of the Criminal Damage Act 1971. Section 5 of that Act provides a special defence of "lawful excuse" and expressly preserves general defences.

3. AGGRAVATED BURGLARY

Definition

4–28   Burglary is the only offence under the Act for which a higher maximum penalty is provided when the offence is committed in aggravating circumstances.

A person commits aggravated burglary if he "commits any burglary and at the time has with him any firearm or imitation firearm, any weapon of offence, or any explosive" (s. 10(1)), and this offence is punishable on conviction on indictment with imprisonment for life (s. 10(2)). It is not triable summarily.[62] The committee regarded the offence as comparable with robbery, which also carries life imprisonment.[63]

The terms "firearm," "imitation firearm," "weapon of offence" and "explosive" are defined or partially defined in section 10 (1).[64] Two of them need discussion here. So does the phrase "at the time has with him."

Firearm

4–29   Apart from saying that " 'firearm' includes an airgun or air pistol," the Act does not define this term. It is extensively defined in the Firearms Act 1968 for purposes of that Act[65]; but that definition does not apply for purposes of the present section.[66] Where it is doubtful whether an article carried by a burglar was a firearm it will often fall within the section in any event as a "weapon of offence."

Weapon of offence

4–30   This means

> "any article made or adapted for use of causing injury to or incapacitating a person, or intended by the person having it with him for such use."

---

[60] The contrary was not suggested in *Collins* [1973] 1 Q.B. 100, where the point was not available for decision. (The point can, of course, be generalised: for instance, an intention, if P will not make a loan, to take his money willy-nilly will be sufficient intention to steal.)

[61] *Collins (Christopher)* [1976] Crim.L.R. 249. (This case has to be read in the light of *D.P.P. v. Humphrys* [1977] A.C.1, on issue estoppel.)

[62] Magistrates' Courts Act 1980, Sched. 1, para. 28(*a*).

[63] *Eighth Report,* para. 80.

[64] See text of s. 10(1) in Appendix 1.

[65] Firearms Act 1968, s. 57(1), read with s. 5(2).

[66] *Cf. Seamark* v. *Prouse* [1980] 1 W.L.R. 698; [1980] 3 All E.R. 26.

This wording is borrowed almost verbatim from the definition of "offensive weapon" for the purpose of the Prevention of Crime Act 1953, which penalises the possession of an offensive weapon in a public place without lawful authority or reasonable excuse.[67] The reference to incapacitation is not in the 1953 definition. It covers articles "such as cords for tying up, gags or pepper."[68] Secondly, the 1953 definition limits the intended use of the weapon to use by the person having it with him, whereas under the present Act the intended use may be use by an accomplice.

It was held in *Williamson*[69] (under the Prevention of Crime Act 1953) **4–31** that whether an article is an offensive weapon is a question of fact for the jury to decide. The trial judge in that case was wrong in ruling that the sheath knife involved was as a matter of law an offensive weapon. The Court of Appeal were certainly justified in pointing out that it would be impossible for the court to "determine in advance" by an appellate ruling "the nature of every knife which may be in a sheath."[70] Yet the proposition that the question whether the article is an offensive weapon is one for the jury is subject to two qualifications. The first is that there may be some cases (although they "must be rare") where "it is possible to say that there is no evidence to the contrary"—meaning, presumably, that the only sensible answer is affirmative; and then the judge may so direct.[71] The second is that relevant authorities yield a number of subsidiary propositions of law which, as they may chance to be relevant, the judge should direct the jury to apply in reaching their decision. The effect of these authorities is suggested in the following paragraphs.

An article is *"made . . . for use for causing injury"* if it was *originally* **4–32** made for such use.[72] It is clear that a cosh is such an article but that a hammer is not; a bayonet obviously is, but a cut-throat razor or carving knife is not.[73]

An article is "adapted for use for causing injury" if it has been *altered* so as to be apt for such use.[74] Whether it must be shown that it was altered *for the purpose* of making it so apt is not clear. It is submitted that in some cases it must. If it were otherwise one in possession of a jagged-edge half of an accidentally broken bottle might be caught by section 10 without proof of his intent to use it to cause injury. The test should be a double one: Is such an article in its altered state ordinarily used for causing injury?[75] If

[67] Prevention of Crime Act 1953, s. 1(1); definition in s. 1(4).
[68] *Eighth Report,* p. 128 (Notes on draft Bill).
[69] (1977) 67 Cr.App. R. 35.
[70] *Ibid.* at p. 39.
[71] *Ibid.* at pp. 38–39. It has been judicially declared that a cosh, a knuckle-duster and a revolver are offensive weapons *per se* (see § 4–32): *Petrie* [1961] 1 W.L.R. 358 at p. 361; [1961] 1 All E.R. 466 at p. 468.
[72] *Cf. Hubbard* v. *Messenger* [1938] 1 K.B. 300 at p. 307 ("constructed or adapted for use for the conveyance of goods").
[73] For the razor, see *Petrie,* above; for the carving knife, *Rapier* (1979) 70 Cr.App. R. 17.
[74] *Cf. Hubbard* v. *Messenger,* above, and many other cases under the Road Traffic and Vehicles (Excise) Acts.
[75] *Cf.Flower Freight Co. Ltd.* v. *Hammond* [1963] 1 Q.B. 275.

not, was it altered for the purpose of such use? An affirmative answer to the latter question will often be a simple inference from the nature of the alteration.

If an article is "made or adapted for use for causing injury or incapacitating a person"—if it is, as it is commonly put, "offensive *per se*"—it need not be proved that the burglar intended it for such use.[76]

4–33   Many things, however, that are not "made or adapted" to injure or incapacitate can be put to such use by one so minded: a razor, a poker or a rope, for instance. If a burglar has such a thing with him there must be affirmative proof that he intended it for such use.[77]

The judge should normally avoid reference in his direction to an intention to use the article to frighten or intimidate; but in a rare case the evidence may justify a finding that the intention was to injure by shock.[78]

4–34   D may commit burglary, having with him an article such as a crow-bar or a torch—that is, an article not "offensive *per se*." If he is suprised by the occupier and uses the article to cause the occupier injury, he will not necessarily be guilty of aggravated burglary. The article will be a weapon of offence only if it was "intended by the person having it with him for [use for causing injury . . .]." If at the time he entered the building D regarded the article as a potential weapon the definition will be satisfied (a conditional intention will plainly be enough); but this would probably be difficult to prove. If not, the article may not qualify as a weapon of offence. It is now well established that, for the purpose of the corresponding definition in the Prevention of Crime Act 1953, the intention to use the article to cause injury must be "formed before the actual occasion to use violence has arisen"[79] and not *"ad hoc."*[80] The same principle should apply in the present context, and not simply because the Theft Act definition is identical in relevant respects. The mischief at which the Prevention of Crime Act is aimed is the carrying of weapons,[81] not their use. Similarly, it may be said, aggravated burglary consists, not in injuring or incapacitating a person in the building that is burgled, but in entering the building with a weapon available for that purpose (or, if an argument offered below[82] is not acceptable, being armed with a weapon while in the building).

---

[76] *Davis* v. *Alexander* (1970) 54 Cr.App.R. 398.
[77] *Petrie,* above.
[78] *Rapier* (1979) 70 Cr.App. R. 17, purporting to apply *Edmonds* [1963] 2 Q.B. 142. The relevant dictum in *Edmonds* (at p. 151) suggests that an intention to frighten may be sufficient where "the frightening [is] . . . of a sort which is capable of producing injury through the operation of shock." But D's *intention* to injure through shock must be required, and not simply the fact that the frightening use of the article is "capable" of causing, or even likely to cause, such injury (see Criminal Justice Act 1967, s. 8).
[79] *Ohlson* v. *Hylton* [1975] 1 W.L.R. 724; [1975] 2 All E.R. 490 (*per* Lord Widgery C.J. at pp. 729, 497 respectively).
[80] *Humphreys* [1977] Crim.L.R. 225.
[81] *Bates* v. *Bulman* [1979] 1 W.L.R. 1190; [1979] 3 All E.R. 170.
[82] § 4–36.

"Has with him"

It appears that, in order that a burglar may be said to have a firearm or **4-35**
weapon of offence "with him" within the meaning of section 10(1) there
must be "a very close physical link" between him and the article and "a
degree of immediate control" over it by him.[83] This test is surely satisfied
(so that D is guilty of aggravated burglary as a principal offender) not only
when D himself has custody of the article but also when, as he anticipates,
it is carried into the building by a companion.[84] The phrase "has with him"
can properly mean only "knowingly has with him."[85] So a burglar who is
ignorant that he has a firearm in his pocket is not guilty of the aggravated
offence. The point is more likely to arise when two or more persons
commit burglary together and one of them has physical possession of an
article within s. 10(1) Then only such of them as know of the article can be
guilty of aggravated burglary.[86] In one case, indeed, something more than
knowledge of the article's presence is necessary. This is the case in which
the article (not being a firearm, imitation firearm or explosive) is a
"weapon of offence" only because D1 intends to use it for causing injury.
For D2 then to be guilty of aggravated burglary he must know of D1's
intention or have that intention himself.

"At the time has with him"

Whether a person is guilty of aggravated burglary depends on whether **4-36**
he has with him a weapon or other article within section 10 "at the time" he
commits burglary. If he is so armed at the time he enters as a trespasser, he
can be convicted of the aggravated offence either (i) on a count alleging
entry with intent or (ii) on a count alleging theft after entry. In case (ii) D
may have entered with intent to steal; but his conviction under section 10
on the basis of entry plus theft will have the same justification as a
conviction under section 9(1)(b): the theft may be easier to prove than the
original intention to commit it.[87] A like solution, however, is not so clearly
acceptable when D, having entered with intent to steal but *without* a
weapon, arms himself with a heavy candlestick when inside and then steals.
Although, once again, he falls within both limb (a) and limb (b) of section
9(1), it is hardly to be supposed that he has committed two offences of
burglary. The right to charge under limb (a) or limb (b) (or under both in
the alternative) is best seen as a procedural amenity and not as involving
the consequence that D commits a fresh burglary when, armed with the
candlestick, he steals. Another way of achieving a conviction of aggravated
burglary in the case of the after-acquired candlestick is to treat burglary as
an offence which continues for as long as D is in the building as a

---

[83] *Kelt* [1977] 1 W.L.R. 1365 at p. 1369; [1977] 3 All E.R. 1099 at p. 1102 (decided under the
Firearms Act 1968, s. 18(1)).
[84] So ruled in *Jones* [1979] C.L.Y. 411 (Judge Solomon).
[85] *Cf. Cugullère* [1961] 1 W.L.R. 858; [1961] 2 All E.R. 343 (decided under the Prevention of
Crime Act 1953, s. 1(1)). See also, as to the mental element involved in "possession,"
Warner v. *Metropolitan Police Commissioner* [1969] A.C. 256.
[86] *Cf. Webley* v. *Webley* [1967] Crim.L.R. 300.
[87] See above, § 4–23.
[88] Even in the light of *Hollis* [1971] Crim.L.R. 525; above, § 4–23.

trespasser; but this does not seem warranted by the terms of section 9. The preferable solution, it is submitted, is to hold section 10 to be satisfied only (i) where a limb (*a*) burglary is alleged and D had the weapon at the time of entry, or (ii) where a limb (*b*) burglary is alleged and he had the weapon both at the time of entry and at the time of the further offence.

CHAPTER 5

OFFENCES OF TAKING NOT AMOUNTING TO THEFT

EACH of the two offences to be considered in this chapter is designed to   **5–01**
deal with a particular kind of mischief that is felt to require a special
sanction by way of exception to the general rule that an unauthorised
taking of property without an intention of permanently depriving of it the
person to whom it belongs is not a criminal offence. As to the mischief
constituted by the taking of motor vehicles and other conveyances and the
need for an exceptional provision in relation to them there is no doubt.
Section 12 in fact re-enacts, in an amended and extended form, an offence
first created in 1930. The need for a special offence to deal with the
removal of articles on display to the public is more controversial.

It will, of course, be understood that a person guilty of either of the
offences about to be discussed may in fact be guilty of the full offence of
theft. This is particularly likely in the case of an offence under section 11;
most people who remove valuable articles from art galleries, museums and
stately homes intend to deprive their owners permanently of them and can
pretend to no right to do so. What sections 11 and 12 do is to provide for
two classes of case: those (common enough in relation to conveyances)
where there is in fact no intention of permanently depriving; and those in
which that intention, though it may well have existed, cannot be proved.

We shall notice in its proper place the provision that a person charged on
indictment with theft may be convicted of an offence under section 12(1)
(normally, an offence of taking a conveyance other than a pedal cycle
without lawful authority). There is no corresponding provision for a
conviction, on a charge of theft, of an offence under section 11. So where
an article has been removed from a place within section 11 and there is any
doubt about the offender's intention or any doubt about proving it, it will
often be expedient to include in the indictment a count charging an offence
under section 11.

1.   REMOVAL OF AN ARTICLE FROM A PLACE OPEN TO THE PUBLIC

Introduction[1]
The clause that eventually became section 11 acquired the popular name   **5–02**
"the Goya clause" while the Bill was before Parliament. This is because
the need for the clause was suggested in particular by the notorious
removal of Goya's portrait of the Duke of Wellington from the National
Gallery. The portrait was returned after four years. Despite evidence that
he had tried to make the Gallery buy the portrait back by paying a large
sum to charity (which was certainly evidence that at the time he took it he
intended to deprive the Gallery permanently, and would now be evidence

---

[1] See *Eighth Report*, para. 57 (ii).

of the same intention for the purposes of theft[2]), the taker was acquitted of
larceny of the portrait. There had been some other cases in recent years of
the temporary removal of articles from public buildings—among them the
removal of the Stone of Scone from Westminster Abbey. Art galleries,
cathedrals and other places housing famous treasures are no doubt
particularly vulnerable to temporary deprivation at the hands of eccentrics,
exhibitionists and people with causes that can be brought to the public
notice by removal of public property.

On balance, having considered arguments for and against the creation of
a new offence, the Committee decided that there should be special
provision for the protection of articles kept in places open to the public.
But they included no such provision in the draft Bill, preferring to
recommend the consideration of special legislation for the purpose. A first
version of "the Goya clause" nevertheless appeared in the Bill presented
to Parliament; and section 11 represents that clause in a much revised
form.

The offence under section 11

5–03   Section 11 renders it an offence in certain circumstances to remove an
article from a place to which the public have access. The offence is
punishable on conviction on indictment with imprisonment for five years
(subs. (4)).

The section is drafted with a complexity disproportionate to the
importance of the offence. The reader is referred to the text of the section
in Appendix 1. What follows here is a statement of the conditions of the
offence, with such commentary or explanation as seems to be required.

The offence under section 11 is committed if, and only if, the following
conditions are satisfied[3]:

5–04   (i) There must be *a building to which the public have access.*
We shall see (in (iv), below) that the section protects articles in the
grounds of a building within the section as well as in the building itself. But
the fact that the public have access to the grounds of a house in order to see
its gardens and model railway is not enough to bring the section into
operation if the public are not also admitted to the building itself for the
purpose mentioned in (ii), below.

> "It is immaterial . . . that the public's access to a building is limited
> to a particular period or particular occasion" (subs. (2)).

It may be that a "building" must have a roof. If so, an exhibition staged
in the ruins of Tintern Abbey or Coventry Cathedral would not be
protected.

5–05   (ii) The public must have access to the building *in order to view the
building or part of it, or a collection or part of a collection housed in it,*

---

[2] s. 6(1), discussed above, § 2–74.
[3] All conditions, and qualifications of them, stated in the following account are justified,
unless otherwise stated, by subs.(1).

including a collection or part of a collection "got together for a temporary purpose."

A trial judge has ruled[4] that the question whether the public have access "in order to view" depends on the purpose of the occupier in giving access rather than on that for which people come in. This is no doubt true; but the principle can only be sensibly applied if the known motives of visitors are allowed to affect the description of the occupier's purposes. If a vicar knows (as surely he must) that many visitors to his church will come in just to look round, he must be construed, it is submitted, as giving access to the public "in order to view," although the primary reason for leaving the church door open is to enable people to enter for devotional purposes.

(iii) If the public have access to a building in order to view a collection **5–06** rather than the building, the *collection* must be one *not "made or exhibited for the purpose of effecting sales or other commercial dealings."*

Where an artist's work is collected and put on show for sale, the application of the section to the collection may depend upon the nature of the building in which the collection is to be viewed. If the works are shown in a shop, there is little doubt that the collection must be regarded as made "for the purpose of effecting sales" even though an interested but impecunious public are welcome to view the collection with no idea of buying. On the other hand, if the collection is exhibited in a building which happens itself to be on show to the public or which contains some other collection which the public come to view and which is not excluded from the section by the motive of sale, the works exposed for sale fall within the section as it were parasitically. A familiar intermediate case is that of the educational institution which puts on a short-term exhibition of the work of a local artist. The public are invited to view the collection for their own pleasure; but the works are priced and the artist hopes to sell them as a result of the public's visits. From one point of view this is a collection "made or exhibited for the purpose of effecting sales"; and it may be safer to treat this contributory purpose as sufficient to prevent the section from applying.

(iv) There must be *a removal of the whole or part of an article from the* **5–07** *building or its grounds.*

If the article is in the building the offence will be complete if it is removed from the building and, for example, hidden in the grounds. But a removal of an article from one part of the building to another or from one part of the grounds to another is not enough.

The word "grounds" is pleasantly untechnical. It could in an exceptional case cause difficulty. D is a gardener employed in the park of a great house to which the public have access, and he lives in a cottage within the park. He removes an article displayed outside the house and places it in the garden of his cottage, or in the cottage itself. Liability here is not as clear as

---

[4] *Barr* [1978] Crim. L.R. 244 (vicar's evidence that his church was open only for devotional purposes and that the cross and ewer taken were displayed simply as aids to devotion; held, no case to answer).

it ought to be. It might not be improper to say that the gardener lives "in a cottage in the grounds of the great house," and that the article has therefore not been removed from the grounds.

5–08   (v) The *article* removed must be one *displayed or kept for display to the public in the building* (or in the part of it that the public come to view) *or in its grounds.*

The point, of course, is that the private belongings of the family who live in the great house, the overcoats and umbrellas of visitors to the museum, the bibles and hymn-books lying around the church, are not accorded special protection against unlawful "borrowing" merely because they happen to be within a building to which the section applies. It seems that an article is "displayed . . . to the public" only if the purpose, or one of the purposes, of its display is that it may be seen by those who are admitted to view the building or a collection housed in it—only if it is, in effect, "exhibited."[5]

An article within the protected class need not at the time of removal be actually on show. It is enough if it is "kept for display"; so an offence is committed by removing from a workshop within an art gallery an old master in the process of being cleaned but intended for exhibition in the gallery.

5–09   (vi) *The removal must in some cases be on a day when the public have access to the building* (subs. (2)), but in most cases the time of removal is immaterial.

This condition as to the time of removal applies when the thing removed is not in the building or grounds as part of a collection intended for permanent exhibition to the public and is not on loan for exhibition with such a collection. The distinction intended is that between "a place, such as the National Gallery, which conducts a permanent exhibition . . . " and "a place such as a stately home which is open only occasionally to the public. . . . "[6] The purpose of making this distinction is to limit an anomaly. A servant or trespasser in an ordinary home not opened to the public view never commits an offence if he temporarily removes an article from it, however precious or priceless the article. By contrast, a servant or trespasser in a stately home sometimes open to the public may commit an offence if he takes something displayed to the public; yet his taking of the article may be quite unconnected with the fact that the public are granted access to the house—that is to say, it may not be an abuse of the privilege that that access constitutes, whereas the abuse of that privilege is the mischief intended to be penalised by the section. This anomaly is to some extent limited by providing, in effect, that if the thing removed is not on permanent exhibition it must be removed on a day when the public have access to it or there will be no offence.

In *Durkin*[7] D removed from an art gallery owned by a local authority a

[5] *Barr,* above.
[6] H.C. Standing Committee H, June 25, 1968: Official Report, col. 56.
[7] [1973] Q.B. 786.

painting forming part of the authority's permanent collection. This painting, like other works in the collection, was not continuously on display; different parts of the collection were exhibited at different times. The painting nevertheless formed part of "a collection intended for permanent exhibition to the public" since the collection was intended to be permanently available for such exhibition, that intention being sufficiently manifested by the authority's settled practice of periodically displaying this and other pictures in the gallery. D was guilty of an offence under section 11(1), although he had taken the painting on a Sunday, when the gallery was closed.

(vii) The removal must be *without lawful authority*.   **5–10**
(viii) The remover must act *without the belief that he has lawful authority for the removal or that he would have it if the person entitled to give it knew of the removal and the circumstances of it* (subs. (3)).
This condition corresponds to the requirement of dishonesty in the offence of theft as that requirement is partially defined in section 2(1)(*a*) and (*b*).[8]

2. TAKING A CONVEYANCE WITHOUT AUTHORITY

Introduction
The unauthorised use of vehicles has long been a social mischief   **5–11**
requiring penal sanctions. The conduct to be controlled may vary in gravity between a thoughtless adolescent joy-riding prank and the use of a handy car for a serious criminal purpose. At either extreme the temporary loss of the vehicle can seriously inconvenience its owner, while the public are in danger from the uninsured use of the vehicle by an often reckless or immature driver. In many cases the police may rightly suspect the taking of a vehicle to be theft but be unable to prove the necessary intention of permanently depriving the owner. In such cases the provable wrong is better described as an unauthorised taking of the vehicle than as a theft of the petrol consumed by its use, which was all that could be charged before the taking of the vehicle was made an offence in itself.
The taking and driving away of a motor vehicle has therefore been an offence since 1930. This offence in an amended form is now extended to all "conveyances." The main purpose of the extension is to provide for yachts, boats and pedal cycles.[9] Section 12 deals separately with conveyances other than pedal cycles and with pedal cycles alone.

Taking a conveyance other than a pedal cycle
Section 12(1) contains what may conveniently be called primary and   **5–12**
secondary offences:

(i) The primary offence is that of taking a conveyance for one's own or another's use without having the consent of the owner or other lawful authority.

[8] Discussed above, §§ 2–81 to 2–83. Compare s. 12(6), the remarks on which at § 5–23, below, apply equally to s. 11(3).
[9] *Eighth Report*, para.83.

(ii) The secondary offence is committed by one who, knowing that a conveyance has been taken without authority, drives it or allows himself to be carried in or on it.

Both offences are punishable with three years' imprisonment on conviction on indictment (subs.(2)).[10]

Offences under subsection (1) and attempts to commit them are deemed for all purposes to be "arrestable offences" (subs.(3)). The powers of arrest without warrant provided by the Criminal Law Act 1967, s. 2, therefore apply; and one who assists an offender by an act done with intent to impede his apprehension or prosecution may be convicted under section 4(1) of the same Act.

A person charged on indictment with theft may be convicted of an offence under section 12(1) (subs.(4)) or, it would seem, of an attempt to commit such an offence, by virtue of the Criminal Law Act 1967, s. 6(3) and (4).

The ingredients of the offences under section 12(1) will be considered under four heads.

(1) "Conveyance"

5–13   Section 12(1) does not apply to pedal cycles (subs. (5)) or to any conveyance constructed or adapted for use only under the control of a person not carried in or on it (subs. (7)(*a*)); but it applies to any other

> "conveyance constructed or adapted for the carriage of a person or persons whether by land, water or air . . . ,"

and the word "drive" is to be construed accordingly (subs. (7)(*a*)). It is clear that any vehicle, vessel or aircraft which, as originally constructed or by virtue of subsequent alteration,[11] makes physical provision for its "driver" to be carried in or on it is within the definition of "conveyance." If it were otherwise the section would not protect, for example, a goods van without a passenger seat.

A horse is not a "conveyance."[12] The section is "directed towards artefacts rather than towards animals."[13]

(2) The prohibited conduct

5–14   (i) The *primary offender* is he who "takes any conveyance for his own or another's use." The word "takes" will be satisfied by any movement

---

[10] An offence or an attempt to commit an offence under s.12 in respect of a motor vehicle may lead to a driving disqualification: Road Traffic Act 1972, s.93 and Sched.4, Pt.III.

[11] See cases decided on similar wording in the Road Traffic Act 1960, s.191(1) (now Road Traffic Act 1972, s.196(1)); *ibid*. Sched. 2, para.2 (now Road Traffic Regulation Act 1967, Sched.5, para.2); Vehicles (Excise) Act 1962, Sched.4, Pt.I, para.7 (now Vehicles (Excise) Act 1971, Sched.4, Pt.I, para.9): especially *French* v. *Champkin* [1920] 1 K.B. 76; *Hubbard* v. *Messenger* [1938] 1 K.B. 300; *Taylor* v. *Mead* [1961] 1 W.L.R. 435; *Flower Freight Co. Ltd.* v. *Hammond* [1963] 1 Q.B. 275.

[12] *Neal* v. *Gribble* (1978) 68 Cr.App.R. 9.

[13] *Ibid.* at p.11. See J. C. Smith at [1978] Crim..L.R. 501 on the failure of the law as drafted to deal with the mischief of riding animals without consent.

intentionally[14] caused (*e.g.* by pushing, by lifting or by releasing a hand-brake). But some movement there must be. It appears that a "taking" for the purposes of the section has two ingredients: (a) an assumption of possession or control, and (b) movement. The Court of Appeal in *Bogacki*[15] said that before a man can be convicted of the primary offence it must be shown

> "that there was an unauthorised taking of possession or control of the [conveyance] by him adverse to the rights of the true owner or person otherwise entitled to such possession or control, coupled with some movement, however small . . . of that [conveyance] following such unauthorised taking."

A person may "take" a conveyance within the meaning of this section **5–15** even though he already has custody of it as a servant or possession as a bailee. This was first revealed in *Wibberley*,[16] decided under the Road Traffic Act 1960, s. 217(1) (the predecessor of s. 12). In that case D was employed to drive a truck. At the end of his day's work he should have returned it to one of his employer's yards. Instead he drove it to his home and, later that evening, used it for his own purposes. His conviction of taking and driving away was upheld. He was in no better position than if he had returned the truck to the yard and later taken it from there without consent.[17] A stronger case than this is *McKnight* v. *Davies*,[18] in which, again, D's duty was to return his lorry to his employer's depot when he had completed his round of deliveries. Instead he drove to a public-house for a drink, drove around elsewhere for his own purposes, and parked the lorry for the night near his home. He returned it to the depot early the next morning. The Divisional Court held that an employed driver can be regarded as "taking" his vehicle

> "if in the course of his working day . . . he appropriates it to his own use in a manner which repudiates the rights of the true owner, and shows that he has assumed control of the vehicle for his own purposes."[19]

Applying such a test the court held that D "took the vehicle when he left the first public house."[20]

---

[14] *Blayney* v. *Knight* (1975) 60 Cr.App.R. 269 (movement caused by accidental pressure on accelerator; no "taking").
[15] [1973] Q.B. 832 at p. 837.
[16] [1966] 2 Q.B. 214.
[17] *Ibid.* at p.219. It seems that D's employer would not have complained if D had parked the truck outside his home until next morning.
[18] [1974] R.T.R. 4.
[19] *Ibid.* at p.8.
[20] *Ibid.* Thus the court avoided the unhappy conclusion that every driver who deviates from his route for the sake of a drink on his way back to base commits an offence under s. 12 unless he thinks that his employer would consent if he knew. More generally: "Not every brief, unauthorised diversion from his proper route . . . in the course of his working day will necessarily involve a 'taking' of the vehicle for his own use" (p.8).

5–16   In so deciding *McKnight* v. *Davies*, the Divisional Court rejected the pre-Act authority of *Mowe* v. *Perraton*[21] as being inconsistent with *Phipps and McGill*,[22] which the court preferred. The latter case was in one respect a stronger one still, for it involved not an employee with mere custody of a vehicle, who could be regarded as wrongfully assuming possession, but a person already in possession as bailee. On condition that he would be back by 9.30 p.m., D borrowed P's car at Dagenham in order to drive to Victoria Station. He did not return that night, but drove the car next day to Hastings. His conviction was upheld. The direction to the jury, that "as from the time he decided not to return the car and drove it off on his own business . . . , if he did not have [P's] permission, he took it and drove it away," was "perfectly proper and accurate" and "supported by . . . *Wibberley*."[23]

The word "takes" thus embraces the notion of entering upon an unauthorised use other than that for which D has custody or possession.[24] This is an extensive reading. Where a motor vehicle is concerned, the unauthorised use can often be prosecuted as an uninsured use; whether any other penal sanction is called for in a case where the vehicle has not been taken "without any reference to the owner"[25] is a matter on which opinions may vary.

5–17   The taking by D must be "for his own or another's use."[26] In *Bow*[27] the Court of Appeal accepted a submission that this involves "that the conveyance should have been used as a conveyance, *i.e.* . . . . as a means of transport."[28] So if D, indulging his sense of humour, pushes P's car on to a double yellow line or without boarding it releases its handbrake so that it runs away down a hill, the offence is not committed. But where, as in *Bow* itself,[29] D moves the conveyance "in a way which necessarily involves its use as a conveyance,"[30] it is immaterial that his motive in doing so is one to which that use is entirely subservient.

The asserted requirement of use "as a conveyance" casts doubt on the decision in *Pearce*.[31] In that case D took a dinghy, placed it on a trailer and towed it away. His conviction under section 12 was upheld. But the dinghy

---

[21] [1952] 1 All E.R. 423. This case had been somewhat painfully distinguished in *Wibberley*, above.
[22] (1970) 54 Cr.App.R. 301.
[23] *Ibid.* at p.304.
[24] For the conflict with the case of *Peart* [1970] 2 Q.B. 672, see below, § 5–22.
[25] See *Peart* [1970] 2 Q.B. 672, at p. 675; *cf. Mowe* v. *Perraton* [1952] 1 All E.R. 423 at p.424.
[26] This phrase is elaborately discussed by White, "Taking the Joy Out of Joy-Riding" [1980] Crim. L.R. 609.
[27] [1977] R.T.R. 6. A gamekeeper used his Land Rover as an obstruction to prevent D, a suspected poacher, from making an escape. D sat in the driving seat of the vehicle and ran the vehicle downhill by releasing the handbrake. His only purpose was to remove the obstruction. Held, a taking "for his own use."
[28] [1977] R.T.R. 6 at p.10.
[29] See n.27, above.
[30] [1977] R.T.R. 6 at p.11. This description of D's conduct in *Bow* is questioned by J. C. Smith [1977] Crim. L.R. at p.178.
[31] [1973] Crim.L.R. 321.

was not "used as a conveyance"; nor was such use necessarily in contemplation. If "stealing a ride" for a person or for goods is the whole mischief aimed at by the section, as *Bow* suggests,[32] *Pearce* must be regarded as wrongly decided. That view of the section, however, is probably too restrictive. The case of a boat "towed away to be used later" was certainly intended to be brought within its scope by the removal of the words "and drives away" during the passage of the Bill[33]—and rightly so. It is thought that the principles asserted in *Bow* will call for some modification and that the correctness of *Pearce* may yet be demonstrated.

Aiding and abetting this offence, like any other, requires full *mens rea*. **5–18** D must be found to have been knowingly a party to the taking of the conveyance (that is, its removal from its original position). His mere voluntary presence when E takes the conveyance is not in itself participation in the taking; nor does his subsequently allowing himself to be carried in the conveyance necessarily establish that participation.[34] To be guilty of aiding and abetting, D must, on general principles, either assist or encourage the taker in the commission of the offence.

(ii) The *secondary offender* is he who knows that the conveyance has **5–19** been taken without authority and "drives it or allows himself to be carried in or on it."

The word "drives" has been considered in many cases under the Road Traffic Acts, including cases under the present section's predecessors. Although the word has to be allowed a wide meaning, the alleged driver of a motor vehicle "must be in the driving seat, or in control of the steering wheel and . . . his activities are . . . not to be held to amount to driving unless they come within the ordinary meaning of that word."[35] A motor vehicle can be driven without starting the engine[36]; but it cannot be driven by merely pushing it while controlling the steering wheel with one hand from the outside.[37] A person in command of the steering wheel and brakes of a vehicle on tow is driving it.[38] If there is any doubt as to whether a person drove a conveyance for the purpose of section 12(1) he can normally be charged with having allowed himself to be carried in or on it. The word "drive" has to be understood as referring to appropriate modes of controlling conveyances generally, and not just those in relation to which the word is normally used.[39]

[32] [1977] R.T.R. 6 at p.10.
[33] H.L.Deb., Vol.291, col.106.
[34] *C. (a minor)* v. *Hume* [1979] Crim. L.R. 328 (where the secondary offence—see text following—could have been, but was not, charged).
[35] *MacDonagh* [1974] Q.B. 448 at p. 452, referring to *Roberts* [1965] 1 Q.B. 85 at p. 88. A merely accidental occurrence cannot be an act of driving: *Blayney* v. *Knight* (1975) 60 Cr.App.R. 269 (above, § 5–14).
[36] *Saycell* v. *Bool* [1948] 2 All E.R. 83; *Floyd* v. *Bush* [1953] 1 W.L.R. 242.
[37] *MacDonagh* [1974] Q.B. 448.
[38] *McQuaid* v. *Anderton* [1980] 3 All E.R. 540; *Caise* v. *Wright* [1981] R.T.R. 49.
[39] s. 12(7)(a) (where the reference to "drive" is rather obscurely expressed, and can be read as also restricting the meaning of the word to "control by a person in or on the conveyance").

5–20   A person does not "allow himself to be carried" in or on a conveyance merely by being present in or on it, even in anticipation of its being moved. There must be some actual movement.[40]

To commit the secondary offence D must know that the conveyance has been taken without authority. The taking may in fact have amounted to theft; and D may know this or may simply know that it has been taken without authority. In either case he is within the section.[41] If he boards the conveyance without knowledge and learns the truth while being carried, he cannot presumably be guilty of the offence unless he remains on board after he has had a realistic opportunity of disembarking; he must, knowing the truth, "allow" himself to be carried.

(3) *The absence of consent or other lawful authority*

5–21   The taking must be without the consent of the owner of the conveyance or other lawful authority. In the case of a conveyance on hire or hire purchase, "owner" means the hirer (see subs. (7)(*b*)), and the fact that the taker does not have the consent of the legal owner is immaterial.[42] The reference to other lawful authority will cover such cases as the removal of a vehicle under statutory power by the police[43] or by a local authority.[44]

The consent required to exclude the offence is a consent actually given, not simply the consent that, as it may later transpire, the owner would have given had he been asked.[45]

5–22   If the owner's consent to the taking of the conveyance is induced by a misrepresentation as to some "fundamental" fact, such as D's identity or the nature of the transaction, it is probable that the consent is vitiated by the fraud. The point was left open in *Peart*.[46] That case decided that deception as to some non-fundamental matter does not affect the consent thereby induced; so that where D deceived P as to the nature and purpose of the journey he proposed to take, it was held that P had consented to D's taking the car in question.

The principle of *Peart* seems to collide with that of *Phipps and McGill*.[47] In *Peart* D's original journey was quite different from that which P had permitted, but the "taking" effected by driving off on this journey was held to be with P's consent. In *Phipps and McGill* D's original journey was the one authorised; but when he embarked on a further journey not authorised by P, he "took" the car without consent. The moral of these cases is that if one proposes to deceive an owner as to the use one wishes to make of his

---

[40] *Miller* [1976] Crim. L.R. 147; *Diggin* (1980) 72 Cr.App.R. 204.
[41] *Tolley* v. *Giddings* [1964] 2 Q.B. 354.
[42] *Tolhurst and Woodhead* (1961) 106 S.J. 16.
[43] See Road Traffic Regulation Act 1967, s. 20, and regulations thereunder.
[44] See Refuse Disposal (Amenity) Act 1978, s. 3.
[45] *Ambler* [1979] R.T.R. 217. But see s. 12(6) (below, § 5–23) as to *belief* that owner would consent.
[46] [1970] 2 Q.B. 672.
[47] (1970) 54 Cr.App.R. 301; see above, § 5–16.

vehicle, it is safer to deceive him about the whole of that use than only to deceive him about part.[48] This cannot be better law than sense.

It seems that a consent given under duress would be no consent for the purposes of this section.[49]

(4) *The exception for honesty; the relevance of intoxication*

Section 12(6) expressly protects from liability anyone who acts in the belief either that he has lawful authority or that the owner, if he knew of the act and its circumstances, would consent. The subsection brings offences under the section into line in this respect with theft. D, it may be said, has acted honestly.[50]   5–23

Authority under a corresponding provision in the Criminal Damage Act 1971 indicates that D may rely on a positive belief within section 12(6) even if it is the result of self-induced intoxication.[51] On the other hand, it has been held that the primary offence is not one of "specific intent"; so conviction cannot be avoided by evidence that D was too drunk to form any intent and did not know he was taking a conveyance without authority or consent.[52] Although there *is* a distinction between ignorance of a fact (that the taking is without consent) and belief, more or less, to the contrary (that the owner would consent), the distinction does not justify the different results produced by the case law. Evidence of intoxication should always be admissible to negative knowledge of the relevant facts. It cannot be doubted that it is admissible in relation to the secondary offence, which expressly requires proof that D knew that the conveyance had been taken without authority.[53]

Taking a pedal cycle

It is a summary offence, punishable with a fine of £50, to take a pedal cycle for one's own or another's use or to ride a pedal cycle knowing it to have been taken without such authority (s. 12(5)). The exception for   5–24

---

[48] It is not suggested that any deception was in fact practised by the accused in *Phibbs and McGill*. Note that in *Peart* "no issue was left to [the jury] as to whether . . . there could have been a fresh taking . . . of this particular van at some time after it was originally driven away" ([1970] 2 Q.B. 672 at p. 675), and the conviction was quashed because of a misdirection on the only issue left to the jury, namely, whether there was at the outset an effective consent to the taking of the van. It seems to be suggested that on a direction canvassing "a fresh taking" a conviction might have been proper. But if there was evidence of only one journey, it is difficult to see at what point a new "taking" (without consent) could be identified; and even if D made, and all along intended to make, two distinct journeys, it would be highly artificial to regard a consent obtained by deception as applying only to the first.
[49] *Cf. Hogdon* [1962] Crim.L.R. 563.
[50] *Cf.* s. 2(1)(*a*) and (*b*). The question is not whether D had lawful authority or whether the owner would have consented; it is whether D so believed: *Clotworthy* [1981] Crim.L.R. 501. He bears no persuasive burden on this issue; he need only raise a reasonable doubt.
[51] *Jaggard* v. *Dickinson* [1981] 2 W.L.R. 118; [1980] 3 All E.R. 716 (Criminal Damage Act 1971, s. 5(2)).
[52] *MacPherson* [1973] R.T.R. 157. For the distinction between offences of "basic intent" and of "specific intent," see *D.P.P.* v. *Majewski* [1977] A.C. 443.
[53] White, *op.cit.* above, n.26, argues that the phrase "for his own or another's use," correctly understood, renders the primary offence one of specific intent.

honesty provided by subsection (6) applies here also. The offences created by subsection (5) are not, of course, arrestable offences.

A difficulty may arise as to the correct classification of a motor-assisted pedal cycle. This was a motor vehicle for the purpose of the replaced offence of taking and driving away a motor vehicle, for which substantial penalties were provided. That offence could be committed by pedalling away such a cycle without using the motor[54]; but when the motor could not be used because of the absence of vital working parts, the vehicle was not a "motor vehicle" within the meaning of that phrase as defined in the Road Traffic Acts.[55] Perhaps a similar distinction can be taken under section 12 as a means of identifying vehicles which at the relevant time are *mere* pedal cycles.

[54] *Floyd* v. *Bush* [1953] 1 W.L.R. 242.
[55] *Lawrence* v. *Howlett* [1952] 2 All E.R. 74.

CHAPTER 6

OBTAINING PROPERTY BY DECEPTION

1. INTRODUCTION TO THE FRAUD OFFENCES

This chapter and Chapters 7 to 10 deal with the contribution made by the   **6–01**
Theft Acts to the control of fraud. The characteristic element of the
offences with which they are concerned is the purpose of the offender to
obtain some economic advantage by a deceptive practice. An unassisted
reader examining the relevant provisions, while readily understanding each
individually, would very likely be baffled as to why they take the form they
do. A brief general introduction to these chapters is required.

The 1968 Act

In the *Eighth Report* the Committee canvassed the arguments for and   **6–02**
against some alternative schemes to provide for offences of criminal
deception.[1] Had the scheme that the Committee favoured been accepted,
there would have been three main provisions. The first, to replace the old
offence of obtaining by false pretences,[2] would have dealt with obtaining
property by deception; this was accepted and is now embodied in section
15, which is the subject of the present chapter. The second would have
been an improved and extended version of the old offence of obtaining
credit by fraud[3]; this was in itself uncontroversial. The third and highly
controversial proposal was for a provision making it an offence, dishonestly and with a view to gain, to induce a person by deception to do or refrain
from doing any act. This was included in the Bill but foundered in the
House of Lords. It was felt that it would effect too wide and vague an
extension of the criminal law. Instead, in place of the second and third of
the offences originally proposed, section 16 was devised to cover obtaining
credit by deception together with so much of the rejected general offence
as was felt to be acceptable. The remnants of section 16, after its partial
repeal by the 1978 Act, are examined in Chapter 9. They deal with a
variety of specialised transactions that probably should not require
individual mention in a well-drafted code.

Sections 17, 19 and 20 contain modified versions, as recommended by   **6–03**
the Committee, of some other pre-existing fraud offences. They are
considered in Chapter 10. It would appear that the Committee desired to
retain the substance of any offences in the replaced legislation that had
anything distinctive to contribute to the control of fraud.[4] The most
important of these, undoubtedly, was falsification of accounts[5]—now

---

[1] *Eighth Report*, paras. 97–100.
[2] Larceny Act 1916, s. 32.
[3] Debtors Act 1869, s. 13.
[4] *Eighth Report*, paras. 102 *et seq.*
[5] Falsification of Accounts Act 1875, s. 2.

re-enacted in modern guise, and under the name of false accounting, in
section 17. On the other hand, it was not proposed that the Act should
contain the whole of this branch of the law. Forgery remains the subject of
its own code.[6] The protection of investors against deceptive inducements to
risk their money with attractive enterprises is the special concern of section
13 of the Prevention of Fraud (Investments) Act 1958 as well as of section
19 of the present Act. And other statutes dealing with particular activities,
transactions or classes of people have their own provisions for the
punishment of fraudulent or even innocently deceptive conduct. The result
is that the collection of provisions in the 1968 Act has an appearance that is
at once partial and miscellaneous.

The 1978 Act

6–04   The most important case of the offence created by section 16 of the 1968
Act was that, under section 16(2)(*a*), where D by deception dishonestly
obtained for himself or another the reduction, or the total or partial
evasion or deferment, of a debt or charge for which he made himself liable.
Happily it is no longer necessary to wrestle with the obscurities of this
provision, to examine the difficult case law to which it gave rise or, in short,
to understand in detail why it was said that the section had "created a
judicial nightmare."[7] It was soon clear that section 16(2)(*a*) was highly
unsatisfactory and must be replaced. Proposals for amending legislation
were made by the Committee in 1977 in their *Thirteenth Report* (with a
draft Bill appended).[8] The outcome was the Theft Act 1978, which
repealed section 16(2)(*a*) and created three new offences.

6–05   There are two ways of expressing simply what the Committee were
seeking to achieve by clause 1 of their draft Bill. First, to use the language
of the old law which had been replaced by section 16(2)(*a*), the aim was to
penalise the obtaining of credit by deception—more precisely, the
obtaining of credit in respect of the payment of money.[9] But the
Committee were not in favour of employing the term "credit" in the
drafting of the offence.[10] The clause might, secondly, be said to be aimed
at the obtaining by deception "of services on which a monetary value is
placed."[11] For an obtaining of credit in respect of a supply of property was
already covered by section 15 of the 1968 Act (at least where an intention
of permanently depriving P existed); and what needed to be dealt with, to
supplement this offence, was a deceptive obtaining on credit of other
valuable benefits such as a hiring of goods, the provision of labour or the
grant of a licence—benefits that might collectively be called "services."

---

[6] Forgery and Counterfeiting Act 1981.
[7] *Per* Edmund-Davies L.J. in *Royale* [1971] 1 W.L.R. 1764 at p. 1767; [1971] 3 All E.R. 1359
at p. 1363.
[8] The Report was preceded by a Working Paper published in August 1974. An excellent
account of the genesis of s.16 and of its history in the courts is provided in Appendix 2 to
the Report.
[9] Working Paper, para. 25.
[10] *Thirteenth Report*, para. 8.
[11] *Ibid.* para. 9.

But the Committee preferred not to employ the term "services" in the drafting of the offence.[12] Instead they offered in clause 1 an offence of dishonestly inducing another by deception to act on any person's promise of payment. This formula, attended by an adequate apparatus of definition, would have achieved the objects described above.

When the Bill was considered by the House of Lords, clause 1 was criticised as too complex and a new clause was substituted, penalising the obtaining of services by deception. After the Bill had passed the Lords, the new clause was hurriedly referred to the Committee, who recommended instead the further version now enacted as section 1 of the 1978 Act. The essential contribution of the Committee at this final stage was to provide a definition of "services" so as to ensure that the offence would be limited, as all along intended, to an obtaining of services "on which a monetary value is placed." On the other hand the offence that emerged was so drafted as not to be limited to deception as to the prospect of payment; nor, in fact, need credit be involved at all. Moreover, section 1 does not (as the Lords amendment did) require the offender to have acted "with a view to gain or an intent to cause loss." The result is an offence not only of completely different design from that originally proposed, but also substantially wider in scope.[13] It is examined in Chapter 7.

Section 2—evading liability by deception—is considered in Chapter 8.   **6–06**
Whereas section 1, at least as originally drafted, was designed to control the deceptive obtaining of credit "at the outset of a transaction"[14] (that is, when liability to pay for services is originally incurred), section 2 is mainly concerned with the obtaining by deception of relief from some existing liability. But it also covers the obtaining by deception of an exemption from, or abatement of, liability to make a payment, which will certainly include some cases of fraud committed before liability is incurred. Section 2 completes the task of replacing section (2)(*a*) of the 1968 Act.

The opportunity was taken at the same time to create, by section 3, a   **6–07**
general offence of making off without payment (in situations in which payment "on the spot" is expected). This deals with the mischief of "bilking," which was only partially, accidentally and artificially covered by sections 1, 15 and 16 of the 1968 Act. This new offence is examined in Chapter 11. It is not an offence requiring proof of a deceptive practice.

2. THE OFFENCE OF OBTAINING PROPERTY BY DECEPTION

The dishonest obtaining by deception of property belonging to another   **6–08**
with the intention of permanently depriving the other of it is punishable on conviction on indictment with 10 years' imprisonment (s. 15(1)).

---

[12] *Ibid.* para. 7.
[13] It is odd that s. 1 was passed without protest, for it is reminiscent of the proposed offence—of inducing a person by deception to do or refrain from doing any act—that was rejected by Parliament 10 years earlier as being too wide (see § 6–02), and wider than that proposal in not requiring a view to gain or an intent to cause loss.
[14] *Thirteenth Report*, para.13.

"For purposes of this section a person is to be treated as obtaining property if he obtains ownership, possesion or control of it . . . " (s. 15(2)). And "deception" is widely defined in section 15(4) so as to include, in effect, any deliberate or reckless deception, howsoever effected. The result of these definitions, and of the adoption in substance of the same large meanings for the expressions "property" and "belonging to another" as they have in the case of theft (s. 34(1)), is to make the present offence a good deal wider than the offence of obtaining by false pretences which it replaced.[15] The main limitations of the repealed offence, by contrast, were: that it applied only to the obtaining of any chattel, money or valuable security; that it applied only when ownership and not merely possession of property was obtained; and that the pretence had to be as to some past or present fact, not including the offender's intentions as to the future.

3.   "OBTAINS PROPERTY BELONGING TO ANOTHER"

Property belonging to another

6–09   The definition of "property" in section 4(1) is made to apply generally for purposes of the Act by section 34(1), so that the offence under section 15 can be committed in respect of any kind of property. There are no provisions, as there are in the case of theft, limiting the circumstances in which land can be the subject of the offence. Nor, for the purposes of this offence, does the reference in section 4(1) to "things in action and other intangible property" present the same difficulties as in the context of theft.[16] Whatever can be transferred by one person to another as property is in practice within section 15, for deception can induce its transfer. So, for instance, a beneficial interest in property under a trust is, it is submitted, itself property within the phrase "things in action and other intangible property," and to induce the assignment of such an interest is therefore to obtain property.

If D, by deception, induces P to pay him more money than he would have paid but for the deception, there is an obtaining of property within the section and D may be convicted even though the precise amount of the excess cannot be specified.[17]

6–10   The property obtained must be property "belonging to another."[18] The wide definition of this phrase in section 5(1) is also made to apply here by section 34(1). It is desirable to notice the force of this in conjunction with the provision that "a person is to be treated as obtaining property if he

---

[15] Larceny Act 1916, s. 32.
[16] See above, § 2–69.
[17] *Levene* v. *Pearcey* [1976] Crim.L.R. 63 (taxi driver telling passenger that normal route is blocked, using longer route and obtaining larger fare).
[18] A mistake in the information or indictment as to the person to whom the property belonged will be immaterial if the defendant nevertheless has enough information to know the nature of the charge; if the victim's identity is material, an error on the point can be cured by amendment: *Etim* v. *Hatfield* [1975] Crim.L.R. 234.

obtains ownership, possession or control of it" (s. 15(2)). The result is that there is an obtaining within section 15 if the effect of D's fraud is that he obtains ownership, possession or control of any property which P owns, possesses or controls or in which P has any proprietary right or interest.[19]

Of course, the normal case will be that in which D induces P to part with property of which P is the owner. It will be enough if D obtains ownership only or possession only. For instance, if D by deception induces P to agree to sell him specific goods in a deliverable state so that, as normally occurs in such a case,[20] the property in the goods passes to D on the making of the contract, D is guilty even if he never acquires possession.[21] Conversely, D may deceive P into lending or hiring goods to him, D's intention being to deprive P permanently of them, and here D is guilty although he does not acquire ownership.

Alternatively, D may himself be the owner and still commit the offence. Two obvious examples are the following:

(i) P contracts to sell goods to D, D using no deception to induce the contract. The circumstances are such that the property in the goods passes before delivery. P retains possession and is entitled to do so until D pays or tenders the price. D by deception induces P to part with possession (*e.g.* he gives P a cheque that he knows to be worthless).

(ii) D pledges goods with P. By deception he induces P to redeliver the goods to him.

Again, neither D nor the person deceived need be the owner. P may have possession or control of Q's goods. If D induces P to part with the goods, intending to deprive both P and Q of them, either P or Q can be named in the indictment as the person to whom the goods belong. It will no doubt be convenient to name P.

Obtaining

Section 15(2) provides that for purposes of the section " 'obtain' **6–11** includes obtaining for another or enabling another to obtain or to retain." The following are examples:

(i) *Obtaining for another.* P has a lien on E's goods and D on E's behalf persuades P to give up possession to him (D) by promising to discharge E's debt. (Note that, as P is the only person whom D intends to deprive, he alone can be named as the person to whom the property belongs.)

(ii) *Enabling another to obtain.* In a similar situation, D prevails on P to deliver the property direct to E. In *Duru*,[22] D deceived P into making a loan to F, which P did by sending a cheque to F's solicitor, E. D had "enabled [E] to obtain" possession or control of the cheque; and it was irrelevant that E was not himself a party to the deception.

---

[19] With one immaterial exception: see s. 5(1).
[20] Sale of Goods Act 1979, s.18, r.1.
[21] By obtaining ownership, D puts himself in a position to pass ownership to a third person, who may buy in good faith and obtain a valid title as against P: Sale of Goods Act 1979, s.23. *Cf. Eighth Report*, para.90.
[22] [1974] 1 W.L.R.2; [1973] 3 All E.R. 715.

(iii) *Enabling another to retain.* E is in possession of P's goods. D deceives P into leaving them with E rather than claiming their return.

It is odd that enabling another to retain is obtaining within the section but that enabling oneself to retain is not. True, in most cases where D, by deception, and with the necessary intention, induces P to let him retain P's property, D will commit theft. But this, considering the overlap that exists between theft and the present offence, hardly explains the discrepancy; and theft may not catch some cases—for instance, if D, P's bailee, induces P by deception to sell him the goods bailed and thus to leave them in his possession, it is possible that he will commit no appropriation until after the goods have ceased to belong to P.[23]

4. Deception

Generally

6–12   "For purposes of this section 'deception' means any deception (whether deliberate or reckless) by words or conduct as to fact or as to law, including a deception as to the present intentions of the person using the deception or any other person" (s. 15(4)).

The words in parenthesis may conveniently be reserved to a discussion of the whole of the mental element of the offence.[24] As a first step in a consideration of the rest of this definition it may be instructive to compare it in a number of respects with the old law.

First, the word "deception" itself should be noticed. It replaces "false pretence" in the Larceny Act 1916, s. 32(1), an expression which was undefined in the statute but about which there existed a mass of case law. The new word has "the advantage of directing attention to the effect that the offender deliberately produced on the mind of the person deceived, whereas 'false pretence' makes one think of what exactly the offender did in order to deceive."[25] There is a hint here that deception may be wider than "false pretence."[26]

Secondly, the reference to a deception "as to law" is included for the avoidance of doubt.[27] It was not settled whether a false statement as to law was a false pretence under the old law.

6–13   Thirdly, the inclusion of "a deception as to . . . present intentions" is the most important change made by this section. In the light of authority

---

[23] See further, Smith, *Theft*, para. 196.

[24] See §§ 6–42, 6–43.

[25] *Eighth Report*, para.87.

[26] And see *ibid.* para. 101 (iv). There has been some discussion as to whether deception can be practised on a machine. See *Davies* v. *Flackett* [1973] R.T.R. 8 (point reserved); "Bystander" (1972) 69 L.S.Gaz. 416; Smith, *ibid.* 576; Lamming (1972) 122 New L.J. 627; Smith, *Theft*, para. 159. It is thought that the answer is clearly no: deception requires an effect on a human mind. Where payment for services is avoided by abuse of a machine (*e.g.* on a car park), the relevant deception offences (Theft Act 1978, ss. 1 and 2) are plainly so worded as to require deception of a person; s. 3 of that Act (making off without payment), on the other hand, is not a deception offence. The use of a false "coin" inserted into a vending machine can be prosecuted as theft of the article dispensed.

[27] *Eighth Report*, para. 101 (ii).

under the Larceny Act, it was essential for the present Act to single out fraudulent promises and other statements as to intention for express reference. It is now, but was not formerly, a criminal offence to obtain property by making a promise that one has no intention of keeping. (Of course to establish such an offence it is vital to prove that the accused did not at the time of the obtaining have the intention that, from his words or conduct, he appeared to have. It is neither necessary nor sufficient to prove that he later decided not to keep it, though the latter fact may be evidence in favour of the conclusion that he never intended to do so.) A further consequence of this change in the law is that the doctrine of *Edgington* v. *Fitzmaurice*[28] now operates in the criminal law as well as in the civil. D's statement that, for example, he intends to use money for a particular purpose is a deception if he does not then have that intention. The definition refers, of course, to "the present intentions of [D] *or any other person.*" So D's statement that E, or the limited company that D represents, intends to do something in the future is also within the definition, if E or the company has not that intention and D either knows this fact or does not believe his statement to be true. We said that this application of *Edgington* v. *Fitzmaurice* was a *further* consequence of the change bought about by the definition. More strictly, it is the basic consequence of that change; false promises are merely the most important practical example of statements about intention.[29]

Fourthly, the words "any deception . . . by words or conduct as to fact" **6–14** reproduce, subject to the use of the word "deception" in place of "false pretence," the meaning of "false pretence" under the old law. There is no doubt that all cases of false pretences are now caught by section 15.[30] For this reason some of the cases decided on the old law will afford useful illustrations of the scope of deception, and especially of deception by conduct. However, deception by conduct is now less important than it used to be. In many of the situations in which convictions had formerly to rest on the discovery of some implied pretence as to fact, the essential wrongdoing was the making of a false promise. Under the present section the false promise can be both the real and the formal basis of the conviction.[31] Thus if D has obtained money from P by promising to marry

---

[28] (1885) 29 Ch.D. 459.
[29] See n.31, below. By "false promise" in the text and in n.31 is meant a promise which, at the time of its being made, the maker does not intend to keep. For important observations as to statements of present intention, expectation or belief implied by the making of promises or forecasts, see cases decided under the Trade Descriptions Act 1968: *Sunair Holidays Ltd.* [1973] 1 W.L.R. 1105; [1973] 2 All E.R. 1233; *British Airways Board* v. *Taylor* [1976] 1 W.L.R. 13; [1976] 1 All E.R. 65.
[30] *Cf. Eighth Report*, para. 101 (iv).
[31] Technically, a false promise must be a "deception . . . by words or conduct . . . as to . . . present intentions," and usually the statement "I intend to do such-and-such" must, strictly, be implied from the speaker's saying "I shall do (or I promise to do) such-and-such." The language of s. 15 compels this slight artificiality by using a conveniently short form of words to cover all promises and statements of intention. But at least this particular artificiality does not obscure the true nature of the deception.

her, he may be convicted if, *and because*, he did not intend to marry her. In the old days he could be convicted only if he was not free to marry her and then only upon the ground that he had said that he was.

Deception by words: fact and opinion; implied facts

6–15   A "deception . . . by words . . . as to fact" involves the making of an untrue statement as to some past or present fact: that the car being sold was first registered in 1978; that the fire giving rise to an insurance claim destroyed the mink coat; and so on. Usually it is easy enough to identify a fact falsely asserted by the words used. But difficulties can occur where the defence is in a position to argue that the statement made was one of opinion rather than of fact; or where the prosecution need to argue that what was false was something implied by D's statements rather than anything he expressly said; and these two situations may occur together.

6–16   (i) *Fact and opinion.* In criminal law as in civil law liability does not normally derive from the giving of an unjustified or exaggerated opinion. A statement of opinion is not a statement of fact. A person seeking to make a sale is not penalised for over-praising his goods so long as he confines himself to statements as to value and quality. But he cannot with impunity assert that the goods have some attribute that is no mere matter of opinion and which it can be demonstrated that they do not have. The difference has been happily expressed as that "between saying that something is gold and saying that something is as good as gold."[32]

6–17   (ii) *Implied facts.* There may be a deception "by words . . . as to fact" although no untrue facts are expressly stated. Ths is because untrue facts may be implied. The assertion of one fact, for example, may be such as to imply the non-existence of some other fact which the maker of the assertion knows to exist and which might affect the mind of the person to whom the statement is made. For instance, a statement about the past fortunes of a business for sale may assert that the average turnover of the business during the past 10 years has been of a certain satisfactory order. This assertion may be literally true; but if the turnover has consistently decreased over the 10 years, so that the volume of business now being done is disastrously small, the concealment of this material fact should (assuming dishonesty) certainly involve the maker of the statement in liability for a "deception . . . as to fact."[33] A neat example of an implied statement is provided by a case in which a car dealer turned back the odometer of a car and displayed a notice saying that the mileage reading

---

[32] Smith and Hogan, *Criminal Law* (1st ed.), p. 410, comparing (*inter alia*) *Bryan* (1857) Dears. & B.265 (opinion; but an unsatisfactory case) and *Ardley* (1871) L.R.1 C.C.R. 301 (fact).

[33] *Cf. Kylsant* [1932] 1 K.B. 442, decided on the wording of the Larceny Act 1861, s.84 ("statement . . . false in any material particular").

"may not be correct." He thereby falsely represented, as the indictment alleged, "that he had no reason to disbelieve" the reading.[34]

(iii) *Expression of opinion implying fact.* A statement that is in form **6–18** one of opinion may likewise imply some fact that can be shown to be untrue. Examples of this are to be found in contract cases. To say that Mr. Smith is "a most desirable tenant" is to seem to assert at least that there are no facts known to the speaker that would justify the view that Mr. Smith does not deserve this description.[35] Similarly, the statement that the shares of a company would be a worth-while investment is in form a value judgment; but it would surely be falsified by proof that the company was unable to pay its creditors and had no apparent means of achieving solvency. Another way of discovering a statement of fact in such cases is to say that D is asserting that he holds the opinion he expresses when in fact he does not hold that opinion at all.[36]

Deception by conduct

Deception by conduct occurs where D's conduct implies a statement **6–19** which is false but which P is induced to rely upon as true. The following are examples of different kinds of fraud depending upon deception by conduct.

(i) When a person sells property he normally implies by his conduct that he has a right to do so and power to give a good title to the thing sold. If he has not, the implication is false. It is likely that the buyer would not buy the property if he knew that the seller had no title or a defective title. If so, what he pays for the property is obtained by deception by conduct (assuming the deception to be "deliberate or reckless").[37]

(ii) The fraud perpetrated by one who wears a uniform to which he is not entitled has long been a classic of the textbooks because of the direction of Bolland B. in *Barnard* in 1837[38]:

> "If nothing had passed in words, I should have laid down that the fact of the prisoner's appearing in the cap and gown would have been pregnant evidence from which a jury should infer that he pretended he was a member of the university. . . . "

There is no reason why this popular illustration of an implied pretence should not survive as a simple example of deception by conduct.

---

[34] *King* [1979] Crim.L.R. 122. *Banaster* (1978) 68 Cr.App.R. 272 illustrates the sometimes subtle distinction between what words mean and what they imply. A minicab driver told a passenger at London Airport that he was "an airport taxi." His conviction of obtaining the fare paid by the deception that it was "the correct fare" was upheld. The jury, it was said, had been rightly allowed to find that the driver's words "implied" that it "was all official." His words could certainly be taken to *mean* that he had some official airport status. It is perhaps questionable whether this plainly *implies* that the fare charged was "correct" (meaning "authorised"?).

[35] *Cf. Smith* v. *Land and House Property Corporation* (1884) 28 Ch.D. 7.

[36] Note that this approach requires very careful drafting of the indictment. The deception charged would be that D falsely represented that he "was of the opinion" or "believed" that such-and-such was the case.

[37] *Cf. Edwards* [1978] Crim.L.R. 49 (squatter "letting" a room).

[38] (1837) 7 C. & P. 784.

6–20   (iii) A similar example is that of the fraud committed by establishing the outward appearance of a genuine business or enterprise and thereby inducing people to supply goods or to pay for non-existent goods or to invest money in a worthless undertaking. Frauds of this kind are often large-scale operations in which several people are involved and they are commonly prosecuted as conspiracies to defraud.[39]

(iv) A person who enters a restaurant and orders a meal impliedly represents by his conduct that he intends to pay for the meal (and, in the ordinary case, that he intends to pay before leaving the restaurant). If he does not so intend, he obtains the meal by deception.[40]

Cheques, cheque cards and credit cards

6–21   The representations involved in the use of cheques, cheque cards and credit cards have recently been considered by the House of Lords in two cases.

(i) *Cheques.* Professor Kenny long ago identified a number of representations as implied by "the familiar act of drawing a cheque."[41] (a) The first implied statement was "that the drawer has an account with [the] bank" upon which the cheque is drawn. There is no doubt that this statement is implied; and it is a convenient representation to allege where the drawer has no such account. (b) The second implied statement was "that [the drawer] has authority to draw on [the account] for [the] amount" for which the cheque is drawn. This implication, it has now been suggested, is incorrect. "A customer needs no authority from his banker to draw a cheque on him; it is the banker who needs authority from the customer to pay it on presentment."[42] It is in any case redundant, being, like the first statement, embraced by the third.[43] (c) In *Metropolitan Police Commissioner* v. *Charles*[44] the majority of their lordships[45] accepted Kenny's third representation, namely:

> "that the cheque, as drawn, is a valid order for the payment of that amount (*i.e.* that the present state of affairs is such that, in the ordinary course of events, the cheque will on its future presentment be duly honoured)."

Kenny went on to point out

> "that it does not imply any representation that the drawer now has money in this bank to the amount drawn for, inasmuch as he may well

---

[39] Conspiracy to defraud is preserved as an offence at common law by the Criminal Law Act 1977, s. 5(2).

[40] See *D.P.P.* v. *Ray* [1974] A.C. 370 (§ 6–25, below)—where there was no offence under s.15, because the intention not to pay was formed after the food had been consumed.

[41] *Outlines of Criminal Law*—see now 19th ed. (1966), p. 359. Kenny cited *Hazelton* (1874) L.R. 2 C.C.R. 134, and his analysis was adopted by the Court of Appeal in *Page* [1971] 2 Q.B. 330 n.

[42] *Per* Lord Diplock in *Metropolitan Police Commissioner* v. *Charles* [1977] A.C. 177 at p. 182; see also *per* Viscount Dilhorne at p. 185.

[43] *Ibid.* at pp. 190–191 (Lord Edmund-Davies).

[44] [1977] A.C. 177.

[45] Lord Diplock restated the drawer's representation to be that "the cheque is one which the bank on which it is drawn is bound, by an existing contract with the drawer, to pay on presentment or, if not strictly bound to do so, could reasonably be expected to pay in the normal course of dealing" (p.182).

have authority to overdraw, or may intend to pay in (before the cheque can be presented) sufficient money to meet it"

—or, it may be added, may expect the account to be sufficiently fed by some other person. This does not mean that the drawer's act simply implies a representation as to the future, a prediction; this would not satisfy the requirement of a "deception . . . as to fact."[46] Rather it implies a statement as to the existence of a "state of affairs" (to repeat Kenny's words) which includes the drawer's present intention or expectation. Nevertheless, it is certainly less pedantic to express it in Viscount Dilhorne's pithy terms: "a man who gives a cheque represents that it will be met on presentment."[47]

The transaction contemplated by Kenny is that where D uses a cheque to obtain property from the payee. When he demands cash from his own bank against his account he thereby represents that he believes the state of his account (no doubt including uncleared effects[48] and overdraft facilities) to be such that he is entitled to draw that amount.

(ii) *Cheque cards and credit cards.* In *Charles* D obtained gambling   **6–22**
chips at a club by giving cheques supported by a cheque card. The use of the card in accordance with specified conditions created an undertaking by D's bank to honour the cheques. So the representation involved in giving the cheques was true; the cheques would undoubtedly be met, whatever the state of D's account. The House of Lords held, however, that when the drawer of a cheque presents a cheque card by way of guarantee, he represents to the payee that he has the bank's authority to use the card in relation to that cheque so as to create a contractual relationship between bank and payee. If the cheque is one which would not be met but for the use of the cheque card, he will lack that authority. The use of the card will then involve a misrepresentation.

In *Lambie*[49] D selected goods in a shop and proposed to pay by Barclaycard. That is to say, she was using the card as a credit card. The shop had the usual agreement with D's bank that the bank would honour a voucher signed by the holder of a current card for a transaction within an agreed limit. D's transaction was within that limit. The shop manageress accepted this form of payment. The House of Lords held, consistently with its decision in *Charles*, that D had represented (falsely, on the facts) that she had authority to contract with the shop on the bank's behalf that the bank would honour the voucher signed by D.

A person dishonestly using a cheque card or credit card is guilty of an offence involving deception only if the payee is deceived by the card-holder's misrepresentation into accepting the cheque or voucher

---

[46] *Pace* Viscount Dilhorne in *Charles* [1977] A.C. 177 at p. 185; *cf.* Smith, *Theft*, para. 166.
[47] [1977] A.C. 177 at p. 186. *Cf. per* Lord Reid in *D.P.P.* v. *Turner* [1974] A.C. 357 at p. 367.
[48] In *Christou* [1971] Crim.L.R. 653, D paid in for the credit of his account cheques which were worthless, as he knew they were or might be. He then drew on the account before those cheques were presented. This was one indivisible deceptive practice.
[49] [1981] 3 W.L.R. 88; [1981] 2 All E.R. 776.

concerned. This aspect of deception is considered below.[50] The discussion may be anticipated by saying that convictions were confirmed in both *Charles*[51] and *Lambie*.[52]

Conduct to conceal facts

6–23   An interesting situation is presented by conduct of D which is intended to work a deception but of which, if the deception is to succeed, P must remain in ignorance. For instance, D may intercept a letter warning P of a fact that would be likely, if known to P, to make him refuse a proposed transaction, or D may hide physical evidence of the fact that P would otherwise see. It would appear to be open to a court to say that such conduct amounts to deception within section 15.[53]

Deception by silence

6–24   In some situations D may be thought to have a moral duty (and may for other purposes have a legal duty) to reveal to P some fact which might affect P's mind in relation to a proposed transaction. Suppose that after forming his intention that P shall be misled by his own ignorance D does nothing active but pursues his dishonest purpose by maintaining silence. If a transaction then ensues in which D obtains property from P, the question may arise whether he has obtained that property by deception.[54]

Before considering particular examples of situations of this kind, the following general observations may be offered. First, before a deception can be found in any such case it must be clear that D's behaviour (however analysed) implied a clear statement by him of the truth or untruth of some proposition—that is, a clear representation. Secondly, the question is not whether D had a duty to reveal facts but only whether—to repeat the first point—he appeared to assert or deny them. But if D is not, according to the law of contract or of tort, under a duty to reveal a fact known to him, it may be the more difficult to interpret his silence as a denial of that fact; and this consideration may contribute to ensuring that the criminal law is not in practice more demanding than the civil. Thirdly, there may in fact be no situation in which mere silence, mere inaction, alone can work a deception within the meaning of the Act. It may be necessary at least to find some other conduct of D in association with which his silence may be interpreted as making a representation.

---

[50] § 6–32.
[51] What was obtained in *Charles* was a pecuniary advantage in the form of D's being "allowed to borrow by way of overdraft" (see below, §§ 6–40 and 9–07) and D was convicted accordingly under s. 16(2)(*b*). He probably had not the intention of permanently depriving the club of the gambling chips, within the meaning of s. 15 (though for an argument to the contrary, see J. C. Smith [1976] Crim.L.R. 330).
[52] The conviction in *Lambie* was under s.16(2)(*a*), since repealed. It might have been under s.15—and should have been: [1981] 3 W.L.R. at p. 91; [1981] 2 All E.R. at p. 779.
[53] A clearer case would be that where D conceals (*e.g.* by painting over) a defect in goods, the goods then being examined by P; in this case the result of the work of concealment is visible to P. *Cf.* the facts of *Cottee* v. *Douglas Seaton (Used Cars) Ltd.* [1972] 1 W.L.R. 1408; [1972] 3 All E.R. 750, a case under the Trade Descriptions Act 1968.
[54] See *Eighth Report*, para. 101 (iv), and a full discussion in Smith, *Theft*, paras. 170–172.

The main relevant authority under the Act is *D.P.P.* v. *Ray*.[55] D entered   **6–25**
a restaurant intending to pay for the meal he was to eat. The
representation implied by his conduct (that he intended to pay) was
therefore true. After he had eaten his meal he decided not to pay and sat,
inactively, at his table until the waiter was out of the room. He then made
his escape without paying. The House of Lords held by a majority that he
had obtained by deception the evasion of his obligation to pay,[56] either
because the initial representation made on entering and ordering the meal
was "a continuing representation which remained alive and operative" and
had become false,[57] or because by remaining at the table after forming his
dishonest intention he continued to make from moment to moment, but
now falsely, the representation that he intended to pay.[58] A corresponding
case under section 15 would be provided by the diner who forms his
decision not to pay for his food between the time of ordering it and the
time of its being served.

D.P.P. v. *Ray* illustrates the situation where D makes an assertion to P   **6–26**
which is true when made but which becomes untrue before the relevant
obtaining. Three other situations may be briefly considered. The first is
that where D makes an assertion which he believes to be true but which is
not. Before he obtains any property from P, D learns that his assertion was
false. He does not correct it. He may probably be interpreted as now
falsely representing that he believes his original assertion to be true, or as
continuing to make (but now falsely) that same assertion. The second
situation is that where P makes clear to D that he assumes some fact to be
true which is material to a negotiation between them. D knows the
assumption is false but, though he does not actively confirm it, he does
nothing to disabuse P. It is thought to be unlikely that a court would hold
D's silence to be "conduct" within the meaning of section 15(4). The third
situation is even clearer. D simply refrains from mentioning to P a fact,
known to D, that might affect P's mind in the transaction proposed
between them. The fact that it will usually be impossible to identify a clear
statement to be inferred from D's silence should suffice to exclude liability,
quite apart from all other considerations, including the consideration that
no civil liability normally arises from simple non-disclosure.

---

[55] [1974] A.C. 370. See also *Nordeng* (1975) 62 Cr.App.R. 123, and commentary by J. C. Smith [1976] Crim.L.R. 196.

[56] Contrary to s.16(2)(*a*), since repealed. The diner who makes off without payment will now be prosecuted under the Theft Act 1978, s. 3: see Chap.11.

[57] *Per* Lord MacDermott (at p. 382).

[58] See *per* Lord Pearson at p. 391; and *cf. per* Lord Morris of Borth-y-Gest at pp. 385–386. It is not suggested that there is any difference of substance between the majority opinions as interpreted here. Lords Reid and Hodson dissented. Lord Reid (at p. 379): "Deception, to my mind, implies something positive. It is quite true that a man intending to deceive can build up a situation in which his silence is as eloquent as an express statement. But what did the accused do here to create such a situation? He merely sat still." Lord Hodson (at p. 389): "Nothing he did after his change of mind can be characterised as conduct which would indicate that he was then practising a deception."

The falsity of the representation

6–27   The representation that D makes by words or conduct must be false if there is to be deception. If D "quite accidentally and, strange as it may sound, dishonestly,"[59] tells the truth, he cannot be convicted under section 15. (He may, however, be convicted of an attempt, even if he obtains what he sets out to obtain.[60])

6–28   The prosecution case may be that the accused obtained a payment by a document containing a number of false particulars—as where he has submitted a claim form for expenses and it is said that some asserted heads of expenditure were fictitious, some rates of expenditure exaggerated, and so on. It has been held to be enough for a conviction that the jury agree that the claim form was incorrect. They need not agree—and therefore need not be directed that they have to agree—on any individual respect in which the form was incorrect.[61] This is puzzling, to say the least. Reduced to absurdity, it means that a person may be convicted of a deception offence although every one of his impugned statements is accepted as true by eleven members of the jury. Only a rule requiring the jury as a whole[62] to agree upon at least one particular statement as false can satisfy basic principle as to the burden of proof.

6–29   Where the burden of proving the falsity of the representation involves proving a negative, there is in commonsense a limit to the quantity of evidence that the prosecution can be expected to adduce on the issue. If D has asserted that such-and-such is the case (*e.g.* the goods he sells cost eight times as much in the big shops), it is enough for the prosecution to speak of limited unsuccessful efforts to verify his assertion (seeking the goods at higher prices in a few shops). Reasonable efforts of that kind having been reported, it is not wrong for the judge to observe to the jury that the defence might be expected to give positive evidence, if it can be given, tending to support the representation.[63]

5.   RELATION BETWEEN THE FALSE REPRESENTATION AND THE OBTAINING

The deception must precede the obtaining

6–30   This proposition should be too obvious to need stating. But it was the sole reason required for the quashing of the conviction in *Collis-Smith*.[64] D had petrol put in the tank of his car at a petrol station. He then falsely stated that he was using the car for business purposes and that his firm would pay for the petrol. This was the substance of the deception charged

---

[59] *Deller* (1952) 36 Cr.App.R. 184, *per* Hilbery J. at p. 191.
[60] Criminal Attempts Act 1981, s. 1, subss. (2) and (3) of which reverse *Haughton* v. *Smith* [1975] A.C. 486.
[61] *Agbim* [1979] Crim.L.R. 171 (with commentator's criticism exactly according with that in the text)—a case of obtaining the execution of a valuable security (s. 20(2)).
[62] That is, the minimum majority to satisfy the Juries Act 1974, s. 17. The same majority, of course, would need to be satisfied as to all other elements of the offence.
[63] *Mandry and Wooster* [1973] 1 W.L.R. 1232; [1973] 3 All E.R. 996, from which the illustrative facts in the text are taken.
[64] [1971] Crim.L.R. 716.

and his appeal against conviction was rightly allowed; the petrol was not obtained by this deception.

The prosecution argued in *Collis-Smith* that after *possession* of property had been obtained D might by a deception then made obtain *ownership*, and that such a transaction would satisfy the section. This argument, it is submitted, was clearly correct in principle (though the court, seemingly anxious to protect criminal practitioners from "difficult points under the Sale of Goods Act," was not prepared to acknowledge this); but it was equally clearly inapplicable in the instant case, in which the property in the petrol must have passed on its being put into the tank.[65]

The effect of the representation on P's mind

(i) *What state of mind must the representation induce?* "To deceive is, I   **6–31** apprehend, to induce a man to believe that a thing is true which is false." This well-known statement by Buckley J. in *Re London and Globe Finance Corporation*[66] was cited with approval in *D.P.P.* v. *Ray*.[67] It appears at first sight to state the obvious and to require no elaboration. Yet there is, on reflection, a good deal of uncertainty attaching to the notion of "believing that a thing is true"; and there has been no judicial consideration of what amounts to "believing" for this purpose.[68] It is submitted that, if indeed "believing" is an appropriate word in this context, it should not be understood only in the sense of firmly accepting the truth of the statement in question. The deception offences can hardly be limited to cases in which P is induced to hold a strong positive belief. P may be well aware that he does not know D, that there are rogues and liars abroad and that D may be one of them. He may act "on the strength" of D's assertion and in reliance upon it, but without in any positive sense either believing or disbelieving it. If D is lying, P is surely "deceived" for the purposes of section 15. It may in fact be better to abandon the word "believe" and to say that to deceive is to induce a man to act in reliance upon a false representation.[69]

---

[65] See above, § 2–36.
[66] [1903] 1 Ch. 728 at p. 732.
[67] [1974] A.C. 370.
[68] The authorities on obtaining by false pretences largely avoided reference to any particular state of mind that the pretence must bring about. It was variously said that it must be proved that by his statement D "did so act on the mind of the prosecutor as that he did thereby obtain money, etc. . . . [and] if in fact the prosecutor was not . . . persuaded [by D's statement] . . . , the charge is not supported" (*Aspinall* (1876) 2 Q.B.D. 48 at p. 57, *per* Brett J.A.); that the offence was committed if "the property was parted with on the faith of the false pretence" (*Jones* (1884) 50 L.T. 726); that it must be shown that P was "influenced by the false pretence and would not have transferred [the goods] but for his reliance on it" (*Russell on Crime* (12th ed.), p. 1184; *cf. Seagrave* (1910) 4 Cr.App.R. 156, as to reliance); that P must have been "induced by" the false statement to part with the property (*Smith* (1915) 11 Cr.App.R. 81). References to P's "believing" D's statement were rare; but see *Grail* (1944) 30 Cr.App.R. 81; *Sullivan* (1945) *ibid.* 132. It may be that the substitution of "deception" for "false pretences" compels closer attention to the point; *cf.* § 6–07, above.
[69] This paragraph was approved by the Court of Appeal in *Lambie* [1981] 1 W.L.R. 78; [1981] 1 All E.R. 332 (reversed on another ground, [1981] 3 W.L.R. 88; [1981] 2 All E.R. 776.

6–32   The test of whether P has been so induced is whether he would have acted as he did if he had known that the representation made by D was false. This question (and not whether P believed D, or why P acted as he did) is therefore the question to which evidence should be directed. This appears from the decisions of the House of Lords in *Metropolitan Police Commissioner* v. *Charles*[70] and *Lambie*,[71] which have already been mentioned for another purpose.[72]

     In *Charles* P accepted D's cheques because they were backed by a cheque card. He would not have done so if he had known that D had no authority to use the card. D's conviction under section 16 of obtaining a pecuniary advantage by deception[73] was upheld. It is quite clear from the evidence that P was at best agnostic on the question of D's right to use the cheque card. Their lordships, in asserting that P "believed" that D was authorised to use it[74] must, on the facts, have been using "belief" to stand for ignorance of the truth plus reliance on the representation of authority; firm acceptance of the truth of that representation was not in question.[75] In *Lambie* the manageress was not asked in evidence whether she would have completed the transaction had she known that the customer was acting dishonestly vis-à-vis the bank, having no authority to use the credit card. But the House of Lords held that the manageress's answer "No" to that question could be assumed; and, simply on that basis, *Charles* was indistinguishable and the customer's conviction of a deception offence was confirmed.[76]

6–33   The situation in a cheque card or credit card case is peculiar in that P stands to lose nothing if D's assertion is untrue; the bank will certainly pay. But this is merely the particular reason why in such a case P is prepared to act without a positive belief in the representation. When in any other situation he acts in reliance on D's representation he may or may not be aware that he is taking a risk as to its truth. It is submitted that in either case, if the representation is untrue, he is "deceived."

---

[70] [1977] A.C. 177.
[71] [1981] 3 W.L.R. 88; [1981] 2 All E.R. 776.
[72] Above, § 6–22. See also *Doukas* [1978] 1 W.L.R. 372; [1978] 1 All E.R. 1061.
[73] For the pecuniary advantage, see below, §§ 6–40, 9–07.
[74] [1977] A.C. 177 at pp. 183, 193.
[75] For analysis of the facts, see J. C. Smith at [1977] Crim. L.R. at pp. 618–619.
[76] [1981] 3 W.L.R. at p. 94; [1981] 2 All E.R. at p. 781. It was said that 'No' was the only possible answer; the alternative would be to suppose that the manageress would be prepared to confess a willingness to be party to a fraud on the bank. But see below, § 6–36. For elaborate criticism of *Charles* and *Lambie*, see J. C. Smith at [1977] Crim.L.R. 617–621 and at [1981] Crim.L.R. 713–717. The essential argument may perhaps be summarised thus: that the payee in a cheque card or credit card case (as witness the evidence in *Charles* and *Lambie*) has no interest in the state of the card-holder's account with his bank, for the very point of the card is to guarantee payment whatever the state of that account; that this is as much as to say that the payee has no interest in whether the user has authority to use the card; that a representation cannot be said to deceive one who is indifferent as to its truth; that the question whether the payee would have accepted payment by means of the card had he actually known of the lack of authority is improperly hypothetical; and that dishonest misuse of a cheque card or credit card in a transaction with a third party should not be held to be an offence of deception. See also A.T.H. Smith, "Criminal Misuse of Cheque Cards and Credit Cards" [1978] J.B.L. 129, especially at pp. 135–136.

In the case of alleged deception by words P will be exactly aware of the representation made by D. The identification of what precisely is implied by conduct, however, may call for quite refined analysis, as the preceding pages have shown; and it cannot be expected that P will necessarily be conscious of, and influenced by, exactly the representation that a well-drawn indictment will later attribute to D. It is customary and convenient to speak (as is done in this chapter) of the effect of D's representation on P's mind. But for some cases this language is not perfectly appropriate. P must, of course, have had a broad sense of what D's conduct conveyed. For the rest, the sufficient questions are: Did D's conduct imply a particular statement? Would P have acted as he did if he had known the contrary of that statement?

(ii) *P's knowledge of falsity or indifference to truth.*   If D makes a false   **6–34**
statement of fact to P, intending thereby to induce P to lend him money or sell him property, and P knows that the statement is false but nevertheless lends the money or sells the property, D is not, despite himself, guilty of obtaining by deception. He may, however, be convicted of attempt.[77]

Another possibility is that P is misled by D's statement but is indifferent to the matter about which the statement is made and therefore transfers property without reliance on it; he would act in the same way even if he knew the truth. Here again, though D may have committed an attempt, he has not committed the full offence under section 15.

On the other hand, if D's representation is a factor operating on P's mind as an inducement to part with his property, the offence is complete. It is irrelevant that other factors also operated on his mind.[78]

Evidence of effective representation

To prove that P was induced to part with his property by the particular   **6–35**
false representation charged, the prosecution are normally obliged to adduce P's evidence to this effect. There are two points here.

(a) First, it is *necessary to charge and prove the representation that operated on P* as the relative inducement. This was not done in *Laverty*.[79] D, having acquired a stolen car, registration number JPA 945C, put different number plates on it—DUV 111C. He sold the car to P. He was charged with obtaining the price from P by the false representation that the car "was the original motor car DUV 111C." There was no evidence that P bought the car in reliance upon the representation that it was the car for which that registration number was originally issued. Nor could it necessarily be inferred that he bought the car because of this representation. His evidence was that he bought it because he thought that P was its owner. The representation charged should have been that D was entitled to sell. D's conviction was quashed.

---

[77] Criminal Attempts Act 1981, s. 1; *Edwards* [1978] Crim.L.R. 49; *cf. Hensler* (1870) Cox 570.
[78] *Cf. e.g. Lince* (1873) 12 Cox 451.
[79] [1970] 3 All E.R. 432.

6–36   (b) Secondly, it is *normally necessary for P to give evidence of the inducement.*[80] The obtaining by the deception charged must, after all, be proved beyond reasonable doubt. P's reliance on the particular representation may, however, be a matter of irresistible inference from other proved facts; and if that is so and P's evidence on the point "is not and cannot reasonably be expected to be available," that reliance may be found as a fact.[81] P should nevertheless be produced as a witness unless his absence can be explained.[82] The conviction in *Lambie* depended, as has been seen,[83] on the confidence of the House of Lords that the manageress, had she been asked, would have said that she would not have accepted Ms Lambie's credit card voucher if she had known that Ms Lambie lacked authority to use the card. But the case can hardly establish an irrebuttable presumption that one who is aware that his customer no longer has a right to use his credit card or cheque card will refuse to accept payment involving its use. The point arises, of course, in a hypothetical way. In practice P will not have known the truth; he will justifiably have regarded the card as guaranteeing payment whatever the position as between D and his bank.[84] But it may not be impossible to persuade P to admit that *had* he known the truth he *might* have been unscrupulous and still accepted that mode of payment. He ought therefore to be available for cross-examination.

The effect of intervening events and transactions

6–37   A common purpose of deception is to induce the victim to enter into a contract, with the effect either that property will automatically pass to the offender (as under many contracts for the sale of goods) or that the victim will subsequently transfer property in performance of the contract. Such a transfer may, of course, occur immediately after the making of the contract or after a considerable lapse of time. The intervention of a contract between the deception and the obtaining of property will not normally affect liability to a conviction.[85] The decisive question is whether the deception was itself an operative factor at the time the property was transferred. A striking instance under the old law was *Martin*.[86] D by false pretences induced P to contract to build him a vehicle. P built and delivered the vehicle, although in the meantime D had countermanded the order. A conviction of obtaining the vehicle by false pretences was upheld, the jury having been entitled to find that the pretence was a continuing one.

---

[80] *Laverty* [1970] 3 All E.R. 432.
[81] *Lambie* [1981] 3 W.L.R. at p. 95; [1981] 2 All E.R. at p. 782; applying *Sullivan* (1945) 30 Cr.App.R. 132; and see *Tirado* (1974) 59 Cr.App.R. 80; *Etim* v. *Hatfield* [1975] Crim.L.R. 234. For criticism of *D.P.P.* v. *Ray* [1974] A.C. 370 (above, § 6–25) on this point, see J.C. Smith, *Theft*, para. 156.
[82] *Tirado*, above (P not able to be brought to this country). In *Etim* v. *Hatfield*, above, post office counter clerks were understandably not called to give evidence about particular giro cheque transactions, which presumably they would not recollect.
[83] Above, § 6–32.
[84] See n.76, above.
[85] *Cf. e.g. Abbott* (1847) 1 Den. 273; *Sanders* [1919] 1 K.B. 550.
[86] (1867) L.R. 1 C.C.R. 56.

The question whether the deception charged still operated at the time of   **6-38**
the transfer is really a compression of two questions: (a) Did D's pretence
continue to the time of the transfer? Was he, that is, still impliedly making
his deceptive statement when he obtained the property? That was the
decisive question in *Martin*. (b) Did P transfer the property under the
still-active influence of the pretence? This is a vital question for cases of the
kind shortly to be mentioned. These two questions reflect the two aspects
of "deception" itself—it takes both a deceiver and a deceived to constitute
a deception. The word differs in this respect from "pretence," which is a
one-sided word by comparison. This difference may justify the courts in
making a fresh start with the cases of delayed obtaining, so as to avoid the
troublesome language of causation that they have formerly used. "Did the
deception still operate?" (in our double sense of that question) is a better
question than those framed in terms of "effective" or "contributing"
causes or of pretences "directly connected" with the obtaining.[87]

Nevertheless such language has been used hitherto by the courts with   **6-39**
little complaint from the writers.[88] Thus, in *Button*,[89] an able runner
obtained a big handicap in a race by pretending to be E, a runner with a
poor record, and won the race. He was held guilty of attempting to obtain
the prize by false pretences. Matthew J. described the pretence as "not too
remote."[90] The opposite result was reached in *Clucas*.[91] In that case it was
held that one who induces a bookmaker to accept a large bet upon a horse
by falsely pretending that he is a commission agent acting on behalf of a
number of persons laying small bets does not by the pretence obtain the
sums paid when the horse wins. It is the backing of the winning horse which
is "the effective cause" of the payment.[92]
It is suggested that in cases like these the appropriate result can be
achieved without classifying the obtaining as a "proximate" or "remote"
consequence, as the case may be, of the pretence. What has to be asked is
whether D, at the time of the obtaining, was making, expressly or
impliedly, any deceptive statement to P and, if so, whether P was at that
time induced to pay the money by that statement.

Deception of P, obtaining from Q
D may deceive P and thereby obtain property from Q or a pecuniary   **6-40**
advantage at Q's expense. If there is "a causal connection"[93] between the
deception and the obtaining D may be convicted under section 15 or

---

[87] These phrases are taken from *Clucas* [1949] 2 K.B. 226.
[88] A notable exception is Turner in *Russell on Crime* (12th ed.), p.1187.
[89] [1900] 2 Q.B. 597.
[90] *Ibid.* at p. 600.
[91] [1949] 2 K.B. 226.
[92] *Ibid.* at p. 230. See also *Lewis* (1922), unreported: see *Russell on Crime* (12th ed.), p.1186
n. A schoolmistress obtained an appointment by misrepresenting her qualifications. She
was acquitted of obtaining her salary by this pretence, "on the ground that she was paid
because of services she rendered, and not because of the falsehood." (There will now be an
offence, in cases like *Clucas* and *Lewis*, under s.16: see below, § 9–09).
[93] *Kovacs* [1974] 1 W.L.R. 370 at p. 373; [1974] 1 All E.R. 1236 at p. 1238; approved in
Metropolitan Police Commissioner v. *Charles* [1977] A.C. 177.

section 16 as may be appropriate. The phrase "causal connection" is rather vague and the scope of the principle may at some time need to be more closely determined; but there was little doubt about the adequacy of the connection in the cases in which the principle has so far been applied:

(a) *Property obtained.* An insurance agent by deception induces P to insure with Q company and may be convicted of thereby obtaining commission from the company in respect of the policy.[94]

(b) *Pecuniary advantage.* D wrongfully uses a cheque card to induce P to accept his cheque. D's bank is thereby obliged to honour the cheque so that his bank account is to that extent overdrawn. D may be convicted of obtaining by deception the pecuniary advantage of being "allowed to borrow by way of overdraft" (s. 16(1) and (2)(*b*)).[95]

6.   The Mental Element

6–41   There are three strands in the mental element of the offence under section 15. D cannot be convicted of the offence unless it is proved:

    (i) that his deception was "deliberate or reckless";
    (ii) that he obtained the property "with the intention of permanently depriving [P] of it"; and
    (iii) that he obtained the property "dishonestly."

"Deliberate or reckless" deception[96]

6–42   "Deception" means "any deception (whether deliberate or reckless) . . . " (s. 15(4)). It has already been observed that the word "deception" is, as it were, a two-sided word; it involves both the making of a deceptive statement and the effect of that statement upon the person to whom it is made. Conformably with the nature of the word they qualify, the words "deliberate" and "reckless" also do double duty. There are two senses, that is to say, in which D may deliberately or recklessly deceive P. He may know or be reckless as to the falsity of the statement; and he may make the statement intending to deceive P or reckless whether P is deceived. There is no doubt that both of these senses of the compressed expression "deception (whether deliberate or reckless)" must be satisfied. On the other hand it would seem that recklessness in both of the relevant respects will suffice. So D is guilty of deception if (a) by words or conduct he makes to P a statement which is false, and (b) he is at least reckless as to its falsity, and (c) he is at least reckless as to its misleading P and (d) it does mislead P. But he is not guilty of deception if, though he makes a false statement, he genuinely believes that P will not be misled by it—if, for instance, he believes that P knows it to be untrue.

6–43   A question arises as to the meaning of "reckless." The House of Lords has held that in some other modern criminal statutes the word includes

---

[94] *Clegg* [1977] C.L.Y. 619 (Judge Beaumont).
[95] Cases cited at n.93; below, § 9–07. Also *Smith* v. *Koumourou* [1979] R.T.R. 355.
[96] See *Eighth Report*, para. 101 (i).

failing to advert to a risk that ought to be obvious—in effect a case of gross negligence.[97] It can be argued that the word has the same meaning in section 15 and that the present offence is committed by one who makes a statement that he crassly fails to recognise may be false and who dishonestly obtains property as a result. This is in fact an unlikely case. One who dishonestly *obtains* by deception (as section 15 requires) is almost bound to have *deceived* dishonestly; he will have realised that his representation might be false and might mislead. The House of Lords decisions mentioned above did not specifically refer to offences of dishonesty or to existing authority requiring more than mere negligence for reckless deception.[98] It is submitted that deception requires at least indifference to the truth of the representation. This would keep the criminal offence in line with ealier House of Lords authority on the tort of deceit.[99]

"With the intention of permanently depriving the other of it"

The effect of this phrase is that, as in the case of theft, there will be no **6–44** offence if D intends by his deception to obtain the property from P only temporarily. D may deceive P into lending him a chattel or letting it to him on hire. If he intends to return it when the period of the loan or hiring is over, he commits no offence under section 15. It is necessary, however, to distinguish carefully between a loan of money and a loan of other property. When D, pretending to be down on his luck, persuades P to lend him £10 in cash, he intends to deprive P permanently of the particular notes and coins handed to him; and, so far as this aspect of the mental element of the offence is concerned, his conduct is within the section although he may intend to repay his debt.[1] And where by deception D obtains a loan from P by cheque, he intends to deprive P permanently of the cheque, for once it is paid it ceases to be in its substance the thing that it was before.[2]

D has the necessary intention for the purpose of section 15 if he intends to deprive P entirely of whatever interest P has in the property. As has been seen,[3] P need only have possession or control of the property or any proprietary right or interest in it, in order to be the victim of this offence. So, for example, if P has a lien on D's goods, and D by deception induces P to deliver the goods to him, intending to defeat the lien, the offence is committed. Similarly, D may trick P into parting with possession of property which P is entitled to possess for a short while only, and this will

---

[97] *Caldwell* [1981] 2 W.L.R. 509; [1981] 1 All E.R. 961 (Criminal Damage Act 1981, s.1); *Lawrence* [1981] 2 W.L.R. 524; [1981] 1 All E.R. 974 (Road Traffic Act 1972, s.2: driving recklessly).

[98] *Staines* (1974) 60 Cr.App.R. 160; *Royle* [1971] 1 W.L.R. 1764; [1971] 3 All E.R. 1359; and see *Waterfall* [1970] 1 Q.B. 148, where the point is expressed to relate to the requirement of dishonesty rather than to that of deception.

[99] *Derry* v. *Peek* (1889) 14 App.Cas. 337. Common law fraud is committed by one who makes a false statement "(1) knowingly, or (2) without belief in its truth, or (3) recklessly, careless whether it be true or false": *per* Lord Herschell at p. 374. Lord Herschell observed that "(3)" is really only an instance of "(2)".

[1] The point is illustrated in *Halstead* v. *Patel* [1972] 1 W.L.R. 661; [1972] 2 All E.R. 147.

[2] *Duru* [1974] 1 W.L.R.2; [1973] 3 All E.R. 715.

[3] Above § 6–10.

be an offence under section 15 even if D intends to return the property to its owner (for whom, indeed, he may have practised the fraud).

6–45   It will be remembered that the expression "with the intention of permanently depriving the other of it" is partially defined for the purpose of theft by section 6.[4] By section 15(3) that section is made to apply also for purposes of section 15 "with the necessary adaptation of the reference to appropriating." Section 6 is therefore to be read for purposes of section 15 as though for the word "appropriating" in section 6(1) there were substituted the words "obtaining by deception." There are obviously some difficulties involved in applying a section that is sufficiently obscure in its primary context to another offence for which it is, in a number of places, even less happily worded. But to deal fully with all the difficulties would be to exaggerate the importance of the section. The following observations may suffice.

(a) Cases in which D obtains *ownership* of P's property by deception "without meaning [P] permanently to lose the thing itself," yet intending "to treat the thing as his own to dispose of regardless of [P's] rights," must be rare indeed.[5] We may construct one, admittedly unlikely, case by way of example. D is hard up. By deception he induces P to sell him a valuable article at a very low price. He merely wants to raise money on the article. He pawns it for a large sum and sends the pawn ticket to P with an apologetic letter.[6]

(b) It is easier to imagine cases in which section 6 might be relevant where D by deception obtains *possession* but not ownership of the property in question. Suppose tht D dishonestly deceives P into giving him possession of some property other than land.[7] The effect of section 6 is that if, though he does not mean P permanently to lose the thing itself, D intends to treat it as his own to dispose of regardless of P's rights, the mental element of the present offence, as of theft, is satisfied. (It will be remembered, however, that if the result of the deception is "a borrowing," s. 6 will apply only if the borrowing "is for a period and in circumstances making it equivalent to an outright taking.") The reader is now invited to consider the first three situations suggested in the discussion of section 6(1) in § 2–74 and to suppose that possession in each situation is obtained by deception. In each case D will on the altered facts have committed an offence under section 15.

(c) If D obtains property by deception, intending to lend it to E for a period and in circumstances making the lending equivalent to an outright disposal, he will be regarded as intending to deprive P permanently (s. 6(1)). So also if he obtains the property intending for his own purposes to part with it under a condition as to its return which he may not be able to

---

[4] See above, §§ 2–73 to 2–77.
[5] In *Duru*, above, the Court of Appeal would if necessary have held s.6(1) to be relevant.
[6] *Cf.* situation (iii) in § 2–74.
[7] As to land, see (d), below.

perform (s. 6(2)). It must be doubtful whether such cases, though provided for by the terms of section 6 as applied to section 15, ever actually arise.

(d) In some of the situations dealt with above, D may be guilty both of **6–46** obtaining property by deception and of theft. But this is not possible if the property is land: you cannot by the same transaction obtain land by deception and also steal it.[8] It is clear, however, that an offence under section 15 can be committed by a deception which obtains an existing interest in land (by the assignment of a lease, for example). But suppose that D by deception induces P to grant him a lease. In this case what D "obtains" must be the land, by obtaining possession of it (s. 15(2)); it is the land which is "property belonging to [P]."[9] The question that might arise is whether a fraudulent lessee can ever be described as intending to deprive a lessor permanently of the land the subject of the demise. What, in particular, if D obtains a very long lease? Leaving aside section 6 for the moment, is there any point short of the assignment of P's whole interest at which the quality of temporariness ceases and that of permanence takes over? If D obtains a lease for 99 years or more it is certainly tempting to say that he intends to deprive P permanently of the land. It cannot be confidently predicted that the courts would yield to this temptation without the aid of section 6: it is sufficient here to hint at the possibility of their doing so. But suppose that P's age and the length of the lease permit D a plausible claim that he did not intend to permanently deprive P personally (let alone his successors in title) of the land. Does D nevertheless intend, within the meaning of section 6(1), to treat the land as his own to dispose of regardless of P's rights? It would not seem so, unless the taking of the lease can be treated as "a borrowing . . . for a period and in circumstances making [the borrowing] equivalent to an outright taking."[10] How ill-adapted, indeed, is the language of section 6 to the offence under section 15! If D by deception obtained a loan of a chattel that he intended to keep for 25 years, there would surely be an offence. Yet if he takes a lease for the same period, an offence can possibly be found only by treating "borrowing" in this context as including any acquisition of possession. Not to do so is to create an unjust distinction; but to do so is to torture language.[11]

Nor does the Act cater in clear terms for the case—surely not a fanciful one—of the person who by deception obtains a tenancy or short lease, intending, when his contractual right is determined by notice or effluxion of time, to claim security of tenure under relevant legislation.

---

[8] See s. 4(2), which limits the circumstances in which land can be stolen, but which does not apply to s.15 (s. 1(3)).

[9] The leasehold interest carved out of P's estate in the land does not exist before it is created by the lease and it never belongs to P. It cannot itself, therefore, be said to be the subject-matter of an offence. *Cf. Chan Wan Lam* [1981] Crim.L.R. 497 (see n.11).

[10] For such a borrowing may amount to treating the property as D's own to dispose of: s. 6(1).

[11] In *Chan Wan Lam* v. *The Queen*, above, where deception induced a government grant of a sub-lease expiring in 1997, three days before expiry of the head lease, the Court of Appeal of Hong Kong considered questions raised in this paragraph and concluded that an offence under the local equivalent of s. 15 could be committed only where D intends to deprive P of the whole of his interest.

"Dishonestly"

6-47   (i) The word "dishonestly" contributes, it is thought, to limiting "reckless" deception to cases in which D is indifferent to the truth of his representation and not merely negligent in making it. This has been discussed above.[12]

(ii) The word "dishonestly" qualifies the phrase "obtains property"; the obtaining must be dishonest. There is no provision in the Act to indicate what "dishonestly" means for this purpose, as section 2 does, at least partially, for the corresponding element in theft. The Committee assumed that D would not obtain property dishonestly if it was property to which he believed himself legally entitled.[13] The rule in relation to the present offence would be analogous to that stated for theft by section 2(1)(a).[14] The supposed legal entitlement upon which D could rely to resist the allegation of dishonesty might be one of several kinds:

(a) D might believe that the property belonged to him and that P was not entitled to retain it.

(b) D might believe that the property belonged to E, for whom he was obtaining it, and that P was not entitled to detain it from E.

(c) D might believe, or it might be the case, that P owed D or E money; and D might believe that the obtaining of the property in question from P was a proper way of enforcing his or E's claim against the defaulting debtor.[15]

Whether a claim of right defence is in fact provided as a matter of law by the word "dishonestly" is uncertain in the light of *Feely*,[16] the application of which to section 15 is discussed in the following paragraphs. One of the many controversial results of that decision is the availability of the argument that, although (by virtue of s. 2(1)(a)) I am innocent of theft if by force I induce P to give me what I wrongly think I have a claim to, it is for the jury to decide whether I am guilty under section 15 if by lying I induce him to do the same. It is hoped that this distinction between the two offences does not exist.[17]

6-48   (iii) As will be recalled, *Feely* decides for the offence of theft that when D does not raise a defence bringing him within section 2(1), the question whether he appropriated the property dishonestly is a question for the jury to decide without the assistance of definition from the court. The basis of this treatment of the issue is the proposition that, the word "dishonestly" being in common use, jurors do not need judicial help to tell them what

[12] § 6–43. Dishonesty and deception are, in fact, separate issues; but they are quite commonly confused or telescoped in the cases. Examples may be found in *Waterfall* [1970] 1 Q.B. 148 (see (1970) 33 M.L.R. 217); *Potger* (1970) 55 Cr.App.R. 42; *Halstead* v. *Patel* [1972] 1 W.L.R. 661; [1972] 2 All E.R. 147; *Greenstein* [1975] 1 W.L.R. 1353; [1976] 1 All E.R. 1; *Lewis* (1975) 62 Cr.App.R. 206.
[13] *Eighth Report*, para. 88.
[14] See the discussion of s.2(1)(a) above, §§ 2–81, 2–82.
[15] *Cf.Williams* (1836) 7 C. & P. 354; and see the discussion, in the context of obtaining by false pretences, by Williams, *Criminal Law—The General Part* (2nd ed.), pp. 330–331.
[16] [1973] Q.B. 530 (above, § 2–87).
[17] The Court of Criminal Appeal in Victoria has held that it does not: *Salvo* [1980] V.R. 401.

amounts to dishonesty. Consistency demands a similar approach to the issue in the context of section 15. The application of that approach required further authority, however. For there were appellate decisions prior to *Feely* which had held that as a matter of law it could be no defence that one had intended to repay a loan obtained by deception[18] or a sum of money obtained across a post office counter by a cheque drawn on an empty giro account.[19] These decisions had not been questioned in *Feely*; and one of them had been relied upon on a related point.[20] There was, too, the consideration that *ex hypothesi* D has been guilty of deliberate or reckless deception in order to obtain property from P to which D maintains no claim of right. The deception itself might be thought to supply a sufficient element of dishonesty.[21]

These doubts as to the general application of *Feely* to section 15 were dispelled by *Greenstein*,[22] which must be taken to overrule, although it did not mention, the pre-*Feely* decisions. D applied for shares being issued to the public. He knew that the issue would be oversubscribed and that shares would be allotted to applicants in proportion to the size of their applications. Cheques had to be sent with applications; an applicant allotted less shares than he applied for would be sent a "return" cheque for the change with the letter of allotment. D applied for very large amounts of shares, sending cheques which could not possibly be met on first presentation—as on the facts he represented they could be—without the help of the proceeds of the issuing houses' own return cheques (which he knew could be speedily cleared). Granted that D obtained the letters of allotment and return cheques by deception, the question was whether this method of conducting "stagging" operations[23] was "dishonest." This was the first prosecution to test that question. The Court of Appeal, citing *Feely*, approved the trial judge's direction that the question was for the jury to decide.[24] This is a remarkable allocation of law-making power to the jury. Speculation is justified as to the kind of precedent the jury's decision constitutes.[25] In case the verdict is indeed some kind of precedent, it had better be mentioned: the jury convicted.

---

[18] *McCall* (1970) 55 Cr.App.R. 175.
[19] *Halstead* v. *Patel* [1972] 1 W.L.R. 661; [1972] 2 All E.R. 147. In *Potger* (1970) 55 Cr.App.R. 42, the Court of Appeal had said that the word "dishonestly" had "a wider ambit" than the phrase "intent to defraud" used in the old law of false pretences. This suggested that a number of situations which under that law were cases of intent to defraud were now as a matter of law to be classified as cases of dishonesty: see especially *Naylor* (1865) L.R. 1 C.C.R. 41; *Carpenter* (1911) 22 Cox 618; and, as to conspiracy to defraud, *Allsop* (1976) 64 Cr.App.R. 29.
[20] See above, § 2–89, n.72.
[21] *Cf.Potger* (1970) 55 Cr.App.R. 42, distinguishing in this respect between deliberate deception and the reckless variety.
[22] [1975] 1 W.L.R. 1353; [1976] 1 All E.R. 1.
[23] Applying for an allotment of shares or stock, in order to sell immediately at a profit—an operation not in itself illegal.
[24] By applying their own standards: [1975] 1 W.L.R. at p. 1359; [1976] 1 All E.R. at p. 6. A statement apparently to the contrary in *Landy* [1981] 1 W.L.R. 355 at p. 365; [1981] 1 All E.R. 1172 at p. 1181, was sought to be explained in *McIvor, The Times*, November 18, 1981; C.A. No. 3488/A/80. The explanation was unconvincing; but it is plain that the Court of Appeal adheres to its statement in *Greenstein*.
[25] D.W. Elliott [1976] Crim.L.R. at pp. 715–716.

7. JURISDICTION

The place of the obtaining

6–49   Where either the person using deception or his victim is not within the jurisdiction, a question can arise as to the jurisdiction of the English court. The court will be competent to try the offence only if it was committed within the jurisdiction and that depends upon the obtaining of the property having occurred here.[26]

(i) *D in England, P abroad*

If D, communicating from England with P who is abroad, deceives P into sending him property that in due course arrives in this country, D will usually "obtain" that property here and not abroad and will thus commit an offence here. The property may, however, be obtained abroad in an exceptional case. This occurred in *Harden*[27] (decided under the Larceny Act 1916, s. 32), where D, in England, wrote to a finance company in Jersey, offering to sell goods for letting on hire-purchase to D's customers. D wrote: "This offer may be accepted . . . within one month . . . by sending your cheque for the net amount." It was held that D thus agreed that the posting of the cheque in Jersey should be equivalent to receipt by him. He therefore obtained the cheque in Jersey and could not be convicted of obtaining it by false pretences in England. This is unsatisfactory; it is curious, to say the least, if by a careful choice of wording D can determine where he commits his crime and thus his amenability to justice.

The Court of Appeal, in *Tirado*,[28] has made it clear that the principle in *Harden* will not be extended. It depends upon a finding that D agreed to accept posting as delivery to himself. In *Tirado* the jury did not so find. D ran an employment agency in Oxford. He obtained bankers' drafts from Morocco, sent on behalf of people for whom he falsely claimed to have jobs in England. He had requested his fee with the client's application form, to be sent through a Moroccan bank or by post. He was held properly convicted of obtaining the drafts in England. One view of what he had written was that he was merely indicating ways of sending the fees that his clients might adopt.[29]

6–50   (ii) *D abroad, P in England*

In the converse case, where ownership in property that the victim dispatches from England passes at the time and place of dispatch, D will have committed an offence within the jurisdiction and can be convicted here if he becomes amenable to process. If ownership does not pass at that time but only when D receives the property abroad, it seems that the English courts will have no jurisdiction.[30]

---

[26] *Harden* [1963] 1 Q.B. 8; *Tirado* (1974) 59 Cr.App.R. 80 (notwithstanding doubts expressed by Lord Diplock in *Treacy* v. *D.P.P.* [1971] A.C. 537 at p.563); *D.P.P.* v. *Stonehouse* [1978] A.C. 55, *per* Viscount Dilhorne at p. 74; *cf. Ellis* [1899] 1 Q.B. 230; *Governor of Pentonville Prison, ex p. Khubchandani* (1980) 71 Cr.App.R. 241.
[27] [1963] 1 Q.B. 8.
[28] (1974) 59 Cr.App.R. 80.
[29] *Ibid.* at p. 87.
[30] See cases cited in n.26, above.

Attempts

(i) *D in England, P abroad* **6–51**

If D in England writes to P abroad in an unsuccessful bid to obtain property by deception, his liability for attempt to commit an offence under section 15 depends on whether there would be jurisdiction to try him for the complete offence if he were successful. For the offence of attempt requires an act done with intent to commit an offence which, if it were completed, would be triable in England and Wales.[31] So (applying the principle stated above) there will be an offence if the attempt was to bring about an obtaining in this country.

(ii) *D abroad, P in England* **6–52**

In *Baxter*,[32] D in Northern Ireland posted a letter to football pool promoters in England making a false claim to a prize. The promoters were suspicious and no prize was paid. D was held to have committed within the jurisdiction an attempt to obtain property by deception by means of a letter transmitted to England and intended to produce an obtaining from a victim within the jurisdiction. The same principle, though applied more subtly on the facts, justified D's conviction of attempt in *D.P.P* v. *Stonehouse*.[33] In that case D was a famous public figure. He insured his life in England in favour of his wife. He then staged the appearance of his death by drowning in Florida and disappeared. The news of his supposed death naturally reached his wife and the insurers, as he intended. The case differs from *Baxter* in that no claim was actually made; but D's false representation was communicated in England so that it could be used by his innocent wife to obtain the assured sum. D was held properly convicted in England of attempting to obtain (that is, to enable his wife to obtain: s. 15(2)) property by deception. The English courts had jurisdiction because "acts constituting an attempt to commit a crime under English law [were] done abroad and intended effects [were] felt in England."[34]

8. LIABILITY OF COMPANY OFFICERS, ETC.

Any director, manager, secretary or other similar officer of a body **6–53** corporate, or any person who was purporting to act in any such capacity, may be proved to have consented to or connived at an offence under section 15 committed by the body corporate. If so, such a person is also guilty of the offence (s. 18(1)).[35]

An officer of a company who actively encourages or participates in the offence will be liable on ordinary principles independently of this provision. Indeed, depending on his status and function in the company, it may be his acts and states of mind which render the company itself guilty of the offence together with him.

Section 18 therefore strikes at the officer who is not guilty as an ordinary

---

[31] Criminal Attempts Act 1981, s. 1(1)(4).
[32] [1972] Q.B. 1.
[33] [1978] A.C. 55.
[34] *Ibid.* at p. 92.
[35] As to bodies corporate managed by their members, see s. 18(2).

principal or accessory party to the offence. It assumes, that is to say, that the company has committed the offence by the conduct of some other officer or officers, but treats as fully liable the officer who inactively acquiesced in what was done. The section therefore involves a striking example of criminal liability for omission.[36]

In order to prove connivance it would seem necessary to show that the officer in question (i) knew what was being done or wilfully closed his eyes to the obvious, and (ii) acquiesced in what was being done by wilfully failing to do what he could reasonably do to prevent it. It is difficult to believe that in practice consent can involve anything less, for consent can hardly be manifested except by active participation or encouragement (with which the section is not concerned) or by wilful passivity.

---

[36] There are numerous precedents for this kind of liability.

CHAPTER 7

OBTAINING SERVICES BY DECEPTION

1. THE OFFENCE

Section 1(1) of the The Theft Act 1978 provides: "A person who by any   **7–01**
deception dishonestly obtains services from another" is guilty of an
offence. The offence carries the following penalties: on conviction on
indictment, up to five years' imprisonment (s. 4(2)); on summary
conviction, up to six months' imprisonment and/or a fine not exceeding (for
the time being) £1,000 (s. 4(3)).

The background to the creation of this offence has been described in
the first part of Chapter 6[1] (Introduction to the Fraud Offences), where
comment was made on its surprising width.

Liability of company officers, etc.

Section 18 of the 1968 Act applies in relation to the offence as it does in   **7–02**
relation to section 15 of the 1968 Act (1978 Act, s. 5(1)).[2]

2. "BY ANY DECEPTION DISHONESTLY OBTAINS"

"By any deception"

The word "deception" has the same meaning here as in section 15 of the   **7–03**
1968 Act—namely, the meaning stated in section 15(4) of that Act (1978
Act, s. 5(2)). The discussion of the word in that context may therefore be
referred to.[3] So may the discussion, in connection with the section 15
offence, of the necessary relationship between the false representation and
the relevant obtaining.[4]

It should be noted that the present offence may be committed by means
of any deception. As explained above,[5] the Committee's original draft
clause limited their proposed offence to deception "going to the prospect
of payment being duly made." But under section 1 as eventually enacted
"services" may be obtained by deception as to any matter, which may or
may not be concerned with the question of payment.

"Dishonestly"

The obtaining of services must be achieved "dishonestly." There is no   **7–04**
need to repeat here what has already been said of the same element in the
offence of obtaining property by deception under section 15 of the 1968
Act.[6]

---

[1] Especially at §§ 6–04, 6–05.
[2] s. 18 is discussed at § 6–53.
[3] §§ 6–12 to 6–29, and §§ 6–42, 6–43.
[4] §§ 6–30 to 6–40.
[5] § 6–05.
[6] §§ 6–47, 6–48.

3. "OBTAINS SERVICES FROM ANOTHER"

7–05   "It is an obtaining of services where the other is induced to confer a benefit by doing some act, or causing or permitting some act to be done, on the understanding that the benefit has been or will be paid for" (subs. (2)).

It was important that the notion of "services" should be broadly understood; hence the explanation in terms simply of the conferring of a benefit by the doing of any act or by causing or permitting any act to be done. But purely gratuitous services (such as lending a lawn-mower or "lending a hand") ought to be excluded; hence the need for a benefit conferred "on the understanding that [it] has been or will be paid for."

"Confer a benefit"

7–06   There are two competing approaches to the reference to P's being induced to "confer a benefit." According to the first approach, which is probably most generally favoured, the reference imports a limiting requirement into the section. It is understood to mean that there are some acts beneficial to D (or to a third party) and some non-beneficial, and that an offence is committed only if deception is used to include the doing, causing or permitting of acts of the former class.[7] It is thought that this approach is erroneous. It renders the offence too vague at its outer edge and promises the introduction of an unsatisfactory and unnecessary issue into prosecutions under the section. The alternative approach may be introduced by observing on the difficulty that would have attended the drafting of the end of section 1(2) if some such notion as that of conferring a benefit had not been employed earlier in the subsection. Some word or short phrase was apparently needed to stand for the thing that "has been or will be paid for." It is thought that "to confer a benefit by [doing, etc.]" is simply a drafting device that makes the phrase "the benefit" available for this purpose. The device need not be understood as modifying the sense of the subsection. Precisely because someone is understood to be prepared to pay for an act or a permission to do an act, the doing or causing of that act or the giving of that permission is perfectly sensibly described as the conferring of a benefit on him.[8] Who else is to be the judge of the matter? If it were not a benefit to him he would not pay for it.

"Doing some act, or causing or permitting some act to be done"

7–07   P may perform, or cause his employee to perform, some professional service, for example, or some work such as driving, building or repairing. Or he may give permission to D (or to E, for whom D uses the deception)

---

[7] See J. R. Spencer, "The Theft Act 1978" [1979] Crim. L.R. 24 at p. 27 ("To some extent as yet uncertain . . . the use of the word 'benefit' cuts down the extreme wideness of the phrases which follow it."); Smith, *Theft*, paras. 224–229 (suggesting the exclusion from the class of benefits of some criminal and some unlawful acts).

[8] Compare the convenient use of the same language in the *Thirteenth Report*, para.9.

to do some act (*e.g.* permission to use equipment, as when D hires a car[9] or the use of a computer, or an amenity such as a tennis court). Many benefits will involve P in both the doing or causing of acts and the giving of permission (*e.g.* the provision of hotel accommodation).

An offence under section 1 is not committed merely by inducing P's **7–08** agreement to confer a benefit. He must actually confer a benefit by doing, or causing or permitting to be done, an act that has been or is to be paid for. It is submitted that this is not P's act of agreement but some act that he will do, or cause or permit to be done, in performance of the agreement. Partial performance should be enough where P abandons performance after discovering the deception or where D, perhaps anticipating detection, disappears and thus frustrates further performance. If detection occurs before anything is done under the agreement, the inducing of the agreement may, of course, depending on the circumstances, be enough to constitute an attempt.

It seems clear that neither P's forbearance to act (as by not enforcing a debt or realising a security) nor his causing an omission (as by instructing his employee not to retake possession of hired goods from D) is "doing some act" within the meaning of section 1(2).

Section 1(2) does not specify that the act be one that is done for, or **7–09** permitted to be done by, the person using the deception. So D may commit an offence under section 1 by obtaining services for E.

"On the understanding that the benefit has been or will be paid for"

The reference to an "understanding" as to payment is a novel one. The **7–10** meaning of this word should rarely cause difficulty. The alleged deception will normally relate to the question of payment and will induce P's "understanding" about the matter; and this will suffice. In an exceptional case, however, where the alleged deception relates to something other than payment, P's understanding that the benefit will be paid for ought surely to be a well-founded understanding. It should be necessary to prove a transaction on the strength of which a reasonable observer would share P's understanding.

The section is no doubt mainly directed to deception relating to payment **7–11** or the prospect of payment. Consideration of such deception may, indeed, have influenced the wording of subsection (2). But the subsection does not provide, as it might easily have done, that P's "understanding that the benefit has been or will be paid for" must itself be induced by deception, or even, for that matter, that the understanding must be false. Notwithstanding the way in which the final words of subsection (2) were introduced in

---

[9] This will be an obtaining of property within the meaning of the 1968 Act, s. 15. But the offence under that section requires an intention of permanently depriving P of the property.

Parliament,[10] those words do nothing to limit the range of relevant deceptions. They simply restrict the benefits that are to be regarded as "services" to benefits for which payment is required. It seems, therefore, that there will be an obtaining of services by deception even where P does an act that D will in fact pay for, being induced to do the act by the deception, for example, that he is dealing with somebody other than D (where it is known that he is unwilling to deal with D) or that D was first-comer among a number of persons seeking the benefit.[11]

Transactions contrary to law or unenforceable

7–12 It does not matter that the transaction is one in respect of which the victim of the deception could not in any case enforce payment. A man may be convicted under the section if he obtains the services of a prostitute without intending to pay her; or if he similarly obtains services which it is positively a criminal offence for his victim to provide.

The wording of the section seems, however, to exclude gaming and wagering contracts. If D bets with a bookmaker on credit, he may perhaps be said to induce the bookmaker to confer a benefit on him by doing an act—namely, by recording the bet. But even if this is so, the act is done on the understanding, not that the benefit "will" be paid for, but only that it "will in a certain event" be paid for. Such a case of contingent "liability" has been omitted by the draftsman. It is, however, within section 16(2) (c) of the 1968 Act.[12]

No view to gain or intent to cause loss is necessary

7–13 If D's deception need not concern the fact or prospect of payment, it is remarkable that he is not required to have acted with a view to gain or an intent to cause loss. As it is, if the above analysis of subsection (2) is correct, the offence may be committed by a person who pays or will pay the proper price for the services he will obtain. A 17-year-old who misrepresents his age in order to gain admission to a cinema showing an X-certificate film appears to commit the offence, so long as his conduct is regarded as dishonest.[13]

[10] Mr. Brynmor John explained that the words "are there to cover two possibilities: . . . the giving of a dud cheque . . . [and] the deception which persuades the victim that he has already been paid" (Standing Committee D, June 27, 1978: Official Report, cols. 4–5).

[11] *Cf.* Parry, "Queue-Jumping and the Theft Bill" (1978) 128 New L.J. 663. (The equivalent point may be made, of course, about the offence of obtaining property by deception.)

[12] Below, § 9–09.

[13] *Cf.* Parry, *loc.cit.,* n.11. For an attempted justification of the omission of any reference to gain or loss, see H.L. Deb., Vol. 394, col. 1647: the omitted phrase produces "inconsistent results when applied to services." The examples given do not, with respect, explain the difficulty.

CHAPTER 8

EVASION OF LIABILITY BY DECEPTION

1. THE OFFENCE[1]

Section 2 of the Theft Act 1978 penalises a range of conduct previously **8–01**
covered or intended to be covered by section 16(2)(*a*) of the 1968 Act.
(The background to the 1978 Act has been described in the first part of
Chapter 6 (Introduction to the Fraud Offences).) Section 2 deals with
deception that secures the remission of existing liability, or induces an
existing creditor to wait for payment or to forgo payment, or obtains
exemption from or abatement of liability. The offence created by the
section attracts the same penalties as the offence under section 1: on
conviction on indictment, up to five year's imprisonment (s. 4(2)); on
summary conviction, up to six months' imprisonment and/or a fine not
exceeding (for the time being) £1,000 (s. 4(3)).

Mere "evasion" of liability not in fact penalised

Under section 16(2)(*a*) of the 1968 Act it was in terms an offence to **8–02**
obtain by deception (among other advantages) the "evasion" of a debt.
This was held to include the "unilateral operation" of obtaining an
opportunity to avoid paying the debt. It did "not connote any activity on
the part of the creditor,"[2] as by consciously releasing the debtor from his
obligation. Even tricking the creditor into turning his back so that the
debtor could steal away sufficed.[3] Nor had the debtor's evasion of his
obligation to be permanent, either in intention or in effect.[4]

The related varieties of fraud covered by section 2 of the 1978 Act are
given the convenient collective name "evasion of liability by deception."[5]
But the language of "evasion" is renounced in the body of the section. The
section does not now penalise the mere unilateral obtaining of an
opportunity to avoid paying[6] but only the obtaining of relief through the
operation of a decision on the part of the creditor as to liability or payment;
and where the creditor is induced to wait for payment or to forgo payment
(s. 2(1)(*b*)) the debtor must have an "intent to make permanent default."

---

[1] For criticism see J.R. Spencer, "The Theft Act 1978" [1979] Crim.L.R. 24 at pp. 34–35.
[2] *D.P.P.* v. *Turner* [1974] A.C. 357; quotations from Lord Reid at p. 366.
[3] *D.P.P.* v. *Ray* [1974] A.C. 370.
[4] *D.P.P.* v. *Turner* [1974] A.C. 357.
[5] It has been said that "the differences between the offences relate principally to the different
situations in which the debtor-creditor relationship has arisen": *Holt and Lee* [1981] 1
W.L.R. 1000 at p. 1003; [1982] 2 All E.R. 854 at p. 856; but this view seems to be without
foundation.
[6] But see section 3 (below, Chapter 11) for the case where "payment on the spot is required
or expected."

Liability of company officers, etc.

8–03   Section 18 of the 1968 Act applies in relation to this offence as it does in relation to section 15 of the 1968 Act (1978 Act, s. 5(1)).[7]

2.   "BY ANY DECEPTION DISHONESTLY SECURES/INDUCES/OBTAINS"

"By any deception"

8–04   The word "deception" has the same meaning here as in section 15 of the 1968 Act—namely, the meaning stated in section 15(4) of that Act (1978 Act, s. 5(2)). The discussion of the word in that context may therefore be referred to.[8] So may the discussion, in connection with the section 15 offence, of the necessary relationship between the false representation and its relevant effect.[9]

"Dishonestly"

8–05   A person charged with an offence under this section must be proved to have acted "dishonestly." Reference may be made to the discussion of this word in the context of section 15 of the 1968 Act.[10]

(i) As under section 15, so here, the word "dishonestly" contributes to limiting "reckless" deception to cases in which D is indifferent to the truth of his statement and not merely negligent in making it.[11] Only if he does not believe in the truth of his representation is that representation "dishonest."[12]

(ii) Under section 15 the word "dishonestly" qualifies "obtains," so that the obtaining of property must be dishonest. Here it qualifies "secures," "induces" or "obtains" (s. 2(1)(a)(b) and (c) respectively) with the like effect. It is possible, therefore, though cases must be rare, that a deceptive evasion of liability otherwise falling within section 2 may not be an offence because D believes that he (or, as the case may be, E, for whose benefit he acts) is legally entitled to the advantage secured or is legally entitled to use the advantage as a means of enforcing a right against P.[13]

(iii) Under section 15 there is, of course, the need for an intention to deprive P of the property obtained by the deception. The present section does not in terms require an intention to secure whatever relevant advantage derives from the deception, but "dishonestly" performs the corresponding function. D does not by deception dishonestly induce P to wait for payment, for example, unless his object in using the deception is that P shall be so induced.[14]

3.   "LIABILITY TO MAKE A PAYMENT"

8–06   Each part of section 2(1) refers to some existing or prospective "liability to make a payment." Such liability may have a contractual, quasi-contractual

---

[7] s. 18 is discussed at § 6–53.
[8] §§ 6–12 to 6–29.
[9] §§ 6–30 to 6–40.
[10] §§ 6–47, 6–48.
[11] See above, § 6–43.
[12] *Waterfall* [1970] 1 Q.B. 148; *Royle* [1971] 1 W.L.R. 1764; [1971] 3 All E.R. 1359.
[13] *Cf.* above, § 6–47 (ii).
[14] *Cf. Locker* [1971] 2 Q.B. 321 (decided under s. 16 of the 1968 Act).

or delictual origin. It may arise in equity, as under a trust. Or it may exist as a matter of public rather than private law. The Committee give as an example of the application of section 2(1)(c) the case of a ratepayer who makes a false statement in order to obtain an abatement of his liability to pay rates.[15]

"Liability" means "legally enforceable liability"

The section is concerned only with "legally enforceable liability" **8–07** (subs. (2)). So, for example, no offence under the section can be committed against a bookmaker or other party to a gaming transaction, against a prostitute, or against a person conducting an unlicensed consumer credit business in respect of a regulated agreement unenforceable by virtue of the Consumer Credit Act 1974, s. 40(1). A minor cannot commit the offence in respect of his "liability" under a contract void under the Infants Relief Act 1874.

There is a partial inconsistency between sections 1 and 2. D may induce P by deception to perform a service for an abated price. If the contract for the service is illegal or *contra bonos mores*, D cannot be convicted under section 2(1)(c) but is liable to conviction under section 1.

A liability is presumably not "legally enforceable" (although it may **8–08** possibly be enforceable by lawful means other than action) if action to enforce it is statute-barred, or if it arises under a contract unenforceable by action for want of a note or memorandum of it signed by or on behalf of the debtor.

Liability for wrongful act or omission

P may claim to have a right to compensation from D in respect of an **8–09** alleged tort or other "wrongful act or omission." So long as D has not "accepted" liability and P has not "established" it, no deception used by D to induce P to abandon his claim or reduce his demand can found an offence under the section (subs. (2)). Once D has accepted liability, however, it seems that he may commit an offence by some ·deception affecting the determination of quantum.[16] It is not clear whether liability may be "accepted" for this purpose even though its admission occurs in negotiations that are properly described as being "without prejudice." It is thought that it may be. The test, it is submitted, should be whether it is clear, from a statement made by D or on his behalf, that liability is not in dispute.

Meaning of "existing liability"

The "existing liability" required by section 2(1)(a) and (b) must, it is **8–10** suggested, be an actual and not merely a potential or contingent liability (*debitum in praesenti*), though payment may be due only in the future (*solvendum in futuro*). The fact that liability to pay under an existing

---

[15] *Thirteenth Report,* para. 15; for further examples, see Appendix 2 to that Report, para. 7.
[16] *Cf. Thirteenth Report,* para. 16.

contract may be conditional upon performance by the other party should not prevent the liability's being "existing" for this purpose. If P has agreed to deliver goods next week against D's promise to pay within the month, D, it is submitted, has an "existing liability." But an insurer or a surety would seem to have only a potential and not an "existing" liability until the occurrence of the insured risk or the default of the primary obligee. The distinction suggested here is not entirely satisfactory, but the rather informal language of the section prompts the manufacture of some artificial dividing line.

4. SECURING REMISSION OF EXISTING LIABILITY

Section 2(1)(a)

8–11   A person commits an offence under section 2(1) who

" . . . by any deception—
(a) dishonestly secures the remission of the whole or part of any existing liability to make a payment, whether his own liability or another's . . . "

This is the case of the debtor who persuades his creditor by a lying hard-luck story to let him off the debt altogether; or that of the purchaser of goods or services who, some time after the bargain is concluded (so that there is an "existing liability"), falsely claims to belong to an association to whose members the supplier customarily gives a discount, with the result that a percentage is knocked off the bill. It is equally an offence if D induces P to remit E's liability rather than some liability of his own.

What mainly distinguishes paragraph (a) of section 2(1) from paragraph (b) is that under paragraph (a) the creditor intends an extinction (in whole or in part) of the debtor's liability, whereas under (b)[17] he intends only a deferment of payment. It must be immaterial that the creditor's agreement to the extinction is not binding on him, because it was obtained by fraud, and that the debtor whose fraud is uncovered may in the result, like the paragraph (b) offender, gain temporary relief only.[18]

Meaning of "remission"

8–12   A "remission" of liability seems to require knowledge on the creditor's part of what is being remitted. It is submitted that the following case is not within section 2 (1)(a). D hires a car from P. The sum that D must pay at the end of the hiring depends in part on the extent to which he has used the car. Before returning the car to P, D tampers with the odometer so that its reading is lower than it should be. P therefore charges a smaller sum than is actually due. This, it is submitted, is not a "remission" of liability. (It may be an "abatement" of liability within the meaning of section 2(1)(c)).

---

[17] If the words "or to forgo payment" at the end of para. (b) are ignored. See below, § 8–16.
[18] Cf. A. T. H. Smith, "Reforming section 16 of the Theft Act" [1971] Crim.L.R. 259 at pp. 262–263. J. C. Smith argues that a "remission" requires an agreement effective in law to destroy the debt, at least in part (as in the case of a composition by D with his creditors): Smith, *Theft*, paras. 234–236; but it does not seem credible that s. 2(1)(a) should be as narrow as this view would make it.

It is further submitted that "remission" of liability also requires knowledge that the liability exists. So where P is persuaded that D has already paid him, he does not "remit" D's liability.[19] (He is induced to "forgo payment" within the meaning of paragraph (b)).

5. INDUCING CREDITOR TO WAIT FOR OR FORGO PAYMENT

Section 2(1)(b)

A person commits an offence under section 2(1) who   8–13

" . . . by any deception— . . .

(b) with intent to make permanent default in whole or in part on any existing liability to make a payment, or with intent to let another do so, dishonestly induces the creditor or any person claiming payment on behalf of the creditor to wait for payment (whether or not the due date for payment is deferred) or to forgo payment . . . "

There are two different cases here. In either of them D may himself be the debtor, or he may be acting (not necessarily with E's authority) to enable E to escape liability. The ensuing discussion will assume that D is the debtor.

Inducing creditor to wait for payment

This is a controversial case. The stalling debtor is not in general guilty of   8–14
a criminal offence, and there is a strong argument that his use of deception should not be distinguished from, say, keeping deliberately out of the creditor's way. At the other extreme it is contended that one who deceives his creditor into waiting for payment should be guilty of an offence even if he intends to pay at some time. The present provision is a compromise between these views. Deceiving the creditor into waiting for payment is an offence only if the debtor intends never to pay. This solution effectively brings paragraph (b) into line with paragraphs (a) and (c): remission, exemption or abatement will inevitably be secured by one who intends to avoid payment altogether. It does not follow that the solution is a virtuous one.[20]

The requirement that P be induced by deception to wait for payment   8–15
does not seem to imply that P need have any alternative. Suppose that D has decided not to pay P. He puts P off most easily by pretending that he is short of ready funds. P says: "Oh, very well; but you must pay next week." This acquiescence means that what P would do if D simply refused to pay him is never put to the test. Probably he could not avoid waiting for payment (though he might promptly resort to litigation and would no doubt refuse credit for further transactions).

P may be induced by deception to wait for payment even if it is true that

---

[19] Smith, *Theft*, para. 236, agrees. *Contra,* G. Syrota [1978] Current Law Statutes Annotated, and (1979) 42 M.L.R. 301 at pp. 304–306; and it must be acknowledged that the Committee seem to have intended "remission" to be understood in a wider, but surely inadmissible, sense: *Thirteenth Report,* para. 16.

[20] See Professor Glanville Williams' powerful Note of Reservation to the *Thirteenth Report* (para. 5 at p. 20); J. R. Spencer, *loc.cit.,* n.1, above, at p. 34.

D could not in any case pay now. This kind of situation was familiar from the case law on section 16(2)(*a*). D owes P money. He induces P to accept a cheque. P is thereby "induced to wait for payment," as is expressly provided by section 2(3). D knows that there is no prospect of the cheque's being met. He has induced P to take the cheque by deception.[21] If he intends to make permanent default and is dishonest, he is guilty of the offence—even, it seems, if he has no present means of paying cash.[22]

D may give his creditor a cheque in accordance with credit terms agreed between them. Even if the cheque is known by D to be worthless, it seems that in such a case the creditor is not induced by deception to take the cheque in payment or, therefore, to wait for payment (despite the terms of s. 2(3)).[23]

Inducing creditor to forgo payment

8–16 The Committee did not explain the difference between remitting liability (paragraph (*a*)) and forgoing payment. A parliamentary request for an explanation received an unconvincing reply.[24] It has already been suggested[25] that a "remission" of liability requires an intention to extinguish a liability of the existence of which the creditor is aware. If this is correct, "remission" does not cover two types of case:

(a) P is induced to give up a claim to payment by being induced to accept that D has no liability. D pretends, for example, that he has paid already[26]; or that he has a set-off; or that the goods P sent did not arrive or were worthless.

(b) P is induced to abandon any hope of payment. He does not agree to the extinction of liability; but he goes further than merely agreeing to wait for payment, for in the circumstances as represented to him he expects never to see it.

Both types of case must be taken to be covered by the phrase "induces [P] . . . to forgo payment," though the language is not ideal.

6.   Obtaining Exemption from or Abatement of Liability

Section 2(1)(c)

8–17 A person commits an offence under section 2(1) who

" . . . by any deception— . . .

(*c*) dishonestly obtains any exemption from or abatement of liability to make a payment";

---

[21] See above, § 6–22.
[22] *D.P.P.* v. *Turner* [1974] A.C. 357.
[23] *Andrews and Hedges* [1981] Crim.L.R. 106 (ruling of Mr. Recorder Sherrard Q.C.).
[24] See H.L.Deb., Vol 389, col. 265. The example of "remission" given on behalf of the Government is an example of "forgoing" according to the distinction suggested in the text, and not one of "remission." But it would be one of "remission" according to the Committee: see note 19, above.
[25] Above, § 8–12.
[26] This was the (unsuccessful) pretence in *Holt and Lee* [1981] 1 W.L.R. 1000; [1981] 2 All E.R. 854: conviction of attempt "to induce [P] to forgo payment" upheld.

and for this purpose he "obtains" any such exemption or abatement if he obtains it for another or enables another to obtain it (subs. (4)).

Examples of this offence occur where D falsely claims to belong to a privileged class of persons (employees of a bus company, students, old age pensioners) and thereby obtains a service free or at a reduced rate; or where by a false statement he procures a rate rebate or a lower assessment to tax than would otherwise have been made on him (or on his principal). It could be objected that D's fraud does not, strictly speaking, affect his liability (to pay the full rate for the service, or to pay the properly assessable tax) but only affects the other party's demand.[27] This objection would destroy paragraph (c) almost entirely. It is submitted that the words of the statute cannot be understood in their strictest sense.[28]

Paragraph (c) does not require an "existing liability." It includes cases   **8–18** where fraud is used at the outset of a transaction. Its language is wide enough, however, to cover a case where D persuades P that his existing liability is smaller than P would otherwise have thought; indeed a false return of income for tax purposes might be such a case. Paragraph (c) therefore overlaps paragraph (b) (as to forgoing payment). It also overlaps section 1, for many cases of obtaining an abatement of liability by deception will involve an obtaining of services by that means.[29]

---

[27] See Smith, *Theft,* para. 239; but he does not apply the objection to a contract (voidable because of a s. 2(1)(c) deception) to supply goods or services at a cheap rate.
[28] See *Thirteenth Report,* para.15.
[29] But if total exemption is obtained, section 1 cannot apply; there is no "understanding that the benefit . . . will be paid for" (s. 1(2)).

CHAPTER 9

OBTAINING A PECUNIARY ADVANTAGE BY DECEPTION

1. THE OFFENCE

9–01   Section 16(1) of the 1968 Act provides:

"A person who by any deception dishonestly obtains for himself or another any pecuniary advantage shall on conviction on indictment be liable to imprisonment for a term not exceeding five years."

Section 16(2) sets out "[t]he cases in which a pecuniary advantage within the meaning of this section is to be regarded as obtained for a person." Those "cases" were originally three in number; but the first, prescribed by the notorious section 16(2)(*a*), has been despatched to a welcome oblivion by the Theft Act 1978, as explained above in the first part of Chapter 6 (Introduction to the Fraud Offences).[1] All that remains is the limited group of cases specified in section 16(2)(*b*) and (*c*), which are examined below.

"Pecuniary advantage"

9–02   It was rightly said in *D.P.P.* v. *Turner* that "we do not have to consider what is meant by pecuniary advantage"[2]—plainly because, by telling us in what case "a pecuniary advantage . . . is to be regarded as obtained," subsection (2) establishes its whole meaning for the purpose of the section. Yet, to deal with the argument (in a case under subs. (2)(*a*)) that a person with no means could gain no pecuniary advantage by evading a debt, Lord Reid further held that the phrase "is to be regarded as obtained" also means "is to be deemed to have been obtained even if in fact there was none"[3] (that is, no pecuniary advantage). This involves treating the phrase "pecuniary advantage" in the section as having both *only* a technical meaning (*i.e.* the meaning, and only the meaning, allowed by subs. (2), read as a definition) and *also* a "natural" meaning (*i.e.* what you would look for by way of pecuniary advantage if subs. (2), read as a deeming provision, did not render this unnecessary)! This is a small miracle of syntax.

Liability of company officers, etc.

9–03   Section 18 applies to offences under section 16. Reference may be made to the text of section 18 in Appendix 1 or to the discussion at § 6–53, above.

2. "BY ANY DECEPTION DISHONESTLY OBTAINS FOR HIMSELF OR ANOTHER"

"By . . . deception . . . obtains for himself or another"

9–04   (i) "*Deception*." Section 16(3) provides that for the purposes of the section "deception" has the same meaning as it has in section 15. It is

---

[1] § 6–04.
[2] [1974] A.C. 357 at p. 364.   [3] *Ibid.* at p. 365.

therefore sufficient to refer to the definition of "deception" in section 15(4) and to the discussion of that definition in the treatment of the offence of obtaining property by deception.[4]

(ii) *"Obtains."* The obtaining of the pecuniary advantage must be a consequence of the deception; once again reference may be made to the discussion of the corresponding point in relation to the offence under section 15.[5]

(iii) *"For himself or another."* The result of the words "for another" is that D may commit the offence by, for example, obtaining by deception for E the granting of an overdraft facility by E's bank (subs. (2)(*b*)) or an opportunity for E to earn remuneration in employment (subs. (2)(*c*)).

"Dishonestly"

A person charged with an offence under section 16 must be proved to have acted "dishonestly." Reference may be made to the discussions of this word in the context of section 15[6] and of the Theft Act 1978, s.2.[7]   **9–05**

3. OVERDRAFTS, INSURANCE POLICIES AND ANNUITY CONTRACTS

Section 16 (2) (b)

A pecuniary advantage is to be regarded as obtained for a person   **9–06**

> "where— . . . (*b*) he is allowed to borrow by way of overdraft, or to take out any policy of insurance or annuity contract,[8] or obtains an improvement of the terms on which he is allowed to do so . . . "
> (s. 16(2)(*b*)).

The reason why borrowing by way of overdraft is mentioned, rather than borrowing generally, is that borrowing will usually involve the transfer of property in the form of money from lender to borrower. When such a transfer is obtained by deception the offence of obtaining property by deception under section 15 is committed. Borrowing by way of overdraft, however, will not, unless cash is drawn, involve the obtaining of anything that can be identified as "property"; the relevant result of the transaction is merely a debit entry in the books of the bank.[9]

"Is allowed to borrow by way of overdraft"

An obvious case within this paragraph is that where by deception D induces his bank manager to sanction an overdrawing (or further overdrawing) of his account. A trial judge has ruled that the offence is complete when the overdraft facility is granted and not only when a   **9–07**

---

[4] See above, §§ 6–12 to 6–29, and §§ 6–42,6–43.
[5] Above, §§ 6–30 to 6–40.
[6] Above, §§ 6–47, 6–48.
[7] Above, § 8–05.
[8] Even a policy or contract void because of the mistake induced by the deception: *Alexander* [1981] Crim.L.R. 183.
[9] *Pace* Judge Paul Clarke in *Watkins* [1976] 1 All E.R. 578 at p. 579.

drawing on the facility causes the account to be debited.[10] This ruling is supported, as the judge observed, by the phrase beginning "or obtains an improvement," which also points to the time when the arrangement is made. The same is true of the reference to the taking out of an insurance policy or an annuity contract.

An extended interpretation of the word "allowed" seems to have been established without argument in *Metropolitan Police Commissioner* v. *Charles*,[11] where D's unauthorised use of a cheque card to guarantee cheques given to E obliged D's bank to honour the cheques, debiting their amounts to D's already overdrawn account. D might perhaps have argued that the additional overdrawing was a consequence of the deception that in the circumstances the bank was obliged to suffer and not one that it could properly be said to have "allowed." The argument would hardly have been meritorious; and the point is surely settled in accordance with the merits by the House of Lords decision in *Charles*. The case is more significant for other points—as to D's deception of E, and as to the obtaining of an advantage at a third party's (the bank's) expense—which have been noticed above.[12]

Paragraph (*b*) seems not to cover the case where D by deception induces his bank not to call in an existing overdraft.[13]

9–08   The words "by way of overdraft" are probably to be strictly construed. An overdraft involves a "drawing" upon an account. It does not cover, therefore, the obtaining of a "bank loan" independently of the existence or creation of an account to be drawn upon. If in making such a loan the bank transfers money to P, there is, as we have said, an obtaining of property. If, on the other hand, the transaction is effected by, for instance, the crediting of some other account, in the same or another bank, with the sum lent (that is, if it is effected by book entries only and not by the transfer of "property"), there seems to be no obtaining either under section 15 or under the present paragraph; but there will be an obtaining of services within the meaning of section 1 of the Theft Act 1978.[14]

4. OPPORTUNITY TO EARN REMUNERATION OR TO WIN MONEY BY BETTING

Section 16(2)(c)

9–09   A pecuniary advantage is to be regarded as obtained for a person

"where— . . . (c) he is given the opportunity to earn remuneration or greater remuneration in an office or employment, or to win money by betting" (s. 16(2)(c)).

---

[10] *Watkins*, above.
[11] [1977] A.C. 177; also *Kovacs* [1974] 1 W.L.R. 370; [1974] 1 All E.R. 1236.
[12] §§ 6–22, 6–32, 6–40.
[13] The case is within the Theft Act 1978, s. 2(1)(*b*) (above, § 8–13), if D acts "with intent to make permanent default"—which must be peculiarly difficult to prove in relation to D's indebtedness to his bank.
[14] See Chap. 7.

There is no doubt at all why this paragraph is included. Under the old law D was not guilty of an offence of obtaining money by false pretences (1) if he obtained employment by deception (as by falsely claiming certain qualifications) and then drew his salary; the salary was paid because of the work done and not because of the deception[15]; or (2) if by a false pretence he induced a bookmaker to accept a bet on a race and then collected the winnings when his horse won.[16] There will probably likewise be no offence now of obtaining property by deception under section 15 in either of these situations. But paragraph (c) ensures that in each case D will commit an offence, not in obtaining the remuneration or winnings, but in obtaining the opportunity to do so; it will, of course, be irrelevant whether D is actually paid.

It may be felt that the wording of paragraph (c) sticks over-closely to the particular cases that revealed the mischief to be remedied. The paragraph certainly has an oddly narrow and selective appearance. This point may be pursued by reference to each of the kinds of case for which paragraph (c) provides.

"Remuneration . . . in an office or employment"

The words "the opportunity to earn remuneration" are substantially   **9–10**
qualified by the words "in an office or employment." The result is that one who by deception obtains the opportunity to earn a financial reward for his services otherwise than in an office or employment is not caught.

"Office" and "employment" are not defined. The preposition "in" no doubt governs them both and somewhat limits the scope of the phrase. It may, for instance, loosely be said that a freelance author is "employed" by publishers to write a book, or that a solicitor is "employed" by his client to perform professional services. But neither the author nor the solicitor earns his remuneration "in" an employment. "Employment" therefore seems to be confined to a fairly narrow range of relationships and may in fact be limited to the relationship of master and servant. The word "office" adds a good deal to the scope of the paragraph by bringing in such things as directorships and public positions which are rewarded with pay.[17] Neither "office" nor "employment," it seems, covers the person privately retained as an independent contractor to perform a particular service. Yet where deception dishonestly obtains the opportunity to earn remuneration, there appears to be no proper ground for distinguishing the office-holder or employee from the independent contractor. The paragraph was drafted with a particular case in mind; but a code such as the present Act is intended to be should not plug gaps in the law, it is respectfully submitted, in this inadequate fashion.

---

[15] *Lewis* (1922) unreported: see above, § 6–39, n.92.
[16] *Clucas* [1949] 2 K.B. 226 (where the winnings were not paid and D was held not guilty of an attempt to obtain by false pretences): see above, § 6–39.
[17] For recent House of Lords discussion of the word "office," see *Edwards* v. *Clinch* [1981] 3 W.L.R. 707. The majority understood the word in a relatively narrow sense in the rather special context of the Income and Corporation Taxes Act 1970, S. 181 (1). For present purposes the dissenting speech of Lord Bridge of Harwich is also suggestive.

"Win money by betting"

9–11   The opportunity to win money by betting is distinguished in the case law from the opportunity to win a prize by competing in a contest. The fraudulent punter was not guilty of obtaining his winnings by false pretences[18]; but the runner fraudulently procuring an excessive handicap was guilty of that offence if he obtained the prize.[19] The explanation lay in the connection between the pretence and the obtaining in each case. No doubt the distinction between the two cases subsists for the purpose of section 15. It does not follow from that that they should be distinguished for the purpose of the present section. Perhaps the explanation for the exclusion of the dishonest runner from paragraph (c) lies in the fact that to have included him would have meant creating a different unjustifiable distinction—namely, that between the runner who competes for a money prize and the runner who competes for something other than money. Section 16 is concerned with pecuniary advantages and paragraph (c) is drafted accordingly.

---

[18] See above, § 9–09 at n.16.
[19] *Button* [1900] 2 Q.B. 597; see above, § 6–39.

CHAPTER 10

OTHER FRAUD OFFENCES

1. FALSE ACCOUNTING

Introduction

Section 17 creates two offences—in short, the falsification of accounts **10–01** and the use of false or deceptive accounts. Both offences are punishable on conviction on indictment with seven years' imprisonment. The section supplements both the law of theft and deception and the law of forgery and using false instruments.

If D fraudulently doctors a cash-book or destroys copy invoices and other sales records, he may not obtain or intend to obtain any property thereby. His conduct may rather be designed to cover up offences already committed. But the particular crime concealed by the false accounting may be hard or impossible to identify; or, though it may be clear, for instance, that D has systematically "milked" an enterprise of which he is a member or an employee, it may not be possible to frame an indictment for theft or to rely solely on a charge of theft.[1] For such reasons as these the criminal law is provided with a weapon which strikes at the falsification of the accounts rather than at the dishonest gain that those accounts assist or conceal.

Again, the destruction or falsification of a document or record under section 17(1)(*a*) may in truth be merely an act of *preparation* for a criminal purpose yet to be accomplished; or the use of a deceptive account under paragraph (*b*) may be an *attempt* to commit some other offence, very likely one of the offences discussed in the preceding four chapters. In this respect offences under section 17 are akin to forgery and using a false instrument, which they considerably overlap. The fabrication or use of false documentation is regarded as a sufficient commitment to the criminal purpose to have the status of a distinct substantive offence. Within the narrow accounting field, section 17 covers conduct not caught by the Forgery and Counterfeiting Act 1981 and is an important ally of that essentially preventive statute.

Falsifying accounts (s. 17(1)(a))

The actus reus

It is an offence under section 17 (1) (*a*) to destroy, deface, conceal or **10–02** falsify any account or any record or document made or required for any accounting purpose, with the *mens rea* hereafter mentioned. It has been

---

[1] Where it is clear that over a period D has stolen money amounting in total to not less than a certain sum, he can be convicted on an indictment charging the theft of that amount between specified dates: see above, § 2–95. But the property stolen must be accurately alleged and proved: *cf. O'Driscoll* [1968] 1 Q.B. 839; commentary at [1967] Crim.L.R. 303. This will not always be possible. It may not be possible, for instance, to prove whether D stole the goods in the shop he managed or money from the till. For observations on the use of "twin" counts charging theft and false accounting, see *Eden* (1971) 55 Cr.App.R. 193.

143

held that a document may be "required" for an accounting purpose if its recipient will in certain events use it for such a purpose although the maker (who is charged with falsification) makes it solely for a non-accounting purpose.[2]

Section 17(2) provides a definition of the act of falsifying. A person is to be regarded as falsifying an "account or other document" if he

(i) makes or concurs in making in it an entry which is or may be misleading, false or deceptive in a material particular, or

(ii) omits or concurs in omitting a material particular from it.[3]

This provision is curious in one respect. The words "account or *other* document" appear to mean that all accounts are documents and exclude from the definition any non-documentary "record." The implication is that the making of a false entry in, or the omission of a material particular from, a non-documentary record is not a falsification of that record for purposes of the section. This can hardly be intended. In the Falsification of Accounts Act 1875, the word "record" did not appear, and it was readily accepted that a mechanical device such as a taximeter was an "account." A driver who drove with his flag up so that the meter did not record the mileage was held to have falsified an account.[4] Such a mechanical device would seem, by accident, to be a "record" but not an "account" under the present Act. The definition in subsection (2) is no doubt a partial one only; a meter can surely be "falsified" by, for instance, being set so as to register at the wrong *rate*. But wherever a non-documentary record is made false merely by the making or omission of a particular *entry,* there would seem to be a *casus omissus* not caught by section 17(1)(*a*).

The above argument would make it desirable ideally to attempt to define "document," for all documentary records *are* within the partial definition in subsection (2). But the meaning of this word is notoriously difficult to pin down,[5] and it is not proposed to make any attempt to define it here, beyond saying that the very existence of the supplementary word "record" suggests that "document" is not intended to have any artificially wide meaning.

The mens rea

10–03   It will be noted that section 17(1)(*a*), read with subsection (2), penalises the making of an entry which "is *or may be* misleading, false or

---

[2] *Attorney-General's Reference (No. 1 of 1980)* [1981] 1 All E.R. 366. A would-be borrower made false statements in a personal loan proposal form addressed to a finance company. If the proposal were accepted, the company would use the form for an accounting purpose. But: (i) Ought not the maker at least to know of the intended use? The decision does not require such knowledge. (ii) The phrase "makes . . . an entry" in the definition of falsification in subs. (2) suggests the making of accounting entries rather than the making of statements about, *e.g.* a person's personal or financial circumstances.

[3] It seems that a particular omitted from a document is not a material particular if there was no duty to enter it in the document: see, *e.g. Keatley* [1980] Crim.L.R. 505 (public house manager: no duty to enter in employer's books details of transactions conducted on his own account in breach of his contract of employment: Judge Mendl).

[4] *Cf. Solomons* [1909] 2 K.B. 980.

[5] See Williams, "What is a Document?" (1948) 11 M.L.R. 150; *Russell on Crime* (12th ed.), pp. 1218 *et seq.*—both in the context of forgery.

deceptive . . . ." The italicised words were added to the Bill during its passage in order to ensure that section 17(1)(*a*) would cover statements recklessly made, as well as those made with positive knowledge of their misleading, false or deceptive nature. The amendment brought paragraph (*a*), so far as it concerns falsification by the making of an entry, into line in this respect with paragraph (*b*).

The offence under section 17(1)(*a*) is not committed unless D acts "dishonestly, with a view to gain for himself or another or with intent to cause loss to another."

Little need here be said about the requirement of dishonesty, which is discussed above in relation to other offences.[6] The falsification may be dishonest although it does not conceal a separate dishonest transaction, as where D makes a false entry in an account in order to conceal a muddle and to put off the evil day of having to sort out the muddle and make good the resulting loss.[7]

The requirement of a view to gain or an intent to cause loss is to be **10–04** understood in the light of the definitions of "gain" and "loss" in section 34 (2)(*a*).[8] Gain and loss "in money or other property" are alone relevant, but the intended gain or loss may be only temporary. So D may, for example, falsify an account in order to facilitate an intended unlawful borrowing from the funds of his employers; and he may be guilty of the offence although he intends to replace what he takes.

It is clear that the "gain" that D has in mind need not be "in view" as a *direct* result of the falsification of the account. In *Wines*,[9] D falsified accounts so as to show inflated profits for the department he managed. According to him his object was to save himself from being dismissed from his job. Under the Falsification of Accounts Act 1875 he was guilty, on his own story, of an act of falsification "with intent to defraud." He would surely now be guilty of falsification "with a view to gain"—that is, with a view to obtaining his continued salary.[10]

Where it is suggested that the gain with a view to which D acted was "a **10–05** gain by keeping what [he] has," it may be supposed, from the plain meaning of the language, that it is necessary to prove that at the time of the falsification D had something to keep and that keeping it was a conscious purpose of the falsification. Suppose that D has committed a fraud for the purpose of relieving himself of other pressing debts. He now falsifies an account in order to cover up his misconduct. He has spent the entire proceeds of that misconduct and is penniless; the only aim of his falsification is to avoid detection. He would not appear to have "a view to gain." Has he, then, acted "with intent to cause loss"? It is not clear that he has. "Loss" is not limited to loss by parting with what one has, but

[6] See above, §§ 2–79, 6–47, 8–05.
[7] *Eden* (1971) 55 Cr.App.R. 193.
[8] See Appendix 1 for the full text.
[9] [1954] 1 W.L.R. 64; [1953] 2 All E.R. 1497.
[10] Compare the view of the Committee in another context: *Eighth Report*, para. 96.

includes also "a loss by not getting what one might get" (s. 34(2)(a)(ii)). If D were not a man of straw, it would be easier than in the case put to say that the victim of the fraud might be misled by the falsification so as not to bring a civil action against D to recover his loss (to get what he might get). In the case of a potential defendant not worth powder and shot this interpretation of the definition of "loss" has a rather strained appearance, though it is possibly acceptable. A further difficulty, however, which exists whether D is penniless or not, is that involved in treating D's intent as being to cause loss, when the only purpose of his falsification was to avoid his detection as a criminal or possible criminal. In a case such as that under discussion it may be difficult to prove that D's intention had anything to do with the future fortunes of his victim. The fact that the victim may be deprived of the chance of recovering against D in an action is no doubt a natural and probable consequence of the falsification. But this is not enough to fix D with an "intent to cause loss"; for nowadays it must be proved that the particular defendant intended or foresaw a relevant consequence of his conduct and not merely that the consequence was the likely result of that conduct.[11] The possibility must therefore be faced that the abandonment of the old language of "with intent to defraud" has had an unhappy result. If the *mens rea* under section 17 were an intent to defraud, the case just discussed would probably cause no difficulty, since in the not dissimilar context of the Forgery Act 1913 "intent to defraud" received an interpretation broad enough to embrace an intention to induce P by deception not to prosecute or take other action available to him.[12]

Use of misleading, false or deceptive accounts (s. 17(1)(b))

10–06   Section 17(1)(b) strikes at the production or use of an account, or of a record or document made or required for an accounting purpose, which, to the knowledge of the producer or user, is or may be misleading, false or deceptive in a material particular. Such production or use in furnishing information for any purpose is an offence if committed with the same *mens rea* as that required under section 17(1)(a), just discussed. The material particular need not be directly connected with the accounting purpose for which the document is made or required; it is sufficient if the document is misleading, false or deceptive in a particular that is material for the purpose for which it is being produced or used—that is, the purpose for which information is being furnished.[13]

This offence is similar to those of altering a forged document under the Forgery Act 1913, s. 6 (now repealed) and using a false instrument under the Forgery and Counterfeiting Act 1981, s. 3. A person "altered" a forged document when he "used" it.[14] The forgery authorities on "uses" may accordingly be relevant for the interpretation of the phrase "makes use of" in the present paragraph.[15]

[11] Criminal Justice Act 1967, s. 8.
[12] *Welham* v. *D.P.P.* [1961] A.C. 103.
[13] *Mallett* [1978] 1 W.L.R. 820; [1978] 3 All E.R. 10.
[14] Forgery Act 1913, s. 6(2).
[15] See in particular *Harris* [1966] 1 Q.B. 184 ("use" by posting a copy).

A document may offend section 17(1)(*b*) notwithstanding that every statement or entry in it is individually true. It may omit facts material to the purpose for which the information is furnished, so as to be effectively false or so that it may mislead those who will rely upon it.[16] If D knows of or suspects the omission and knows that because of it the document may be misleading in some material respect, he is as guilty as if the document contained a positive lie.

Liability of company officers, etc.

Section 18 applies to offences under section 17. The reader may refer to   **10–07**
the text of section 18 in Appendix 1 or to the discussion at § 6–53, above.

2.   FALSE STATEMENTS BY COMPANY DIRECTORS, ETC.

If a company director, intending to deceive members or creditors of the   **10–08**
company about its affairs, is party to the publication of a written statement or account which to his knowledge is or may be misleading, false or deceptive in a material particular, he is guilty of an offence carrying seven years' imprisonment on conviction on indictment. Section 19, which so provides, applies in fact to all officers of bodies corporate or of unincorporated associations and to all persons purporting to act as such.

The offence replaces that previously provided by the Larceny Act 1861, s. 84. Its specialised application makes it inappropiate for full discussion here. It is better considered in the wider context of provisions concerned with the liability of company officers and the control of investment frauds, which matters are outside the scope of this book.

3.   SUPPRESSION OF DOCUMENTS. PROCURING EXECUTION OF VALUABLE SECURITIES

Section 20 preserves, with certain amendments desirable to achieve   **10–09**
conformity with other provisions in this part of the Act, offences formerly found in the Larceny Acts of 1861 and 1916. These offences are best regarded as supplementary to offences already considered, as will be indicated in the descriptions of them which follow. They do not call for more than brief treatment. The reader is referred to the text of the Act in Appendix 1 for the full terms of the section. The offences created by it are punishable on conviction on indictment with imprisonment for seven years.

Suppression, etc., of certain documents

Section 20(1) concerns the destruction, defacement or concealment of   **10–10**
certain classes of document—namely:

(i) any "valuable security"; this phrase is defined in very wide terms by subsection (3)[17];

---

[16] *Cf. Kylsant* [1932] 1 K.B. 442; *Birshirgian* (1936) 25 Cr.App.R. 176.
[17] It means "any document creating, transferring, surrendering or releasing any right to, in or over property, or authorising the payment of money or delivery of any property, or evidencing the creation, transfer, surrender or release of any such right, or the payment of money or delivery of any property, or the satisfaction of any obligation."

(ii) any will or other testamentary document;

(iii) any original document of or belonging to, or filed or deposited in, any court of justice or any government department.

The *mens rea* of the offence is the same as that required for an offence of falsifying accounts under section 17(1)(*a*), and the discussion in that context need not be repeated. Indeed the two offences have very much in common. The destruction or concealment of a deed or a will, like that of an accounting document, may be a mere act of preparation with a view to the eventual accomplishment of a fraudulent purpose. The main value of section 20(1)[18] is to provide a sanction against the preparatory act where the essence of the matter is a fraudulent purpose in contemplation rather than, for instance, the offence of criminal damage that may also be involved.[19]

Procuring execution of valuable securities

10–11   Section 20(2) renders it an offence, dishonestly and with a view to gain or with intent to cause loss, by any deception to procure the execution of a valuable security.

"Deception" has the same meaning in this context as in the offence of obtaining property by deception[20] (subs. (3)). The procuring must be *by* the deception; the discussion of the relation between a false representation and the obtaining of property required for an offence under section 15 applies here with necessary modifications.[21]

"Valuable security" is defined in very wide terms by subsection (3).[22] The word "execution" is a shorthand expression for an extensive range of acts spelt out in subsection (2), the text of which should be consulted. They include (to offer some extreme examples) the destruction of a valuable security and the signing of a paper in order that it may be converted into a valuable security. The purpose referred to by the words "in order that" may be that of the accused alone and not that of the person deceived into signing; indeed, a typical deception which the subsection certainly covers is a deception as to the very nature of the document being signed.[23] Nor, according to old authority, need the "valuable security" into which the document is intended to be converted be one which will in fact be valid if put to use.[24]

The *mens rea* of this offence is once again the same as that required under section 17(1)(*a*), and once again the reader can be referred to the earlier discussion.[25]

---

[18] If it has any value in practice. It is doubtful whether there were any modern prosecutions under the corresponding repealed provisions: see *Eighth Report*, para. 106.

[19] *Cf. ibid.*

[20] See above, §§ 6–12 *et seq.*

[21] See above, §§ 6–30 *et seq.*

[22] See n. 16, above.

[23] *Cf. Graham* (1913) 8 Cr.App.R. 149.

[24] *Graham*, above.

[25] Above, §§ 10–03 to 10–05.

Section 20 (2) supplements the main provisions of this part of the Act in 　**10–12**
two ways.

(i) First, it strikes at conduct analogous to obtaining property or services
by deception. The characteristic aim of a fraud within section 20(2) will be
the imposition of some liability upon the victim or a third person[26] (as
when D procures P's signature to a deed, a cheque or a guarantee); but this
will not necessarily involve the obtaining of property or services either
immediately or at all. So section 20(2) enlarges the range of fraudulent
practices rendered criminal by the two Theft Acts.

(ii) Secondly, the ultimate aim of one who by deception procures the
execution of a valuable security may in fact be the obtaining of property or
of some other advantage by use of the valuable security in question.
Section 20(2) therefore in effect makes a separate substantive offence out
of conduct which may be preparatory to the commission of one of the
offences discussed in earlier chapters.

[26] *Cf. Thornton* [1964] 2 Q.B. 176 at p. 182.

CHAPTER 11

MAKING OFF WITHOUT PAYMENT

1. The Offence. Power of Arrest

11–01   An offence is committed by "a person who, knowing that payment on the spot for any goods supplied or service done is required or expected from him, dishonestly makes off without having paid as required or expected and with intent to avoid payment of the amount due" (Theft Act 1978, s. 3(1)). The offence is punishable on conviction on indictment with up to two years' imprisonment (s. 4(2)(*b*)), and on summary conviction with up to six months' imprisonment and/or a fine not exceeding (for the time being) £1,000 (s. 4(3)).

The change in the law effected by section 3

11–02   Criminal law sanctions are not generally provided against the dishonest debtor. Section 3 makes an exception for one who, by physically removing himself from the scene at which his obligation arises, may effectively put himself beyond his creditor's grasp. The mischief is commonly termed "bilking." Only certain examples of it were formerly subject to control. Section 3 provides a comprehensive sanction. The following paragraphs explain the change in the law that has taken place.

(i) *Theft or no theft.* If D dishonestly makes off without paying for goods supplied to him, he is not guilty of theft if the property in the goods has already passed to him and the supplier has ceased to have possession or control of them.[1] The present section, therefore, apart from extending the law, avoids nice questions of civil law even in a case where it may in fact be possible to prove theft.

(ii) *Original or supervening dishonesty.* When D runs out of a restaurant without paying for his meal, conviction under section 15 of the 1968 Act requires proof that his intention not to pay was formed before he obtained the food, so that it may be found that he obtained it by deception as to his intention to pay.[2] Exactly the same point applies under section 1 of the 1978 Act, as to obtaining services by deception. Under the present section there is no need to prove that a prior deception induced the supply of goods or the rendering of the service.

11–03   (iii) *Making off achieved by deception or otherwise.* Formerly, where prior deception could not be proved (and property in the goods, if any, had passed) D might still be guilty, under section 16 of the 1968 Act, of

---

[1] See above, § 2–35. It is assumed that D has not got the goods by the supplier's mistake in circumstances bringing the case within s. 5(4) of the 1968 Act (above, § 2–30). No one, in any case, wants to rely on s. 5(4) if something simpler will do.
[2] See above, § 6–13.

obtaining the evasion of his debt by deception. As a result of the decision of the House of Lords in *D.P.P.* v. *Ray*,[3] he might be convicted of this offence if, having decided to make off from the restaurant, garage forecourt or barber's shop without paying, he waited until P (a person aware of his transaction) had turned his back, and then fled. P was to be treated as relevantly deceived and D's evasion as being effected by the deception. But if D simply made off upon deciding not to pay, or if P happened to be out of the way from the time of D's decision until his acting upon it, there was no offence because no deception. The distinction and the extensive notion of deception upon which it turned were equally disreputable. There should be an offence in all of these situations or in none. There is now an offence in all.

Power of arrest

Unlike the offences created by sections 1 and 2 of the 1978 Act, which **11–04** carry a maximum penalty of five years' imprisonment, this offence is not an arrestable offence within the meaning of the Criminal Law Act 1967, s. 2(1). A special power of arrest without warrant is therefore provided in respect of anyone who is or, with reasonable cause, is suspected to be, committing or attempting to commit the offence (s. 3(4)). This is a so-called "citizen's arrest" power; the waiter, hotel receptionist or petrol pump attendant may arrest the customer who is "making off" or attempting to do so. The arrest must be made, however, while the offender is still "making off"; there is no power to arrest a person who is, or is suspected of being, "guilty of the offence"[4] but who is no longer (suspected to be) "committing" it. The problem of determining when the "making off" ends could possibly arise. It is not one that can be resolved by a general formula.[5]

2. THE DETAILS OF THE OFFENCE

There must be some "goods supplied" or "service done"

(i) *Goods supplied.* The section is particularly designed to cover the kind **11–05** of sale transaction under which property in the goods inevitably passes before payment is expected—the transfer of petrol from pump to fuel tank, for example, or the service of a meal to a diner who will pay after eating. But it will also apply to a delivery of goods in anticipation of the passing of property. A common case is that of the wrapping and pricing of goods at a supermarket food counter, the goods being handed to the customer to be paid for at the cashier's desk. These goods are plainly "supplied" at the food counter although they are not yet "sold"; so that if the customer dishonestly leaves without paying, he commits the present offence, which is thus an alternative to a charge of theft. This does not mean that the

---

[3] [1974] A.C. 370.
[4] *Cf.* Criminal Law Act 1967, s. 2(3) and (4).
[5] *Cf.* "the course of the stealing" in s. 22(1) of the 1968 Act.

standard case of shoplifting is an offence under section 3; goods simply exposed for sale are not "goods supplied."

"Goods" has the meaning stated in section 34(2)(*b*) of the 1968 Act (s. 5(2)).

11–06   (ii) *Service done.* The definition of "an obtaining of services" by section 1(2) is not matched by a definition of "service done" in section 3(1). Nor is the shift from "services" to "[a] service" explained. It is submitted, however, that "service done" should be liberally interpreted, as "obtains services" is broadly defined. For example, permitting a person to use a tennis court in a public park or a rowing boat on a private lake should be regarded as the doing of a service, even though nothing is done apart from the giving of permission to use the amenity. But something in the way of permission (if only a permission to be inferred from deliberate inaction) appears to be necessary. The section does not cover a making off from a cinema or dance hall that has been clandestinely entered through a back door or window. An amenity thus involuntarily provided is not a "service done."[6]

"Service done" must cover the letting of goods on hire, as it will also cover the letting of a room in a guest house or hotel.

Transactions contrary to law or unenforceable

11–07   Making off without having paid is no offence if the supply of goods or the doing of the service was contrary to law or if the service done is such that payment is not legally enforceable (s. 3(3)).

The contract under which the goods are supplied or the service done may itself be "contrary to law."[7] Thus, it may be an offence to supply the goods in question (*e.g.* a flick knife) or to do the service; or to conduct the sale in a particular manner (*e.g.* in contravention of the Mock Auctions Act 1961); or to supply the goods to the particular customer served (*e.g.* intoxicating liquor to a minor).

11–08   The supply of goods or the doing of the service may be "contrary to law" because of some breach of the law committed in carrying out the transaction.[8] All depends upon the correct construction of the statutory provision that is contravened: is it intended to affect the contract in performance of which the contravention occurs, or does it merely impose penalties for the contravention?[9] A new jurisprudence on this difficult question could well arise from the present section. It will merely be observed here, by way of example: (a) that the lack of a necessary licence—*e.g.* a street trader's or hackney carriage driver's licence—will very probably take the transaction outside section 3; (b) that a serious

---

[6] See *Thirteenth Report,* para. 21.
[7] See this heading in Treitel, *An Outline of the Law of Contract* (2nd ed.), pp. 159 *et seq.*
[8] The topic is not suitable for full treatment here. See Chitty, *Law of Contracts* (24th ed.), Chap. 16, especially at paras. 1012 *et seq.*
[9] *St. John Shipping Corporation* v. *Joseph Rank Ltd.* [1957] 1 Q.B. 267.

breach of the Motor Vehicles (Construction and Use) Regulations may render the doing of a service "contrary to law"[10]; but (c) that it can hardly be intended that a relatively trivial breach of the same Regulations should render a taxi-driver's contract with his passenger "contrary to law" so that he cannot in theory sue for his fares or in practice arrest the passenger for an offence under section 3.[11]

Services for which payment is not legally enforceable include, most **11–09** obviously, services under contracts void by statute (*e.g.* gaming contracts) or as being contrary to public policy (*e.g.* the services of a prostitute or other "immoral" services).

The meaning of "payment" in section 3(1)[12]

There are three references to "payment" in section 3(1): payment on the **11–10** spot must be required or expected from D; D must make off without having paid (which must mean "without having made payment") as required or expected; and he must do so with intent to avoid payment. "Payment" presumably bears the same meaning throughout the subsection. It seems that the word must be understood in a very wide sense. The section is obviously not intended for the protection only of establishments that are known to require payment in cash. The smart hotel that welcomes card-holders, the restaurant that will accept luncheon vouchers, the shop that is known to take cheques from customers who provide evidence of identity—these must be within the section as well as the taxi-driver and hot-dog stall proprietor who obviously expect cash. It is therefore suggested that references to "payment" (from or by D) in section 3(1) are to be understood as references to any transaction acceptable to P as constituting "payment" in a broad sense and, if not then discharging D's liability, capable in fact of maturing into such discharge. On this view, payment by cheque (at least one with a prospect of being met on presentment) or, for example, by credit card, will be "payment."[13]

To express the matter in another way, the suggestion is that "payment on the spot" is required or expected from the customer if he ought before leaving to make an effective gesture of payment[14] within the range of gestures acceptable to the creditor; that he makes off "without having paid as required or expected" if he leaves without having made such a gesture; and that he makes off "with intent to avoid payment" if his aim in making off is to avoid the making of an effective payment gesture at that time.

---

[10] As in *Ashmore, Benson, Pease & Co. Ltd.* v. *A.V. Dawson Ltd.* [1973] 1 W.L.R. 828 (overloading lorry).
[11] *Cf. St. John Shipping Corporation* v. *Joseph Rank Ltd.*, above, at p. 281.
[12] This passage has been redrafted in an attempt to meet criticism by G. Syrota, "Are Cheque Frauds Covered by Section 3 of the Theft Act 1978?" [1980] Crim. L.R. 413, at pp. 415–417.
[13] This suggestion derives some support from the fact that there is no provision in s. 3 corresponding to s. 2(3), according to which, for purposes of s. 2(1)(*b*), a creditor who is induced to accept a cheque or other security for money by way of conditional satisfaction is to be treated not as being paid but as being induced to wait for payment.
[14] Or, possibly, a gesture of payment, whether effective or not: see below, § 11–13.

D must know that "payment on the spot is required or expected"

11–11   Payment "on the spot" is payment "then and there"—that is, before leaving the place at which the goods are on that occasion supplied or the service is on that occasion done. It also includes "payment at the time of collecting goods on which work has been done or in respect of which service has been provided" (s. 3(2)). It does not matter that the car has been repaired on an earlier day or that the clothes have been dry-cleaned off the premises from which they are being collected.

The phrase "required or expected" is an informal way, it is submitted, of expressing the fact that payment on the spot is, strictly speaking, a matter of contractual obligation. An alternative reading is to understand "expected" to mean "looked for, if not strictly required." But if payment now is not strictly required, the amount payable is not yet "due," as later in the subsection it is assumed to be.[15] The fact is that transactions covered by the section are mainly of a very informal type. The terms governing payment will rarely be express; rather, the obligation to pay on the spot will derive from common usage and be a matter of common understanding. If the debtor shares the understanding, he knows that such payment is expected. If he thinks that he enjoys credit terms, he cannot be guilty of the offence, however dishonest he may be. If, conversely, he has in fact been served on credit terms, but believes that payment on the spot is required, again he cannot commit the offence; for one cannot "know" what is not the case.

"Makes off without having paid"

11–12   The phrase "makes off" seems to be simply an atmospherically loaded synonym for "leaves" or "goes away." There need be no haste or stealth. The "making off" may even occur with the knowledge and assistance of the creditor's staff, as where a cool customer calls for his hat and coat, requests that a cab be summoned for him and sends his compliments to the chef. The opportunity to leave without paying may be obtained by deception (*e.g.* on the pretext of going to get money, or by giving counterfeit coin in pretended payment). It is probable that there is a "making off" in such a case.[16]

11–13   It has been suggested that a person "makes off without having paid as required or expected" if he leaves without having made an effective gesture of payment within the range of gestures acceptable to the creditor. The person who leaves foreign coins in the newsvendor's tray or gives forged banknotes for his petrol has surely not "paid." Some difficulty is

---

[15] A third explanation of the word "expected" is possible—namely, that it covers a case in which payment *now* is required (the amount is "due") but payment *at this very place* is looked for though not required.

[16] *Cf.* Smith, *Theft*, para. 242. But Bennion argues that "makes off" has a "natural meaning" that requires "guilty haste (or something like it)," and that giving a dud cheque and leaving is for this reason not within s. 3: [1980] Crim.L.R. 670.

[17] § 11–10.

[18] Stolen money is a different case. The innocent creditor acquires a good title to stolen currency passed to him. The payment gesture is effective.

caused, however, by the case of one who gives in purported payment a cheque that he realises will not be met on presentment. One view of this case is that it involves no "making off."[19] It is supposed, however, that this is not correct. Then it seems, on the one hand, odd to say that one who dishonestly gives a bad cheque thereby "pays." Indeed, it is not easy to find a satisfying point of distinction between the case of a bad cheque and that of counterfeit currency; if the former is a case of "payment," the suprising general proposition might follow that even ineffective payment gestures are "payment" within the meaning of section 3 (1). If the case under consideration were charged under section 3, it would certainly be tempting to yield to common sense and to say that no payment has been made. On the other hand, it is precisely for the case of the bad cheque dishonestly given that section 2(3) is at pains to provide, for purposes of section 2(1)(b), that the creditor who is given a cheque is to be treated not as being paid but as being induced to wait for payment; and the silence of section 3 on this point may possibly imply that the contrary is intended for purposes of that section.[20] Moreover, a charge under section 3 might be regarded as improperly avoiding the need to prove an "intent to make permanent default," which is required under section 2(1)(b). The latter provision is surely intended to be used in a bad cheque case.[21] It is hoped that good prosecution practice will ensure that the point does not arise for decision. In case this hope is disappointed, the view is offered here that common sense provides the preferable solution: a payment gesture must be an effective one.[22]

"With intent to avoid payment of the amount due"

Section 3 does not require an intent to make permanent default. The phrase "intent to avoid payment," read in its context and in the light of the contrast with section 2(1)(b), clearly means an intention to avoid the on-the-spot payment known to be required.[23] It is that intention that causes the leaving to have the quality of a "making off." If D intended to pay later, his defence on a charge under section 3 must be that he did not make off "dishonestly."   **11–14**

D may, on the other hand, think that payment has already been made, by himself or a companion. In this case, not knowing there is an "amount due," he cannot be said to intend to avoid payment of it.   **11–15**

A similar defence may be made by a customer who pays or tenders less than the sum charged on the ground that that sum is excessive. He may claim that the price (not notified or negotiated in advance) is unreasonable;

---

[19] See n. 16, above.
[20] *Cf.* n. 13, above.
[21] Syrota, *loc. cit.*, n. 12, above, argues that one who gives a dud cheque has "paid" (conditional payment) "as required or expected" (*i.e.* "on the spot").
[22] It may be effective without being honest. If the cheque is met although D thought it would not be, he has surely paid on the spot (if "payment" in s.3(1) has the kind of meaning suggested for it). His gesture of payment is effective in spite of him. And see note 18.
[23] *Cf. Corbyn* v. *Saunders* [1978] 1 W.L.R. 400 at p. 403c; [1978] 2 All E.R. 697, at p. 699g.

or that defects in the goods or service reduce what he is legally obliged to pay. His contention in either case is that what he pays or tenders is the whole "amount due" and that his making off is not, therefore, with intent to avoid payment of that amount. (But this kind of defence is perhaps more easily accommodated under the issue of dishonesty.)

"Dishonestly"

11–16   Reference may be made to the discussion of the word "dishonestly" in the context of the offence of theft.[24] The general principle is that it is for the jury or the magistrates as judges of fact to say whether the accused's conduct was "dishonest" within the meaning of that word as "an ordinary word of the English language," applying for this purpose "the current standards of ordinary decent people."[25]

11–17   Two kinds of case may be mentioned as likely examples of problems for the trier of fact:

(i) D has left his hotel without paying his bill. He claims that he needed for other purposes all the ready cash he had on him and that he intended to pay the bill within a few days. If the jury or justices think that this may be true, they will have to face the further question whether D acted "dishonestly" in leaving as he did.

(ii) D has left a restaurant without paying the bill. He claims to have done so because he was angry over some discourtesy, or because the food and service were so bad as to elicit an extreme protest from him. Once again there are two questions. May he be telling the truth? If so, was his making off "dishonest"?

[24] Above, §§ 2–86 to 2–91.
[25] *Feely* [1973] Q.B. 530.

CHAPTER 12

BLACKMAIL

1. INTRODUCTION

BEFORE the passing of the Act the term "blackmail" was not a term of art in   **12–01**
English law. The word had been used by lawyers as a convenient way of
referring to a number of offences contained in the Larceny Act 1916,
ss. 29–31, where, however, the word did not appear. By laymen it was
understood to mean the obtaining of some advantage by the use of
improper threats, especially threats to make use of information discreditable to the victim. The layman's use of the word was naturally looser than
the lawyer's; but layman and lawyer were not far apart in their
understanding of what amounted to blackmail, and they both regarded the
kinds of conduct they had characteristically in mind as among the most
serious criminal or moral offences.

The complex statutory provisions replaced by section 21 of the present   **12–02**
Act have been aptly described as "an ill-assorted collection of legislative
bric-à-brac which the draftsman of the 1916 Act put together with scissors
and paste."[1] There was a considerable number of offences, carrying widely
different maximum penalties. These offences, by their own terms and still
more by virtue of their interpretation at the hands of the courts,
overlapped to a perplexing and unsatisfactory degree. The overlap was, if
anything, rendered more serious by the fact that the most important of the
provisions were so drafted as to involve fundamentally different
approaches to one of the central problems of this part of the law. That
problem, shortly expressed, is this: from what point of view, in considering
the lawful or unlawful character of a demand with menaces, is the
propriety of or justification for the relevant conduct to be judged? Should
the fact that what D demands is rightfully due to him be relevant? If it
should, should it be relevant that, though what D demands is not
something to which he has a valid claim, yet he thinks it is? If blackmail can
be committed even by demanding something to which D is (or believes he
is) entitled, by what criterion is the propriety of his using a particular threat
to support his demand properly to be judged—by his own subjective
opinion, or by an objective standard, whether represented by the terms of
a statute or by the opinion of a court or jury? To these questions the
Larceny Act, as interpreted, afforded no clear or consistent answers.

Questions of the kind mentioned in the preceding paragraph may be   **12–03**
plausibly answered in a number of different ways. The Act provides a
unified and tolerably coherent solution. In order to achieve this solution
and a general simplification of the law, the Committee largely dispensed

[1] Hogan [1966] Crim.L.R. 474.

with the language of the repealed provisions. The only words of importance preserved from the Larceny Act are the words "demand" and "menaces," which reflect the language of the Larceny Act 1916, ss. 29(1)(i) and 30. Apart from the use of these two words, the offence now called "blackmail" is new both in form and in approach. It proceeds in fact from the necessity that the Committee felt "to go back to first principles and to consider as a matter of policy what kind of conduct should amount to blackmail."[2]

The problem of policy was answered thus. Any demand with menaces should, prima facie, be condemned, and it should be caught by the Act if its purpose is a property gain or loss. But honesty should win exemption; the Act does not strike at the conscientious mind. One should be entitled to plead, in effect: "I thought my demand was justified and my pressure acceptable"; such language comes as close as the subject-matter allows to the notion of honesty. This solution inevitably proved controversial.[3]

2. DEFINITION OF BLACKMAIL. GENERAL OBSERVATIONS

The statutory definition[4]

12–04   There are three ingredients of the crime of blackmail:

(i) D must make a "demand with menaces."

(ii) The demand with menaces must be "unwarranted"; and it will be unwarranted unless D makes it "in the belief—(a) that he has reasonable grounds for making the demand; and (b) that the use of the menaces is a proper means of reinforcing the demand."

(iii) D must make the demand "with a view to gain for himself or another or with intent to cause loss to another."

The crime is thus defined in section 21(1). Some slight assistance in the interpretation of "demand" and "menaces" is afforded by subsection (2). Subsection (3) provides a maximum penalty of fourteen years' imprisonment on conviction on indictment. Blackmail is not triable summarily.[5]

General observations

12–05   The ingredients of the offence require to be separately considered. First, however, some general observations may be helpful.

The application of section 21 is likely to cause difficulty, and its policy to give rise to possible concern, only rarely. Most of the cases for which provision is required and for which the section will in practice be used can readily be seen to fall within its terms. D threatens to publish discreditable

---

[2] *Eighth Report,* para. 115.

[3] For the controversy, see *Eighth Report,* paras. 108 *et seq.*; McKenna, "Blackmail: a Criticism" [1966] Crim.L.R. 467; Hogan, "Blackmail: Another View," *ibid.* at p. 474; H.L.Deb., Vol. 289, cols. 212 and 230 (debate on Second Reading of the Bill); *ibid.* Vol.290, col. 524 (clause considered in Committee); *ibid.* Vol. 291 (clause considered on Report); H.C. Deb., Vol. 763, col. 1435 (debate in Second Reading Committee); and consideration of clause in Standing Committee H, June 25 and 27, 1968: Official Report, cols. 77 and 81. During the passage of the Bill the scope of the offence created by s. 21 was slightly increased by amendment of the definitions of "gain" and "loss" in s. 34(2)(a).

[4] See the text of s. 21 in Appendix 1.

[5] Magistrates' Courts Act 1980, Sched.1, para. 28(a).

details about P's private life unless P pays him for silence; a corrupt policeman threatens to lay a fictitious charge against P but suggests that the charge may be avoided by a suitable payment; a thug offers his "protection" to a club or café proprietor while two or three large demi-thugs lounge in the doorway; a shop proprietor is told that a bomb has been hidden on his premises and will be allowed to go off unless he hands over a stated amount in cash: in cases like these the fact that a crucial issue in the offence of blackmail is cast in subjective terms will have a splendid irrelevance. The worst cases that ought to be blackmail are clearly blackmail.

Even if what D threatens is something that may lawfully be done (or that he thinks may be lawfully done), this is never by itself enough to protect him if his threat to do it is a means of reinforcing a demand. D is perfectly entitled, as a matter of law, to tell P's wife of P's adultery, and there may be circumstances in which he may regard it as the morally correct thing to do. Further, he may properly warn P that he proposes to tell P's wife of the adultery. What he cannot do is to invoke these liberties as a sufficient ground for using them as a means of extortion.

Only when D claims that what he demands is in some way his due does **12–06** the subjective test adopted in the section begin to affect the matter. Only when D can plausibly say something like: "I thought the sum I named was properly due to me," *and* "I thought my threat was a proper way of getting it"—only then can his demand with menaces escape the condemnation of the section. At this point we have clearly approached the very borderline of blackmail on any view of what should be included in a crime so named. Very occasionally a person of low moral standards, holding or claiming to hold unusually liberal views as to the means which it is permissible to use to obtain what seems to be his due, may escape a conviction that he would have suffered had an objective criterion been embodied in the section.[6] There is a converse possibility—that a person of unusually high moral standards and veracity on oath may suffer a conviction merely because he has failed to live up to his own standards and has made a demand with menaces not "warranted" by his own beliefs! But this is surely an academic rather than a real life possibility.

A more important limitation of the scope of blackmail than the use of **12–07** the subjective test of propriety is the requirement that D's demand be made with a view to gain or with intent to cause loss. Gain and loss mean only "gain or loss in money or other property" (s. 34(2)(*a*)). So it is not blackmail[7] to demand, with whatever supporting threats, the custody of a child, the victim's sexual favours, a release from lawful custody or the withdrawal of evidence proposed to be given in support of a prosecution. Differing views may be held as to the propriety of excluding all such

---

[6] But see § 12–28, below.
[7] Though it may be some other offence.

demands from the offence. The point is stressed here because it is one that it is desirable to have in mind throughout a consideration of the other aspects of blackmail, which must now be discussed.

3. The Making of a Demand with Menaces

The demand

12–08   It must be clear from the circumstances that D is demanding something (some act or omission) from P. But it is not necessary that he should actually use language such as invariably carries the force of a demand. "It is not necessary that the language should be explicit," observed Lord Reading C.J. in *Studer*[8]; "it may be in language only a request." He might have added, with the facts of that case in mind, that it may on its face be only a suggestion made for P's benefit. D told P that £250 was the sum he would need from P in order that he might induce a detective to withdraw an otherwise inevitable charge against P; but D was guilty of demanding money with menaces, for the detective and the alleged charge were both fictitious. D was menacing P with talk of a supposed peril and demanding £250 as the price of its evasion. The case was but a subtle and unusual version of the more familiar transaction of which *Collister and Warhurst*[9] is a modern example. There police officers threatened to bring a bogus charge against P but made it clear that he would avoid the charge by a payment. Although their demand was not express, it was implicit in their words and conduct,[10] and they too were guilty of demanding money with menaces.

12–09   Words, in fact, are not necessary at all, so long as D's conduct conveys a demand. If D holds a gun at the head of P's sleeping child and points at a safe of which P alone knows the combination, D's conduct is as eloquent as words could be and there is a strong prima facie case of blackmail. (If the gun were pointed at P himself or at his waking child, so that P or the child were put in fear, the natural offence to charge would be assault with intent to rob. There is a clear overlap between that offence and blackmail.)

The act or omission demanded

12–10   Section 21(2) expressly provides that "the nature of the act or omission demanded is immaterial." This provision was included in the draft Bill "in order to avoid any argument that, because the offence depends on the

---

[8] (1915) 11 Cr.App.R. 307; see also *Robinson* (1796) 2 Leach 749.
[9] (1955) 39 Cr.App.R. 100.
[10] The threat was to arrest P on a charge of importuning. One of the accused said to P: "This is going to look very bad for you." A meeting was arranged for the following day, and it was made clear to P that a report on his alleged conduct would be typed but would be used only if P failed to keep the appointment. When he met the accused the next day, P was asked if he had brought anything with him. Pilcher J.'s direction to the jury (39 Cr.App.R. 100 at p. 102), approved on appeal (*ibid.* at p. 105), remains of value on the meaning of a demand: it was enough if the jury were satisfied "that, although there was no express demand . . . , the demeanour of the accused and the circumstances of the case were such that an ordinary reasonable man would understand that a demand . . . was being made upon him . . . ."

demand being made with a view to gain or with intent to cause loss, the thing demanded must be property."[11]

Some examples of demands for different kinds of act and omission will be given in the last part of this chapter.[12]

The making of the demand

Section 21 requires only that a demand with menaces be made, not, of course, that it be complied with. But equally, if the demand is complied with the offence is nonetheless committed.   **12–11**

A question which may occasionally arise and which on one set of facts has reached the House of Lords is whether the full act of making a demand with menaces involves the effective communication of the demand to P. A letter sent to P may miscarry; a message may remain undelivered; P may not hear D's words or observe his gestures. The question is whether the posting of the letter, the entrusting of the message, the speaking of the words, the making of the gestures, or some or any of these, amount to the making of the demand which it is D's purpose to convey.

In *Treacy* v. *D.P.P.*[13] the House of Lords, by a majority, held that a demand conveyed by a letter is made when the letter is posted, so that where the letter is addressed to a victim abroad, its being posted in England completes an offence of blackmail within the jurisdiction. Lord Hodson's opinion to this effect (in which Lord Guest concurred) depended mainly on the consideration that the act of posting would formerly have constituted a complete offence under the Larceny Act 1916, s. 29(1)(i)[14]; and Lord Diplock applied what he conceived to be the linguistic sense of "ordinary literate men and women": a man in ordinary conversation, he thought, would say "I have made a demand" as soon as he had posted a letter containing a demand.[15]   **12–12**

Lords Reid and Morris of Borth-y-Gest dissented. Each gave a number of examples of factual situations illustrating the proposition that "[a] demand is not made until it is communicated."[16] This proposition would seem to be true at least of the case of a message entrusted by D to E for delivery to P, whether the message is oral or in writing. The effect of *Treacy* may be to make a special rule for the case where E is the Post Office,[17] although the majority did not expressly rely on any peculiarity of the post as a means of transmission.

---

[11] *Eighth Report*, p. 131 (notes on draft Bill).
[12] Below, § 12–34.
[13] [1971] A.C. 537; discussed by Pace (1971) 121 New L.J. 242.
[14] [1971] A.C. 537 at pp. 557–558. The offence under s. 29(1)(i), however, was that of *uttering* a letter or writing demanding property with menaces.
[15] [1971] A.C. 537 at p. 565.
[16] *Ibid.* at p. 556, *per* Lord Morris of Borth-y-Gest. Their Lordships' examples are at pp. 550 and 555–556.
[17] But see Smith, *Theft*, para. 304.

12–13   The case of an oral utterance which fails to communicate a demand requires separate consideration. If the words are incapable of being heard by any victim, it is submitted that no demand is made.[18] But if D shouts "Your money or your life!" at P, D probably does, as a matter of language, "make a demand with menaces" even if P is stone deaf. In any event, it would be unsatisfactory to have one rule for words which P does not hear and another for words which he does not understand, and it seems clear that if P does hear the words but does not understand their demanding or threatening implications, D has made a demand with menaces so long as an ordinary person in P's position would have understood what D was intending to convey.[19]

A letter posted abroad

12–14   In *Treacy* v. *D.P.P.*[20] "it appears that all their Lordships were disposed to hold that had it been a case of a demand dispatched abroad which had arrived in England, there would have been jurisdiction here to try the offence . . . ."[21] There are two ways of achieving this result consistently with the actual decision in *Treacy*. The method preferred by Lord Diplock avoids the substantive question of when and where the demand is made. In his view, there being in section 21 no "geographical limitation on where the described conduct of the offender takes place or where its consequences take effect," the offender may be convicted in England if either the conduct or the consequences occur there.[22] The second method involves holding that a demand conveyed by post continues to be "made" until the letter reaches its addressee. Thus the demand would be "made" within the jurisdiction although it originates abroad. This possibility was left open by the Court of Appeal and by Lord Hodson.[23] It is supported by a combination of the Court of Appeal's reference to "the inchoate nature of [blackmail] and its similarity to an attempt"[24] and the decision of the same court in *Baxter*[25] that attempt is itself an offence that continues from the time when it is first committed until the time when it fails.

Attempted blackmail

12–15   If a blackmailing demand is "made" as soon as it is spoken or dispatched beyond recall, the possibility of a case of attempted blackmail is limited to

---

[18] Edwards (1952) 15 M.L.R. at p. 346, puts the case of the loudspeaker, concealed in P's house, that fails to function when D seeks by means of it to convey a demand to P; surely a mere attempt. (But if the words are heard by an unintended victim and affect him as a demand with menaces, the offence will be complete.)

[19] See to the same effect John Stephenson J. in *Treacy* in the Court of Appeal: [1971] A.C. 537 at p. 543.

[20] [1971] A.C. 537.

[21] *Baxter* [1972] 1 Q.B. 1 at p. 13, *per* Sachs L.J.

[22] [1971] A.C. 537 at pp. 559–564.

[23] *Ibid.* at pp. 543 and 558 respectively.

[24] *Ibid.* at p. 545.

[25] [1972] 1 Q.B. 1 (above, § 6–52). In this case convictions in England of attempts to obtain property by deception by means of letters posted in Northern Ireland and received in Liverpool were upheld.

fanciful situations such as those where D is affected by a stammer or interrupted in the act of posting.[26] In fact there is some authority for the proposition that there cannot be an attempt to demand,[27] blackmail being itself "in substance an attempt to obtain money."[28] Whether this proposition is wholly justified (fanciful situations apart) will depend upon the way in which some of the questions discussed above are worked out in a developing case law.

The menaces

Under the Larceny Act 1916, ss. 29(1)(i)[29] and 30,[30] the word "menace"   **12–16** was given a wide meaning. In the leading case of *Thorne* v. *Motor Trade Association*,[31] Lord Wright said:

> "I think the word 'menace' is to be liberally construed and not as limited to threats of violence but as including threats of any action detrimental to or unpleasant to the person addressed. It may also include a warning that in certain events such action is intended."

There is no doubt that the word is intended to have a wide meaning in section 21 also. The possible varieties of menace are innumerable. Apart from threats of physical violence (to P or to some other person), of prosecution or of the revelation of criminal conduct or sexual misbehaviour (whether real or pretended), all of which have already been referred to in this chapter, we may add a few examples suggested by important cases under the old law: a threat to publish attacks on a company calculated to lower the value of its shares[32]; a threat to reveal that P has not honoured a debt[33]; a threat to place P on a trade association's "stop list" unless he pays a fine imposed by the association for breach of its rules[34]; a threat not to give evidence in an action.[35] These are but illustrations thrown up by the chances of earlier litigation.

Although menaces may take many forms, not every trivial threat will   **12–17** satisfy the section. The Committee in fact chose the word "menaces" in preference to "threats" because they regarded the former word as the

---

[26] And see n. 18, above.
[27] *Moran* (1952) 36 Cr.App.R. 10 at p. 12 (criticised by Edwards (1952) 15 M.L.R. at p. 346; by Smith [1961] Crim.L.R. at p. 445; and by Williams, *Criminal Law—General Part* (2nd ed.), p. 615, n.9, instancing the case of the letter that does not arrive); *Treacy* in the Court of Appeal:[1971] A.C. 537 at p. 554; and in the House of Lords, *per* Lord Hodson, *ibid.* at p. 558 (the proposition is "correct as a general rule").
[28] [1971] A.C. 537 at p. 545, *per* John Stephenson J.; and see text above, at n. 24.
[29] The offence was that of uttering a letter or writing "demanding of any person with menaces, and without any reasonable or probable cause, any property or valuable thing."
[30] The offence was committed by one who "with menaces or by force demands of any person anything capable of being stolen with intent to steal the same."
[31] [1937] A.C. 797 at p. 817.
[32] *Boyle and Merchant* [1914] 2 K.B. 339.
[33] *Norreys* v. *Zeffert* [1939] 2 All E.R. 187.
[34] *Thorne* v. *Motor Trade Association* [1937] A.C. 797.
[35] *Clear* [1968] 1 Q.B. 670.

stronger of the two.[36] "Give me £50 or I shall tickle you with this feather" is not on the face of it a threat strong enough for blackmail even if P is known to be ticklish. In one case[37] a student had offered shopkeepers, for a modest contribution to charity, copies of a poster guaranteeing protection from rag activities that might inconvenience them. The jury were directed that as a matter of commonsense no "menaces" were involved. It is indeed in most cases a matter of commonsense; and normally, it has been held, the jury can be left to apply the word "menaces" as "an ordinary English word" according to their own understanding of it.[38]

12–18   There is one question, however, on which, in an exceptional case, the jury will need assistance—namely, the question how far the actual or possible fortitude of the victim enters into the evaluation of the threat used. The point was considered in *Clear*,[39] decided under the Larceny Act 1916, s. 30.[40] The Court of Appeal reviewed earlier cases and held that "threats and conduct of such a nature and extent that the mind of an ordinary person of normal stability and courage might be influenced or made apprehensive so as to accede unwillingly to the demand would be sufficient for a jury's consideration."[41] But that section also required an intent to steal on the part of D, and this requirement may to some extent have controlled the meaning to be given to the word "menaces" in the Larceny Act. Only in rare cases could a person be credited with an intent to steal—that is, in effect, to obtain property from P without his consent—when he had used a threat incapable of affecting an ordinarily firm mind. Such cases are not impossible, however. If D knows that P is an unusually timid person or exceptionally vulnerable to a particular kind of pressure, he may expect him to succumb to a threat that would have no chance of affecting a stronger character or a person in different circumstances, and he may choose P as his victim for that reason. The "ordinary person" doctrine, therefore, although liberally enough applied to the facts of *Clear* itself, had an inherent weakness in its own statutory context. The different context of section 21 may justify the rejection, or at least a modification, of the doctrine. It is suggested that a test along the following lines might be just and workable: (a) that a threat may amount to "menaces" within the meaning of section 21 if, on all the facts known to D, including the nature and circumstances of P, it is a threat that might be capable of reducing P's ability to resist the demand; and (b) that if D knows nothing special about P, P may for this purpose be taken to be a person neither by nature nor by reason of circumstances unusually susceptible to

---

[36] *Eighth Report,* para. 123. This view was "notwithstanding the wide meaning given to 'menaces' in *Thorne's* case" (above, at n. 31).
[37] *Harry* [1974] Crim.L.R. 32.
[38] *Lawrence and Pomroy* (1971) 57 Cr.App.R. 64.
[39] [1968] 1 Q.B. 670.
[40] See n. 30, above.
[41] [1968] 1 Q.B. 670 at p. 679.

pressure. If P were known to be dangerously allergic to feathers, a threat to tickle him with one might after all be "menaces."

The source of the threatened evil

To be guilty of blackmail D must make or be party to the making of a demand with menaces; but "it is . . . immaterial whether the menaces relate to action to be taken by the person making the demand" (s. 21(2)). An example of a menace relating to action to be taken by another has already been seen in the case of *Studer*[42] (though in that case the circumstances were extreme in that both the threatened action and the person who would take it were fictitious).   **12–19**

4. THE DEMAND WITH MENACES MUST BE "UNWARRANTED"

It is as well to set out the relevant part of section 21(1) again. Blackmail depends upon the making of an *unwarranted* demand with menaces;   **12–20**

> "and for this purpose a demand with menaces is unwarranted unless the person making it does so in the belief—
> (*a*) that he has reasonable grounds for making the demand; and
> (*b*) that the use of the menaces is a proper means of reinforcing the demand."

Burden of proof

The passage quoted above from section 21(1) is merely a part of the definition of blackmail. It has nothing to say about the incidence of the burden of proof in relation to any ingredient of the offence. The section says that a demand with menaces is unwarranted unless D has certain beliefs when he makes the demand. It does not say that he shall be presumed not to have had those beliefs unless he affirmatively proves that he did. The unwarranted nature of the demand is one of the ingredients of the crime of blackmail. The principle is now firmly established[43] that the prosecution must prove every ingredient of a criminal offence and that they have as part of this task the burden of negativing beyond reasonable doubt any circumstance, of which there is evidence worthy of consideration, that might afford ground for an acquittal.[44] There is nothing in the language of section 21(1) to distinguish, in this respect, between D's assertion that he held the relevant beliefs and the assertion of any other accused person that he acted, for instance, in self-defence,[45] or under duress[46] or in a state of sane automatism.[47]   **12–21**

---

[42] Above, § 12–08. *Cf. Smith* (1850) 1 Den. 510.
[43] *Woolmington* v. *D.P.P.* [1935] A.C. 462; and cases elaborating the fundamental rule stated by that case: *e.g.* the cases cited in nn. 45 to 47, below.
[44] The principle is of course subject to express statutory exceptions and to a common law exception in relation to the defence of insanity.
[45] *Lobell* [1957] 1 Q.B. 547.
[46] *Bone* [1968] 1 W.L.R. 983.
[47] *Bratty* v. *Attorney-General for Northern Ireland* [1963] A.C. 386.

12–22   It is submitted, then, that before there can be a conviction of blackmail the jury must be satisfied that D did not hold the relevant beliefs.[48] This does not mean that it will always be necessary for the prosecution to take special steps for the purpose of satisfying the jury on this issue. The prosecution need not negative the existence of a belief of which there is no evidence. The effect of the section is to place on D an evidential burden. Unless he introduces evidence, worthy of consideration, to the effect that he held the beliefs required by the section, the jury will be bound to find that the demand with menaces was unwarranted. Accordingly no direction to the jury on the topic will be required.[49]

This, at any rate, is the position in most cases; it is not certain that it is the position in all. There may occasionally be a case in which, having heard the prosecution evidence, the jury are of the opinion not only that D *did* have reasonable grounds for making the demand (this may well be undisputed), but also that the use of the menaces *was* a proper means of reinforcing the demand. Strictly speaking, the jury's view of the justice of the demand and the propriety of the menaces is irrelevant under the section. Yet if the jury take a view favourable to the accused on both matters, are they not entitled to suppose that he took the same view himself when he made the demand?[50]

Belief in reasonable grounds for making the demand

12–23   D's belief that he has reasonable grounds for making the demand may be justified on any view. If P owes him money or ought to pay him compensation for a tort, it is reasonable for D to demand payment of the debt or of a reasonable sum by way of compensation, and D's belief that he had reasonable grounds for making his demand follows almost automatically from the fact that such grounds existed.

Difficulty arises only when D did not in fact have reasonable grounds for making his demand (or cannot give credible evidence to the effect that he did) or when there is room for doubt as to whether he had such grounds.

12–24   The section draws no distinction between the different kinds of grounds that D may believe to exist for the making of his demand. He may believe, wrongly as a matter of *fact,* that what he demands is due (he believes P owes him money, but P has in fact paid him). He may believe, but be wrong in his *opinion,* that a certain sum constitutes reasonable compensation for P's tort (actual or supposed). He may believe, wrongly as a matter

---

[48] Yet see the *Eighth Report,* para. 121, where the Committee consider whether, under the new law, persons in the position of accused persons in two cases decided under the Larceny Act "would *establish*" the beliefs required by s. 21. (Italics supplied.) It is assumed that the word "establish" (and similar language in the same passage) was used *per incuriam.*

[49] *Lawrence and Pomroy* (1971) 57 Cr.App.R. 64; *Harvey* (1980) 72 Cr.App.R. 139 at p. 142 (no "live issue").

[50] Even so, once a demand with menaces has been proved (and assuming evidence of a view to gain or an intent to cause loss), a submission that the accused has no case to answer may not ever be technically correct, because of the way in which s. 21(1) is worded. But the jury might at the end of the prosecution case be invited to stop the case if they take a view of D's conduct strongly favourable to him.

of *law,* that P is bound to pay him a certain sum. He may believe, but be, in the opinion of others, wrong in his *moral judgment,*[51] that he is entitled to demand the act or omission that he demands of P. Any of these types of belief, if genuinely held, will be within the section.

To escape liability D must have believed that he had reasonable grounds **12–25** for making the particular demand that he made. If the sum demanded is disproportionate to the claim asserted or to the interest that D is seeking to protect, the likelihood that D believes himself entitled to make the demand naturally diminishes. The point may be illustrated by reference to a question litigated under the old law. The question was whether it was lawful for a trade association to demand from one of its members or from some other person the payment of a fine for a breach of the association's rules, the demand being supported by a threat to place the member or other person on the association's "stop list" if he did not pay the fine. Under the Larceny Act 1916, s. 29(1)(i), the legality of such a demand depended on whether it was made with "reasonable . . . cause." It was ultimately held that it was so made if the sum demanded was a reasonable sum having regard to the legitimate business interests of the association.[52] The test was purely objective. Under section 21 the question becomes whether D himself (perhaps the secretary of the association) believes the sum is a reasonable sum to demand, or at least believes that the association's decision to impose the fine renders it lawful and reasonable for him to demand it on behalf of the association (for this would be quite consistent with his personally considering that the sum is too great).

There is no requirement that D's belief be reasonable. In holding the **12–26** belief that he holds, D may reveal himself as eccentric or unusually stupid or grossly careless or deficient in moral sense; but this will be quite irrelevant. The test applied to determine whether the demand with menaces is "unwarranted" is entirely subjective. D himself sets the standard.

The unreasonableness of D's alleged belief goes only to its credibility. His suggestion that he acted under a particular belief may strain credulity too far. The jury may take the view that no one could have believed that the law was as D asserts he believed it to be. They may consider that D's demand for compensation was so plainly extortionate that D cannot have

---

[51] Contrast s. 2(1)(*a*), under which, for the purposes of theft, an appropriation of property is not to be regarded as dishonest if D believes that he has *in law* the right to deprive P of the property. A moral "claim of right," although possibly never a defence to a charge of theft, can provide a partial answer to a charge of blackmail. So, for instance, D, an employee of P, may claim that he thought himself morally entitled to demand a rise in wages, without alleging that he had any contractual right to a rise. And a lady in the position of the defendant in *Bernhard* [1938] 2 K.B. 264 (referred to in the text, below) would not be reduced, as she was under the Larceny Act 1916, s. 30, to claiming that as a result of an error of law she thought she had an enforceable claim against P for money promised to her for a past immoral consideration; she would now say that she thought she was morally justified in pressing her claim.
[52] *Thorne* v. *Motor Trade Association* [1937] A.C. 797.

believed he was entitled to so large a sum. In these cases D will be convicted because of the jury's utter disbelief and not because of their disapproval. That at least is the theory upon whch a conviction of blackmail should rest. In practice, of course, the jury's own standards are likely to be important in conditioning their willingness to give credence to D's evidence; and in that sense their disapproval is not completely irrelevant.

Belief in the propriety of using the menaces

12–27   It will commonly be much harder for D to allege with any plausibility that he believed the use of the menaces to be a proper means of reinforcing his demand than it will be to allege a belief in reasonable grounds for making the demand. "I thought that P owed me money" or "I thought the sum I demanded was reasonable compensation" will often enough be convincing statements. But D's evidence obviously becomes less attractive at the point where he has to add: "and I thought it proper to seek to make P pay by threatening to reveal that as a solicitor he had misappropriated his client's money."

The prevailing view (and that of the jury) may be that a threat to expose P's fraud, or to bring criminal proceedings, or to announce to the world that he defaults on his debts of honour, is not a proper means of reinforcing a demand—even where what is demanded is due or believed to be due. But the general view is irrelevant—except to the extent that it provides a standard whereby to judge whether D himself may genuinely have believed the use of the menaces to be "proper." The question of D's own belief must be left to the jury.[53]

12–28   It was held in *Harvey*[54] that no act known by D to be unlawful can be believed by him to be "proper" (even though he may hold it to be "justified"). There has as yet been no further authoritative elucidation of the meaning of "proper." The Committee suggested that the word "directs the mind to a consideration of what is morally and socially acceptable."[55] With this in mind it has been argued that whether D believed his use of the menaces to be "proper" requires reference to his understanding of general opinion. Did he believe that it was "morally and socially acceptable" by prevailing standards?[56] According to this test, the question would be, not whether D took an indulgent view of his own conduct (the argument assumes that he always would), but whether he thought that other people would do so. He might genuinely think that they would; he might, in the jury's view, be wrong; and in such a case, but only in such a case, the subjective character of the offence would operate in his favour. This

[53] *Harvey* (1980) 72 Cr.App.R. 139.
[54] (1980) 72 Cr.App.R. 139.
[55] *Eighth Report*, para. 123.
[56] Smith, *Theft*, paras. 325 *et seq.*; see also Law Commission Working Paper No. 61, *Offences relating to the Administration of Justice*, para. 82.

argument is attractive.[57] It has perhaps been partly vindicated by the decision in *Harvey* and may yet be generally adopted. In the only other reported case so far, however, the jury were told that D's guilt or innocence depended upon "his own opinion as to whether he was acting rightly or wrongly." Such a direction can produce a striking acquittal, as the case shows.[58]

The Committee, to test the likely operation of the section, took the situations in the famous cases of *Bernhard*[59] and *Dymond.*[60] In the former case a Hungarian lady demanded money that had been promised to her in consideration of her past services as P's mistress. She threatened that if he did not pay her she would expose him to his wife, and to the public by means of a newspaper advertisement. In *Dymond,* D claimed payment (of an unspecified amount) from P for an alleged indecent assault upon her. Her threats were that P would "gett summons" and that she would "let the town knowed all about your going on." The Committee anticipated that under the new law "Dymond probably (assuming the facts were as the defence wished to prove[61]) and Bernhard certainly, would easily establish[61] that they believed that they had reasonable grounds for making the demand."[62] This would clearly be to achieve the easier half of their tasks. Each would now have to allege further that she believed her threats were a proper means of reinforcing her demand for payment. Each, in her righteous indignation, may conceivably have believed so; but she would find it a harder matter to give satisfactory evidence on this point than on the other.   **12–29**

Whether D will succeed on this issue may depend in part on such matters as his standard of education, his intelligence and his social environment. Miss Dymond's illiteracy and Mrs. Bernhard's foreign extraction might be material to support the suggestion that they did not have an accurate sense of what was "proper." Conversely, if D is in business in the City, he may find it hard to assert a belief in the propriety of threatening to publish among P's social circle the fact that P had not paid a trading debt. He, though not Miss Dymond, would know that such a thing is not "done," and he would probably himself believe that a threat to do it is an improper way of seeking to recover the debt.   **12–30**

---

[57] It is more attractive than a similar interpretation of "belief that he has reasonable grounds for making the demand." There seems less ground for arguing, in relation to this belief, that the inquiry concerns D's judgment of other people's (or the law's) view of what is reasonable.

[58] *Lambert* [1972] Crim.L.R. 422. D told P, whom he suspected of having an affair with his wife, that £250 would buy D's rights to the wife (the report says "[P's] rights," presumably in error); if P would not pay, D would tell P's wife and employer of his suspicions. D was acquitted of blackmail.

[59] [1938] 2 K.B. 264.

[60] [1920] 2 K.B. 260.

[61] But see above at n. 48, at to the propriety of this language.

[62] *Eighth Report,* para. 121.

12–31   In assessing the genuineness of D's alleged belief, both the nature of the demand and the precise threat used must of course be taken into account. "A threat to do some harm disproportionate to the amount of a disputed claim would be strong evidence of the absence of any belief in the propriety of the threat."[62]

5.   A VIEW TO GAIN OR AN INTENT TO CAUSE LOSS

"With a view to gain . . . or with intent to cause loss"

12–32   A demand with menaces is not blackmail unless made with a view to gain for oneself or another or with intent to cause loss to another. This language has been considered in the context of offences under section 17, and the reader is referred to that discussion.[63] It has already been observed[64] that the requirement of a view to gain or an intent to cause loss constitutes an important limitation of the scope of blackmail. Gain and loss "in money or other property" are the only aims of D's demand relevant to his guilt under section 21. Some examples of cases excluded by this aspect of the definition of blackmail have already been given.[64]

"Gain or loss in money or other property"

12–33   Although " 'gain' and 'loss' are to be construed as extending only to gain or loss[65] in money or other property" (s. 34(2)(a)), both words are given artificially wide meanings. By section 34(2)(a)(i), " 'gain' includes a gain by keeping what one has, as well as a gain by getting what one has not." By sub-paragraph (ii), " 'loss' includes a loss by not getting what one might get, as well as a loss by parting with what one has."

12–34   Blackmail therefore covers much more than simply demands for the transfer of money or other property. The following demands seem all to be among those capable of being blackmail:

(i) A demand that P pay a debt. It has been argued that no "gain" to D or "loss" to P occurs when P pays to D what he owes him.[66] This argument may in any case have been affected by the amendments to the Bill that caused "gain" to include "getting" what one has not and "loss" to include "parting with" what one has. That point aside, however, it is thought that the argument is wrong in principle. The gravamen of the offence of blackmail is the use of menaces, not conceived by D to be "proper," to reinforce a demand (and "the nature of the act or omission demanded is immaterial" (s. 21(2)). Even a just demand should not be *so* supported. There is in fact no difficulty in regarding D as having "gained" by the payment or transfer to him of money or property to which he is entitled; and to do so accords with the intention of the framers of the Act.[67]

---

[63] Above, §§ 10–04, 10–05.
[64] Above, § 12–07.
[65] "Whether temporary or permanent."
[66] Hogan [1966] Crim.L.R. 474 at p. 476.
[67] *Eighth Report*, para. 119. This point appears to have passed *sub silentio* in *Lawrence and Pomroy* (1971) 57 Cr.App.R. 64, in a manner according with the view expressed here; and a circuit judge has expressly ruled to the same effect: *Parkes* [1973] Crim.L.R. 358. (The harrassment of contract debtors by, *inter alia*, demands accompanied by alarming threats may now be prosecuted summarily under the Administration of Justice Act 1970, s. 40.)

(ii) A demand that P give D a job, in which D will earn a salary. D has a view to gain.[68]

(iii) A demand that P permit D to take indecent photographs of her, D's purpose being to sell prints of the photographs. Here too D has a view to gain.

(iv) A demand that P abandon a claim against D for money or other property. D has a view to gain by keeping what he has or an intent to cause loss to P by P's not getting what he might get.

(v) A demand by D that P deceive Q into abandoning a claim against E. The section does not require the intended loss to be a loss to the person of whom the demand is made; and a view to gain "for another" is sufficient.

(vi) A demand that P destroy letters written by D to P. P will suffer "a loss by parting with what [he] has."[69]

---

[68] *Cf.* in a very different context the reference, at § 10–04, above, to *Wines* [1954] 1 W.L.R. 64. But a demand that P appoint D to an honorary office will not be blackmail.
[69] *Cf. Eighth Report,* para. 117.

CHAPTER 13

HANDLING

1. DEFINITION

13–01 SECTION 22(1) defines the offence of handling stolen goods:

> "A person handles stolen goods if (otherwise than in the course of the stealing) knowing or believing them to be stolen goods he dishonestly receives the goods, or dishonestly undertakes or assists in their retention, removal, disposal or realisation by or for the benefit of another person, or if he arranges to do so."

Section 22(2) provides a maximum penalty of imprisonment for 14 years on conviction on indictment.[1]

The word "handling" is a term of art.[2] The offence may be committed without physically touching the stolen goods; and one may physically handle them, even with guilty knowledge, without committing the offence. The ways in which the offence may be committed are defined by the section. Those ways are various; but despite the variety the section creates a single offence.[3]

2. STOLEN GOODS

There must be stolen goods

13–02 Whatever variety of the offence be in question, the property concerned must at the time of the alleged handling be "stolen goods" within the meaning of the section. One example of the offence occurs when a person "believing them to be stolen goods . . . dishonestly receives the goods" or does one of a number of acts in relation to them. This wording does not render guilty of handling a person who deals with goods which he wrongly believes to be stolen at the time of his act.[4] Another variety of handling is that committed by one who arranges to receive stolen goods or, for instance, to dispose of them. It is clear that for this purpose the goods must be stolen before the arrangement is made.[5]

---

[1] Handling stolen goods from an offence not committed in the United Kingdom was originally triable only on indictment (s.29(2): repealed). It is now triable either way: Magistrates' Courts Act 1980, Sched.1, para.28.

[2] Under the Larceny Act 1916, s. 33, the corresponding offence was limited to the "receiving" of goods. The offence was extended by the Criminal Law Act 1967, s. 4(7), so as to be almost as wide as the present offence. The word "handling" was introduced by the Theft Act merely as the name of the offence. It does not (*pace Smythe* (1980) 72 Cr.App.R. 8 at p.13) represent a "new concept" or lend itself to interpretation.

[3] *Griffiths* v. *Freeman* [1970] 1 W.L.R. 659; [1970] 1 All E.R. 1117. For a powerful critique of the handling provisions, see I. D. Elliott (1977) 26 I.C.L.Q. 110 at pp. 135–144 (including, however, a misreading at p. 138, n.170, of § 13–31, below).

[4] *Haughton* v. *Smith* [1975] A.C. 476. But he can be convicted of attempted handling: Criminal Attempts Act 1981, s. 1(2)(3); reversing *Haughton* v. *Smith* in this respect.

[5] Contrast *McDonough* (1962) 47 Cr.App.R. 37 (incitement to receive stolen goods).

"Stolen"

Section 24(4) gives an extended meaning to the word "stolen." Its effect   **13-03**
is that, for the purpose (among others) of the offence of handling, goods
are to be regarded as stolen not only if they have been the subject of theft
as defined in section 1, but also if they have been obtained by blackmail or
by deception (that is, by an offence under section 15).[6] Moreover,
references in the relevant provisions of the Act to stolen goods include the
proceeds of dealings with such goods by a thief or handler, as is mentioned
immediately below. Throughout this chapter, therefore, as in those
provisions, the words "steal," "stolen," "theft" and "thief" are all to be
understood in correspondingly wide senses.

The theft need not have occurred in England and Wales, nor since the
commencement of the Act. It is sufficient if (a) the goods were
appropriated or obtained anywhere and at any time by a transaction
satisfying the definition of theft in section 1, of obtaining property by
deception in section 15 or of blackmail in section 21 *and* (b) that
transaction was an offence when it was committed in the country where it
was committed.[7]

"Goods" and their proceeds

"[Goods] . . . includes money and every other description of property   **13-04**
except land, and includes things severed from the land by stealing"
(s. 34(2)(*b*)). Handling can therefore be committed in respect of every-
thing except land.

There is a complicated provision (s. 24(2)) to secure that the taint of the
theft may apply to the proceeds of stolen goods and that the offence of
handling shall extend to proceeds so tainted as to the original goods. The
reader is referred to the text of this provision in Appendix 1. The following
are some illustrations of its effect.[8]

(a) A steals goods. (i) He sells them for £1,000 in cash. The goods and   **13-05**
the £1,000 are now both "stolen goods." (ii) B receives part of the £1,000
knowing that it represents stolen goods. He is guilty of handling. (iii) With
the rest of the £1,000 A buys a *car*. This too is "stolen." C, knowing the
truth, undertakes to dispose of the car for A. He is guilty of handling. So is
D, who buys the car, if he has guilty knowledge, for the car "at [one] time
represented the stolen goods in the hands of the thief" (s. 24(2)(*a*)).

(b) A steals £1,000 in £1 notes. (i) A owes B £500 and pays him with £500
of the stolen money. B knows it is stolen and is therefore a handler. If B
buys *goods* with the £500, those goods are "stolen," as will be money he
receives on a resale of those goods. (ii) A pays the remaining £500 to C for

---

[6] See *e.g. Dabek* [1973] Crim.L.R. 527 (goods obtained on credit by deception as to matters
relevant to the giving of credit: "stolen" goods).

[7] s. 24(1)(4). It would seem that the prosecution must prove as a fact the relevant matters of
foreign law in order to show that the theft was an offence thereunder. *Cf. Naguib* [1917] 1
K.B. 359 as to the proof of foreign marriages in bigamy cases. Questions as to foreign law
are nevertheless for the judge to decide: Administration of Justice Act 1920, s. 15;
Hammer [1923] 2 K.B. 786.

[8] And for discussion of a case which called for careful analysis of s.24(2), see n.44, below.

services rendered. C does not know the money is stolen and is therefore not a handler. C buys *goods* with his £500. Those goods are not "stolen," for they do not represent "stolen goods in the hands of a handler" (s. 24(2)(*b*)).

13–06   (c) A by deception obtains a cheque for £1,000 from his employer. Being so obtained, the cheque is "stolen." (i) A pays the cheque into his bank account. The *bank balance* (as a thing in action and therefore "goods" within the meaning of section 34(2)(*b*))[9] may be goods representing the cheque in the hands of A as being the proceeds of his disposal or realisation of them; if so, it is "stolen."[10] (ii) A draws *£300 cash* from the account and pays it to B. B may thus receive "stolen goods." There is no difficulty about this if the bank account has been fed only by stolen cheques or consisted only of the proceeds of stolen goods.[11] But in the case of an account fed by both "stolen" and "honest" money, the prosecution must be able to prove, by reference to the history of the account, that the cash was capable of representing stolen goods. This may perhaps be possible even if honest money in the account could alone cover the withdrawal; but it would need to be shown that A intended to withdraw stolen rather than honest money.[12] (iii) A gives C *a cheque for £300* drawn on the account. C may cash this cheque or the cheque may be collected for the credit of his bank account. If so the discussion in (ii) above applies to the cash or to the resulting debt owed to C by his bank as it applies to the cash considered in (ii). But it is not clear that it applies to the cheque itself. To be "stolen" the cheque must "represent . . . [the original cheque] in the hands of [A] as being the proceeds of [a] disposal or realisation . . . of . . . [the bank balance] representing [the original cheque]": s. 24(2)(*a*). But the cheque now drawn by A is surely not the *proceeds* of such a disposal or realisation but rather the means of effecting one.[13]

Proof that the goods are stolen

13–07   On a charge of handling, then, the prosecution must prove that the goods were stolen within the above extended sense of the word. Sometimes they will be able to show clearly how the goods were stolen and by whom. Sometimes the fact that they were stolen will be established by the evidence of the person to whom they belong as to the manner in which they were lost,[14] though without necessarily identifying the thief. Exceptionally the fact that they were stolen may be the proper inference from evidence that establishes the identity neither of the victim nor of the thief. In

---

[9] *Attorney-General's Reference* (*No.* 4 *of* 1979) (1980) 71 Cr.App.R. 341 at p.348.
[10] Unless the victim of the theft has ceased, because of a mixing of funds, to have a right to restitution: see the discussion by J.C. Smith at [1981] Crim.L.R. 52, referring to s. 24(3) (below, § 13–11).
[11] *Attorney-General's Reference*, above, at p. 348.
[12] *Ibid.* at p.349. *B's* intention to receive stolen money or his belief that it was stolen is no evidence as to its stolen character: *ibid.*; see below, § 13–07.
[13] But see the court's tentative view on the point: *ibid.*
[14] As to evidence by statutory declaration in proceedings for handling goods stolen in the course of transmission, see s. 27(4).

particular, the circumstances in which the alleged handler acquired the goods (at a gross undervalue, for example, in a place where such goods are not normally sold) may be fairly capable of only one interpretation as to their history.[15] The court may know of those circumstances from the reported statements of the accused himself, which are of course admissible against him. But his account of what he was told about the goods is mere hearsay and inadmissible even against him.[16] Nor, it has been held, is his own belief or conclusion that they were stolen admissible to prove that they were—even if his conclusion seems "fair and safe to rely upon."[17] Yet it has also been said that "whether a belief has any evidential value must depend upon the facts of the case"[18]; and on the strength of this dictum it is still perhaps open to argument in a suitable case that D's own experience in the relevant trade renders his opinion effectively that of an expert and admissible on that account as evidence of the character of the goods.[19]

An inference of theft should not be too lightly drawn from circumstances **13–08** of suspicion. The unknown "thief" may have believed he had a right to the goods[20]; furtive behaviour and false explanations may conceal some other sinister truth than that the goods were stolen. Or it may be that the goods were indeed stolen, but by the accused himself; in which case a conviction of handling would only rarely be proper.[21] On the other hand, the fact of theft has to be proved against the alleged handler, not against the thief, and an acquittal of the alleged thief is not necessarily inconsistent with the conviction of another person of handling.[22]

When goods cease to be stolen goods
Even assuming, however, that the goods are proved to have been stolen **13–09** at some time before the act by which D is alleged to have handled them, it is possible that they were not *still* stolen goods at the time of D's act; and in

---

[15] *Sbarra* (1918) 13 Cr.App.R. 118 (by a side door during the night); *Hulbert* (1979) 69 Cr.App.R. 243 (clothing in quantity bought for low prices in pubs); *McDonald* (1980) 70 Cr.App.R. 288 (television set bought for £90 from unidentified man in betting shop); see also *Overington* [1978] Crim.L.R. 692.
[16] *Hulbert*, above; and see *Marshall* [1977] Crim.L.R. 106.
[17] *Hulbert*, above (the words quoted are from p.247); *Overington*, above; *Attorney-General's Reference (No. 4 of 1979)* (1980) 71 Cr.App.R. 341 (above, n.12); and see Crown Court rulings in *Porter* [1976] Crim.L.R. 58; *Hack* [1978] Crim.L.R. 359. Cases in which the stolen character of goods has been inferred from D's conduct (*e.g.* hiding them, as in *Young* v. *Spiers* (1952) 36 Cr.App.R. 200) must now be treated with caution to the extent that such conduct may reflect hearsay or D's belief; A.T.H. Smith, "Theft and/or Handling" [1977] Crim.L.R. 517 at pp. 521–523; but the seminal case of *Fuschillo* [1940] 2 All E.R. 489 is perhaps unaffected in this respect.
[18] *McDonald*, above, *per* Lawton L.J. at p.290.
[19] See Stone, "Proof that Goods are Stolen" (1979) 129 N.L.J. 1018 at p.1019, citing *Gibbons* [1971] V.R. 79; and *cf.*, as to the identity of drugs, *Chatwood* [1980] 1 W.L.R. 874; [1980] 1 All E.R. 467. The topic is reviewed by Scott, "Controlling the Reception in Evidence of Unreliable Admissions" [1981] Crim. L.R. 285.
[20] See above, § 2–81. In *Farrell* [1975] 2 N.Z.L.R. 753, the supposed thief had been acquitted of theft on the ground of insanity; in *Walters* v. *Lunt* [1951] 2 All E.R. 645, he was under the age of criminal responsibility.
[21] See below, §§ 13–27 to 13–29.
[22] *Close* [1977] Crim. L.R. 107, depends upon this proposition but is a very puzzling application of it on the facts.

such a case D is not guilty of the offence. Section 24(3) describes two classes of situation in which this could be the case.

(i) The first situation is that in which, before the handling, the goods "have been restored to the person from whom they were stolen or to other lawful possession or custody."

Restoration to the person from whom the goods were stolen may be taken to mean a return to his possession or to that of his agent. No act by or on behalf of the victim of the theft falling short of a deliberate exercise of control over the goods will suffice to amount to a restoration of them. So, for example, cartons of cigarettes stolen from a company by an employee and placed by him in the company's lorry were not "restored" to the company by the acts of the company's security officer in initialling the cartons for the purpose of identification and of police officers in following the lorry to where the cigarettes were sold by the thief to D; they were still "stolen" when D bought them.[23]

The phrase "the person from whom they were stolen" is somewhat casual, since property may be stolen from a variety of persons having disparate interests in it.[24] Whether the phrase refers to the person, if any, specified as the victim in the indictment or to any person who might have been so specified is rendered less important than it might have been[25] by the additional reference to other lawful possession or custody.

13–10   Goods are "restored" to lawful possession or custody, notwithstanding the inappropriateness of the verb, if they are "taken by a police officer in the course of his duty and reduced into possession by him."[26] The principle that such restoration will deprive the goods of their "stolen" status can therefore embarrass police operations. For instance, police officers seize goods in the hands of the thief. The thief then co-operates with them to trap D, an intending receiver. D receives the goods from the thief and is promptly arrested. If it can be proved that D's arrangement to receive the goods was made after the goods were stolen[27] and before they came into the hands of the police, D can be convicted of handling on an indictment carefully drafted. But if no arrangement occurring in that period can be proved, there can be no conviction of handling, because the goods were not "stolen" when they were received.[28] In some cases, however, it is less clear whether the goods have been restored to lawful possession. In *Attorney-General's Reference (No. 1 of 1974)*[29] a police constable found in

---

[23] *Greater London Metropolitan Police Commissioner* v. *Streeter* (1980) 71 Cr.App.R. 113; contrast *Villensky* [1892] 2 Q.B. 597.

[24] s. 1(1) read with s. 5; s. 15(1) read with s. 5(1).

[25] *Cf.Schmidt* (1866) L.R. 1 C.C.R. 15; *Villensky* [1892] 2 Q.B. 597. As to naming the victim in the indictment, see below, § 13–32, at nn.1, 2.

[26] *Attorney-General's Reference (No.1 of* 1974) [1974] Q.B. 744 at p. 750. (It is doubtful whether the word "custody" adds much in the present context. In *Attorney-General's Reference* the words "possession," "custody" and "control" were used interchangeably by Lord Widgery C.J. (at p. 753)).

[27] See above, § 13–02, at n.5.

[28] As to liability for attempt, see above, n.4.

[29] [1974] Q.B. 744.

an unattended car packages of clothing that he suspected were stolen (as they indeed proved to be). He removed the rotor arm from the car to immobilise it, and kept watch. When D appeared and tried to start the car, the constable questioned him. He gave an implausible explanation and was arrested. The trial judge directed D's acquittal on a charge of handling, ruling that the goods were no longer "stolen" when D came to the car. On a reference under the Criminal Justice Act 1972, s.36, however, the Court of Appeal's opinion was that whether the constable had taken possession of the goods "depended primarily on [his] intentions." Had he made up his mind to "reduce them into his possession or control, take charge of them so that they could not be removed and so that he would have the disposal of them"? Or did he act as he did simply to ensure that he would be able to question the driver about the goods when he appeared, having meanwhile an open mind as to whether the goods were to be seized? This was an issue that should have been left for the jury's determination.[30]

(ii) Secondly, the goods will cease to be stolen when the person from   **13–11** whom they were stolen "and any other person claiming through him have . . . ceased as regards those goods to have any right to restitution in respect of the theft." For instance, the owner of goods which have been obtained from him by deception may, on discovering the fraud, affirm the transaction in question and so lose all title to the goods; a third party may have acquired a good title to the goods by virtue of some exception to the rule *nemo dat quod non habet*; or, exceptionally, the owner's title may have been extinguished by the expiration of six years following a conversion not "related to the theft."[31]

3.   WHAT CONDUCT AMOUNTS TO HANDLING

Assuming that D has the appropriate *mens rea*, he will be guilty of handling   **13–12** if he[32]:

(a) receives stolen goods; or
(b) arranges to receive them; or
(c) undertakes or assists in their retention, removal, disposal or realisation by or for the benefit of another person; or
(d) arranges to act as in (c).

(a) Receiving

Before 1968 the corresponding offence under the old law was limited to   **13–13** receiving and was called by that name. Receiving involved nothing less than the acquisition of exclusive control of the property or of joint

---

[30] *Ibid.* at pp. 753–754. In the light of the Court of Appeal's opinion, some pre-Act cases on the present topic are now of little, if any, authority; especially *King* [1938] 2 All E.R. 662.
[31] Limitation Act 1980, ss.2, 3(2), 4.
[32] But "otherwise than in the course of the stealing." As to the thief, see below, §§ 13–27 to 13–29.

possession with the thief or another receiver.[33] Handling is now a much wider offence, but presumably the meaning of receiving itself remains as before.[34] If D examines goods in the thief's presence while negotiating with him, he does not thereby handle them in the technical sense. On the other hand if, for example, the thief leaves the goods with D by way of loan or on approval, D handles when he knowingly accepts the possession so given to him; *a fortiori* if he acquires possession of the goods by gift or purchase.

(b) Arranging to receive

13–14   If D negotiates with C, a thief, for the purchase of the stolen goods, D is not on this account guilty of handling. What is required is at least an arrangement to receive (or to do some other act that amounts to handling under head (c), below). But the conclusion of a bargain between C and D will normally involve at least an arrangement by D to receive the goods and therefore a complete offence. There must be an arrangement by D to acquire possession on his own account. Consequently, if D, when he buys from C, arranges for C to deliver the goods direct to E, a sub-purchaser, D presumably does not "arrange to receive" the goods, though it appears that he "undertakes or assists in their . . . realisation by or for the benefit of [C]."[35]

Making an offer to buy from the thief, with a view to taking delivery if the offer is accepted, is an attempt to handle (an attempt to arrange to receive).

(c) Undertaking or assisting in[36] retention, removal, disposal or realisation

13–15   Once he has accomplished his theft the thief faces major problems for which he may need all manner of facilities. The goods may need to be stored. They may have to be carried to a place of safety or to the purchaser. Gold and silver articles may require melting down. Stolen cars require new number-plates and registration documents and the execution of skilled work to conceal their identity. Contact must be made with "fences" and negotiations conducted. Anyone who assists in or undertakes any of these or similar operations for the thief or for another handler is guilty of handling if he knows or believes the goods to be stolen and acts dishonestly. The net is flung very wide.

The act undertaken or assisted in must be "by or for the benefit of another person." This vital phrase qualifies each of the four nouns "retention," "removal," "disposal" and "realisation."[37] The whole phrase is commonly recited, without attention to its meaning, even when part of it cannot apply. In fact, it is submitted, what the handler "undertakes" must be an act "for the benefit of another person"; and what he "assists in" must

---

[33] *Hobson* v. *Impett* (1957) 41 Cr.App.R. 138; *Frost and Hale* (1964) 48 Cr.App.R. 284.

[34] See *Smythe* (1980) 72 Cr.App.R. 8.

[35] See *Deakin* [1972] 1 W.L.R. 1618; [1972] 3 All E.R. 803, commented upon below, § 13–16, para. (iv).

[36] "Undertaking" is intended to refer to one who acts on his own, "assisting in" to one who acts in concert with the thief or another handler: *Eighth Report*, para. 128.

[37] *Sloggett* [1972] 1 Q.B. 430.

be an act done *either* "by . . . another person" *or* "for the benefit of another person."[38]

It has been held that a sale of goods by D to E is a realisation of them which D "undertakes . . . for the benefit of" E.[39] With respect, it is thought that this decision is unfortunate. An act should not be regarded as done "for" a person's benefit just because that person in fact benefits from it.

(i) *Retention.* It has been held that the meaning of "retain" is a matter of law. The word means "keep possession of, not lose, continue to have."[40] The Court of Appeal held in *Brown*[41] that, where D knows that stolen goods are on his premises, mere failure to reveal them to police officers who are searching for them may be evidence that he has permitted the goods to remain on his premises and is thereby assisting in their retention, but cannot itself amount to so assisting. To have held otherwise would have been to encroach on the principle that one is not bound to answer police questions.[42] On the other hand, it appears from *Pitchley*[43] that one who discovers that property he is holding for another is stolen property must be active to disburden himself of it. D received money from his son and paid it into his own post office savings bank account on his son's behalf. According to him he realised only afterwards that the money was stolen. Even on that basis he was held rightly convicted of handling, for after learning the truth he made no withdrawal from the account and had been "assisting in the retention of the money."[44]

13–16

(ii) *Removal.* This word obviously covers anyone carrying or transporting stolen goods for another's benefit or assisting therein. An illustration may conveniently be given here, however, of the fact that D's act need not

---

[38] For a slightly more restricted reading, see J. R. Spencer, "The Mishandling of Handling" [1981] Crim.L.R. 682. Blake [1972] Crim.L.R. 494, assumes that "by" and "for the benefit of" were intended to have the functions indicated in the text. But he feels (unnecessarily, it is submitted) that the statutory wording cannot grammatically achieve that intention. Although it is a fair point that the draftsman might have studied the structure of his sentence more closely, Blake's own reading of "by" ("through the agency, means, instrumentality, or causation of" [another]) must surely be rejected.

[39] *Bloxham* [1981] 1 W.L.R. 659; [1981] 2 All E.R. 647, a decision justly condemned by Spencer, *loc.cit.*, n.38.

[40] *Pitchley* (1972) 57 Cr.App.R. 30. (The headnote is misleading as to the facts.)

[41] [1970] 1 Q.B. 105.

[42] *Rice* v. *Connolly* [1966] 2 Q.B. 414. In *Brown*, above, D said to the police "Get lost!" But this made no difference.

[43] See n.40, above.

[44] It should surely have been, if anything, "undertaking the retention of a thing in action," namely, a debt owed to D by the bank. The argument would be that that debt was the proceeds of a realisation of the stolen money: see s. 24(2). In fact it is highly doubtful whether the precise wording of s. 24(2) was satisfied in *Pitchley*. S. 24(2)(*b*) comes closest to applying. At first sight the thing in action may appear to "represent . . . the stolen goods in the hands of a *handler* . . . ." But for this purpose the thing must be "the proceeds of [a] realisation of . . . the stolen goods handled by him." At the time of the realisation, however, D did not know the money was stolen and therefore the goods realised were not "goods *handled* by him." It is thought that, if the premise upon which this footnote is based is correct, the conviction should have been quashed. There is a tendency even among lawyers to think of credit at the bank as being "money" for the purposes of the Act; in *Pitchley* there are many references in the judgment to "money in the savings book" (*sic*). But "money in the bank" is a loose expression. See above, § 2–09, at nn.30, 31.

be done solely for another's benefit. For instance, D may help C to carry C's stolen goods into D's shop, there to negotiate. In doing so D "assists in their . . . removal . . . by [C]," and is surely guilty although he acts for his own purposes.

(iii) *Disposal*. This word is apt to cover a wide range of acts, including destruction, dumping, transformation by heat or by chemical means and distribution by way of gift.

(iv) *Realisation*. Realisation of goods occurs when they are exchanged for money or anything else of value.[45] Realisation for the benefit of another typically occurs when an agent sells on behalf of a principal.[46] Where the thief himself sells stolen goods, the buyer may perhaps be described as assisting in their realisation, though normally it would seem more appropriate to charge him with receiving or arranging to receive them. In one case, however, the Court of Appeal regarded the buyer's conduct as accurately described by an indictment alleging that he undertook the realisation of the goods.[47] There certainly was a realisation by the seller; but it is a remarkable use of language to say that the buyer "undertook" that act.

(d) Arranging to act as in (c)

13–17   If D merely arranges to do or assist in doing any of the kinds of things referred to under the preceding head he will be guilty of the complete offence of handling. The Act is indeed remarkable, here as in theft, in the extent to which it treats as major substantive offences transactions of a preliminary or accessory character. It would be as well to bear this in mind in interpreting the word "arranges." Very little formality and precision need attend an arrangement—nothing in the nature of a contract or solemn promise. But there should be an element of finality.

To illustrate the problem and the kind of approach suggested, we may take the case of D who says that he is prepared to lend a hand in carrying some parcels from C's house to a lorry outside. It is suggested that—(i) if a time is fixed, there is an arrangement, however casually made; (ii) if all that occurs is D's expression of willingness in principle, there is no arrangement within the section; (iii) in any intermediate case the court should be most wary of finding an arrangement. Whether D has arranged to assist depends as a matter of degree on the details of the case. If, for instance, all is finally settled except the time of the operation, which C will communicate to D, it would not be improper to say that D has arranged to assist.

---

[45] For a trial judge's ruling giving "realisation" a fairly broad meaning and on the facts of the case permitting an omission to prevent payment to another to amount to assisting in realisation by that other, see *Tamm* [1973] Crim.L.R. 115.

[46] As to a sale as realisation "for the benefit of" the buyer, see *Bloxham* [1981] 1 W.L.R. 659; [1981] 2 All E.R. 647 (above § 13–15).

[47] *Deakin* [1972] 1 W.L.R. 1618; [1972] 3 All E.R. 803. Even if the buyer's receipt of the goods is described in this way, the handling is over once that receipt has occurred: see *Figures* [1976] Crim.L.R. 744 (goods bought abroad and carried to England; no handling in England).

It may be noted that, the act of arranging being the complete offence, it will be mere mitigation that D in the end decided not to lend his assistance.

4. THE MENTAL ELEMENT

Knowledge or belief

Handling is committed by one who knows or believes that the goods are **13–18** stolen. Only knowledge or belief on the part of the person charged will satisfy the requirements of the section; it is not sufficient that any reasonable person would have realised that the goods were stolen.[48] What is required, of course, is knowledge of or belief in *facts* which result in the goods having as a matter of law a stolen character. D may know or believe that the goods have been acquired in some way amounting to an offence of theft or obtaining by deception or by blackmail; but he may not know in just what kind of circumstances they were acquired, or he may positively believe in facts which, if true, would indeed result in the goods being stolen, but which are not the true facts. He will still be guilty: there is no need for him to identify the class of "theft" concerned.

Nor need D know the nature of the goods with which he is dealing. It is enough if he knows or believes, for instance, that the goods in the unopened suitcase he is looking after are stolen goods.[49]

"The knowledge . . . need not be such knowledge as would be acquired **13–19** if the prisoner had actually seen the lead stolen; it is sufficient if you think the circumstances were such . . . as to make the prisoner believe that it had been stolen." So said Bramwell B. in a case[50] under the old law, though the word "believing" was not in the statute. Obviously it was never necessary for D to have witnessed the theft; he might "know" by credible report. He may now no doubt "believe"—which section 22 expressly allows to suffice—on the strength of any evidence.

But what amounts to "believing" for this purpose? It has to be submitted that the help given by appellate decisions on this subject is inadequate[51] and that judicial pronouncements on "belief" and on its relationship to "wilful blindness" are unsatisfactory. Below are offered, in turn, (a) a brief discussion untrammelled by authority and (b) a summary of the case law with comments.

(a) *Belief and wilful blindness: a recommended view.* The language of **13–20** "belief" is often used in criminal statutes, without definition from Parliament or commentary from judges. Such language is in fact full of difficulty.[52] In the present context it obviously refers at one extreme to a

---

[48] *Atwal* v. *Massey* (1971) 56 Cr.App.R. 6; *Stagg* [1978] Crim.L.R. 227; *Bellenie* [1980] Crim.L.R. 437.
[49] *McCullum* (1973) 57 Cr.App.R. 708.
[50] *White* (1859) 1 F. & F. 665.
[51] Compare the strong comments of Professor J.C. Smith at [1980] Crim L.R. 437, and of J. Beaumont, "Knowledge and Belief in Handling Stolen Goods" (1978) 142 J.P.N. 527.
[52] See Griew in Glazebrook (ed.), *Reshaping the Criminal Law*, 57 at pp. 69–76.

firm conclusion, with or without adequate evidence, that the goods are stolen. This may be called "strong" belief that the goods are stolen. Such a state of mind shades off into others—for instance, into less confident belief that the goods are stolen (the condition, perhaps, of thinking that the goods are "probably" stolen and being prepared to act on this assumption until it is contradicted): this is another state of mind surely within the section. It is hardly distinguishable from a certain kind of strong suspicion (realising that "very likely" the goods are stolen); and such suspicion itself shades down by imperceptible degrees to mild suspicion (realising that "maybe" they are stolen). Under certain conditions a state of suspicion is regularly treated in criminal law as "knowledge of the second degree" and as satisfying a statutory requirement of "knowledge."[53] This occurs when the actor can be described as exhibiting "wilful blindness": despite his suspicion, he shuts his eyes to an available means of knowledge, carefully refraining from inquiry lest he learn what he does not care to know. There is no doubt that the words "knowing or believing" in section 22 are intended to embrace cases of "wilful blindness." But care is needed in giving content to that phrase. If suspicion is strong and inquiry easy to make, there should be no difficulty (D is offered goods at a very low price in a pub by a man he has never met; if his suspicions are aroused, he should ask questions before buying.[54]) On the other hand, suspicion may be only slight and not such in the circumstances as to justify the affront or embarrassment that an inquiry would cause (D feels that the circumstances are unusual and open to various interpretations; but the seller is highly respectable and the goods are not very valuable). Then it would seem wrong to condemn the failure to investigate by calling the suspicion "knowledge" or "belief." Somewhere between these two situations the line ought to be drawn.

13–21   (b) *Belief and wilful blindness: the law as declared by the courts.* Appellate pronouncements imply, first of all, a slightly different function for "wilful blindness." They assert, what is plain, that suspicion is not an additional state of mind satisfying the section, alternative to knowledge and belief.[55] Rather, according to the Court of Appeal, a jury may infer D's knowledge or belief that the goods were stolen from the fact that, suspecting as much, he "deliberately closed his eyes to the circumstances," and they may be so directed; but it is a misdirection to advise them that, on such facts, they must as a matter of law find such knowledge or belief.[56] On this basis, "wilful blindness" is not itself a case of knowledge (as it is regularly said to be in other contexts) or of belief. Instead it is merely

---

[53] *Roper* v. *Taylor's Central Garage* [1951] 2 T.L.R. 284.
[54] The Committee gave this as an example of "believing" (*Eighth Report*, para. 134).
[55] *Grainge* [1974] 1 W.L.R. 619; [1974] 1 All E.R. 928; *Griffiths* (1974) 60 Cr.App.R. 14 (explaining *Atwal* v. *Massey* (1971) 56 Cr.App.R. 6); *Smith (Albert)* (1976) 64 Cr.App.R. 217.
[56] *Griffiths,* above. The Court of Appeal has repeatedly reaffirmed *Grainge* and (especially) *Griffiths* and insisted that they be followed: *Reeves* (1978) 68 Cr.App.R. 331; *Pethick* [1980] Crim.L.R. 242; *Lincoln, ibid.* 575.

evidence of one or other of them. (But this suggests that D may have two states of mind—suspicion and belief; whereas in fact he has only one. It also permits the jury to decline a finding of knowledge or belief in a case which in other contexts would be said to be one of knowledge). Secondly, the question is whether D "positively believed" that the goods were stolen; it is not enough that he believed that they were probably stolen or that it was more likely than not that they were,[57] or that he suspected, however strongly, that they were.[58] (To which it may, with respect, be objected: (i) that this requirement of firm conviction will exclude cases that ought to be within the offence of handling; and (ii) that it seems to make little sense to treat turning a blind eye as evidence of firm conviction; for your blind eye is only really significant when you think the fact probable or likely—when you are sure, you may as well look.[59]) But, thirdly, the trial judge should not in fact try "to tell the jury what they should understand by the word 'believing' "; for "except in most unusual cases juries are capable of understanding what is meant by the word . . . ."[60] (It is submitted, however, that without consistent instruction different jurors, and indeed different justices, may understand the word to embrace rather different mental states. Some, unaided, may suppose that belief that the goods are probably stolen is enough. It is curious that the court should, as it were in the same breath, declare that this is an error and assert that it is preferable to take no steps to avoid it. The lay tribunal, it is submitted, requires clearer guidance than the present approved direction[61] will give them.)

Time of knowledge or belief

In a case of *receiving* the offence is not committed unless D knows or believes at the time he receives the goods that they are stolen.[62] And the same must be true of an *arranging* to receive or to do any of the other acts listed in the section; the guilty knowledge or belief must exist at the time of the arranging. But there is no reason why it should exist when D begins *assisting* in, or *undertaking*, one of those acts; to continue the assistance or the operation involved in the undertaking[63] after learning or divining the truth must surely be an offence. This will be no less the case where the undertaking, itself originally innocent, follows upon an innocent receiving. D receives the goods and then begins to deal with them for the benefit of

13–22

---

[57] *Reader* (1977) 66 Cr.App.R. 33.
[58] *Pethick*, above. Unless, indeed, "the suspicion amounted to belief": *Bellenie* [1980] Crim.L.R. 437 (but how can "suspicion" be stronger than belief in a probability?).
[59] But apparently there are those who find dealing in stolen goods acceptable, and believe it to be less dangerous, if the origin of the goods, though well understood, is not made explicit ("stolen," "nicked"); and those who suppose that whatever is not spelt out in words is not known. See S. Henry, *The Hidden Economy*, pp. 56–57.
[60] *Smith (Albert)*, above; *Ismail* [1977] Crim.L.R. 557; *Reader*, above.
[61] The *Griffiths* direction: see above, at n.56.
[62] *Alt* (1972) 56 Cr.App.R. 457; *Grainge* [1974] 1 W.L.R. 619; [1974] 1 All E.R. 928; *Smythe* (1980) 72 Cr.App.R. 8 (receiving is "a single finite act").
[63] "Undertakes" must be allowed to mean "conducts" rather than "takes on" or "embarks upon."

another; he handles them when he continues to deal with them after learning that they are stolen.[64]

Proof of knowledge or belief

13–23   Where D has handled goods there may be little or no evidence tending directly to prove that he knew or believed them to be stolen; but the prosecution may be assisted in this proof by one or both of two principles, the first judge-made, the second statutory.

(i) *"Recent possession."* On a charge under the old law of receiving stolen goods knowing them to have been stolen, if the prosecution proved that D received the goods and that they were *recently* stolen, it was proper to direct the jury that they could convict if they heard from D no innocent explanation of his possession which they thought might reasonably be true. The jury were not bound to convict in such a case even if D gave no explanation; it was merely open to them to infer guilty knowledge, if they thought fit, from possession of recently stolen goods.[65] A similar direction remains appropriate under the Act in a case of receiving (and no doubt also in a case of arranging to receive). But it would not be right to use such a direction in relation to all modes of handling. Mere porterage is not on a par with the acquisition of exclusive control when it comes to considering the probability that the handler knew the history of the goods; and in *Sloggett*[66] it was said that the so-called (but abominably so-called) "doctrine of recent possession" had "nothing to do" with a count in that case alleging assistance in retention.

It should be noted that D's possession of recently stolen goods may justify the inference either that he was a guilty handler or that he was the original thief.[67] Where the evidence is consistent with either explanation, both offences should be charged and the matter left to the jury.[68]

13–24   (ii) *Other goods or other conviction.* The statutory aid to the proof of *mens rea* is to be found in section 27(3). This renders admissible, "for the

---

[64] As in *Pitchley* (1972) 57 Cr.App.R. 30 (subject to the special doubt about that case expressed in n.44 above). If D is a bona fide purchaser, no subsequent dealing with the goods by him after learning that they are stolen can be theft: s. 3(2) (above, § 2–54). But he may be guilty of handling if, for instance, he deals with the goods for the benefit of a sub-purchaser (*Bloxham* [1981] 1 W.L.R. 659; [1981] 2 All E.R. 647); for s. 3(2) does not protect against liability for handling. *Quaere* whether this result was intended?

[65] The leading case is *Schama and Abramovitch* (1914) 11 Cr.App.R. 45. The principle is one of common sense rather than of legal doctrine: see *D.P.P.* v. *Nieser* [1959] 1 Q.B. 254 at pp. 266–267, *per* Diplock J. What amounts to a "recent" theft may depend on the nature of the thing stolen. In *Mason* [1980] 3 W.L.R. 617; [1980] 3 All E.R. 777, D admitted acquiring possession of antique silver wine coasters five months after they were stolen; the jury were held entitled to infer guilty knowledge.

[66] [1972] 1 Q.B. 430 at p. 433.

[67] *Smythe* (1980) 72 Cr.App.R. 8 at p.11.

[68] *Seymour* [1954] 1 W.L.R. 678. The authority of this case need not be taken to be affected either by the fact that in certain circumstances a person can now be guilty of handling property that he himself originally stole (see below, § 13–29) or by the observations of Lord Widgery C.J. in *Stapylton* v. *O'Callaghan* [1973] 2 All E.R. 782, considered in n.89, below. On an indictment for handling alone, it is unnecessary to direct the jury that the prosecution must establish that D was not the thief and did not receive the goods in the course of the stealing, unless an issue as to this arises on the evidence: *Griffiths* (1974) 60 Cr.App.R. 14.

purpose of proving that [D] knew or believed the goods to be stolen goods," two classes of evidence:

"(a) evidence that he has had in his possession, or has undertaken or assisted in the retention, removal, disposal or realisation of, stolen goods[69] from any theft taking place not earlier than twelve months before the offence charged[70]; and

(b) . . . evidence that he has within the five years preceding the date of the offence charged been convicted of theft or of handling stolen goods."

The subsection is to be strictly construed. It does not render admissible the details of the transactions that it lets in; so, for example, evidence of D's possession of other stolen goods is not to include evidence showing that he knew or believed them to be stolen.[71] It has been cogently objected that what is thus excluded is evidence of the very fact that makes the admitted transaction relevant to the issue of *mens rea* in the case being tried; that what the subsection, so interpreted, permits is evidence from which, taken alone, unsafe inferences of fault may be drawn; and that therefore "the fair prosecutor should be slow to rely upon it."[72]

Certain conditions must be satisfied before evidence becomes admissible **13–25** under section 27(3): (i) D must be being proceeded against[73] only for handling stolen goods; (ii) evidence must first be given of D's having committed an act of handling in relation to the goods the subject of the charge; and (iii) a conviction can be proved under paragraph (b) only if D[74] has had seven days' notice in writing of the intention to prove it. Subject to these conditions the evidence is admissible at any stage of the proceedings—that is, at committal proceedings as well as on trial.

To say that the evidence is admissible is not to say that it will necessarily be admitted. The judge retains a discretion to exclude it if that is necessary for the sake of ensuring a fair trial.[75] In exercising that discretion in a case involving a number of handling counts, the judge must bear in mind that the evidence will be relevant only where there is an issue as to D's knowledge or belief that the goods were stolen, but not relevant to any count in which, for example, the only or primary issue concerns D's alleged

---

[69] The words "stolen goods" have the same wide meaning here as they have in s. 22: s. 27(5).
[70] The evidence may relate to goods from a theft taking place after the offence charged: *Davis* [1972] Crim.L.R. 431. Evidence relating to possession of other stolen goods will also be admissible at common law, whether or not it is within s. 27(1)(a), if there is a substantial nexus between the offences: *ibid.*; Cross, *Evidence* (5th ed.), p.400.
[71] *Bradley* (1979) 70 Cr.App.R. 200.
[72] J.C. Smith, [1980] Crim.L.R. 174.
[73] This refers to the proceedings before the court at the time when the evidence is tendered; it is immaterial that some other offence was charged in the same indictment but has been severed and awaits trial: *Anderson* [1978] Crim.L.R. 223 (Judge Stroyan Q.C.).
[74] Or, no doubt, his solicitor: *cf. Bott* [1968] 1 All E.R. 1119. It is not essential for the notice to refer to the section : *Airlie* [1973] Crim.L.R. 310.
[75] *Knott* [1973] Crim.L.R. 36. See *Herron* [1967] 1 Q.B. 107 and *List* [1966] 1 W.L.R. 9; [1965] 3 All E.R. 710, for examples of a situation in which the discretion to exclude should be exercised.

possession of the goods. If the evidence is admitted, the judge must take care to ensure that the jury realise to what issue it is relevant.[76]

Dishonesty

13–26 No one can be guilty of handling unless he acts dishonestly; and the dishonesty—like the knowledge or belief that the goods are stolen—must coincide with the relevant act of handling. D receives goods knowing they are stolen and intending to take them to the police; later he decides to keep them; he is not guilty of handling. For it is obviously no offence to receive stolen goods with the intention of handing them to the police or to their owner. This can be stated as a matter of law notwithstanding that it is said to be for the jury to say whether conduct is dishonest.[77]

The word "dishonestly" in section 22(1) may give rise to an exceptional defence of mistake as to the criminal law. D may plead thus: True, I knew the facts; but I thought as a matter of law that C's act was no offence and that C had acquired a perfectly valid title to the goods. It is submitted that if this plea may be true, D should be acquitted of handling on the ground that he is not proved to have acted dishonestly.

5.   THE RELATIONSHIP BETWEEN HANDLING AND THEFT[78]

The thief as handler

13–27 If D1 and D2 are both parties to a theft, either or both of them may do acts generally prohibited as handling. D1 may take goods from P's house and hand them to D2 who is waiting outside: D2 thus "receives the goods." D1 and D2 may each carry some of the stolen goods away from the scene: then each "assists in their . . . removal . . . for the benefit of" the other. To avoid the liability of a thief for handling in such situations, it is provided that the acts prohibited by section 22(1) shall be handling only if done "otherwise than in the course of the stealing."[79]

The phrase will first be considered on principle. It seems clear that "the course of the stealing" must last for some time beyond the first moment of appropriation or obtaining: "the stealing" cannot simply mean "that which renders the goods stolen," for the goods must already be stolen if an offence of handling is to be in question at all. Presumably what is referred to is the total process of *effective* appropriation, including the "get-away." But it is not at all clear how long "the course of the stealing" lasts. If D1 and D2 take silver goods, drive them 50 miles, melt them down and contract over the telephone to sell the metal to E (without, as it were, pausing for breath), at what point does their "stealing" cease? It is

---

[76] *Wilkins* [1975] 2 All E.R. 734.
[77] *Feely* [1973] Q.B. 530 (above, § 2–87). Harvey [1972] Crim.L.R. 213 reports an anonymous trial at which Shaw J. ruled that D does not *dishonestly* assist in the realisation by the thief of stolen goods where he acts as intermediary between owner and thief for the payment of ransom money for the goods. But this was before *Feely* was decided.
[78] A.T.H. Smith, "Theft and/or Handling" [1977] Crim.L.R. 517.
[79] The stealing in question is that by which the goods first acquire their stolen character. A person who subsequently deals with them may be guilty of theft as well as of handling, notwithstanding the parenthesis in s. 22(1): *Sainthouse* [1980] Crim.L.R. 506; and below, § 13–30.

suggested that its "course" must be over at the latest when they are "clean away," if not before—though this is, inevitably, to use one vague phrase to set a limit to the scope of another for the purposes of just one kind of factual situation. If the suggestion is correct, each of the thieves will be guilty of handling at least during the later stages of their journey and thereafter.

Pitham and Hehl[80] is the only directly relevant case so far reported. One   **13–28**
M offered to sell to D the furniture of a man who was in prison. This offer was a complete appropriation. The rest of the facts are not quite clear, but it appears that D inspected the furniture on two occasions before buying it and taking it away. His act of handling was held to have occurred "otherwise than in the course of the stealing." The Court of Appeal referred to arguments such as that conducted above but found it unnecessary to pass upon them. This seems to confirm that the theft and the handling were on separate occasions—though it does not explain why the course of the stealing was not regarded as continuing until the offer for sale was accepted. If the facts have been misunderstood and the two events occurred on the same occasion, the decision would be difficult to reconcile with the robbery case of *Hale*,[81] according to which an appropriation (and therefore "the time of" the stealing) is not a mere momentary event but endures for some time, obviously varying with the circumstances. It is not clear whether "the course of the stealing" within the meaning of section 22 and "the time of" the stealing within the meaning of section 8 are the same period. If they are, it seems that one who receives or relevantly deals with goods during the continuance of the appropriation must himself (subject to *mens rea*) be a secondary party to the theft. Participating in "the course of" the stealing, he is thus immune from handling liability. *Pitham and Hehl* seems to assume that this is so; D's liability for handling was assumed to depend upon the fact that the course of M's stealing was over.

A former rule that a person could not be guilty both of stealing and of   **13–29**
receiving the same goods has not survived the combination of the Criminal Law Act 1967 (which abolished all rules peculiar to felony) and the Theft Act.[82] Once beyond "the course of the stealing," therefore, a person guilty of theft may commit an offence of handling the same goods or part of them. D, a thief, may, for example, the "course of the stealing" being over:
(i) "undertake" acts within section 22(1) for the benefit of E, an accomplice in the theft, or "assist" in the performance of such acts by E;
(ii) receive the goods or part of them from another party to the theft, or from a handler, or from an innocent party into whose hands they have come;
(iii) give or sell the goods to E, a handler, or to F, an innocent party, and

[80] (1976) 65 Cr.App.R. 45.
[81] (1978) 68 Cr.App.R. 415 (above, § 3–08).
[82] *Dolan* (1975) 62 Cr.App.R. 36.

then help E or F to dispose of the goods (or retain or remove them for E or F)[83];

(iv) be liable as a secondary party to a handling by E (whether that handling is a receiving from D himself[84] or from another person, or some other act within section 22(1)).

The handler as thief

13–30 Whenever an act of handling amounts to an appropriation of property belonging to another with the intention of permanent deprivation, the handler will also be guilty of theft. The Committee observed that this would "often" be the case, because the handler's act would be "likely" to be an appropriation. An appropriation by receiving was the only illustration they gave.[85] But an act of "retention, removal, disposal or realisation" may equally be an appropriation.[86] For the purposes of theft, the appropriation need not be made "for the thief's own benefit" (s. 1(2)); and it cannot be said that, because P is already deprived, the handler does not intend to deprive P permanently; for on that argument even a receiver would not steal. The possibility is, therefore, that all handlers steal who actually deal with the goods themselves.[87]

In *Stapylton* v. *O'Callaghan*[88] D was tried on informations charging respectively theft and handling (by receiving) of a driving licence. It was clear that the licence had been stolen and that D, in whose possession it was found not long afterwards, had come by it dishonestly and that he intended to keep it. But it was not clear how D had acquired the licence. The magistrate, apparently treating the two informations as mutually exclusive and not being satisfied as to which was appropriate, dismissed both. The Divisional Court directed a conviction of theft, because, even if D was not the original thief, he "dishonestly possessed himself of the licence and intended to keep it" and was guilty of theft in so doing. Of course he may have been guilty of handling also.[89]

13–31 In this discussion of the handler as thief it has been assumed that the original "thief" did not acquire ownership by his crime. But if that crime was obtaining property by deception or blackmail he may have done so; in which case the handler will not be guilty of theft, for the goods will no

---

[83] *Cf. Eighth Report*, para.131.
[84] *Carter Patersons and Pickfords Carriers Ltd.* v. *Wessel* [1947] K.B. 849.
[85] *Eighth Report*, para.132.
[86] *Sainthouse* [1980] Crim.L.R. 506.
[87] This would exclude one who only "arranges" to receive or to deal with the goods, and perhaps some who only "assist in" rather than "undertaking" an act within the section. But any of these might be a secondary party to someone else's theft.
[88] [1973] 2 All E.R. 782.
[89] A passage at the end of the judgment of Lord Widgery C.J. (at p. 784), taken literally, suggests that in any case where the circumstances show D to be guilty of theft, it would be inappropriate to consider the alternative charge of handling ("with the added penalty that might arise"). This observation should be regarded as confined to cases like that in which it was made. Where D *is* guilty of handling goods which (*ex hypothesi*) are already stolen, a conviction of handling better expresses his part in the total transaction than a conviction of theft (unless, exceptionally, he was also the original thief: see above, § 13–29).

longer belong to the victim of the original offence, unless the "thief's" title has been avoided before the handling occurs.

Some handlers (*e.g.* some who undertake retention or removal) will be assisting the thief or another handler to escape apprehension or prosecution. If that is the purpose or one of the purposes of the handling,[90] the handler will also be guilty, under the Criminal Law Act 1967, s. 4(1), of assisting an offender.

6.   INFORMATIONS AND INDICTMENTS

Section 22(1) creates a single offence and an information simply alleging   **13–32** handling contrary to the section is not bad for duplicity. But where D may be embarrassed by an absence of particulars as to the mode of handling alleged, the information should set out particulars or an application for particulars should be acceded to.[91]

Similarly, although a conviction may be had upon an indictment in which the particulars of offence allege simply that D dishonestly handled certain goods, knowing or believing them to be stolen,[92] the particulars ought to allege the mode of handling it is proposed to establish, with adequate detail.[93] Where a particular mode is alleged (*e.g.* receiving), there cannot be a conviction of a different species of handling (*e.g.* assisting in removal)[94]—or there cannot, at any rate, without amendment of the indictment. Where the mode is uncertain, there should be separate counts to cover different modes.[95] It is neither necessary nor helpful, however, to cover every possible alternative[96]; normally two counts are the most required, one alleging receiving, the other alleging an act within the second part of section 22(1).[97]

A count alleging an undertaking or assisting in the retention, removal, disposal or realisation of goods or an arranging to do so should include the words "by or for the benefit of another."[98]

The particulars of a count for handling should include an averment of knowledge or belief that the goods were stolen.[99]

There are some cases in which it is necessary to name the owner of the stolen goods in the indictment—cases, that is to say, "where the property is of a common and indistinctive type" and "where, unless the ownership be

---

[90] *Cf. Andrews and Craig* [1962] 1 W.L.R. 1474; [1962] 3 All E.R. 961; *Brown* [1965] Crim.L.R. 108.

[91] *Griffiths v. Freeman* [1970] 1 W.L.R. 659; [1970] 1 All E.R. 1117.

[92] *Ikpong* [1972] Crim.L.R. 432; *Kirby* (1972) 56 Cr.App.R. 758; *Pitchley* (1972) 57 Cr.App.R. 30.

[93] *Alt* (1972) 56 Cr.App.R. 457.

[94] *Nicklin* [1977] 1 W.L.R. 403; [1977] 2 All E.R. 444, in which the principles stated in this paragraph were reaffirmed.

[95] *Sloggett* [1972] 1 Q.B. 430; *Marshall* (1971) 56 Cr.App.R. 263.

[96] *Ikpong*, above.

[97] *Willis and Syme* [1972] 1 W.L.R. 1605; [1972] 3 All E.R. 797; *Deakin* [1972] 1 W.L.R. 1618; [1972] 3 All E.R. 803, where, at pp. 1624 and 808 respectively, a formula is offered of particulars of a count alleging handling within the second part of s.22(1).

[98] *Sloggett*, above. (In some cases the words "by or" will strictly be inappropriate. See above, § 13–15).

[99] *Amos* [1971] Crim.L.R. 352.

assigned in the particulars of the charge, the accused may be at a loss to understand fully the nature of the charge which he has to meet."[1] But this certainly does not mean that whenever the goods are of a common type, the attribution of ownership will be a material averment so that the prosecution must fail if that ownership is not proved; on the facts it may be immaterial from whom the goods were stolen.[2]

13–33 Where it is alleged that D either stole or received goods attributable to a particular theft, the goods should be the subject of a separate handling count which is to be treated as alternative to any theft, robbery or burglary count relating to those goods. There may sometimes need to be a compendious count covering a "hoard" of goods, possibly received over a period of time; this will be when particular goods are not identifiable as the proceeds of particular thefts. But where some at least of the goods in a compendious count are shown to have been received on different occasions from different thefts, a single conviction on that count of handling all the goods cannot be substituted for defective convictions of the thefts. In such a case the indictment should have been differently drawn.[3]

13–34 Section 27 contains provisions permitting the charging in one indictment, and the trial together, of any number of persons alleged to have handled, whether at different times or at the same time, goods deriving from the same theft (s. 27(1)); and the conviction of any of two or more accused indicted for jointly handling any stolen goods if he handled all or any of the goods, whether or not he did so jointly with any of the other accused (s. 27(2)).[4] The latter provision permits the conviction of two persons jointly charged who are proved to have been guilty of successive handlings of the same goods.[5]

7. ADVERTISING REWARDS FOR RETURN OF GOODS STOLEN OR LOST

13–35 It is convenient to mention here that section 23 (which reproduces a pre-existing offence) prohibits the use of certain words—*e.g.* words to the effect "no questions asked"—in public advertisements of rewards for the return of stolen or lost goods. The offence may be committed by the advertiser, the printer or the publisher. It carries a maximum fine on summary conviction of £100.[6]

---

[1] *Gregory* (1972) 56 Cr.App.R. 441, where a late amendment of the assertion as to ownership was improper as giving rise to a risk of injustice.
[2] *Deakin,* above, referring to r. 6(1) of the Indictment Rules scheduled to the Indictments Act 1915, which had, however, been revoked by the Indictment Rules 1971 and not replaced.
[3] *Smythe* (1980) 72 Cr.App.R. 8.
[4] See *Eighth Report,* pp. 132–133 (notes on draft Bill).
[5] *French* [1973] Crim.L.R. 632.
[6] For the fascinating history behind this provision and its forebears, see Hall, *Theft, Law and Society* (2nd ed.), pp. 70–76.

CHAPTER 14

GOING EQUIPPED

1. DEFINITION. POWER OF ARREST

IT is an offence for a person to have with him, when not at his place of
abode, any article for use in the course of or in connection with any
burglary, theft or cheat[1] (s. 25(1)) or any offence under section 12(1)—that
is, in effect, an offence of taking a conveyance other than a pedal
cycle (s. 25(5)).

The offence is punishable on conviction on indictment with imprisonment for three years (s. 25(2)). Where it is committed "with reference to
the theft or taking of motor vehicles" the offender may be disqualified for
holding or obtaining a driving licence.[2] An offence under section 25 may
justify an order under section 43 of the Powers of Criminal Courts Act
1973, operating to deprive the offender of his rights, if any, in the article
involved, on the ground that it was intended by him to be used for the
purpose of committing, or facilitating the commission of, an offence.

As the maximum penalty for an offence under section 25 is less than five
years' imprisonment, the offence is not an arrestable offence within the
meaning of the Criminal Law Act 1967, s. 2. A power to arrest without
warrant anyone who is, or who with reasonable cause is suspected to be,
committing an offence under the section is therefore specially provided by
section 25(4).

2. THE DETAILS OF THE OFFENCE

The articles covered by the section

The Committee offer a convenient list of typical articles covered by the
section:

> "The offence will apply, for example, to firearms and other offensive
> weapons, imitation firearms, housebreaking implements, any articles
> for the purpose of concealing identity (for example, masks, rubber
> gloves and false car number-plates) and . . . car keys and confidence
> tricksters' outfits"[3];

and it will apply to a vehicle for use in getting to or from the place of a
crime. Indeed it can be any article whatsoever so long as it is intended for a
relevant criminal purpose.

"When not at his place of abode"

It is important to stress that the offence is limited to occasions when the
possessor of the article is not at his place of abode. The professional

14-01

14-02

14-03

---

[1] That is, an offence of obtaining property by deception under s. 15 (s. 25(5)).
[2] Road Traffic Act 1972, Sched. 4, Pt. III, para. 3.
[3] *Eighth Report,* para. 148.

burglar is safe in his possession of the tools of his trade as long as he keeps them at home. No doubt the possession at home of a burglar's kit or of a confidence trickster's outfit is some indication of a general intention to use that equipment; but when the intending offender takes his equipment with him away from home it will usually be safe to regard him as having a particular crime in contemplation or at least as intending to use the equipment on that occasion if an opportunity to do so presents itself, and it is at this point that the section becomes an acceptable and very important weapon in the armoury of crime control. The section in fact goes a little further than this. For D may, for instance, make his mask or skeleton key at his place of work, intending to take it home to add to his stock-in-trade. Nevertheless, if caught at work in possession of an article capable of being shown to have an intended criminal use covered by the section, he is clearly within the section.

One is "at his place of abode" only if he is on a site where he intends to abide; so a person who has equipment for theft with him in a vehicle in which he lives commits an offence under the section except when the vehicle is on such a site.[4]

"Has with him"

14–04   The cross-heading above section 25 ("Possession of housebreaking implements etc.") must be intended simply to indicate the provision of the old law that is here replaced.[5] The marginal note to the section ("Going equipped for stealing, etc.") seems to offer a brief hint of the mischief with which the section deals. The language of the marginal note, though not having the status of a definition,[6] is useful. Having an article with one, within the meaning of this section, is probably narrower than having it in one's possession. To adopt the language of a case decided under the Firearms Act 1968, it probably requires "a very close physical link and a degree of immediate control" over the article.[7] This test will be satisfied where D is carrying the article (about his person or in his vehicle) or where he is responsible for its being in a place where it is immediately available for his use—in a word, where he is "equipped" with it. We may add a further case—namely, that where D1 and D2 are in company and D1 has with him an article within the section; then, it seems, D2 also has it "with him" if, but only if,[8] he knows that D1 has it[9] *and* he is jointly with D1 a party to a relevant enterprise in which the article will be available for use.[10]

"For use in the course of or in connection with" an offence

14–05   D must have an article with him "for use in the course of or in connection with" one of the stated offences. This means that he must

---

[4] *Bundy* [1977] 1 W.L.R. 914; [1977] 2 All E.R. 382.
[5] Larceny Act 1916, s. 28(2).
[6] *D.P.P.* v. *Schildkamp* [1971] A.C. 1, cited in *Kelt* (below).
[7] *Kelt* [1977] 1 W.L.R. 1365 at p. 1369; [1977] 3 All E.R. 1099 at p. 1102. In this case the Court of Appeal pointed out that the terms of the Firearms Act 1968 plainly drew a distinction between having a firearm with one and having it in one's possession.
[8] *Cf. Lester and Byast* (1955) 39 Cr.App.R. 157; *Harris* [1961] Crim.L.R. 256.
[9] *Cf. Webley and Webley* [1967] Crim.L.R. 300.
[10] *Cf. Thompson* (1869) 11 Cox 362; *Jones* [1979] C.L.Y. 411 (above, § 4–35).

intend the article to be used for an offence yet to be committed, though not necessarily that it should be used by himself or for a particular offence already determined upon.[11] The use of the phrase "in connection with" widens the scope of the section by providing for a case in which an article is intended for use in preparation for a crime or, for instance, in escaping after it has been committed.[12]

The contemplated offences

The article may be intended for use in the course of or in connection with   **14-06**
any:

(i) *burglary*

The offence of "possessing housebreaking implements"[13] by night was a weapon of long standing in the armoury of preventive justice; and the main function of the broader generalisation achieved in section 25 no doubt remains the control of the intending burglar. Not that the section is used only when a criminal enterprise has proceeded no further than the stage of preparation. Sometimes it cannot be proved, although it is the case, that a person was involved in a burglary, and a conviction under section 25 is all that can be obtained. And a burglar may sometimes be convicted of both the preparatory and the substantive offences; and in such a case, although it was all one criminal activity, it has been held, surprisingly, that consecutive sentences of imprisonment are not improper.[14]

(ii) *theft*

Taking a conveyance contrary to section 12(1) is treated as theft for this purpose (s. 25(5));

(iii) *cheat—that is, an offence under section 15*   **14-07**

It must be proved that the accused intended, with the help of the article (either in the commission of the offence or in its preparation), to obtain property dishonestly by deception.

One kind of case has occasioned difficulty. D is employed as a salesman. He furnishes himself with articles of his own with the intention of selling them to customers as though they are his employer's goods. He will then keep the proceeds. Has he the articles with him for use in connection with an offence under section 15? In *Rashid*[15] D was a British Rail steward; the articles were bread and tomatoes for use in making sandwiches for sale on a train. D's conviction was quashed because the jury should have been told that, in order to convict, they must find an intention to commit an offence against the customer under section 15 rather than (as the judge had told them) a fraud on D's employers. But the Court of Appeal thought that a customer would not care whose materials had been used in the sandwiches and that his purchase would not be made in reliance on the deception.

---

[11] *Ellames* (1974) 60 Cr.App.R. 7.
[12] *Ibid.;* Smith and Hogan, *Criminal Law* (4th ed.), p. 597.
[13] See cross-heading above s. 25. See latterly, Larceny Act 1916, s. 28 (2).
[14] *Ferris* [1973] Crim.L.R. 642, cogently criticised by D.A. Thomas at p. 643.
[15] [1977] 1 W.L.R. 298; [1977] 2 All E.R. 237.

They were inclined to think the prosecution misconceived. In *Doukas*,[16] however, where a hotel wine waiter intended to sell his own wine instead of the hotel's, a differently constituted Court of Appeal thought that the hypothetical customer must be reasonably honest and would not, if he knew the truth, be party to the intended fraud on the hotel.[17] They thought that that must be the view of a reasonable jury. Both courts stated that the result of a particular case must depend on the circumstances—especially on the nature of the article for sale. But, whatever the special circumstances, if the jury were asked whether D realised that a potential customer *might* have declined to purchase if he knew the truth,[18] the likely answer must be that he did; and that, it is submitted, should suffice for a conviction.

In *Mansfield*[19] D's intention was to obtain a job by producing driving documents that did not belong to him. Thus in due course he would obtain wages. But the wages (as opposed to the job) would not be obtained by the deception,[20] and the documents were not, therefore, "for use . . . in connection with [a] cheat."

Proof of the criminal purpose

14–08 The fact that D intended the article to be used in the course of or in connection with one of the stated offences must be proved by the prosecution. Commonly that intention will be suggested forcibly enough by the nature of the article and the circumstances in which D had it with him; and then an explanation from D seems called for. This common sense proposition is rendered statutory in relation to a limited class of articles by section 25(3), which provides that

> "proof that [D] had with him an article made or adapted for use in committing a burglary, theft or cheat shall be evidence that he had it with him for such use."

Some comments may be made upon this provision.

14–09 First, it seems to do little if anything more than state the obvious. The subsection surely means merely that possession of an article of the kind to which it refers is in itself evidence from which a jury *may* infer the necessary criminal purpose. Even in the absence of a credible explanation consistent with innocence, possession of an article within the subsection is only "evidence" of such a purpose and is not necessarily conclusive. Still less does such evidence place on D a burden of positively persuading the jury of his innocent purpose.[21] No doubt he must come forward with some explanation if he can; and perhaps subsection (3) will in some cases justify

---

[16] [1978] 1 W.L.R. 372; [1978] 1 All E.R. 1061.
[17] *Cf.* the opinion of the House of Lords on a related point in *Lambie* [1981] 3 W.L.R. 88; [1981] 2 All E.R. 776; above, § 6–32.
[18] According to the Court of Appeal in *Rashid*, the question is whether D realised that a customer *"would* have declined to purchase." But, with respect, it should be enough that D proposes to take a risk; *vide* the word "reckless" in s. 15(4), and *cf.* above, § 6–42.
[19] [1975] Crim.L.R. 101.
[20] See above, § 6–39, n. 92.
[21] See on subs. (3), *Eighth Report*, paras. 151–153.

strong comment from the trial judge upon an accused's failure to give evidence. But, apart from this last possible effect upon the judge, it is submitted that the position would have been the same without the subsection.

Secondly, the phrase "made . . . for use . . . " may be unfortunate. As noted earlier in the context of aggravated burglary, an article is to be regarded as "made" for a particular use if it was originally made for such use.[22] But there are many articles, which have long been known as "house-breaking implements" and are probably meant to be within the scope of subsection (3), which are not in the normal sense "made" for housebreaking. Assuming subsection (3) to have any substantial value at all, it may therefore be necessary to give the phrase "made . . . for use . . ." a special meaning here, and one different from that which we have assumed it to bear in section 10. This indeed seems to be implied by the Committee's reference in this context to skeleton keys, possession of which "in itself calls for explanation by the accused."[23] A locksmith may make a skeleton key for a perfectly legitimate purpose. If such a key is in D's possession when not at his place of abode, it is surely not the Committee's intention that the application of subsection (3) should depend upon whether D is a locksmith and, if he is, on proof of his purpose in making the key; or, if D is not a locksmith, on proof of the source of the key and of the original purpose of its making.

In summary, subsection (3) appears to distinguish needlessly and   **14–10** clumsily between different kinds of case. It is submitted that the question in all cases should be—and is—whether the circumstances taken together amount to evidence of a relevant criminal purpose. If three men are found late at night in a van with a torch and some carpenter's tools, and each man has a stocking in his pocket, there is clearly evidence of an intention to wear the stocking on the head. An explanation is called for—no less in this case than in a case within the terms of subsection (3), however interpreted. It is suggested that such a case will be dealt with in practice identically with a case within the subsection, except that it will not be proper to direct the jury in terms of subsection (3).[24]

---

[22] See above, § 4–32 on s. 10(1)(b).
[23] Eighth Report, para. 151.
[24] Harrison [1970] Crim.L.R. 415.

CHAPTER 15

HUSBAND AND WIFE

1. The Spouse as Offender

15–01 The Act applies in relation to the parties to a marriage as if they were not married (s. 30(1)), so that a husband can commit any offence under the Act against his wife or in connection with her property, and vice versa. Any argument to the effect that if the parties were not married the victim would have no interest in the property that is the subject-matter of the alleged offence is defeated by the same subsection, which requires any interest derived from the marriage to be treated as if it subsisted independently of the marriage.

The subsection does not, of course, affect general doctrines of the criminal law relating to husband and wife. The defence of marital coercion will be as available to a wife on a prosecution under the Act as on other prosecutions[1]; and husband and wife will no more be able to conspire together to commit an offence under the Act than they are able to conspire to commit other offences.[2]

2. The Spouse as Prosecutor. The Prosecution of Spouses

15–02 Section 30(2) assimilates the position of the married to that of the unmarried in another respect and is not limited to offences under the Act. It provides that "a person shall have the same right to bring proceedings against that person's wife or husband for any offence (whether under this Act or otherwise) as if they were not married."

This provision, however, is subject to a restriction on some prosecutions imposed, in respect of prosecutors generally, by section 30(4).[3] This provides that certain proceedings are to be instituted only by or with the consent of the Director of Public Prosecutions save in special cases. The proceedings in respect of which the limitation is imposed are proceedings against a person "for any offence of stealing or doing unlawful damage to property which at the time of the offence belongs to that person's husband or wife, or for any attempt, incitement or conspiracy to commit such an offence." The phrase "belongs to" in this passage is to be interpreted in accordance with section 5(1) (s. 34(1)), which is discussed in the chapter on theft.[4]

---

[1] Criminal Justice Act 1925, s. 47; Williams, *Criminal Law—General Part* (2nd ed.), pp. 764–768.
[2] Criminal Law Act 1977, s. 2(2)(*a*).
[3] The subsection operated to render the proceedings a nullity in *Withers* [1975] Crim.L.R. 647.
[4] See above, §§ 2–19 to 2–21.

The restriction on prosecution does not apply— **15–03**

(i) if the accused spouse is charged with committing the offence jointly with the other spouse (an example would be the case in which a wife is alleged to have stolen with her husband partnership property belonging to him and his partner); or

(ii) "if by virtue of any judicial decree or order (wherever made)" the spouses "are at the time of the offence under no obligation to cohabit"[5] (s. 30(4), proviso (a)).

The restriction would, on the other hand, appear to apply (unless the case falls within either of these exceptions) even where the marriage is at an end before the institution of proceedings, for the subsection is expressed in terms of marriage "at the time of the offence."

Subsection (4) does not in general prevent the arrest without warrant, or the issue or execution of a warrant for the arrest, of a person for any offence, or the remand in custody or on bail of a person charged with any offence.[6] But the spouse-victim cannot himself or herself arrest without warrant for an offence within the subsection, and a warrant of arrest cannot be issued on an information laid by him or her without the Director's consent (subs. (5)[7]).

3. THE SPOUSE AS WITNESS

Section 30 (3) provides that where proceedings are brought against a   **15–04**
person, otherwise than by his or her wife or husband, for an offence "committed . . . with reference to " the wife or husband or to property belonging to[8] her or him, "the wife or husband shall be competent to give evidence at every stage of the proceedings, whether for the defence or for the prosecution, and whether the accused is charged solely or jointly with any other person."

But the wife or husband, though competent, is not compellable either to give evidence or to disclose any communication made to her or him during the marriage by the accused, unless she or he would be so compellable at common law (proviso (a)). The exception made for a case where the spouse would be compellable at common law was based on *Lapworth*,[9] in which the Court of Criminal Appeal decided that a wife, being at common law (by way of exception to the general rule) a competent prosecution witness where her husband is charged with personal violence against her, is also compellable in such a case. But *Lapworth* has been overruled since the Act was passed. The House of Lords has held[10] that the rule in *Leach* v.

---

[5] See *Woodley* v. *Woodley* [19781] Crim.L.R. 629 (proviso applies to divorce judge's committal order suspended on terms that husband do not molest wife or approach within 200 yards of her home).
[6] Prosecution of Offences Act 1979, s. 6(2)(a).
[7] Added by the Criminal Jurisdiction Act 1975, s. 14(4) and Sched. 5, and amended by the Prosecution of Offences Act 1979, s. 11(1) and Sched. 1.
[8] *Cf.*, above, text at n. 4.
[9] [1931] 1 K.B. 117.
[10] *Hoskyn* v. *Metropolitan Police Commissioner* [1979] A.C. 474.

$R.$[11] is of general application: the conferment of competence on a spouse as a prosecution witness does not of itself render her or him compellable; and, because partly of fears for the future of the marriage if one spouse is forced to testify against the other and partly of repugnance at the idea of such compulsion,[12] the rule is that even the competent spouse is not compellable. The same may be true of a spouse as a witness for the defence.[13] At common law a spouse was not competent as a defence witness except when competent as a witness for the prosecution[14]—that is, notably, in cases of violence against herself or himself. If even in such a case competence does not imply compellability,[15] there would be no case in which one spouse could be compelled to give evidence either against the other or for her or him (or for her or his co-accused) in proceedings within section 30(3). The prosecution may not comment on the failure of the accused's spouse to give evidence (proviso (b)).

An offence may be committed "with reference to" a spouse or his or her property although it is not an offence "against" the spouse or the property; and it need not be an offence under the Act.[16] Where a wife forged her husband's signature to contractual documents, her offences under the Forgery Act 1913 were offences "with reference to" the husband, for if the signatures had been genuine or authorised his rights and obligations would have been directly affected.[16]

15–05   Section 30(2) declares a spouse who prosecutes pursuant to that subsection to be a competent witness for the prosecution at every stage of the proceedings. But he or she will not be compellable.[17]

Subsections (2) and (3) of section 30 were intended as interim provisions.[18] When the Act was passed the Committee were engaged upon a wider review of the law of evidence in criminal cases; they have since reported, proposing changes in the law relating to the accused's spouse as a witness.[19]

---

[11] [1912] A.C. 305. The case concerned the effect of a statutory provision enabling an accused's spouse to be called as a witness without the accused's consent in certain cases (Criminal Evidence Act 1898, s. 4(1)).

[12] See, however, the powerful dissent of Lord Edmund-Davies in *Hoskyn*, above, at pp. 499 *et seq.*

[13] See Cross, *Evidence* (5th ed.), pp. 178–179.

[14] *Sergeant* (1826) Ry. & M. 352; Cross, *op. cit.* pp. 166–167.

[15] But the policy arguments invoked where one spouse is asked to testify *against* the other are not available in this case.

[16] *Noble* [1974] 1 W.L.R. 894; [1974] 2 All E.R. 811.

[17] *Cf. Leach* v. *R.* [1912] A.C. 305.

[18] *Eighth Report*, paras. 197–199.

[19] *Eleventh Report, Evidence (General)* (Cmnd. 4991), paras. 143–157 and Draft Criminal Evidence Bill, cl. 9.

CHAPTER 16

RESTITUTION AND COMPENSATION

1.   TITLE TO PROPERTY

SECTION 31(2) provides that the title to property that has been stolen or   **16–01**
obtained by fraud or other wrongful means shall not be affected by reason
only of the conviction of the offender. It was formerly the law that if goods
were stolen and a title to the goods was acquired by a third party by
purchase in market overt, the effect of a conviction of the thief after such
purchase was to cause the property in the goods to revest in the original
owner or his personal representative. There was no justification for the
continuance of this rule in modern times. The relevant statutory
provisions[1] were repealed by the Act. Section 31(2) ensures, if express
provision for the purpose was required, that the title to property shall
depend on the operation of civil law principles and not on the outcome of
criminal proceedings.

2.   RESTITUTION AND COMPENSATION[2]

Not only is the title to property which has been the subject of an offence to   **16–02**
be unaffected by criminal proceedings against the offender. It is also clear
that disputes concerning the title to such property are not appropriate for
litigation in those proceedings. Nevertheless it is desirable to make
available to criminal courts procedures whereby, in cases where no dispute
as to title appears to exist, they may make orders for the restoration of
property or for the compensation of losers at the conclusion of their
proceedings. Special provisions for this purpose are contained in section
28, as amended.[3]
   The powers of the court under section 28 may be exercised where

> "goods have been stolen and either a person is convicted of any
> offence with reference to the theft (whether or not the stealing is the
> gist of his offence) or a person is convicted of any other offence but
> such an offence as aforesaid is taken into consideration in determining
> his sentence . . . ." (s. 28(1)).

   In this context, as in that of handling, the words "stealing," "theft" and
so on refer to offences of obtaining property by deception and blackmail as
well as to theft, and to such offences whether committed in England or
Wales or abroad (s. 28(6)). "Goods" means all kinds of property except
land, but including things severed from the land by stealing (s. 34(2)(*b*)).

---

[1] Sale of Goods Act 1893, s. 24(1); and see Larceny Act 1916, s. 45.
[2] Macleod, "Restitution under the Theft Act 1968" [1968] Crim.L.R. 577; Thomas,
   Principles of Sentencing (2nd. ed.), pp. 331–334.
[3] Amended by the Criminal Justice Act 1972, s. 6 and Sched. 5, and by the Criminal Law Act
   1977, s. 65 and Sched 12. References to s. 28 hereafter are references to the section as
   amended.

The exact scope of the phrase "any offence with reference to the theft" is not clear. It obviously includes handling. It may include offences such as conspiracy to steal, or assisting the thief contrary to the Criminal Law Act 1967, s. 4(1). The phrase "taken into consideration in determining sentence" has in a related context been held to be the "well-known term of legal art" referring to the conventional procedure for the admission on conviction of further offences to which the offender invites the court to have regard in sentencing.[4]

The convicting court[5] may on the conviction, even if the passing of sentence is in other respects deferred, make any of a number of orders. These will be set out and briefly discussed; after which we shall deal with some matters relevant to the section as a whole.

Restoration of the stolen goods

16-03   Section 28(1)(*a*) empowers the court to order anyone having possession or control of stolen goods to restore them to anyone entitled to recover them from him.

Such an order can be made by the court of its own motion. But it is unlikely to be made in practice without an application. Most commonly that application will be made by the police, who may wish for their own protection to have the formal authority of a court order for the return of the goods to the victim of the offence. More commonly still, no doubt, the police will return the goods to the owner at the conclusion of the criminal proceedings without any order for that purpose being made. But this course can have its hazards.[6] Where the proceedings end in an acquittal the police, seeking judicial sanction for parting with the property to a particular claimant, must take separate proceedings for the purpose in a magistrates' court under the Police (Property) Act 1897.[7] Where there has been a conviction, an application to the convicting court under section 28(1)(*a*) is clearly more convenient. The paragraph may be of similar service to anyone other than the police who may have possession of stolen property in his hands at the end of a trial.

16-04   Of course an application for restoration may be made by the victim of the offence or anyone else claiming to be entitled to recover the property. It is not appropriate to consider at length the problems of title that could theoretically arise on such an application. For the jurisdiction of the court under this section, which is entirely discretionary, should not be exercised in any case raising difficult questions of civil law. To embark upon such questions would be beyond the proper province of a criminal court (as of

---

[4] *D.P.P.* v. *Anderson* [1978] A.C. 964 at p. 977 (Powers of Criminal Courts Act 1973, s. 39: criminal bankruptcy).
[5] But where a magistrates' court commits an offender to the Crown Court for sentence, the power to make an order under s. 28 passes to the Crown Court and is not to be exercised by the committing court: Criminal Justice Act 1967, s. 56(5); *Blackpool JJ., ex p. Charlson and Gregory* [1972] 1 W.L.R. 1456; [1972] 3 All E.R. 854.
[6] See, *e.g. Winter* v. *Bancks* (1901) 84 L.T. 504.
[7] See below § 16–14. For an illustration of the value of such proceedings to the police, see *Bullock* v. *Dunlap* (1876) 2 Ex.D. 43.

this book). The court will make an order only in a clear case.[8] Normally such a case will be one in which it is apparent that neither the offence itself nor any subsequent dealing with the property by the offender has had any effect upon the title to the property.[9] It may be anticipated, therefore, that the vast majority of orders will be made in cases of theft in the narrow sense. But they may also be made in some cases of obtaining property by deception or blackmail in which the original offender is caught before disposing of the property obtained by the offence.[10] Where a person guilty of obtaining by deception or blackmail has transferred the property to a third person (other than a person convicted of handling) there is always liable to be an issue as to title between the transferee and the original owner; for the offender may have acquired a voidable title by his offence and, if he has, may have passed a good title to his transferee[11] before his own title was avoided by the act of the victim.

Goods representing the stolen goods

The convicted person (the thief or a handler) may be proved to have   **16–05** property into which the stolen property or some part of it has been directly or indirectly converted, as by the spending of stolen money or the sale of stolen goods. A person entitled to recover such identifiable proceeds of the stolen property from the convicted person may obtain an order under section 28(1)(b) that those proceeds be delivered or transferred to him.[12] Such an order, in contrast to orders under paragraphs (a) and (c), requires an application by the person in whose favour it is to be made. He must be able to show a right under the civil law to "follow" the stolen goods into the goods that represent them. It must be clear that he can do this, for it will not be appropriate for the court to decide difficult questions of the law of tracing for the purpose of enabling itself to make an order.

---

[8] *Ferguson* [1970] 1 W.L.R. 1246; [1970] 2 All E.R. 820 (applying to s. 28 the principles laid down in *Stamp* v. *United Dominions Trust (Commercial) Ltd.* [1967] 1 Q.B. 418, for the exercise of the corresponding jurisdiction under the Larceny Act 1916, s. 45, and the Magistrates' Courts Act 1952, s. 33); *Church* (1970) 55 Cr.App.R. 65.
   A possible reason for the refusing of an order even when the question of title is clear would be the claim of the possessor that, believing in his good title to the goods, he has improved them since acquiring them. On the making of an order under para. (a) he would not be able to obtain an allowance for the improvement, as he would in proceedings against him for wrongful interference: Torts (Interference with Goods) Act 1977, s. 6(1).

[9] Mann, *The Legal Aspect of Money* (3rd ed.), p. 4, says that "it is an open question whether money passed and accepted bona fide from hand to hand as currency is 'money' for the purpose of an order for restitution" (referring to "money" in the definition of "goods" in s. 34(2)(b), and citing *Moss* v. *Hancock* [1899] 2 Q.B. 11). It is submitted that this is the wrong question. The question should be whether anyone is "entitled to recover" the money from its possessor; and the answer might well turn on the negotiable character of money as currency (*cf.* coins as curios: *Moss* v. *Hancock,* above).

[10] *Cf.* the situations in *George* (1901) 65 J.P. 729; *Cohen* (1907) 71 J.P. 190. In each of these cases property found in the possession of the prisoner was identifiable as the proceeds of property obtained by false pretences (*cf.* s. 28(1)(b), below). The prisoner's title to the property had been avoided, not by the conviction (*cf.* s. 31(2)), but by the victim's disaffirmation of the transaction between himself and the prisoner. In *Cohen* the order was made against the opposition of the prisoner's trustee in bankruptcy.

[11] By virtue of the Sale of Goods Act 1979, s. 23, or of corresponding common law principles.

[12] Orders may be made under both paragraph (b) and paragraph (c) of s. 28(1), but not so that the person in whose favour the orders are made recovers in total more than the value of the stolen goods: s. 28(2).

Money in the possession of the convicted person

16–06   The convicted person may not have been found in possession of the stolen goods, but it may be clear that had they been in his possession some person (usually the victim of the offence) would have been entitled to recover them from him. In such a case the court may,[13] under section 28(1)(*c*), order a sum not exceeding the value of the stolen goods to be paid, out of the convicted person's money taken out of his possession on his apprehension, to any person who, if those goods were in the possession of the convicted person, would be entitled to recover them from him.[14]

The Criminal Justice Act 1972, s. 6(3), provides that an order under paragraph (*c*) may be made "without any application being made in that behalf or on the application of any person appearing to the court to be interested in the property concerned."

D may be convicted of handling part only of a larger quantity of stolen goods. If all the goods the subject of the conviction have been recovered, it is an incorrect exercise of discretion to make an order under paragraph (*c*) for the payment to P of money found on D so as to compensate P for the loss of the other goods with which, so far as his conviction shows, D was not concerned.[15]

The operation of paragraph (*c*) depends upon the hypothesis that *if* the convicted person had possessed the stolen goods the person in whose favour the order is to be made *would* have been entitled to recover them from him. But the victim of theft will usually be entitled to recover the stolen goods from almost anyone in possession of them. It does not seem right to make any convicted person liable to pay their value simply by notionally attributing possession to him. To be so liable he should surely be guilty either of the substantive offence or of a handling that amounts to the tort of conversion. Most convicted persons within the section will be so guilty, but not all. It is submitted that the paragraph should be interpreted (or at least applied, by virtue of the court's discretion) in this limited way.

16–07   For an order to be made against a person under paragraph (*c*) the money must have been "taken out of his possession on his apprehension." This does not mean that it must actually have been found on his person at the time of his arrest. First, it may be found elsewhere, though in his "possession." In *Ferguson*[16] it was in a safe deposit box at Harrods store, the box being in his name and he holding the key. Secondly, it may be found some time after the arrest. In *Ferguson* the Court of Appeal had no doubt that there was power to make an order under the paragraph in respect of money found and taken 11 days after the arrest. This reading—the result of "giving the words 'on his apprehension' a

---

[13] With no obligation to have regard to the convicted person's means (*cf.* compensation orders, below, § 16–16): *Lewis* [1975] Crim.L.R. 353.
[14] See n. 12, above.
[15] *Parker* [1970] 1 W.L.R. 1003; [1970] 2 All E.R. 458. In fact there may be no power to make an order in these circumstances; the point was reserved in *Parker*.
[16] [1970] 1 W.L.R. 1246; [1970] 2 All E.R. 820.

common-sense meaning"[17]—is quite strikingly expansive. Perhaps the decision stretches this far and no farther: that money will be "taken out of [D's] possession on his apprehension" if it is in his legal possession (on his person; in his house or his safe deposit box; in the keeping of his servant) both when he is arrested and when it is found and taken, he being still in custody when the latter event occurs.

Although the police may lawfully have taken money out of a person's possession on his apprehension, they do not have power to retain it pending trial solely in anticipation that the court may on his conviction make an order under paragraph (c).

Compensation for a bona fide purchaser or lender

The person against whom an order for restoration of the stolen goods is **16–08** made under section 28(1)(a) may be one who has in good faith bought the goods from the convicted person or has in good faith lent money to the convicted person on the security of the goods. Section 28(3) provides that in such a case the court may order the payment of compensation to the purchaser or lender out of the convicted person's money taken out of his possession on his apprehension. The compensation is not to exceed the amount paid for the goods or the amount owed in respect of the loan. The Criminal Justice Act 1972, s. 6(3),[19] applies to this subsection as to section 28(1)(c).

Summary procedure for use in clear cases

The point has been made several times above that the jurisdiction under **16–09** section 28 is only to be exercised in very clear cases.[20] The procedure is an essentially summary one, to be exercised as a matter of convenience at the tail-end of a criminal trial. No procedure is provided for giving notice to a person not already before the court that he may make a claim or that an order under section 28(1)(a) may be made against him. Such a person, even though not concerned in the criminal trial, may, of course, know of the proceedings and be present for the purpose of making or resisting an application; and there is no doubt that he may be heard in person or by counsel.[21] But a third party to whom, for instance, money found in the convicted person's possession might belong has no *locus standi* before the court and might be unjustly affected by an order for payment of that money to the victim of the theft. Nor does the criminal court have the necessary machinery (especially the process of discovery) for resolving issues as to title.[22]

---

[17] [1970] 1 W.L.R. at p. 1248; [1970] 2 All E.R. at p. 821.
[18] *Malone* v. *Metropolitan Police Commissioner* [1980] Q.B. 49.
[19] See above, § 16–06.
[20] See cases cited in n. 8 above.
[21] *Cf. Macklin* (1850) 5 Cox 216.
[22] See *Ferguson* [1970] 1 W.L.R. 1246; [1970] 2 All E.R. 820. And see *Church* (1970) 55 Cr.App.R. 65, suggesting questions as to the rights of an insurance company which has paid the victim of the theft under a policy covering the stolen goods.

Materials on which and time at which order to be made

16–10   The summary nature of the procedure is further emphasised by the provisions of section 28 as to the materials on which an order under the section is to be made and as to the time for making the order.

Section 28(4) provides that none of the powers conferred by the section is to be exercised

> "unless in the opinion of the court the relevant facts sufficiently appear from evidence given at the trial or the available documents,[23] together with admissions made by or on behalf of any person in connection with any proposed exercise of the powers . . . ."

For the purpose of section 28 (4) the trial comes to an end when sentence is passed,[24] so that there is no power to make an order based on facts appearing from evidence given after that time. And an order under section 28(1) must be made "on the conviction," which has been said to mean "immediately after the conviction." [25] All in all, the intention seems to be that the court is not to resolve disputed questions of title upon the basis of the evidence, documents and admissions referred to in section 28(4), but rather that that material, to justify an order, should reveal that there is no dispute to be resolved.

Suspension of orders

16–11   There are provisions for the suspension of orders under section 28 to allow time for appeal.

Where any order under the section is made *by a magistrates' court*, it is automatically suspended unless (in the case of an order made under subsection (1)(*a*) or (*b*)) the court directs otherwise because it is of the opinion that title to the property affected by the order is not in dispute. The suspension is for the period for the time being prescribed by law for the giving of notice of appeal against a decision of a magistrates' court, or until the determination of an appeal of which notice was given during that period.[26]

Where *on conviction on indictment* "an order for the restitution of property to a person" is made, there is a similar automatic suspension of the order (Criminal Appeal Act 1968, s. 30(1), as amended by Sched. 3 to the present Act). Any order under section 28 is to be treated as an order for the restitution of property within the meaning of section 30 of the Criminal Appeal Act (s. 28(5)). The suspension occurs unless the trial court directs otherwise for the reason mentioned above. It lasts for 28 days or until the determination of any appeal.

---

[23] For the meaning of this phrase, see the full text of s. 28(4) in Appendix 1.
[24] *Church* (1970) 55 Cr.App.R. 65.
[25] *Ibid.* The language of Lord Esher M.R. in *Justices of the Central Criminal Court* (1886) 18 Q.B.D. 314 at p. 318 remains appropriate; " . . . it seems that the order can, and what is more, ought to be, made practically at the time of the trial; I do not say that it must be made at the minute, but it must be made as one of the conclusions of the trial."
[26] Criminal Justice Act 1972, s. 6(5).

There is a provision for the further suspension, in case of appeal to the House of Lords, of orders not quashed by the Court of Appeal.[27]

Appeals

Orders made on conviction on indictment

If a person convicted on indictment successfully appeals against his   **16–12** conviction an order made on that conviction under section 28, if it has been suspended pending the appeal, will not take effect[28]; and even if the conviction is not quashed, the Court of Appeal on such an appeal may annul or vary the order.[29]

The convicted person may also appeal against the order itself.[30] But a person who has been refused an order or a third party claiming to be prejudiced by an order has no right of appeal,[31] though in an appropriate case he may apply for judicial review (certiorari).[32]

Orders made on summary conviction

A convicted person against whom an order under section 28 is made by a magistrates' court may appeal to the Crown Court against the order by way of an appeal against sentence.[33] And any person aggrieved by an order of a magistrates' court under section 28 may appeal to the Divisional Court by way of case stated on the ground that the order is wrong in law or is in excess of jurisdiction.[34]

Enforcement of orders under section 28

An order made under section 28 by the Crown Court will be enforceable   **16–13** by committal for contempt.[35]

Disobedience to an order made by a magistrates' court, other than an order for the payment of money, may be punished under the Magistrates' Courts Act 1980, s. 63(3). The person in default may be ordered to pay a

---

[27] Criminal Appeal Act 1968, s. 42(1) (to which also s. 28(5)—see text above—applies).
[28] Criminal Appeal Act 1968, s. 30(2) (Court of Appeal); *ibid*. s. 42(2)(*a*) (House of Lords); Criminal Justice Act 1972, s. 6(4)(*a*) (order made in respect of offence taken into consideration).
[29] Criminal Appeal Act 1968, s. 30(4).
[30] *Parker* [1970] 1 W.L.R. 1003; [1970] 2 All E.R. 458, referring to s. 28(5) and to the Criminal Appeal Act 1968, s. 30(4). Reference might also have been made to ss. 9 and 50(1) of the latter Act, and may now be made to the Criminal Justice Act 1972, s. 6(4)(*b*) (as to appeal against an order in respect of an offence taken into consideration), to support the view that such an appeal lies as an appeal against "sentence."
[31] He cannot appeal either to the criminal division (*Elliot* [1908] 2 K.B. 452) or to the civil division (*Justices of the Central Criminal Court* (1886) 18 Q.B.D. 314) of the Court of Appeal. (But the Criminal Appeal Rules 1968 contemplate that the Court of Appeal may wish a person "immediately affected by an order of the judge of the court of trial" to be represented at the hearing of a convicted person's appeal: rr. 22(2)(*a*), 25(1). A clearer right to be heard was formerly provided: Criminal Appeal Rules 1908, r. 9, now revoked.) The absence of a right of appeal is another reason why an order should not be made under s. 28 except in a clear case: *cf. Stamp* v. *United Dominions Trust (Commercial) Ltd.* [1967] 1 Q.B. 418 at p. 430.
[32] See, *e.g. London County JJ., ex p. Dettmer & Co.* (1908) 72 J.P. 513.
[33] Magistrates' Courts Act 1980, s. 108(1)(3).
[34] *Ibid.* s. 111.
[35] R.S.C. Ord. 52. *Cf. Wollez* (1860) 8 Cox 337.

sum not exceeding £50 for every day during which he is in default[36] or a sum not exceeding £1,000, or may be committed to custody until he has remedied his default[37] or for a period not exceeding two months.

Other procedures

16–14　　　There are some other procedures available either for the restoration of stolen property to its rightful owner or for the compensation by order of the criminal courts of the victims of offences under the Act.

Procedures relating to stolen property

It has already been mentioned[38] that the police often act quite informally by returning stolen property to the owner after the termination of criminal proceedings. Alternatively either the police or any person claiming the property can invoke the Police (Property) Act 1897, under which a magistrates' court may make an order for the delivery of the property to the person appearing to the court to be the owner.[39] If the owner cannot be ascertained the court may make "such order . . . as to the . . . court may seem meet."[40]

An order under the Police (Property) Act does not prevent a person taking proceedings for the recovery of property against any person in possession of it as a result of the order, but such proceedings must be brought within six months of the order.[41] In the case of property that has not been the subject of an order under section 28 or under the 1897 Act, a person claiming to be entitled to it is of course left to his civil remedies, which are unaffected by the fact that an order under section 28 has been refused or not applied for.[42]

Compensation[43]

16–15　　　Under section 35 of the Powers of Criminal Courts Act 1973, a person convicted of an offence may be ordered by the convicting court[44] to make an order "requiring him to pay compensation for any personal injury, loss or damage resulting from that offence or any other offence which is taken into consideration[45] by the court in determining sentence" (subs. (1)); and

---

[36] But not more than £1,000 in all.
[37] But not more than two months in all.
[38] Above, § 16–03.
[39] "Owner" means owner in its ordinary popular meaning of the person entitled to the goods: *Raymond Lyons & Co. Ltd.* v. *Metropolitan Police Commissioner* [1975] Q.B. 321. The court should not make an order under the Act except in a straightforward case where there is no real issue of law or difficulty in determining whether a person is the owner: *ibid.* at p. 326.
[40] Police (Property) Act 1897, s. 1(1). Regulations under *ibid.* s. 2(1) provide for the disposal of property whose owner has not been ascertained and in respect of which no order of a competent court has been made: see Stone's *Justice's Manual* (1981), Vol. 3, p. 6542
[41] Police (Property) Act 1897, s. 1(2)
[42] *Cf. Ex p. Davison* (1896) 60 J.P. 808; *Scattergood* v. *Sylvester* (1850) 15 Q.B. 506.
[43] Brazier, "Appellate Attitudes Towards Compensation Orders" [1977] Crim.L.R. 710; Thomas, *Principles of Sentencing* (2nd ed.), pp. 326–331.
[44] But see n. 5, above, reading that note as applying to compensation orders as to orders under s. 28.
[45] That is, is the subject of formal "t.i.c." procedure: *cf. D.P.P.* v. *Anderson* [1978] A.C. 964 (above, n. 4).

in the case of an offence under the Theft Act, "where the property . . . is recovered, any damage to the property[46] occurring while it was out of the owner's possession shall be treated . . . as having resulted from the offence, however and by whomsoever the damage was caused" (subs. (2)).

Compensation orders made by a magistrates' court are subject to a maximum of £1,000[47] in respect of any offence of which the court has convicted the offender, and in effect, where compensation is ordered in respect of offences taken into consideration by a magistrates' court, the total compensation in respect of all offences may not exceed £1,000 multiplied by the number of offences of which the offender has been convicted (subs. (5)).

The section does not require an application from the party to be **16–16** compensated before a compensation order may be made; but where there is an issue as to whether the particular loss has been suffered (*e.g.* whether particular goods were stolen) the court should not make an order except on an application on behalf of the victim and on evidence of the loss.[48] If stolen goods are recovered undamaged and unreduced in value, there can be no order for compensation in favour of the victim of the theft.[49] But an innocent purchaser from a thief or from a handler may have had to return the goods to their owner, and if so he will have suffered a "loss . . . resulting from the [theft or handling] offence" within the meaning of section 35(1).[50]

In determining the amount of compensation to be paid, a court must take the offender's means into account so far as they appear or are known to the court (subs. (4)), and an order should not be made when there is real doubt as to whether the offender can pay within a reasonable time.[51] But an order may be made against an offender without present means on the strength of his earning capacity, and there may be good moral reasons for making one.[52]

An order should be made only in a simple case[53] where the legal position is quite clear.[54] Only realistic orders should be made, not including orders involving payments over a long period or orders that may be counter-

---

[46] Not, in case of taking a car without consent contrary to s. 12, other property damaged by the offender when driving the car: *Quigley* v. *Stokes* [1977] 1 W.L.R. 434; [1977] 2 All E.R. 317 (see subs. (3)).
[47] Substituted for £400 by the Criminal Law Act 1977, s. 60.
[48] *Kneeshaw* [1975] Q.B. 57.
[49] *Sharkey* [1976] Crim.L.R. 388; *Cadamarteris* [1977] Crim.L.R. 236 (stolen car dismantled and resprayed, but no loss proved; *sed quaere?*).
[50] *Howell* (1978) 66 Cr.App.R. 179 (handling).
[51] *Inwood* (1974) 60 Cr.App.R. 70; *O'Donoghue* (1974) 66 Cr.App.R. 116n.; *Webb* (1979) 1 Cr.App.R. (S.) 16. But the court may allow time to pay and direct payment by instalments: Powers of Criminal Courts Act 1973, s. 34; Magistrates' Courts Act 1980, s. 75. As to imprisonment in default of payment, see *Bunce* (1977) 66 Cr.App.R. 109 (reviewing statutory provisions, for guidance of Crown Court judges).
[52] *Bradburn* (1973) 57 Cr.App.R. 948; *Kneeshaw*, above.
[53] *Bradburn*, above; *Oddy* [1974] 1 W.L.R. 1212; [1974] 2 All E.R. 666; *Kneeshaw*, above.
[54] *Inwood*, above.

productive by resulting in the commission of further offences to enable the compensation to be paid.[55]

A compensation order must relate to injury, loss or damage suffered by a particular person as a result of a specific offence, and must be for a specific amount that has been agreed or proved as the correct amount.[56] It may include a sum by way of interest.[57]

A compensation order does not justify a reduction in sentence, for which it is not a substitute.[58]

---

[55] *Bradburn*, above; *Daly* [1974] 1 W.L.R. 133; [1974] 1 All E.R. 290; *Inwood*, above; *Oddy*, above; *Wylie* [1975] R.T.R. 94; *Whenman* [1977] Crim.L.R. 430; see also *Wilkinson* (1979) 1 Cr.App.R. (S.) 69; *Shenton* (1979) 1 Cr.App.R. (S.) 81. But see *Workman* (1979) 1 Cr.App.R. (S.) 335 (D had house etc. purchased in part with proceeds of offences).
[56] *Inwood*, above; *Oddy*, above; *Vivian* (1978) 68 Cr.App.R. 53; *Cornwell* (1979) 1 Cr.App.R. (S.) 19. Joint and several orders, though possible. are to be avoided if substantial justice can be achieved by orders made severally: *Grundy and Moorhouse* [1974] 1 W.L.R. 139; [1974] 1 All E.R. 292.
[57] *Schofield* [1978] 1 W.L.R. 979; [1978] 2 All E.R. 705.
[58] *Lovett* (1870) 11 Cox 602; *Ironfield* (1971) 55 Cr.App.R. 91; *Inwood*, above; *Oddy*, above; *Stapleton and Lawrie* [1977] Crim.L.R. 366; *Miller* (1976) 68 Cr.App.R. 56 n. (in which most of the above principles were reaffirmed); *Copley* (1979) 1 Cr.App.R. (S.) 55.

APPENDIX 1

Theft Act 1968

(1968 c. 60)

Arrangement of Sections

Definition of "theft"

SECT.
1. Basic definition of theft.
2. "Dishonestly".
3. "Appropriates".
4. "Property".
5. "Belonging to another".
6. "With the intention of permanently depriving the other of it".

Theft, robbery, burglary, etc.

7. Theft.
8. Robbery.
9. Burglary.
10. Aggravated burglary.
11. Removal of articles from places open to the public.
12. Taking motor vehicle or other conveyance without authority.
13. Abstracting of electricity.
14. Extension to thefts from mails outside England and Wales, and robbery, etc. on such a theft.

Fraud and blackmail

15. Obtaining property by deception.
16. Obtaining pecuniary advantage by deception.
17. False accounting.
18. Liability of company officers for certain offences by company.
19. False statements by company directors, etc.
20. Suppression, etc. of documents.
21. Blackmail.

Offences relating to goods stolen, etc.

22. Handling stolen goods.
23. Advertising rewards for return of goods stolen or lost.
24. Scope of offences relating to stolen goods.

Possession of house-breaking implements, etc.

25. Going equipped for stealing, etc.

Enforcement and procedure

26. Search for stolen goods.
27. Evidence and procedure on charge of theft or handling stolen goods.
28. Orders for restitution.
29. Jurisdiction of quarter sessions, and summary trial.

209

General and consequential provisions

SECT.

30. Husband and wife.
31. Effect on civil proceedings and rights.
32. Effect on existing law and construction of references to offences.
33. Miscellaneous and consequential amendments, and repeal.

Supplementary

34. Interpretation.
35. Commencement and transitional provisions.
36. Short title, and general provisions as to Scotland and Northern Ireland.

SCHEDULES:

Schedule 1—Offences of taking, etc. deer or fish.
Schedule 2—Miscellaneous and consequential amendments.
Schedule 3—Repeals.

An Act to revise the law of England and Wales as to theft and similar or associated offences, and in connection therewith to make provision as to criminal proceedings by one party to a marriage against the other, and to make certain amendments extending beyond England and Wales in the Post Office Act 1953 and other enactments; and for other purposes connected therewith.   [26th July 1968]

Definition of "theft"

Basic definition of theft

17–01   **1.**—(1) A person is guilty of theft if he dishonestly appropriates property belonging to another with the intention of permanently depriving the other of it; and "thief" and "steal" shall be construed accordingly.

(2) It is immaterial whether the appropriation is made with a view to gain, or is made for the thief's own benefit.

(3) The five following sections of this Act shall have effect as regards the interpretation and operation of this section (and, except as otherwise provided by this Act, shall apply only for purposes of this section).

"Dishonestly"

17–02   **2.**—(1) A person's appropriation of property belonging to another is not to be regarded as dishonest—

(a) if he appropriates the property in the belief that he has in law the right to deprive the other of it, on behalf of himself or of a third person; or

(b) if he appropriates the property in the belief that he would have the other's consent if the other knew of the appropriation and the circumstances of it; or

(c) (except where the property came to him as trustee or personal representative) if he appropriates the property in the belief that the person to whom the property belongs cannot be discovered by taking reasonable steps.

(2) A person's appropriation of property belonging to another may be dishonest notwithstanding that he is willing to pay for the property.

"Appropriates"
3.—(1) Any assumption by a person of the rights of an owner amounts to **17–03** an appropriation, and this includes, where he has come by the property (innocently or not) without stealing it, any later assumption of a right to it by keeping or dealing with it as owner.

(2) Where property or a right or interest in property is or purports to be transferred for value to a person acting in good faith, no later assumption by him of rights which he believed himself to be acquiring shall, by reason of any defect in the transferor's title, amount to theft of the property.

"Property"
4.—(1) "Property" includes money and all other property, real or **17–04** personal, including things in action and other intangible property.

(2) A person cannot steal land, or things forming part of land and severed from it by him or by his directions, except in the following cases, that is to say—

(a) when he is a trustee or personal representative, or is authorised by power of attorney, or as liquidator of a company, or otherwise, to sell or dispose of land belonging to another, and he appropriates the land or anything forming part of it by dealing with it in breach of the confidence reposed in him; or

(b) when he is not in possession of the land and appropriates anything forming part of the land by severing it or causing it to be severed or after it has been severed; or

(c) when, being in possession of the land under a tenancy, he appropriates the whole or part of any fixture or structure let to be used with the land.

For purposes of this subsection "land" does not include incorporeal hereditaments; "tenancy" means a tenancy for years or any less period and includes an agreement for such a tenancy, but a person who after the end of a tenancy remains in possession as statutory tenant or otherwise is to be treated as having possession under the tenancy, and "let" shall be construed accordingly.

(3) A person who picks mushrooms growing wild on any land, or who picks flowers, fruit or foliage from a plant growing wild on any land does not (although not in possession of the land) steal what he picks, unless he does it for reward or for sale or other commercial purpose.

For purposes of this subsection "mushroom" includes any fungus, and "plant" includes any shrub or tree.

(4) Wild creatures, tamed or untamed, shall be regarded as property; but a person cannot steal a wild creature not tamed nor ordinarily kept in captivity, or the carcase of any such creature, unless either it has been reduced into possession by or on behalf of another person and possession of it has not since been lost or abandoned, or another person is in course of reducing it into possession.

"Belonging to another"

17–05 **5.**—(1) Property shall be regarded as belonging to any person having possession or control of it, or having in it any proprietary right or interest (not being an equitable interest arising only from an agreement to transfer or grant an interest).

(2) Where property is subject to a trust, the persons to whom it belongs shall be regarded as including any person having a right to enforce the trust, and an intention to defeat the trust shall be regarded accordingly as an intention to deprive of the property any person having that right.

(3) Where a person receives property from or on account of another, and is under an obligation to the other to retain and deal with that property or its proceeds in a particular way, the property or proceeds shall be regarded (as against him) as belonging to the other.

(4) Where a person gets property by another's mistake, and is under an obligation to make restoration (in whole or in part) of the property or its proceeds or of the value thereof, then to the extent of that obligation the property or proceeds shall be regarded (as against him) as belonging to the person entitled to restoration, and an intention not to make restoration shall be regarded accordingly as an intention to deprive that person of the property or proceeds.

(5) Property of a corporation sole shall be regarded as belonging to the corporation notwithstanding a vacancy in the corporation.

"With the intention of permanently depriving the other of it"

17–06 **6.**—(1) A person appropriating property belonging to another without meaning the other permanently to lose the thing itself is nevertheless to be regarded as having the intention of permanently depriving the other of it if his intention is to treat the thing as his own to dispose of regardless of the other's rights; and a borrowing or lending of it may amount to so treating it if, but only if, the borrowing or lending is for a period and in circumstances making it equivalent to an outright taking or disposal.

(2) Without prejudice to the generality of subsection (1) above, where a person, having possession or control (lawfully or not) of property belonging to another, parts with the property under a condition as to its return which he may not be able to perform, this (if done for purposes of his own and without the other's authority) amounts to treating the property as his own to dispose of regardless of the other's rights.

Theft, robbery, burglary, etc.

Theft

17–07 **7.** A person guilty of theft shall on conviction on indictment be liable to imprisonment for a term not exceeding ten years.

Robbery

17–08 **8.**—(1) A person is guilty of robbery if he steals, and immediately before or at the time of doing so, and in order to so, he uses force on any person or puts or seeks to put any person in fear of being then and there subjected to force.

(2) Any person guilty of robbery, or of an assault with intent to rob, shall on conviction on indictment be liable to imprisonment for life.

Burglary

9.—(1) A person is guilty of burglary if— **17–09**

(*a*) he enters a building or part of a building as a trespasser and with intent to commit any such offence as is mentioned in subsection (2) below; or

(*b*) having entered any building or part of a building as a trespasser he steals or attempts to steal anything in the building or that part of it or inflicts or attempts to inflict on any person therein any grievous bodily harm.

(2) The offences referred to in subsection (1) (*a*) above are offences of stealing anything in the building or part of a building in question, of inflicting on any person therein any grievous bodily harm or raping any woman therein, and doing unlawful damage to the building or anything therein.

(3) References in subsections (1) and (2) above to a building shall apply also to an inhabited vehicle or vessel, and shall apply to any such vehicle or vessel at times when the person having a habitation in it is not there as well as at times when he is.

(4) A person guilty of burglary shall on conviction on indictment be liable to imprisonment for a term not exceeding fourteen years.

Aggravated burglary

10.—(1) A person is guilty of aggravated burglary if he commits any **17–10** burglary and at the time has with him any firearm or imitation firearm, any weapon of offence, or any explosive; and for this purpose—

(*a*) "firearm" includes an airgun or air pistol, and "imitation firearm" means anything which has the appearance of being a firearm, whether capable of being discharged or not; and

(*b*) "weapon of offence" means any article made or adapted for use for causing injury to or incapacitating a person, or intended by the person having it with him for such use; and

(*c*) "explosive" means any article manufactured for the purpose of producing a practical effect by explosion, or intended by the person having it with him for that purpose.

(2) A person guilty of aggravated burglary shall on conviction on indictment be liable to imprisonment for life.

Removal of articles from places open to the public

11.—(1) Subject to subsections (2) and (3) below, where the public have **17–11** access to a building in order to view the building or part of it, or a collection or part of a collection housed in it, any person who without lawful authority removes from the building or its grounds the whole or part of any article displayed or kept for display to the public in the building or that part of it or in its grounds shall be guilty of an offence.

For this purpose "collection" includes a collection got together for a temporary purpose, but references in this section to a collection do not apply to a collection made or exhibited for the purpose of effecting sales or other commercial dealings.

(2) It is immaterial for purposes of subsection (1) above, that the public's access to a building is limited to a particular period or particular occasion; but where anything removed from a building or its grounds is there otherwise than as forming part of, or being on loan for exhibition with, a collection intended for permanent exhibition to the public, the person removing it does not thereby commit an offence under this section unless he removes it on a day when the public have access to the building as mentioned in subsection (1) above.

(3) A person does not commit an offence under this section if he believes that he has lawful authority for the removal of the thing in question or that he would have it if the person entitled to give it knew of the removal and the circumstances of it.

(4) A person guilty of an offence under this section shall, on conviction on indictment, be liable to imprisonment for a term not exceeding five years.

Taking motor vehicle or other conveyance without authority

17–12   **12.**—(1) Subject to subsections (5) and (6) below, a person shall be guilty of an offence if, without having the consent of the owner or other lawful authority, he takes any conveyance for his own or another's use or, knowing that any conveyance has been taken without such authority, drives it or allows himself to be carried in or on it.

(2) A person guilty of an offence under subsection (1) above shall on conviction on indictment be liable to imprisonment for a term not exceeding three years.

(3) Offences under subsection (1) above and attempts to commit them shall be deemed for all purposes to be arrestable offences within the meaning of section 2 of the Criminal Law Act 1967.

(4) If on the trial of an indictment for theft the jury are not satisfied that the accused committed theft, but it is proved that the accused committed an offence under subsection (1) above, the jury may find him guilty of the offence under subsection (1).

(5) Subsection (1) above shall not apply in relation to pedal cycles; but, subject to subsection (6) below, a person who, without having the consent of the owner or other lawful authority, takes a pedal cycle for his own or another's use, or rides a pedal cycle knowing it to have been taken without such authority, shall on summary conviction be liable to a fine not exceeding fifty pounds.

(6) A person does not commit an offence under this section by anything done in the belief that he has lawful authority to do it or that he would have the owner's consent if the owner knew of his doing it and the circumstances of it.

(7) For purposes of this section—

(*a*) "conveyance" means any conveyance constructed or adapted for the carriage of a person or persons whether by land, water or air, except that it does not include a conveyance constructed or adapted for use only under the control of a person not carried in or on it, and "drive" shall be construed accordingly; and

(*b*) "owner", in relation to a conveyance which is the subject of a hiring agreement or hire-purchase agreement, means the person in possession of the conveyance under that agreement.

Abstracting of electricity

13.   A person who dishonestly uses without due authority, or dishonestly causes to be wasted or diverted, any electricity shall on conviction on indictment be liable to imprisonment for a term not exceeding five years. **17–13**

Extension to thefts from mails outside England and Wales, and robbery etc. on such a theft

14.—(1) Where a person— **17–14**

(*a*) steals or attempts to steal any mail bag or postal packet in the course of transmission as such between places in different jurisdictions in the British postal area, or any of the contents of such a mail bag or postal packet; or

(*b*) in stealing or with intent to steal any such mail bag or postal packet or any of its contents, commits any robbery, attempted robbery or assault with intent to rob;

then, notwithstanding that he does so outside England and Wales, he shall be guilty of committing or attempting to commit the offence against this Act as if he had done so in England or Wales, and he shall accordingly be liable to be prosecuted, tried and punished in England and Wales without proof that the offence was committed there.

(2) In subsection (1) above the reference to different jurisdictions in the British postal area is to be construed as referring to the several jurisdictions of England and Wales, of Scotland, of Northern Ireland, of the Isle of Man and of the Channel Islands.

(3) For purposes of this section "mail bag" includes any article serving the purpose of a mail bag.

Fraud and blackmail

Obtaining property by deception

15.—(1) A person who by any deception dishonestly obtains property belonging to another, with the intention of permanently depriving the other of it, shall on conviction on indictment be liable to imprisonment for a term not exceeding ten years. **17–15**

(2) For purposes of this section a person is to be treated as obtaining property if he obtains ownership, possession or control of it, and "obtain" includes obtaining for another or enabling another to obtain or to retain.

215

(3) Section 6 above shall apply for purposes of this section, with the necessary adaptations of the reference to appropriating, as it applies for purposes of section 1.

(4) For purposes of this section "deception" means any deception (whether deliberate or reckless) by words or conduct as to fact or as to law, including a deception as to the present intentions of the person using the deception or any other person.

Obtaining pecuniary advantage by deception

17–16   **16.**—(1) A person who by any deception dishonestly obtains for himself or another any pecuniary advantage shall on conviction on indictment be liable to imprisonment for a term not exceeding five years.

(2) The cases in which a pecuniary advantage within the meaning of this section is to be regarded as obtained for a person are cases where—

[(a) *any debt or charge for which he makes himself liable or is or may become liable (including one not legally enforceable) is reduced or in whole or in part evaded or deferred; or*]

(b) he is allowed to borrow by way of overdraft, or to take out any policy of insurance or annuity contract, or obtains an improvement of the terms on which he is allowed to do so; or

(c) he is given the opportunity to earn remuneration or greater remuneration in an office or employment, or to win money by betting.

(3) For purposes of this section "deception" has the same meaning as in section 15 of this Act.

[*Subsection (2)(a) was repealed by the Theft Act* 1978, *s.*5(5).]

False accounting

17–17   **17.**—(1) Where a person dishonestly, with a view to gain for himself or another or with intent to cause loss to another,—

(a) destroys, defaces, conceals or falsifies any account or any record or document made or required for any accounting purpose; or

(b) in furnishing information for any purpose produces or makes use of any account, or any such record or document as aforesaid, which to his knowledge is or may be misleading, false or deceptive in a material particular;

he shall, on conviction on indictment, be liable to imprisonment for a term not exceeding seven years.

(2) For purposes of this section a person who makes or concurs in making in an account or other document an entry which is or may be misleading, false or deceptive in a material particular, or who omits or concurs in omitting a material particular from an account or other document, is to be treated as falsifying the account or document.

Liability of company officers for certain offences by company

17–18   **18.**—(1) Where an offence committed by a body corporate under section 15, 16 or 17 of this Act is proved to have been committed with the consent or connivance of any director, manager, secretary or other similar officer of the body corporate, or any person who was purporting to act in any such capacity, he as well as the body corporate shall be guilty of that offence, and shall be liable to be proceeded against and punished accordingly.

(2) Where the affairs of a body corporate are managed by its members, this section shall apply in relation to the acts and defaults of a member in connection with his functions of management as if he were a director of the body corporate.

False statements by company directors, etc.

19.—(1) Where an officer of a body corporate or unincorporated association (or person purporting to act as such), with intent to deceive members or creditors of the body corporate or association about its affairs, publishes or concurs in publishing a written statement or account which to his knowledge is or may be misleading, false or deceptive in a material particular, he shall on conviction on indictment be liable to imprisonment for a term not exceeding seven years.   **17–19**

(2) For purposes of this section a person who has entered into a security for the benefit of a body corporate or association is to be treated as a creditor of it.

(3) Where the affairs of a body corporate or association are managed by its members, this section shall apply to any statement which a member publishes or concurs in publishing in connection with his functions of management as if he were an officer of the body corporate or association.

Suppression, etc. of documents

20.—(1) A person who dishonestly, with a view to gain for himself or another or with intent to cause loss to another, destroys, defaces or conceals any valuable security, any will or other testamentary document or any original document of or belonging to, or filed or deposited in, any court of justice or any government department shall on conviction on indictment be liable to imprisonment for a term not exceeding seven years.   **17–20**

(2) A person who dishonestly, with a view to gain for himself or another or with intent to cause loss to another, by any deception procures the execution of a valuable security shall on conviction on indictment be liable to imprisonment for a term not exceeding seven years; and this subsection shall apply in relation to the making, acceptance, indorsement, alteration, cancellation or destruction in whole or in part of a valuable security, and in relation to the signing or sealing of any paper or other material in order that it may be made or converted into, or used or dealt with as, a valuable security, as if that were the execution of a valuable security.

(3) For purposes of this section "deception" has the same meaning as in section 15 of this Act, and "valuable security" means any document creating, transferring, surrendering or releasing any right to, in or over property, or authorising the payment of money or delivery of any property, or evidencing the creation, transfer, surrender or release of any such right, or the payment of money or delivery of any property, or the satisfaction of any obligation.

217

Blackmail

17–21 **21.**—(1) A person is guilty of blackmail if, with a view to gain for himself or another or with intent to cause loss to another, he makes any unwarranted demand with menaces; and for this purpose a demand with menaces is unwarranted unless the person making it does so in the belief—

(*a*) that he has reasonable grounds for making the demand; and

(*b*) that the use of the menaces is a proper means of reinforcing the demand.

(2) The nature of the act or omission demanded is immaterial, and it is also immaterial whether the menaces relate to action to be taken by the person making the demand.

(3) A person guilty of blackmail shall on conviction on indictment be liable to imprisonment for a term not exceeding fourteen years.

Offences relating to goods stolen, etc.

Handling stolen goods

17–22 **22.**—(1) A person handles stolen goods if (otherwise than in the course of the stealing) knowing or believing them to be stolen goods he dishonestly receives the goods, or dishonestly undertakes or assists in their retention, removal, disposal or realisation by or for the benefit of another person, or if he arranges to do so.

(2) A person guilty of handling stolen goods shall on conviction on indictment be liable to imprisonment for a term not exceeding fourteen years.

Advertising rewards for return of goods stolen or lost

17–23 **23.** Where any public advertisement of a reward for the return of any goods which have been stolen or lost uses any words to the effect that no questions will be asked, or that the person producing the goods will be safe from apprehension or inquiry, or that any money paid for the purchase of the goods or advanced by way of loan on them will be repaid, the person advertising the reward and any person who prints or publishes the advertisement shall on summary conviction be liable to a fine not exceeding one hundred pounds.

Scope of offences relating to stolen goods

17–24 **24.**—(1) The provisions of this Act relating to goods which have been stolen shall apply whether the stealing occurred in England or Wales or elsewhere, and whether it occurred before or after the commencement of this Act, provided that the stealing (if not an offence under this Act) amounted to an offence where and at the time when the goods were stolen; and references to stolen goods shall be construed accordingly.

(2) For purposes of those provisions references to stolen goods shall include, in addition to the goods originally stolen and parts of them (whether in their original state or not),—

(*a*) any other goods which directly or indirectly represent or have at any time represented the stolen goods in the hands of the thief as being the proceeds of any disposal or realisation of the whole or part of the goods stolen or of goods so representing the stolen goods; and

(*b*) any other goods which directly or indirectly represent or have at any time represented the stolen goods in the hands of a handler of the stolen goods or any part of them as being the proceeds of any disposal or realisation of the whole or part of the stolen goods handled by him or of goods so representing them.

(3) But no goods shall be regarded as having continued to be stolen goods after they have been restored to the person from whom they were stolen or to other lawful possession or custody, or after that person and any other person claiming through him have otherwise ceased as regards those goods to have any right to restitution in respect of the theft.

(4) For purposes of the provisions of this Act relating to goods which have been stolen (including subsections (1) to (3) above) goods obtained in England or Wales or elsewhere either by blackmail or in the circumstances described in section 15(1) of this Act shall be regarded as stolen; and "steal", "theft" and "thief" shall be construed accordingly.

Possession of housebreaking implements, etc.

Going equipped for stealing, etc.

25.—(1) A person shall be guilty of an offence if, when not at his place of abode, he has with him any article for use in the course of or in connection with any burglary, theft or cheat. **17–25**

(2) A person guilty of an offence under this section shall on conviction on indictment be liable to imprisonment for a term not exceeding three years.

(3) Where a person is charged with an offence under this section, proof that he had with him any article made or adapted for use in committing a burglary, theft or cheat shall be evidence that he had it with him for such use.

(4) Any person may arrest without warrant anyone who is, or whom he, with reasonable cause, suspects to be, committing an offence under this section.

(5) For purposes of this section an offence under section 12(1) of this Act of taking a conveyance shall be treated as theft, and "cheat" means an offence under section 15 of this Act.

Enforcement and procedure

Search for stolen goods

26.—(1) If it is made to appear by information on oath before a justice of the peace that there is reasonable cause to believe that any person has in his custody or possession or on his premises any stolen goods, the justice may grant a warrant to search for and seize the same; but no warrant to search for stolen goods shall be addressed to a person other than a constable except under the authority of an enactment expressly so providing. **17–26**

(2) An officer of police not below the rank of superintendent may give a constable written authority to search any premises for stolen goods—

(a) if the person in occupation of the premises has been convicted within the preceding five years of handling stolen goods or of any offence involving dishonesty and punishable with imprisonment; or

(b) if a person who has been convicted within the preceding five years of handling stolen goods has within the preceding twelve months been in occupation of the premises.

(3) Where under this section a person is authorised to search premises for stolen goods, he may enter and search the premises accordingly, and may seize any goods he believes to be stolen goods.

[(4) *Repealed by the Criminal Justice Act* 1972, s.64(2), *Sched.*6.]

(5) This section is to be construed in accordance with section 24 of this Act; and in subsection (2) above the references to handling stolen goods shall include any corresponding offence committed before the commencement of this Act.

Evidence and procedure on charge of theft or handling stolen goods

17–27   27.—(1) Any number of persons may be charged in one indictment, with reference to the same theft, with having at different times or at the same time handled all or any of the stolen goods, and the persons so charged may be tried together.

(2) On the trial of two or more persons indicted for jointly handling any stolen goods the jury may find any of the accused guilty if the jury are satisfied that he handled all or any of the stolen goods, whether or not he did so jointly with the other accused or any of them.

(3) Where a person is being proceeded against for handling stolen goods (but not for any offence other than handling stolen goods), then at any stage of the proceedings, if evidence has been given of his having or arranging to have in his possession the goods the subject of the charge, or of his undertaking or assisting in, or arranging to undertake or assist in, their retention, removal, disposal or realisation, the following evidence shall be admissible for the purpose of proving that he knew or believed the goods to be stolen goods:—

(a) evidence that he has had in his possession, or has undertaken or assisted in the retention, removal, disposal or realisation of, stolen goods from any theft taking place not earlier than twelve months before the offence charged; and

(b) (provided that seven days' notice in writing has been given to him of the intention to prove the conviction) evidence that he has within the five years preceding the date of the offence charged been convicted of theft or of handling stolen goods.

(4) In any proceedings for the theft of anything in the course of transmission (whether by post or otherwise), or for handling stolen goods from such a theft, a statutory declaration made by any person that he despatched or received or failed to receive any goods or postal packet, or that any goods or postal packet when despatched or received by him were

in a particular state or condition, shall be admissible as evidence of the facts stated in the declaration, subject to the following conditions:—

    (*a*) a statutory declaration shall only be admissible where and to the extent to which oral evidence to the like effect would have been admissible in the proceedings; and

    (*b*) a statutory declaration shall only be admissible if at least seven days before the hearing or trial a copy of it has been given to the person charged, and he has not, at least three days before the hearing of trial or within such further time as the court may in special circumstances allow, given the prosecutor written notice requiring the attendance at the hearing or trial of the person making the declaration.

(5) This section is to be construed in accordance with section 24 of this Act; and in subsection (3) (*b*) above the reference to handling stolen goods shall include any corresponding offence committed before the commencement of this Act.

Orders for restitution

28.—(1) Where goods have been stolen, and either a person is convicted **17–28** of any offence with reference to the theft (whether or not the stealing is the gist of his offence) or a person is convicted of any other offence but such an offence as aforesaid is taken into consideration in determining his sentence, the court by or before which the offender is convicted may on the conviction [(whether or not the passing of sentence is in other respects deferred)] exercise any of the following powers—

    (*a*) the court may order anyone having possession or control of the goods to restore them to any person entitled to recover them from him; or

    (*b*) on the application of a person entitled to recover from the person convicted any other goods directly or indirectly representing the first-mentioned goods (as being the proceeds of any disposal or realisation of the whole or part of them or of goods so representing them), the court may order those other goods to be delivered or transferred to the applicant; or

    (*c*) the court may order that a sum not exceeding the value of the first-mentioned goods shall be paid, out of any money of the person convicted which was taken out of his possession on his apprehension, to any person who, if those goods were in the possession of the person convicted, would be entitled to recover them from him.

(2) Where under subsection (1) above the court has power on a person's conviction to make an order against him both under paragraph (*b*) and under paragraph (*c*) with reference to the stealing of the same goods, the court may make orders under both paragraphs provided that the person in whose favour the orders are made does not thereby recover more than the value of those goods.

(3) Where under subsection (1) above the court on a person's conviction makes an order under paragraph (*a*) for the restoration of any goods, and it

appears to the court that the person convicted has sold the goods to a person acting in good faith, or has borrowed money on the security of them from a person so acting, the court may order that there shall be paid to the purchaser or lender, out of any money of the person convicted which was taken out of his possession on his apprehension, a sum not exceeding the amount paid for the purchase by the purchaser or, as the case may be, the amount owed to the lender in respect of the loan.

(4) The court shall not exercise the powers conferred by this section unless in the opinion of the court the relevant facts sufficiently appear from evidence given at the trial or the available documents, together with admissions made by or on behalf of any person in connection with any proposed exercise of the powers; and for this purpose "the available documents" means any written statements or admissions which were made for use, and would have been admissible, as evidence at the trial, the depositions taken at any committal proceedings and any written statements or admissions used as evidence in those proceedings.

(5) Any order under this section shall be treated as an order for the restitution of property within the meaning of sections 30 and 42 of the Criminal Appeal Act 1968 (which relate to the effect on such orders of appeals).

(6) References in this section to stealing are to be construed in accordance with section 24(1) and (4) of this Act.

[*Subsections* (1) (*other than the words in square brackets*), (2) *and* (3) *are printed as substituted by the Criminal Justice Act* 1972, *s.* 64(1), *Sched.* 5. *The words in square brackets in subsection* (1) *were added by the Criminal Law Act* 1977, *s.* 65(4), *Sched.*12.]

Jurisdiction of quarter sessions, and summary trial
17–29   **29.**—[(1) *Repealed by the Courts Act* 1971, *s.*56, *Sched.*11.]
[(2) *Repealed by the Criminal Law Act* 1977, *s.*65(5), *Sched.*13.]

General and consequential provisions

Husband and wife
17–30   **30.**—(1) This Act shall apply in relation to the parties to a marriage, and to property belonging to the wife or husband whether or not by reason of an interest derived from the marriage, as it would apply if they were not married and any such interest subsisted independently of the marriage.

(2) Subject to subsection (4) below, a person shall have the same right to bring proceedings against that person's wife or husband for any offence (whether under this Act or otherwise), as if they were not married, and a person bringing any such proceedings shall be competent to give evidence for the prosecution at every stage of the proceedings.

(3) Where a person is charged in proceedings not brought by that person's wife or husband with having committed any offence with reference to that person's wife or husband or to property belonging to the wife or husband, the wife or husband shall be competent to give evidence at every stage of the proceedings, whether for the defence or for the

prosecution, and whether the accused is charged solely or jointly with any other person:

Provided that—

(*a*) the wife or husband (unless compellable at common law) shall not be compellable either to give evidence or, in giving evidence, to disclose any communication made to her or him during the marriage by the accused; and

(*b*) her or his failure to give evidence shall not be made the subject of any comment by the prosecution.

(4) Proceedings shall not be instituted against a person for any offence of stealing or doing unlawful damage to property which at the time of the offence belongs to that person's wife or husband, or for any attempt, incitement or conspiracy to commit such an offence, unless the proceedings are instituted by or with the consent of the Director of Public Prosecutions:

Provided that—

(*a*) this subsection shall not apply to proceedings against a person for an offence—

(i) if that person is charged with committing the offence jointly with the wife or husband; or

(ii) if by virtue of any judicial decree or order (wherever made) that person and the wife or husband are at the time of the offence under no obligation to cohabit [*and*

(*b*) *Repealed by the Criminal Jurisdiction Act* 1975, *s.* 14(5), *Sched.*6.]

(5) Notwithstanding [section 6 of the Prosecution of Offences Act 1979] subsection (4) of this section shall apply—

(*a*) to an arrest (if without warrant) made by the wife or husband, and

(*b*) to a warrant of arrest issued on an information laid by the wife or husband.

[*Subsection* (5) *was added by the Criminal Jurisdiction Act* 1975, *s.*14(4), *Sched.*5. *The words in square brackets were substituted by the Prosecution of Offences Act* 1979, *s.*11(1), *Sched.*1.]

Effect on civil proceedings and rights

31.—(1) A person shall not be excused, by reason that to do so may   **17–31** incriminate that person or the wife or husband of that person of an offence under this Act—

(*a*) from answering any question put to that person in proceedings for the recovery or administration of any property, for the execution of any trust or for an account of any property or dealings with property; or

(*b*) from complying with any order made in any such proceedings;

but no statement or admission made by a person in answering a question put or complying with an order made as aforesaid shall, in proceedings for an offence under this Act, be admissible in evidence against that person or (unless they married after the making of the statement of admission) against the wife or husband of that person.

(2) Notwithstanding any enactment to the contrary, where property has been stolen or obtained by fraud or other wrongful means, the title to that

or any other property shall not be affected by reason only of the conviction of the offender.

Effect on existing law and construction of references to offences

17–32   **32.**—(1) The following offences are hereby abolished for all purposes not relating to offences committed before the commencement of this Act, that is to say—

(*a*) any offence at common law of larceny, robbery, burglary, receiving stolen property, obtaining property by threats, extortion by colour of office or franchise, false accounting by public officers, conceal- ment of treasure trove and, except as regards offences relating to the public revenue, cheating; and

(*b*) any offence under an enactment mentioned in Part 1 of Schedule 3 to this Act, to the extent to which the offence depends on any section or part of a section included in column 3 of that Schedule;

but so that the provisions in Schedule 1 to this Act (which preserve with modifications certain offences under the Larceny Act 1861 of taking or killing deer and taking or destroying fish) shall have effect as there set out.

(2) Except as regards offences committed before the commencement of this Act, and except in so far as the context otherwise requires,—

(*a*) references in any enactment passed before this Act to an offence abolished by this Act shall, subject to any express amendment or repeal made by this Act, have effect as references to the corresponding offence under this Act, and in any such enactment the expression "receive" (when it relates to an offence of receiving) shall mean handle, and "receiver" shall be construed accordingly; and

(*b*) without prejudice to paragraph (*a*) above, references in any enactment, whenever passed, to theft or stealing (including refer- ences to stolen goods), and references to robbery, blackmail, burglary, aggravated burglary or handling stolen goods, shall be construed in accordance with the provisions of this Act, including those of section 24.

Miscellaneous and consequential amendments, and repeal

17–33   **33.**—(1) The Post Office Act 1953 shall have effect subject to the amendments provided for by Part I of Schedule 2 to this Act and (except in so far as the contrary intention appears) those amendments shall have effect throughout the British postal area.

(2) The enactments mentioned in Parts II and III of Schedule 2 to this Act shall have effect subject to the amendments there provided for, and (subject to subsection (4) below) the amendments made by Part II to enactments extending beyond England and Wales shall have the like extent as the enactment amended.

(3) The enactments mentioned in Schedule 3 to this Act (which include in Part II certain enactments related to the subject matter of this Act but already obsolete or redundant apart from this Act) are hereby repealed to

the extent specified in column 3 of that schedule; and, notwithstanding that the foregoing sections of this Act do not extend to Scotland, where any enactment expressed to be repealed by Schedule 3 does so extend, the Schedule shall have effect to repeal it in its application to Scotland except in so far as the repeal is expressed not to extend to Scotland.

(4) No amendment or repeal made by this Act in Schedule 1 to the Extradition Act 1870 or in the Schedule to the Extradition Act 1873 shall affect the operation of that Schedule by reference to the law of a British possession; but the repeal made in Schedule 1 to the Extradition Act 1870 shall extend throughout the United Kingdom.

Supplementary

Interpretation

34.—(1) Sections 4(1) and 5(1) of this Act shall apply generally for   **17–34** purposes of this Act as they apply for purposes of section 1.

(2) For purposes of this Act—

(*a*) "gain" and "loss" are to be construed as extending only to gain or loss in money or other property, but as extending to any such gain or loss whether temporary or permanent; and—

    (i) "gain" includes a gain by keeping what one has, as well as a gain by getting what one has not; and

    (ii) "loss" includes a loss by not getting what one might get, as well as a loss by parting with what one has;

(*b*) "goods", except in so far as the context otherwise requires, includes money and every other description of property except land, and includes things severed from the land by stealing.

Commencement and transitional provisions

35.—(1) This Act shall come into force on the 1st January 1969 and, save   **17–35** as otherwise provided by this Act, shall have affect only in relation to offences wholly or partly committed on or after that date.

(2) Sections 27 and 28 of this Act shall apply in relation to proceedings for an offence committed before the commencement of this Act as they would apply in relation to proceedings for a corresponding offence under this Act, and shall so apply in place of any corresponding enactment repealed by this Act.

(3) Subject to subsection (2) above, no repeal or amendment by this Act of any enactment relating to procedure or evidence, or to the jurisdiction or powers of any court, or to the effect of a conviction, shall affect the operation of the enactment in relation to offences committed before the commencement of this Act or to proceedings for any such offence.

Short title, and general provisions as to Scotland and Northern Ireland

36.—(1) This Act may be cited as the Theft Act 1968.   **17–36**

[(2) *Repealed by the Northern Ireland Constitution Act* 1973, *s.* 41(1), *Sched.* 6.]

(3) This Act does not extend to Scotland or . . . to Northern Ireland, except as regards any amendment or repeal which in accordance with section 33 above is to extend to Scotland or Northern Ireland.

[*The words omitted in subsection* (3) *were repealed by the Northern Ireland Constitution Act* 1973, *s.* 41(1), *Sched.* 6.]

SCHEDULES

Section 32 SCHEDULE 1

OFFENCES OF TAKING, ETC. DEER OR FISH

Taking or killing deer

17–37 [1. *Repealed by the Deer Act* 1980, *s.* 9(2). *For s.* 1 *of the Deer Act* 1980, *see above,* § 2–08.]

Taking or destroying fish

17–38 2.—(1) Subject to subparagraph (2) below, a person who unlawfully takes or destroys, or attempts to take or destroy, any fish in water which is private property or in which there is any private right of fishery shall on summary conviction be liable to a fine not exceeding fifty pounds or, for an offence committed after a previous conviction of an offence under this subparagraph, to imprisonment for a term not exceeding three months or to a fine not exceeding one hundred pounds or to both.

(2) Subparagraph (1) above shall not apply to taking or destroying fish by angling in the daytime (that is to say, in the period beginning one hour before sunrise and ending one hour after sunset); but a person who by angling in the daytime unlawfully takes or destroys, or attempts to take or destroy, any fish in water which is private property or in which there is any private right of fishery shall on summary conviction be liable to a fine not exceeding twenty pounds.

(3) The court by which a person is convicted of an offence under this paragraph may order the forfeiture of anything which, at the time of the offence, he had with him for use for taking or destroying fish.

(4) Any person may arrest without warrant anyone who is, or whom he, with reasonable cause, suspects to be, committing an offence under subparagraph (1) above, and may seize from any person who is, or whom he, with reasonable cause, suspects to be, committing any offence under this paragraph anything which on that person's conviction of the offence would be liable to be forfeited under subparagraph (3) above.

Section 33(1)(2) SCHEDULE 2

MISCELLANEOUS AND CONSEQUENTIAL AMENDMENTS

PART I

Amendments of Post Office Act 1953

17–39 1. The Post Office Act 1953 shall have effect subject to the amendments provided for by this Part of this Schedule (and, except in so far as the contrary intention appears, those amendments have effect throughout the British postal area).

2. Sections 22 and 23 shall be amended by substituting for the word "felony" in section 22(1) and section 23(2) the words "a misdemeanour", and by omitting the words "of this Act and" in section 23(1).

3. In section 52, as it applies outside England and Wales, for the words from "be guilty" onwards there shall be substituted the words "be guilty of a misdemeanour and be liable to imprisonment for a term not exceeding ten years".

4. In section 53 for the words from "be guilty" onwards there shall be substituted the words "be guilty of a misdemeanour and be liable to imprisonment for a term not exceeding five years".

5. In section 54, as it applies outside England and Wales,—
   (a) there shall be omitted the words "taking, embezzling", and the words "taken, embezzled", where first occurring;
   (b) for the words "a felony" there shall be substituted the words "an offence" and the word "feloniously" shall be omitted;
   (c) for the words from "be guilty" to "secreted it" there shall be substituted the words "be guilty of a misdemeanour and be liable to imprisonment for a term not exceeding fourteen years".

6. In sections 55 and 58(1), after the word "imprisonment", there shall in each case be inserted the words "for a term not exceeding two years".

7. In section 57—
   (a) there shall be omitted the words "steals, or for any purpose whatever embezzles", and the words from "or if" onwards;
   (b) for the word "felony" there shall be substituted the words "a misdemeanour".

8. After section 65 there shall be inserted as a new section 65A—

"Fraudulent use of public telephone or Telex system.
   65A. If any person dishonestly uses a public telephone or telex system with intent to avoid payment (including any such system provided, under licence, otherwise than by the Postmaster General), he shall be guilty of a misdemeanour and be liable on summary conviction to imprisonment for a term not exceeding three months or to a fine not exceeding one hundred pounds or to both, or on conviction on indictment to imprisonment for a term not exceeding two years."

9. Section 69(2) shall be omitted.

10. For section 70 there shall be substituted the following section—

"Prosecution of certain offences in any jurisdiction of British postal area.
   70.—(1) Where a person—
   (a) steals or attempts to steal any mail bag or postal packet in the course of transmission as such between places in different jurisdictions in the British postal area, or any of the contents of such a mail bag or postal packet; or
   (b) in stealing or with intent to steal any such mail bag or postal packet or any of its contents, commits any robbery, attempted robbery or assault with intent to rob;
then, in whichever of those jurisdictions he does so, he shall by virtue of this section be guilty in each of the jurisdictions in which this subsection has effect of committing or attempting to commit the offence against section 52 of this Act, or the offence referred to in paragraph (b) of this subsection, as the case may be, as if he had done so in that jurisdiction, and he shall accordingly be liable to be prosecuted, tried and punished in that jurisdiction without proof that the offence was committed there.

   (2) In subsection (1) above the reference to different jurisdictions in the British postal area is to be construed as referring to the several jurisdictions of England and Wales, of Scotland, of Northern Ireland, of the Isle of Man, of the Channel Islands; and that subsection shall have effect in each of those jurisdictions except England and Wales."

11. In section 72 there shall be added as a new subsection (3)—

"(3) In any proceedings in England or Wales for an offence under section 53, 55, 56, 57 or 58 of this Act, section 27(4) of the Theft Act 1968 shall apply as it is expressed to apply to proceedings for the theft of anything in the course of transmission by post; and in the case of proceedings under section 53 of this Act a statutory declaration made by any person that a vessel, vehicle or aircraft was at any time employed by or under the Post Office for the transmission of postal packets under contract shall be admissible as evidence of the facts stated in the declaration subject to the same conditions as under section 27(4) (*a*) and (*b*) of the Theft Act 1968 apply to declarations admissible under section 27(4)".

12. In section 87(1), the definition of "valuable security" shall be omitted but, except in relation to England and Wales, there shall be substituted:—

" 'valuable security' means any document creating, transferring, surrendering or releasing any right to, in or over property, or authorising the payment of money or delivery of any property, or evidencing the creation, transfer, surrender or release of any such right or the payment of money or delivery of any property, or the satisfaction of any obligation."

Part II

Other amendments extending beyond England and Wales

Act amended	Amendment
17–40 The Extradition Act 1873 (36 & 37 Vict. c. 60)	In the Schedule (additional list of extradition crimes) for the words "the Larceny Act 1861" there shall be substituted the words "the Theft Act 1968".
The Public Stores Act 1875 (38 & 39 Vict. c. 25)	For section 12 (incorporation of parts of Larceny Act 1861) there shall be substituted:— "(1) Any person may arrest without warrant anyone who is, or whom he, with reasonable cause, suspects to be, in the act of committing or attempting to commit an offence against section 5 or 8 of this Act. (2) If it is made to appear by information on oath before a justice of the peace that there is reasonable cause to believe that any person has in his custody or possession or on his premises any stores in respect of which an offence against section 5 of this Act has been committed, the justice may issue a warrant to a constable to search for and seize the stores as in the case of stolen goods, and the Police (Property) Act 1897 shall apply as if this subsection were among the enactments mentioned in section 1(1) of that Act."
The Army Act 1955 (3 & 4 Eliz. 2, c. 18)	For section 44(1)(*b*) there shall be substituted— "(*b*) handles any stolen goods, where the property stolen was public or service property, or".

Act Amended	*Amendment*

The Army Act 1955—*cont.*
(3 & 4 Eliz. 2, c. 18)
	For section 45 (*b*) there shall be substituted—
	   "(*b*) handles any stolen goods, where the property stolen belonged to a person subject to military law, or".
	In section 138(1) for the words from "receiving" to "stolen" there shall be substituted the words "handling it".
	In section 225(1) after the definition of "Governor" there shall be inserted—
	   " 'handles' has the same meaning as in the Theft Act 1968";
	and for the definition of "steals" there shall be substituted—
	   " 'steals' has the same meaning as in the Theft Act 1968, and references to 'stolen goods' shall be construed as if contained in that Act".

The Air Force Act 1955 (3 & 4 Eliz. 2, c. 19)	The same amendments shall be made in sections 44, 45, 138 and 223 as are above directed to be made in the corresponding sections of the Army Act 1955, except that in the amendment to section 45(*b*) "air-force law" shall be substituted for "military law".
The Naval Discipline Act 1957 (5 & 6 Eliz. 2, c. 53)	For section 29(*b*) there shall be substituted— "(*b*) handles any stolen goods, where the property stolen was public or service property, or". In section 76(1) for the words from "receiving" to "embezzling" there shall be substituted the word "handling". In section 135(1) the same amendments shall be made as are above directed to be made in section 225(1) of the Army Act 1955.
The Army and Air Force Act 1961 (9 & 10 Eliz. 2, c. 52)	Section 21 shall be omitted.

[*Entry relating to the Road Traffic Act* 1962, *Sched.* 1, *Part II; repealed by the Road Traffic Act* 1972, *s.* 205(1) *Sched.* 9.]

PART III

Amendments limited to England and Wales

Act amended	*Amendment*	
The Gaming Act 1845 (8 & 9) Vict. c. 109)	In section 17 (punishment for cheating at play, etc.) for the words "be deemed guilty of obtaining such money or valuable thing from	**17–41**

229

Act Amended	*Amendment*
The Gaming Act 1845—*cont.* (8 & 9) Vict. c. 109)	such other person by a false pretence" and the following words there shall be substituted the words— "(*a*) on conviction on indictment be liable to imprisonment for a term not exceeding two years; or (*b*) on summary conviction be liable to imprisonment for a term not exceeding six months or to a fine not exceeding two hundred pounds or to both".

[*Entry relating to the Pawnbrokers Act* 1872, *s.* 38: *repealed by the Consumer Credit Act* 1974, *s.* 192(3)(*b*), *Sched.* 5.]

The Bankruptcy Act 1914 (4 & 5 Geo. 5, c. 59)	In section 166 (admissions on compulsory examination, etc., not to be admissible as evidence in proceedings for certain offences) for the words following "against that person" there shall be substituted the words "or (unless they married after the making of the statement or admission) against the wife or husband of that person in any proceeding in respect of an offence under the Theft Act 1968".
The House to House Collections Act 1939 (2 & 3 Geo. 6, c. 44)	In the Schedule (offences for which a conviction is a ground for refusing or revoking a licence under the Act to promote a collection for charity) for the entry relating to the Larceny Act 1916 there shall be substituted:— "Robbery, burglary and blackmail".

[*Entry relating to the Magistrates' Courts Act* 1952, *Sched.* 1, *para.* 8: *repealed by the Criminal Law Act* 1977, *s.*65(5), *Sched.* 13.]

The Visiting Forces Act 1952 (15 & 16 Geo. 6 & 1 Eliz. 2, c. 67)	In the Schedule there shall be inserted in paragraph 1 (*a*) after the word "buggery" the word "robbery", and in paragraph 3 there shall be added at the end— "(*g*) the Theft Act 1968, except section 8 (robbery)".
The Finance Act 1965 (1965 c. 25)	In Schedule 10, in the Table in paragraph 1, for the words "Sections 500 to 505" there shall be substituted the words "Sections 500 to 504".
The Finance Act 1966 (1966 c. 18)	In Schedule 6, in paragraph 13, for the words "Sections 500 to 505" there shall be substituted the words "Sections 500 to 504", and the words from "together with" to "the said section 505" shall be omitted.

[*Entry relating to the Criminal Law Act* 1967, *Sched.* 1: *repealed by the Courts Act* 1971, *s.* 56, *Sched.* 11.]

Act Amended	*Amendment*
The Firearms Act 1968 (1968 c. 27)	Schedule 1 (offences in connection with which possession of a firearm is an offence under section 17(2)) shall be amended, except in relation to a person's apprehension for an offence committed before the commencement of this Act, by substituting for paragraph 4— "4. Theft, burglary, blackmail and any offence under section 12(1) (taking of motor vehicle or other conveyance without owner's consent) of the Theft Act 1968": by omitting paragraph 7: and by substituting in paragraph 8 for the words "paragraphs 1 to 7" the words "paragraphs 1 to 6".

SCHEDULE 3

Repeals

[*This Schedule repealed penal enactments superseded by this Act and obsolete and redundant enactments and effected certain consequential repeals. It is not reprinted in this edition.*]   **17–42**

APPENDIX 2

Theft Act 1978
(1978 c. 31)

Arrangement of Sections

SECT.
1. Obtaining services by deception.
2. Evasion of liability by deception.
3. Making off without payment.
4. Punishments.
5. Supplementary.
6. Enactment of same provisions for Northern Ireland.
7. Short title, commencement and extent.

An Act to replace section 16(2)(*a*) of the Theft Act 1968 with other provision against fraudulent conduct; and for connected purposes.

[20th July 1978]

Obtaining services by deception

1.—(1) A person who by any deception dishonestly obtains services from another shall be guilty of an offence.   **18–01**

(2) It is an obtaining of services where the other is induced to confer a benefit by doing some act, or causing or permitting some act to be done, on the understanding that the benefit has been or will be paid for.

Evasion of liability by deception

18–02   **2.**—(1) Subject to subsection (2) below, where a person by any deception—

(*a*) dishonestly secures the remission of the whole or part of any existing liability to make a payment, whether his own liability or another's; or

(*b*) with intent to make permanent default in whole or in part on any existing liability to make a payment, or with intent to let another do so, dishonestly induces the creditor or any person claiming payment on behalf of the creditor to wait for payment (whether or not the due date for payment is deferred) or to forgo payment; or

(*c*) dishonestly obtains any exemption from or abatement of liability to make a payment;

he shall be guilty of an offence.

(2) For purposes of this section "liability" means legally enforceable liability; and subsection (1) shall not apply in relation to a liability that has not been accepted or established to pay compensation for a wrongful act or omission.

(3) For purposes of subsection (1)(*b*) a person induced to take in payment a cheque or other security for money by way of conditional satisfaction of a pre-existing liability is to be treated not as being paid but as being induced to wait for payment.

(4) For purposes of section (1)(*c*) "obtains" includes obtaining for another or enabling another to obtain.

Making off without payment

18–03   **3.**—(1) Subject to subsection (3) below, a person who, knowing that payment on the spot for any goods supplied or service done is required or expected from him, dishonestly makes off without having paid as required or expected and with intent to avoid payment of the amount due shall be guilty of an offence.

(2) For purposes of this section "payment on the spot" includes payment at the time of collecting goods on which work has been done or in respect of which service has been provided.

(3) Subsection (1) above shall not apply where the supply of the goods or the doing of the service is contrary to law, or where the service done is such that payment is not legally enforceable.

(4) Any person may arrest without warrant any one who is, or whom he, with reasonable cause, suspects to be, committing or attempting to commit an offence under this section.

Punishments

18–04   **4.**—(1) Offences under this Act shall be punishable either on conviction on indictment or on summary conviction.

(2) A person convicted on indictment shall be liable—

(*a*) for an offence under section 1 or section 2 of this Act, to imprisonment for a term not exceeding five years; and (*b*) for an offence under section 3 of this Act, to imprisonment for a term not exceeding two years.

(3) A person convicted summarily of any offence under this Act shall be liable—

(*a*) to imprisonment for a term not exceeding six months; or

(*b*) to a fine not exceeding the prescribed sum for the purposes of [section 32 of the Magistrates' Courts Act 1980] (punishment on summary conviction of offences triable either way: £1,000 or other sum substituted by order under that Act),

or to both.

[*The words in square brackets in subsection* (3) *were substituted by the Magistrates' Courts Act* 1980, *s.*154(1), *Sched.*7.]

Supplementary

5.—(1) For purposes of sections 1 and 2 above "deception" has the same   **18–05** meaning as in section 15 of the Theft Act 1968, that is to say, it means any deception (whether deliberate or reckless) by words or conduct as to fact or as to law, including a deception as to the present intentions of the person using the deception or any other person; and section 18 of that Act (liability of company officers for offences by the company) shall apply in relation to sections 1 and 2 above as it applies in relation to section 15 of that Act.

(2) Sections 30(1) (husband and wife), 31(1) (effect on civil proceedings) and 34 (interpretation) of the Theft Act 1968, so far as they are applicable in relation to this Act, shall apply as they apply in relation to that Act.

(3) In the Schedule to the Extradition Act 1873 (additional list of extradition crimes), after "Theft Act 1968" there shall be inserted "or the Theft Act 1978"; and there shall be deemed to be included among the descriptions of offences set out in Schedule 1 to the Fugitive Offenders Act 1967 any offence under this Act.

(4) In the Visiting Forces Act 1952, in paragraph 3 of the Schedule (which defines for England and Wales "offences against property" for purposes of the exclusion in certain cases of the jurisdiction of United Kingdom courts) there shall be added at the end—

"(*j*) the Theft Act 1978".

(5) In the Theft Act 1968 section 16(2)(*a*) is hereby repealed.

Enactment of same provisions for Northern Ireland

6. An Order in Council under paragraph 1(1)(*b*) of Schedule 1 to the   **18–06** Northern Ireland Act 1974 (legislation for Northern Ireland in the interim period) which contains a statement that it operates only so as to make for Northern Ireland provision corresponding to this Act—

(*a*) shall not be subject to paragraph 1 (4) and (5) of that Schedule (affirmative resolution of both Houses of Parliament); but

(*b*) shall be subject to annulment by resolution of either House.

Short title, commencement and extent

18–07 **7.**—(1) This Act may be cited as the Theft Act 1978.

(2) This Act shall come into force at the expiration of three months beginning with the date on which it is passed.

(3) This Act except section 5(3), shall not extend to Scotland; and except for that subsection, and subject also to section 6, it shall not extend to Northern Ireland.

INDEX

ACCOUNTS
falsifying, *see* Falsification of Accounts
Advertising Rewards, 13–35, 17–23
Agent
innocent, burglary by, 4–15
property, receiving, 2–25—2–27
theft by, 2–25—2–27, 2–67
Aggravated Burglary, 17–10
article made for causing injury, 4–32
firearm, using, 4–29
having weapon "with him," 4–35
lesser offence, 1–09
meaning, 4–28, 17–10
penalty, 4–28
weapon, using, 4–30—4–34
Annuity Contract
deception, obtained by, 9–06, 17–16
Arrest
going equipped, 14–01
making off without payment, 11–04, 18–03
spouse, by, 15–03
taking conveyance, 5–12
Art Gallery. *See* Place open to the Public,
Removal of Article from.
Assault
robbery, on charge of, 1–09
with intent to rob, 1–09, 3–03, 17–08
Attempt
complete offence, proof of, 1–10
property, to obtain by deception, 6–51,
6–52

BAILEE
theft by, 2–24, 2–40, 2–55
Bank
account as property, 2–09
balance, theft of, 2–12, 2–13
loan, obtaining, 9–08
overdraft as pecuniary advantage,
9–06—9–08
Betting
pecuniary advantage, as, 9–09, 9–11,
17–16
Bicycle
taking without consent, 5–24, 17–12
Blackmail, 17–21
attempted, 12–15
burden of proof, 12–21, 12–22
demand, 12–08
belief in reasonable grounds for making,
12–23—12–26
conduct, by, 12–09
examples of, 12–34

Blackmail—*cont.*
demand—*cont.*
letter posted abroad, 12–14
making of, 12–11—12–13
oral, 12–13
sorts of, 12–10
unwarranted, 12–20
demanding with menaces, 12–02, 12–03
gain, with view to, 12–07, 12–32, 12–33
lay meaning, 12–01
loss, intent to cause, 12–07, 12–32, 12–33
menaces,
action to be taken by another, 12–19
belief in propriety of using,
12–27—12–31
effect on victim, 12–18
examples, 12–16, 12–17
meaning, 12–16
other enactments, reference to in, 17–32
penalty, 12–04
scope of, 12–05—12–07
statutory meaning, 12–02, 12–04
Building
meaning, 4–17
Burglary, 17–09
accident, by, 4–26
aggravated. *See* Aggravated Burglary.
building,
meaning, 4–17—4–21
caravan, of, 4–22
electricity, abstracting, not, 4–24
entry gained by fraud, 4–09
going equipped for, 14–06
grievous bodily harm, intent to inflict,
4–26
houseboat, from, 4–22
inhabited vehicle or vessel, 4–22
innocent agent, through, 4–15
instrument entering, 4–16
intent to steal, 4–24, 4–25
Larceny Act, in, 4–01
lesser offence, 1–09
licence to enter, 4–07
meaning, 4–02
modes of, 4–23
other enactments, referred to in, 17–32
part of building, 4–17—4–21
flat as part, 4–19
shop, parts of, 4–20
penalty, 4–02
rape, intent to commit, 4–27
trespasser, entry as, 4–04—4–09, 4–14
belief in right to enter, 4–10

Burglary—*cont.*
  trespasser, entry as—*cont.*
    invitation to enter, 4–11—4–13
    trial, mode of, 4–03
    unlawful damage, intent to do, 4–27
CARAVAN
  burglary of, 4–22
Cheat
  common law, abolition of, 17–32
  going equipped for, 14–07, 17–25
Cheque
  drawn from partly stolen goods, 13–06
  obtaining by deception, 6–44
  representations implied by, 6–21
  theft of, 2–14
Cheque Card
  representations implied by, 6–22
  use, effect of, 6–32
Church. *See* Place Open to the Public,
  Removal of Articles from
Company
  evasion of liability by deception by officer,
    8–03, 18–05
  false accounts, use of, 10–06, 17–17,
    17–18, 18–05
  false statement by director, 10–08, 17–19
  obtaining by deception by officer, 6–53,
    7–02, 17–15, 17–18, 18–05
  pecuniary advantage obtained by
    deception by, 9–03, 17–16, 17–18
Compensation
  amount of, 16–16
  injury or damage, for, 16–15
  power of court, 16–16
  sentence, not affecting, 16–16
Conveyance, Taking without Authority,
    5–11—5–24, 17–12
  aiding and abetting, 5–18
  allowing oneself to be driven, 5–19, 5–20
  arrestable offence, 5–12
  consent obtained by misrepresentation,
    5–22
  consent, without, 5–21
  conveyance, meaning, 5–13
  driving, 5–19
  going equipped for, 14–06
  honest belief in consent, 5–23
  horse, not including, 5–13
  pedal cycle, 5–24
  penalty, 5–12
  primary offence, 5–12, 5–14
  secondary offence, 5–12, 5–19
  taking, 5–14
    authorised person, by, 5–15, 5–16
    for own use, 5–17
  theft charge, or, 1–11
Copyright
  theft of, 2–69

Corporation Sole
  property belonging to, 2–34, 17–05
Credit Card
  representations implied by, 6–22
  use, effect of, 6–32, 6–36
Credit, Obtaining by Deception, 6–05 *et
    seq.*, 18–01 *et seq.*
Criminal Law Revision Committee
  Eighth Report, 1–04, 6–02
  Thirteenth Report, 6–04

DECEPTION. *See* Property Obtained by
    Deception
Deer
  theft of, 2–08, 17–37
Dishonesty, 17–02
  belief in a right to deprive, 2–81, 2–82
  consent, belief in victim's, 2–83
  discovery of owner, 2–82
  evasion of liability, 8–05
  falsification of accounts, 10–03
  handling, 13–26
  making off without payment, 11–16, 11–17
  obtaining pecuniary advantage by
    deception, 9–05
  obtaining property by deception, 6–47,
    6–48
  obtaining services by deception, 7–04
  ordinary meaning, 1–14
  proof of, 2–80
  residual function of, 2–86, 2–87
  standards of, 2–88—2–91
  theft, in, 2–79—2–91
  willingness to pay for property, 2–85

ELECTRICITY
  abstracting, 2–98, 17–13
  burglary and, 4–24
  theft of, 2–15
Embezzlement
  meaning, 2–01
Employment
  deception, obtained by, 9–09, 9–10, 17–16
Equitable Interest
  under agreement, theft of, 2–22, 17–05
Evidence
  husband and wife, by, 15–04, 17–30
  incriminating questions, 1–06, 17–31
Explosive
  meaning, 17–10
Extortion
  office or franchise, by, abolition of, 17–32

FALSE ACCOUNTS, use of, 10–01, 10–06,
    17–17
Falsification of Accounts, 6–03, 10–01, 17–17
  actus reus, 10–02
  company officer, 10–07, 17–18

Falsification of Accounts—*cont.*
  dishonesty, 10–03
  document as account, 10–02
  "falsifying," 10–02
  "gain," 10–04
  "loss," intent to cause, 10–05
  mens rea, 10–03
Firearm
  going equipped with, 14–02
  meaning, 4–29, 17–10
Fish
  theft of, 2–08, 17–38
Flowers
  theft of, 2–05, 17–04
Fraudulent Conversion
  meaning, 2–01
Fruit
  theft of, 2–05, 17–04

GOING EQUIPPED, 17–25
  article for use in offence, 14–05, 14–09
  articles covered, 14–02
  burglary, for, 14–06
  cheat, for, 14–07
  contemplated offences, 14–06
  "having article with him," 14–04
  meaning, 14–01
  motor vehicles, connected with, 14–01
  penalty, 14–01
  possessor of article to be away from
    abode, 14–03
  proof of purpose, 14–08—14–10
  taking conveyance, for, 14–06
  theft, for, 14–06

HANDLING STOLEN GOODS, 17–22—17–24
  acquittal of alleged thief, 13–08
  advertising rewards, 13–35, 17–23
  arranging to receive, 13–14
  "by or for the benefit of another person,"
    13–15
  dishonesty, 13–26
  evidence to be admitted, 13–24, 13–25,
    17–27
  "goods," 13–04—13–06, 17–34
  goods ceasing to be stolen, 13–09—13–11
    loss of title to, 13–11
    restoration to lawful possession, 13–10
  goods to be stolen, 13–02
    proof of, 13–07, 13–08
  handler as thief, 13–30, 13–31
  indictment, 13–32—13–34
  information alleging, 13–32
  knowledge or belief in theft, 13–18—13–21
    proof of, 13–23
    suspicion, 13–20
    time of, 13–22
    wilful blindness, 13–20, 13–21

Handling Stolen Goods—*cont.*
  meaning, 13–01
  mens rea, 13–18—13–26, 17–26
  offering to buy from thief, 13–14
  other enactments, reference to in, 17–32
  penalty, 13–01
  receiving, 13–13
  recent possession, 13–23
  restitution, 17–28
  "stolen," 13–03
  theft and, 2–70, 13–27—13–31
  theft, place of, 13–03
  theft, verdict of, 1–09
  undertaking or assisting, 13–15
    arranging, 13–17
    retention, removal, disposal or
      realisation, in, 13–16
Horse
  conveyance, not, 5–13
Human Body
  theft of, 2–16
Husband and Wife, 17–30
  arrest by spouse, 15–03
  compellability, 15–04, 15–05
  competence, 15–04
  conspiracy, 15–01
  evidence of, 15–04, 15–05
  joint offence, 15–03
  marital coercion, 15–01
  offence with reference to spouse's
    property, 15–04
  prosecution by spouse, 15–02, 15–03
  spouse as offender, 15–01
  witness, spouse as, 15–04, 15–05

INDICTMENT
  duplicity, defective for, 2–96
  handling, for, 13–32—13–34
  lesser offence, 1–08
  theft, for, 2–92—2–97
    continuous offence, 2–94
    general deficiency, 2–95
    single activity, charge for, 2–93
Information
  handling, for, 13–32
  theft, for, 2–92—2–97
Insurance Policy
  deception, obtained by, 9–06, 17–16

LAND
  deception, obtained by, 6–46
  personal representative, theft by, 2–05
  severance, 2–05
  squatting, 2–06
  theft of, 2–04, 17–04
  things annexed to, 2–04, 17–05
  things deposited on, 2–04
  things growing on, 2–05, 2–06
  trustee, theft by, 2–05

Larceny
  meaning, 2–01
  statute, 1–04
Lease
  obtaining by deception, 6–46
  tenant, theft by, 2–05, 17–04
Liability, Evaded by Deception, 6–06, 8–01,
    18–02
  company officer, 8–03
  deception, 8–04
  dishonesty, 8–05
  existing liability, 8–10
    abatement of, 8–12
    remission of, 8–11, 8–12
  inducing creditor to forgo payment, 8–16
  inducing creditor to wait for payment,
    8–13, 8–15
  liability to make payment, 8–06
    abating, 8–17
    exemption from, obtaining, 8–17
    legally enforceable, 8–07
    statute barred, 8–08
  meaning, 8–01
  mere evasion, 8–02
  penalty, 8–01
  wrongful act or omission, liability for, 8–09

Mail Bags
  offences, 1–06, 17–14
Making off without Payment, 6–07, 11–01,
    18–03
  bad cheque, paying with, 11–13
  deception, achieved by, 11–03
  deception, time of, 11–02
  dishonesty, 11–16, 11–17
  goods supplied, 11–05
  intent to avoid payment, 11–14
  knowledge of amount due, 11–15
  "making off," 11–12, 11–13
  meaning, 11–01
  "payment," 11–10
  payment on the spot, 11–11
  penalty, 11–01
  power of arrest, 11–04
  service done, 11–06
  theft, and, 11–02
  transaction contrary to law, 11–07—11–08
  unenforceable transaction, 11–07
Menaces, Demanding with. See Blackmail.
Money
  meaning, 2–09
Mushrooms
  theft of, 2–05, 17–04

Overdraft
  pecuniary advantage, as, 9–06—9–08,
    17–16

Pecuniary Advantage Obtained by
    Deception, 9–01, 17–16
  betting, by, 9–09, 9–11, 17–16
  company officer, 9–03
  deception, 9–04
  dishonesty, 9–05
  "for himself or another," 9–04
  meaning, 9–01
  obtaining, 9–04
  overdraft, 9–06—9–08
  repealed in part, 6–04
  "pecuniary advantage," 9–02
  remuneration, opportunity to earn, 9–09
    office of employment, in, 9–10
  theft charge, on, 1–11
Pedal Cycle
  taking without consent, 5–24, 17–12
Place open to the Public, Removal of Article
    from, 5–02—5–10, 17–11
  article to be displayed, 5–08
  building, public having access to, 5–04
    in order to view, 5–05, 5–06
  "Goya clause," 5–02
  penalty, 17–11
  removal, 5–07
  removal without authority, 5–10
  time of removal, 5–09
Plant
  meaning, 17–04
  theft of, 2–05, 17–04
Police
  search, authority to, 1–06, 17–26
Postal Packets
  offences, 1–06, 17–14
Procuring Execution of Valuable Securities,
    10–11
Property obtained by Deception, 6–08,
    17–15
  attempts,
    jurisdiction, 6–51, 6–52
  belonging to another, 6–10, 17–05
  company officer, 6–53, 17–18
  deception, 6–08, 6–12
    business, appearance of, 6–20
    cheque card or credit card, 6–22, 6–32,
      6–36
    cheques, 6–21
    conduct, by, 6–19
    conduct to conceal facts, 6–23
    deliberate or reckless, 6–42, 6–43
    fact and opinion, 6–16
    fact, as to, 6–15
    false pretence, and, 6–12, 6–14
    false representation, 6–27—6–29
    implied facts, 6–17
    law, as to, 6–12
    obtaining, to precede, 6–30
    opinion implying fact, 6–18

Property Obtained by Deception—*cont.*
  deception—*cont.*
    present intentions, as to, 6–13
    restaurant, ordering meal in, 6–20, 6–25
    silence, by, 6–24, 6–25
    title, as to, 6–19
    uniform, by wearing, 6–19
  deception and obtaining from different
    persons, 6–40
  dishonesty, 6–47, 6–48
  effect of representation, 6–31—6–34
  Eighth Report, in, 6–02
  events and transactions after deception,
    6–37—6–39
  evidence of effective representation, 6–35,
    6–36
  evidence of inducement, 6–36
  intention to permanently deprive,
    6–44—6–46
  jurisdiction, 6–49—6–52
  lease, 6–46
  mental element, 6–41
  obtaining, 6–11
    for another, 6–11
    temporary, 6–44
  owner, by, 6–10
  penalty, 6–08
  place of obtaining, 6–49
  proof of representation, 6–35
  property, 6–09
  retaining, 6–11
  theft, and, 2–66, 6–44—6–46
  Thirteenth Report, in, 6–04
  victim's knowledge of falsity, 6–34
Public Telephone
  dishonestly using, 2–98, 17–39

RESTAURANT
  intent to pay in, 6–20, 6–25
Restitution, 17–28
  application for, 16–04
  enforcement of order, 16–13
  goods representing stolen goods, 16–05
  materials on which order made, 16–10
  money in possession of convicted person,
    16–06, 16–07
  offences affected, 16–02
  powers of court, 16–02
  stolen goods, of, 16–03
  summary procedure, 16–09
  suspension of order, 16–11
    appeal, on, 16–12
  time at which order made, 16–10
Robbery, 14–08
  assault, charge of, 1–10
  claim of right, 3–02
  common law, abolition of, 17–32
  fear, putting person in, 3–06

Robbery—*cont.*
  force at time of stealing, 3–08
  force in order to steal, 3–10
  force, use of, 3–03—3–05
  future force, 3–06
  Larceny Act, in, 3–01
  lesser offence, 1–09
  meaning, 3–01
  theft, proof of, 3–02
  victim of, 3–07

SEARCH WARRANTS, 1–06, 17–26
Services, Obtaining by Deception, 6–05,
  18–01
  benefit, conferring, 7–06
  company officer, 7–02
  deception, 7–03
  dishonesty, 7–04
  doing, causing, or permitting act, 7–07,
    7–08
  for another, 7–09
  meaning, 7–01
  no view to gain or intent to cause loss,
    7–13
  penalty, 18–04
  "services," 7–05
  transactions contrary to law, 7–12
  understanding that payment be made,
    7–10, 7–11
  unenforceable transaction, 7–12
Shares
  theft of, 2–69
Stolen Property
  return of, 16–14 *and see* Compensation;
    Restitution
Suppression of Documents, 10–10

TELEPHONE
  dishonestly using, 2–98, 17–39
Telex
  dishonestly using, 2–98, 17–39
Theft
  agent for sale, by, 2–67
  appropriation, 2–37—2–70, 17–03
  bailee, by, 2–55
  bona fide purchaser, by, 2–54
  consent facilitating, 2–59
  consent preventing, 2–58
  conversion, and, 2–39, 2–40
  custodian, by, 2–55
  duration of, 2–45
  early stage, at, 2–48—2–50
  finder, by, 2–53
  handling, by, 2–70
  intention, and, 2–43, 2–44
  meaning, 2–37
  omissions as, 2–46, 2–47

Theft—*cont.*
  attempted, 2–48
  borrowing not, 2–71
  conditional intent, 2–76, 2–78
  consent of victim, 2–57—2–67
    fraud, obtained by, 2–60
  copyright, of, 2–69
  corporation sole, property belonging to,
    2–34, 17–05
  definition, 2–02
  "dishonestly," 2–79—2–91, 17–02 *and see*
    Dishonesty
  duress, by, 2–67
  electricity, of, 2–15
  garage, from, 2–36
  going equipped for, 14–06, 17–25 *and see*
    Going Equipped
  handling, and, 13–27—13–31
  human body, of, 2–16
  inchoate transactions, 2–48—2–50
  informations and indictments, 2–92—2–97
  intention to permanently deprive,
    2–71—2–78, 17–06
    examples, 2–74
    meaning, 2–73
    "permanently," 2–72
    treating as own to dispose of,
      2–74—2–77
  land, of, 2–04—2–06, 17–04
  laudable motive, 2–91
  lesser offence, 1–09
  making off without payment and, 11–02
  money, of, 2–09
  obtaining a pecuniary advantage by
    deception proved, 1–11
  obtaining by deception, and, 2–66,
    6–44—6–46
  obtaining ownership by deception, 2–63,
    2–64
    delivery, followed by, 2–65
  obtaining possession by deception, 2–61,
    2–62
  owner, by, 2–41, 2–42
  part of a whole, of, 2–97
  penalty, 2–02, 17–07
  possession, by taking, 2–51—2–55
    possession, without, 2–56
  procedural rules, 2–92
  property belonging to another, 2–03,
    2–18—2–36, 17–05

Theft—*cont.*
  property belonging to another—*cont.*
    appropriation, at time of, 2–35, 2–36
    possession or control, 2–19, 2–20
    proprietary right or interest, 2–21, 2–22
    trust property, 2–23
  property got by another's mistake,
    2–30—2–33
    deception, 2–33
    legal obligation, under, 2–31
  property received from or on account of
    another, 2–24—2–29
    improper profit, 2–29
    obligation, under, 2–25—2–27
  sale or return, goods on, 2–67
  shares, of, 2–69
  shops, in, 2–35
  taking a conveyance, conviction of, 1–11
  things in action, 2–10—2–14, 2–68, 2–69
  trade marks, of, 2–69
  trade secrets, of, 2–17, 2–69
  voidable transactions, 2–67
  wild creatures, of, 2–07, 2–08, 17–04
Theft Act
  civil law, reference to, 1–13
  layman interpreting, 1–13
  simplification, aimed at, 1–12
Things in action, 2–10—2–14, 17–04
  bank accounts, 2–12, 2–13
  cheques, 2–14
Trade Marks
  theft of, 2–69
Trade Secrets
  theft of, 2–17, 2–69
Treasure Trove
  concealing, 17–32
Trespass
  meaning, 4–05
Trial
  mode of, 1–07
  verdicts, 1–08
Trust
  property, theft of, 2–23, 17–05

UNIFORM
  wearing, deception by, 6–19

WILD CREATURES, 2–07, 2–08, 17–04, 17–37,
  17–38
Witness. *See* Husband and Wife